A WORKBOOK
FOR ARGUMENTS

A Complete Course in Critical Thinking

Second Edition

A WORKBOOK
FOR ARGUMENTS

A Complete Course in Critical Thinking

Second Edition

David R. Morrow
&
Anthony Weston

Hackett Publishing Company, Inc.
Indianapolis/Cambridge

For further information, please address
    Hackett Publishing Company, Inc.
    P.O. Box 44937
    Indianapolis, Indiana 46244-0937

    www.hackettpublishing.com

Cover design by Deborah Wilkes
Interior design by Elizabeth L. Wilson

Library of Congress Cataloging-in-Publication Data
Morrow, David R.
  A workbook for arguments : a complete course in critical thinking / David R.
Morrow & Anthony Weston. — Second edition.
      pages cm
Also contains the entire text of the fourth edition of Weston's Rulebook, while
supplementing this core text with extensive further explanations and exercises.
  Includes index.
  ISBN 978-1-62466-427-4 (pbk.) — ISBN 978-1-62466-428-1 (cloth)
  1. Critical thinking. 2. Reasoning. 3. Logic. 4. Persuasion (Rhetoric)
  5. English language—Rhetoric. I. Weston, Anthony, 1954– II. Weston,
Anthony, 1954– Rulebook for arguments. III. Title.
  BF441.M687 2015
  168—dc23   2015019230

Contents

Part 1

Part 2

Part 3

Contents

Preface to the Second Edition

A Workbook for Arguments builds on Anthony Weston's *Rulebook for Arguments* to offer a complete textbook for a course in critical thinking. Like the first edition, the *Workbook* contains the entire text of the fourth edition of the *Rulebook* while supplementing this core text with extensive further explanations and exercises:

Homework exercises adapted from a wide range of actual arguments from newspapers, philosophical texts, literature, movies, YouTube videos, and other sources.

Practical advice to help students succeed when applying the *Rulebook*'s rules to the examples in the homework exercises.

Suggestions for further practice that outline activities students can do by themselves or with classmates to improve their critical thinking skills or that point them to online resources to do the same.

Detailed instructions for in-class activities and take-home assignments designed to engage students in critical thinking.

An appendix on mapping arguments, a topic not included in the *Rulebook*, that introduces students to this vital skill in evaluating or constructing complex and multi-step arguments.

Model responses to odd-numbered exercises, including commentaries on the strengths and weaknesses of selected model responses as well as further discussion of some of the substantive intellectual, philosophical, and ethical issues raised by the exercises.

This second edition improves on the first by offering

Updated and improved homework exercises to ensure that the examples continue to resonate with today's students. About one-third of the exercises in the book have been replaced with updated, better tested, or more science-focused examples. The exercises carried over from the first edition have not been changed.

An increased focus on scientific reasoning throughout the text, including homework exercises and in-class activities covering a range of scientific disciplines. Nearly every exercise set in the first six chapters includes at least one example of scientific reasoning. (Exercise 5 in each exercise set is a scientific example. See the model responses to Exercise 5 in each set for discussion of scientific reasoning.) The goal of dispersing these examples across the text is to make it clearer to students how scientific reasoning dovetails with critical thinking more generally.

Two new in-class activities that ask students to analyze arguments in their original form, rather than in the simplified form found in the exercise sets. Look for these activities in Part III.

A Rulebook for Arguments will continue to be available in its original brief and slim format, while in this greatly expanded version it can be used as a full-scale textbook in its own right.

The *Rulebook* first appeared in 1986—nearly thirty years ago. When it first came out, we had no idea how much interest there would be in such a book, a little rule-based handbook for argumentation on the model of Strunk and White's classic *The Elements of Style*. It turned out there was a great deal of interest! Since then the *Rulebook* has gone through four editions and has become a bit of a classic itself. It has been used in classes across the curriculum, from high schools and law schools to graduate schools and community colleges, and in the study not just of critical thinking but also of rhetoric, applied ethics, journalism, and many other subjects. It has been translated into ten languages—plus bootlegged into a few more—and even transcribed into braille.

The field of critical thinking has also changed dramatically since the '80s. Then commonly called "informal logic," at least by philosophers, it was relatively new, still half-wishing to be formal logic and accustomed mainly to treating the wider realm of reasoning as a matter mostly of avoiding "fallacies," a grab-bag of seemingly random types of mistakes. Now, by contrast, critical thinking is a field in its own right, much better tuned to the variety and texture of actual argumentation and focused not merely or mainly on pitfalls to be avoided but on the underlying principles of *good* argumentation. In some small ways, the *Rulebook* may have helped to forward this wider-angled and more constructive vision of critical thinking. In any case its rules, quite on purpose, represent just such principles.

Rulebook has always been a slim little volume, though: always supplementary, appealing both to writers who want a brief argument handbook on their shelves alongside *The Elements of Style* and to students and classroom instructors who need, in the words of the original Preface, "a list of reminders and rules . . . a treatment that students can consult and understand on their own and that therefore does not claim too much class time." It has fulfilled that role very well. The *Workbook*, by contrast, was intended for instructors who wanted to devote more time—or an entire course—to the principles of critical thinking.

The success of the first edition of the *Workbook* suggests that the field is ready for a full-fledged textbook in the same key as the *Rulebook*. Here the same rules are laid out, but then systematically elaborated and practiced, first in sets of exercises specific to nearly every rule and then in general exercises keyed to each of the *Rulebook*'s chapters. Here you can make the rules your own by using them repeatedly in the context of real-world arguments. While the *Rulebook* will continue to be published on its own, there is now a much more developed alternative as well—you hold it in your hands.

Especially for beginning students, learning to apply these rules effectively requires a great deal of practice. That is why this *Workbook* is full of exercises! But it also requires more than just practice. It requires guidance, too. To that end, Part II of the *Workbook* provides model responses (sometimes several different model responses) to every odd-numbered exercise—half of the execises in this book—along with detailed commentaries on those model responses. In our view, these model responses and commentaries are almost as important a part of the textbook as Part I. Key themes are more thoroughly explained and reviewed there, and sometimes new themes are introduced there as well. Thus, Part II can be key to a richer and fuller learning. Be sure to check it out! Instructors are encouraged to make the relevant model responses part of their classes' regular assigned reading as well.

The *Rulebook* is authored by Anthony Weston, and appears here, though divided into pieces, almost exactly as it also appears in its fourth edition. The *Workbook* sections that develop and apply each of the rules, along with the model responses (Part 2) and critical thinking activities (Part 3), are authored by David Morrow in close collaboration with Anthony Weston.

Deborah Wilkes, publisher of Hackett Publishing Company, has guided this project from the beginning with a perfect combination of editorial acumen, flexibility, and good humor. Thanks also to Liz Wilson, Hackett's production director, for her intrepid assistance throughout the production process, and to Jennifer Albert for her eagle-eyed copyediting. Multiple publisher's reviewers looked over the emerging *Workbook* at various points as well. For many suggestions and much useful critical feedback (see Rule 38!) we are grateful to Patricia Allen, Massachusetts Bay

Community College; Peter Amato, Drexel University; Christian Bauer, Sacramento City College; Lisa Bellantoni, Albright College; Jason Burrows, Hennepin Technical College; Joanne Ciulla, University of Richmond; Cynthia Gobatie, Riverside Community College; Conan Griffin, Florida Gulf Coast University; Julianna Griffin, Florida Gulf Coast University; Kenya Grooms, DePaul University; John Ellingwood Kay, San Francisco State University; Paul Mattick, Adelphi University; George Pullman, Georgia State University; Ryan Scherbart, Cabrillo College; Michael Strawser, University of Central Florida; and Daniela Vallega-Neu, University of Oregon. What errors and infelicities remain, of course, should be laid only to us—and we'd be delighted to hear about them, along with any other suggestions and reactions to this text. Please send feedback to us in care of the publisher.

Meantime, we wish all the best to every user of this book. Use it well—and use it often!

AW, DM

Note about Companion Web Site

There is a companion Web site for this book at

http://www.hackettpublishing.com/workbookforarguments

which contains links to relevant online and printed resources. Many of the exercise sets point you to this Web site for additional practice, and a few point you to the Web site for the exercises themselves. The Web site also contains ideas for additional critical thinking activities.

Introduction

What's the point of arguing?

Many people think that arguing is simply stating their prejudices in a new form. This is why many people also think that arguments are unpleasant and pointless. One dictionary definition for "argument" is "disputation." In this sense we sometimes say that two people "*have* an argument": a verbal fistfight. It happens often enough. But it is not what arguments really are.

In this book, "to give an argument" means to offer a set of reasons or evidence in support of a conclusion. Here an argument is not simply a statement of certain views, and it is not simply a dispute. Arguments are efforts to *support* certain views with reasons. Arguments in this sense are not pointless; in fact, they are essential.

Argument is essential, in the first place, because it is a way of finding out which views are better than others. Not all views are equal. Some conclusions can be supported by good reasons; others have much weaker support. But often we don't know which are which. We need to give arguments for different conclusions and then assess those arguments to see how strong they really are.

Here argument is a means of *inquiry*. Some philosophers and activists have argued, for instance, that the factory farming of animals for meat causes immense suffering to animals and is therefore unjustified and immoral. Are they right? We can't necessarily tell just by consulting our current opinions. Many issues are involved—we need to examine the arguments. Do we have moral obligations to other species, for instance, or is only human suffering really bad? How well can humans live without meat? Some vegetarians have lived to very old ages. Does this show that vegetarian diets are healthier? Or is it irrelevant when you consider that some non-vegetarians also have lived to very old ages? (You might make some progress by asking whether vegetarians live to old age at a higher *rate*.) Or might healthier people tend to become vegetarians, rather than vice versa? All of these questions need to be considered carefully, and the answers are not clear in advance.

Argument is essential for another reason too. Once we have arrived at a conclusion that is well supported by reasons, we use arguments to explain and defend it. A good argument doesn't merely repeat conclusions. Instead it offers reasons and evidence so that other people can make up their minds for themselves. If you become convinced that we should indeed change the way we raise and use animals, for example, you must use arguments to explain how you arrived at your conclusion. That is how you will convince others: by offering the reasons and evidence that convinced *you*. It is not a mistake to have strong views. The mistake is to have nothing else.

Argument grows on you

Typically we learn to "argue" by *assertion*. That is, we tend to start with our conclusions—our desires or opinions—without a whole lot to back them up. And it works, sometimes, at least when we're very young. What could be better?

Real argument, by contrast, takes time and practice. Marshaling our reasons, proportioning our conclusions to the actual evidence, considering objections, and all the rest—these are acquired skills. We have to grow up a little. We have to put aside our desires and our opinions for a while and actually *think*.

School may help—or not. In courses concerned with teaching ever-larger sets of facts or techniques, students are seldom encouraged to ask the sorts of questions that arguments answer. Sure, the Constitution mandates an Electoral College—that's a fact—but is it still a good idea? (For that matter, was it ever a good idea? What were the reasons for it, anyway?) Sure, many scientists believe that there is life elsewhere in the universe, but why? What's the argument? Reasons can be given for different answers. In the end, ideally, you will both learn some of those reasons and also learn how to weigh them up—and how to seek out more yourself.

Mostly, again, it takes time and practice. This book can help! Moreover, the practice of argument turns out to have some attractions of its own. Our minds become more flexible, open-ended, and alert. We come to appreciate how much difference our own critical thinking can really make. From everyday family life to politics, science, philosophy, and even religion, arguments are constantly offered to us for our consideration, and we may in turn offer back our own. Think of argument as a way to make your own place within these unfolding, ongoing dialogues. What could be better than *that*?

Outline of this book

This book begins by discussing fairly simple arguments and moves to extended arguments and their use in essays and oral presentations at the end.

Chapters I–VI are about composing and assessing *short* arguments. Short arguments simply offer their reasons and evidence briefly, usually in a few sentences or a paragraph. We begin with short arguments for several reasons. First, they are common: in fact so common that they are part of everyday conversation. Second, longer arguments are usually elaborations of short arguments, or a series of short arguments linked together. If you learn to write and assess short arguments first, then you can extend your skills to longer arguments in essays or presentations.

A third reason for beginning with short arguments is that they are the best illustrations both of the common argument forms and of the typical mistakes in arguments. In longer arguments it can be harder to pick out the main points—and the main problems. Therefore, although some of the rules may seem obvious when first stated, remember that you have the benefit of a simple example. Other rules are hard enough to appreciate even in short arguments.

Chapter VII guides you into sketching and then elaborating an extended argument, considering objections and alternatives as you do. Chapter VIII guides you from there into writing an argumentative essay. Chapter IX then adds rules specifically about oral presentation. Again, all of these chapters depend on Chapters I–VI, since extended arguments like these essentially combine and elaborate the kinds of short arguments that Chapters I–VI discuss. Don't skip ahead to the later chapters, then, even if you come to this book primarily for help writing an essay or doing a presentation. At the very least, read through the shaded sections of the earlier chapters—the parts from the *Rulebook for Arguments,* on which this book is based—so that when you arrive at those later chapters you will have the tools you need to use them well. Instructors might wish to assign Chapters I–VI early in the term and Chapters VII–IX when the time comes for essays and presentations.

Three appendixes close out Part 1 of the *Workbook.* The first is a listing of fallacies: types of misleading arguments that are so tempting and common, they even have their own names. The second offers three rules for constructing and evaluating definitions. The third, which is not included in the original *Rulebook,* covers argument mapping, which is a powerful technique for understanding how the pieces of an argument fit together. Use them when you need them!

Part 2 of the *Workbook* offers model responses to the odd-numbered exercises in nearly every exercise set. Most model responses have commentaries that explain the strengths and weaknesses of each response.

Part 3 of the *Workbook* contains longer critical thinking activities that build on the rules and exercises in Part 1. Some of these you can do on your own. Others you will need to do in class or with a group of classmates.

How to use the *Workbook*

Throughout Part 1 of this book, you will notice that some passages have a shaded bar beside them. The passages with the sidebar come from Anthony Weston's *Rulebook for Arguments*. The passages without the sidebar are only in the *Workbook for Arguments*. The additions in Part 1 consist mainly of exercise sets designed to help you learn how to apply the lessons from the passages with the sidebars. You can get the main ideas of each chapter by reading just the passages with the sidebars. Before attempting an exercise set, though, be sure to read both the *Rulebook* text before it and the "Tips for success" that accompany the exercise set.

After you have completed an exercise set—or at any rate, after you've given it your best shot—take a look at the model responses for that exercise set. (You'll find the model responses in Part 2.) We strongly encourage you to read them even if you don't need help doing the exercises. The model responses often contain important further discussions. Moreover, part of their aim, considered as a whole, is to paint a wide-ranging and compelling picture of critical intelligence at work. The spirit of critical thinking is just as vital as the letter, so to speak, and in the *Workbook* you will find both.

Every exercise set ends with a suggestion about how to get more practice applying the skills used in that exercise set. Many of these suggestions are most effective if you work in a group. If you find that you consistently want more practice, form a study group with some of your classmates.

From time to time, your instructor may have you complete one of the critical thinking activities from Part 3. These activities are designed to be especially enjoyable and engaging and to help you connect the material in this book to your own life. Be sure to find out whether your instructor has any additional or alternative instructions for the activity, or if he or she wants you to complete one of the variations listed at the end of the activity's assignment sheet.

Critical thinking is a skill—and like most skills, it's a skill that you can always improve, even if you're already good at it. Reading about guidelines for critical thinking, such as the rules presented in this book, is an important part of honing your skill, but there is no substitute for practice. (That could even be Rule 46: Practice, practice, practice.) The aim of this workbook is to give you an opportunity for guidance, practice, and feedback. With some persistence and hard work, you'll find yourself thinking more clearly and more critically than ever.

Part 1

Part 1

Chapter I

Short Arguments: Some General Rules

Arguments begin by marshaling reasons and organizing them in a clear and fair way. Chapter I offers general rules for composing short arguments. Chapters II–VI discuss specific *kinds* of short arguments.

Identify premises and conclusion

The very first step in making an argument is to ask yourself what you are trying to prove. What is your conclusion? Remember that the conclusion is the statement for which you are giving reasons. The statements that give your reasons are your *premises*.

Consider these lines from Winston Churchill:

> I am an optimist. It does not seem to be much use being any-thing else.

This is an argument—as well as an amusing quip—because Churchill is giving a *reason* to be an optimist: his premise is that "It does not seem to be much use being anything else."

Premises and conclusion are not always so obvious. Sherlock Holmes has to explain one of his deductions in "The Adventure of Silver Blaze":

> A dog was kept in the stalls, and yet, though someone had been in and fetched out a horse, [the dog] had not barked. . . . Obviously the . . . visitor was someone whom the dog knew well.[1]

Holmes has two premises. One is explicit: the dog did not bark at the visitor. The other is a general fact that Holmes assumes we know about dogs: dogs bark at strangers. Together these premises imply that the visitor was not a stranger. It turns out that this is the key to solving the mystery.

When you are using arguments as a means of inquiry, you sometimes may start with no more than the conclusion you wish to defend. State it clearly, first of all. Maybe you want to take Churchill a step farther and

---

1. Sir Arthur Conan Doyle, "The Adventure of Silver Blaze," in *The Complete Sherlock Holmes* (Garden City, NY: Garden City Books, 1930), p. 199.

argue that you and I should be optimists too. If so, say so explicitly. Then ask yourself what reasons you have for drawing that conclusion. What reasons can you give to prove that we should be optimists?

You could appeal to Churchill's authority. If Churchill recommends optimism, who are we to quibble? This appeal will not get you very far, however, since equally famous people have recommended pessimism. You need to think about the question on your own. Again, what is *your* reason for thinking that we should be optimists?

One reason could be that optimism boosts your energy to work for success, whereas if you feel defeated in advance you may never even try. Optimists are more likely to succeed, to achieve their goals. (Maybe this is what Churchill meant as well.) If this is your premise, say so explicitly.

This book offers you a ready list of different forms that arguments can take. Use this list to develop your premises. To defend a generalization, for instance, check Chapter II. It will remind you that you need to give a series of examples as premises, and it will tell you what sorts of examples to look for. If your conclusion requires a deductive argument like those explained in Chapter VI, the rules outlined in that chapter will tell you what types of premises you need. You may have to try several different arguments before you find one that works well.

Exercise Set 1.1: Distinguishing premises from conclusions

Objective: To give you practice distinguishing premises from conclusions in other people's arguments.

Instructions: Rewrite each argument below, underlining the conclusion of each argument and putting brackets around each premise.

Tips for success: Distinguishing premises from conclusions is sometimes more of an art than a science. We wish people were always clear about the premises and conclusions of their argument, but that's just not the case. Therefore, learning to distinguish premises from conclusions takes practice. As you practice, there are two strategies that you should keep in mind.

The first strategy is simply to ask yourself what the author of this argument is trying to convince you to believe. The claim that the author is trying to get you to believe is the argument's conclusion. Then you can ask what *reasons* the author gives to try to convince you. These will be the argument's premises.

The second strategy for distinguishing premises from conclusions is to look for *indicator words*. Some words or phrases are *conclusion indicators*. These are words or phrases that tell you that you're about to read or hear the conclusion of an argument. Other words or phrases are *premise indicators*. These tell you that you're about to read or hear a premise. Here's a sample of the most common conclusion and premise indicators:

Conclusion Indicators	**Premise Indicators**
therefore	because
thus	since
hence	given that
so	for
consequently	on the grounds that
this shows that	this follows from

You'll start to notice more indicator words as you get better at analyzing arguments.

Two more pieces of advice: First, don't rely solely on indicator words. Some arguments will not use any indicator words. Others will use indicator words in other ways. Some words, like *because, since,* and *so,* have many other uses; not every use of *because* indicates that you're about to hear a premise. When in doubt, fall back on our first strategy: ask yourself whether the author is giving you a reason for the conclusion. If your answer is no, you haven't found a premise, even if the sentence includes *because* or *since.*

Second, don't assume that everything in a passage is either a premise or a conclusion. Not all passages contain arguments. Some passages are telling stories, describing things, giving explanations, issuing commands, making jokes, or doing other things besides giving reasons for a conclusion. Even in passages that do contain arguments, some sentences or clauses will provide background information, make side comments, and so on. Again, the key is to ask yourself, "Is this sentence stating a conclusion or giving me a reason to believe that conclusion?" If it is doing either, it's part of an argument; if not, it's not.

Sample

[In order to prosper, a democracy needs its citizens to be able to carry out their responsibilities competently.] [Being a competent citizen requires familiarity with the basics of math, natural science, social science, history, and literature, as well as the ability to read and write well and the ability to think critically.] [A liberal education is essential to developing these skills.] Therefore, <u>in order for a democracy to prosper, its citizens must get a liberal education.</u>

Adapted from: Steven M. Cahn, letter to the editor, New York Times, *May 21, 2004*

The markings in this sample problem indicate that the last sentence is the conclusion and that each of the first three sentences is a separate premise. Although each sentence in this letter to the editor expresses either a premise or a conclusion, remember that many passages contain sentences (or parts of sentences) that are neither premises nor conclusions. You don't need to bracket or underline those (parts of) sentences.

1. Racial segregation reduces some persons to the status of things. Hence, segregation is morally wrong.

    Adapted from: Martin Luther King, Jr., "Letter from a Birmingham Jail," Liberation: An Independent Monthly, *Jun 1963*

2. While performing an autopsy on a dead sea turtle, Dr. Stacy found shrimp in the turtle's throat. Sea turtles can only catch shrimp if the turtles are stuck in nets with the shrimp. Therefore, the dead sea turtle was probably caught in a net.

    Adapted from: Shaila Dewan, "Animal Autopsies in Gulf Yield Mystery," New York Times, *Jul 14, 2010, http://www.nytimes.com/2010/07/15/science/ earth/15necropsy.html*

3. Most people experience no side effects from the yellow fever vaccine. People with egg allergies shouldn't get the yellow fever vaccine, though, because some part of the vaccine is grown inside eggs.

    Adapted from: Division of Vector Borne Infectious Diseases, "Vaccine | CDC Yellow Fever," Centers for Disease Control and Prevention, http://www.cdc.gov/ncidod/dvbid/YellowFever/vaccine/

4. There are two ways of settling a dispute: by discussion and by physical force. Since the first way is appropriate for human beings and the second way appropriate for animals, we must resort to force only when we cannot settle matters by discussion.

Adapted from: Cicero, De Officiis *11*

5. Positron-emission tomography, better known as PET, is a method for examining a person's brain. Before undergoing PET, the patient inhales a gas containing radioactive molecules. The molecules are not dangerous for the patient because they break down within a few minutes, before they can do any damage.

Adapted from: Bryan Kolb and Ian Q. Wishaw, Fundamentals of Human Neuropsychology, *5th ed. (New York: Worth Publishers, 2003), 161*

6. The head of the spy ring is very dangerous. He is also exceptionally clever and a master of disguise. He has a dozen names and a hundred different appearances. But there is one thing he cannot disguise: he is missing the tip of his little finger. So, if you ever meet a man who is missing the top joint of his little finger, you should be very careful!

Adapted from: The 39 Steps, *directed by Alfred Hitchcock (London: Gaumont British, 1935)*

7. Some people buy college degrees on the Internet because they're trying to pretend that they went to college. That's a waste of money, since it's easy to make a college degree on your computer, and a degree that you make yourself is just as good as a degree that you bought on the Internet.

Adapted from: "Fake Degrees in Government," The Onion, *Oct 18, 2006, http://www.theonion.com/articles/fake-degrees-in-government,15092/*

8. People are created equal and endowed with unalienable rights. Governments exist to protect those rights. When a government violates those rights, people have a right to rebel against that government and create a new one. The king of Great Britain has repeatedly violated the rights of the American colonists. Thus, the American colonists have a right to rebel against the king of Great Britain.

Adapted from: U.S. Declaration of Independence

9.   In the film *Interstellar*, the main characters travel through a "wormhole," which is a tunnel through space-time that would enable space travelers to zip from one part of the universe to another. In theory, wormholes are possible, but it's probably impossible to use wormholes to travel around the universe. Keeping wormholes open long enough to travel through them would require enormous amounts of "negative enery," and it's probably impossible to generate that much negative energy.

Adapted from: Mike Wall, "Interstellar's Science: Is Wormhole Travel Possible?" LiveScience, Nov 24, 2014, http://www.livescience.com/48890-interstellar-movie-wormhole-travel-feasibility.html

10.   The only remaining question was why the man had been murdered. Was it a politically motivated crime or a private one? I thought right away that it must be a privately motivated crime. Political assassins move quickly and flee. But in this case, the murderer's footprints are all over the room, showing that he had spent quite a while in this room.

Adapted from: Arthur Conan Doyle, A Study in Scarlet (London: Ward Lock & Co., 1888; repr., London: Penguin, 2001), 138

Model responses for odd-numbered exercises can be found on page 287.

Need more practice? Take a look at the editorials, op-eds, and letters to the editor on the Web site for your favorite newspaper. Most of these will contain arguments. Working by yourself or with a classmate, identify the premises and conclusions in those arguments.

Rule 2

Develop your ideas in a natural order

Short arguments are usually developed in one or two paragraphs. Put the conclusion first, followed by your reasons, or set out your premises first and draw the conclusion at the end. In any case, set out your ideas in an order that unfolds your line of thought most clearly for the reader.

Consider this short argument by Bertrand Russell:

The evils of the world are due to moral defects quite as much as to lack of intelligence. But the human race has not hitherto discovered any method of eradicating moral defects. . . .

Intelligence, on the contrary, is easily improved by methods known to every competent educator. Therefore, until some method of teaching virtue has been discovered, progress will have to be sought by improvement of intelligence rather than of morals.[2]

Each sentence in this passage prepares the way for the next one, and then the next one steps smoothly up to bat. Russell begins by pointing out the two sources of evil in the world: "moral defects," as he puts it, and lack of intelligence. He then claims that we do not know how to correct "moral defects," but that we do know how to correct lack of intelligence. Therefore—notice that the word "therefore" clearly marks his conclusion—progress will have to come by improving intelligence.

Getting an argument to unfold in this smooth sort of way is a real accomplishment. It's not easy to find just the right place for each part—and plenty of wrong places are available. Suppose Russell instead argued like this:

The evils of the world are due to moral defects quite as much as to lack of intelligence. Until some method of teaching virtue has been discovered, progress will have to be sought by improvement of intelligence rather than of morals. Intelligence is easily improved by methods known to every competent educator. The human race has not hitherto discovered any means of eradicating moral defects.

These are the same premises and conclusion, but they are in a different order, and the word "therefore" has been omitted before the conclusion. Now the argument is much harder to understand, and therefore also much less persuasive. The premises do not fit together naturally, and you have to read the passage twice just to figure out what the conclusion is. Don't count on your readers to be so patient.

Expect to rearrange your argument several times to find the most natural order. The rules discussed in this book should help. You can use them to figure out not only what kinds of premises you need but also how to arrange them in the best order.

---

2. Bertrand Russell, *Skeptical Essays* (1935; repr., London: Allen & Unwin, 1977), p. 127.

Exercise Set 1.2: Outlining arguments in premise-and-conclusion form

Objective: To give you practice rewriting arguments in a clear, logical structure.

Instructions: Each of the following passages contains an argument. Put the premises in a natural, meaningful order, and write them out in a numbered list. Then, write the conclusion at the end of the list.

Tips for success: It's often helpful to outline arguments in premise-and-conclusion form. This involves several steps.

First, identify the premises and the conclusions, just as you did in Exercise Set 1.1.

Then, put the premises in a meaningful order—that is, an order that helps you understand how the premises connect with one another and with the conclusion. In many cases, there won't be a single best ordering. Try a few different orderings and pick the one that makes the most sense to you.

When you have settled on a meaningful order for the premises, write the premises down in a numbered list. It's helpful to make each premise a complete sentence, replacing pronouns like *him* or *it* with the names of the people or things they stand for.

Finally, write the conclusion at the end of the list. Some logicians draw a line between the premises and the conclusion, much like the line that mathematicians draw between an arithmetic problem and its answer. This line shows that the premises "add up" to the conclusion. Other logicians write *therefore* or include the symbol ∴ (which means *therefore*) before the conclusion.

Sample

Some companies are creating genetically modified animals, such as salmon, that provide more meat for consumers. If genetically modified salmon escaped into the wild, they would compete with "natural" salmon for food. Natural salmon, though, have been honed by natural selection to flourish in the wild. Genetically modified salmon are not designed to flourish in the wild. Thus, non-genetically modified salmon would outcompete genetically modified salmon if genetically modified salmon escaped into the wild.

Adapted from: "Dawn of the Frankenfish," The Economist, Jun 10, 2010

(1) If genetically modified animals escaped into the wild, they would compete with "natural" salmon for food.

(2) Natural salmon have been honed by natural selection to flourish in the wild.

(3) Genetically modified salmon are not designed to flourish in the wild.

Therefore, (4) Non-genetically modified salmon would outcompete genetically modified salmon if genetically modified salmon escaped into the wild.

This argument already presents its ideas in a natural order. The only thing needed to put it into premise-and-conclusion form is to identify the premises, put them in a numbered list, and add "therefore" before the conclusion.

The first sentence in the passage is not a premise in the argument. Its purpose is to provide context for the argument, not to give a reason to accept the conclusion. We do not need to include it in our outline of the argument.

---

1. Although he's only halfway through his basketball career, LeBron James will eventually surpass Michael Jordan in MVP awards, All-Star appearances, total points scored, and many other records. It is quite possible that he'll win as many championships as Jordan did. So far, Jordan is the greatest basketball player of all time. So, LeBron will eventually become the greatest player of all time.

Adapted from: David Lariviere, "LeBron James Will Eventually Top Michael Jordan as Basketball's Greatest Player," Forbes.com, May 24, 2013, http://www.forbes.com/sites/davidlariviere/2013/05/24/lebron-james-will-eventually-top-michael-jordan-as-basketballs-greatest-player/

2.   Someone who can't get enough to eat clearly lives in poverty. But someone who can't afford the things that his or her society regards as necessities also lives in poverty. Wealthier societies will regard more things as necessities than poorer societies. Thus, the "poverty line," which is the amount of money someone must have to count as "non-poor," will be higher in a wealthier society than in a poorer society.

Adapted from: David Phillips, Quality of Life: Concept, Policy, and Practice
(Abingdon, UK: Routledge, 2006), 110

3.   A team of researchers led by Brendan Nyhan at Dartmouth wanted to study the effects of giving parents information on the safety of vaccines. They gave some parents information from the Centers for Disease Control and Prevention stating that there is no evidence that vaccines cause autism. Other parents received no information about vaccine safety. When compared to parents who received no information, parents who received information were no more likely to vaccinate their children. Nyhan and his colleagues concluded that simply providing information about vaccine safety does not increase the proportion of parents who get their children vaccinated.

Adapted from: Maria Konnikova, "I Don't Want to Be Right," New Yorker, May 16, 2014, http://www.newyorker.com/science/maria-konnikova/i-dont-want-to-be-right

4.   Smaller high schools are better than larger high schools since smaller high schools have been shown to have higher graduation rates and a higher proportion of students going on to college. New York City has broken a number of large high schools up into several smaller schools.

Adapted from: David M. Herszenhorn, "Gates Charity Gives $51 Million to City to Start 67 Schools," New York Times, Sep 18, 2003, http://www.nytimes.com/2003/09/18/nyregion/gates-charity-gives-51-million-to-city-to-start-67-schools.html

5.   In 1908, something flattened eight hundred square miles of forest in a part of Siberia called Tunguska. Theories abound about "the Tunguska event." Some people say it was a UFO. Some even say it was a tiny black hole. Recently, however, scientists discovered

that a lake in the area has the shape of an impact crater that would have been created by an asteroid or comet. So, the Tunguska event was caused by an asteroid or comet.

Adapted from: Paul Rincon, "Fire in the Sky: Tunguska at 100," BBC News, Jun 30, 2008, http://news.bbc.co.uk/2/hi/science/nature/7470283.stm

6. There is a "generation gap" in Americans' knowledge of politics. That is to say, older people know more about politics than younger people. This is not the result of older people generally being more interested in politics than younger people. Opinion polls from the 1940s through the mid-1970s show that younger people used to be at least as well informed about politics as the older people of their time were.

Adapted from: Robert D. Putnam, Bowling Alone (New York: Simon & Schuster, 2000), 36

7. All cars should have a spear mounted on the steering wheel, aimed directly at the driver's chest. After all, we should do everything we can to encourage cautious driving. Since people behave much more cautiously when they know that their life is on the line, steering wheel–mounted spears would make people drive much more cautiously.

Adapted from: Steven E. Landsburg, The Armchair Economist (New York: Simon & Schuster, 1994), 5

8. Human nature is not inherently good. Human nature consists of those human traits that are spontaneous; these things cannot be learned. Thus, if something can be learned, then it is not part of human nature. Yet, goodness is not spontaneous; people must learn how to be good.

Adapted from: Xunzi, Xunzi, in Readings in Classical Chinese Philosophy, 2nd ed., edited by Philip J. Ivanhoe and Bryan W. van Norden (Indianapolis: Hackett Publishing Company, 2005), 298–99

9. It is possible for someone to wonder whether her life is meaning-ful even if she knows that she has enjoyed her life. This shows that a meaningful life is not the same as an enjoyable life. At the same

time, someone who is alienated from her life or feels like her life is pointless, even if she is doing things that might seem worthwhile from an objective perspective, is not leading a meaningful life. This shows that a meaningful life is not the same as a life spent on objectively worthwhile projects. All of this shows that neither enjoyment nor objectively worthwhile projects, considered separately from the other, are sufficient for a meaningful life.

Adapted from: Susan Wolf, "Happiness and Meaning: Two Aspects of the Good Life,"
Social Philosophy & Policy *14 (1997), 211*

10. Suppose that Tim learns that his grandfather had done something terrible in the 1920s, several years before the birth of Tim's mother. Suppose also that Tim has invented a time machine. While it may seem that Tim could go back in time and kill his grandfather to prevent him from doing this terrible thing, in fact, it is impossible for Tim to kill his grandfather. The past has already happened. It cannot be changed. Since Tim's grandparents had Tim's mother, who went on to have Tim, it must be the case that Tim did not kill his grandfather.

Adapted from: David Lewis, "The Paradoxes of Time Travel," American
Philosophical Quarterly *13 (1976), 149–50*

Model responses for odd-numbered exercises can be found on page 290.

Need more practice? Following the steps described in the "Tips for success" section, outline the arguments from Exercise Set 1.1 in premise-and-conclusion form. Work with a friend or classmate if you want to be able to compare your work with someone else's. For even more practice, do the same thing with the arguments in the editorials, op-eds, and letters to the editor that you found on your favorite newspaper's Web site.

For a more sophisticated way to show the relationships among premises in an argument, see Appendix III: Argument Mapping (p. 268). Argument maps are especially helpful in understanding complex arguments.

Exercise Set 1.3: Analyzing visual arguments

Objective: To help you recognize short arguments in visual materials.

Instructions: Go to the companion Web site for this book. Click on the link for "Chapter I" and then on the link for "Exercise Set 1.3." You will get a list of links to images and videos. Write a premise-and-conclusion outline of the argument that you think the image or video is trying to communicate.

Tips for success: We are constantly bombarded by visual material—from billboards to artwork to online videos—that aims to persuade us of something. Sometimes the material tries to persuade us to do something or to want something. Sometimes it tries to persuade us to believe something. You can think of many of these materials as *visual arguments*. They don't necessarily present their premises and conclusions in words, but many of them still can be read as offering reasons in support of conclusions—that is, as arguments.

When you're thinking about a visual argument, it's entirely up to you to present the argument's ideas in a natural order. The first thing you'll need to do is determine the conclusion of the visual argument. What is the argument trying to get you to do or believe? Then you'll need to ask yourself whether the picture or video offers you reasons to believe that conclusion. If so, these will be the premises of the argument.

To identify these premises, think about what the connection is between the images that you are seeing and the conclusion that those images are meant to support. To take an extremely simple case, suppose an advertisement shows an athlete enjoying a Sprite. The conclusion of this visual argument is that you ought to drink Sprite too. What is the connection between the image of the athlete drinking Sprite and the claim that you ought to drink it? If the athlete takes a sip after a hard game or workout, perhaps the message is that Sprite is especially refreshing. In that case, the argument might be something like this: "Sprite is especially refreshing. You like refreshing drinks. Therefore, you ought to drink Sprite." Or maybe the athlete is sitting around with her friends, and they are all having a good time and drinking Sprite. In that case, the message might be that hip young adults—especially people who like this particular athlete's sport—drink Sprite and that if you want to be like these people, you should drink Sprite too.

Different people are likely to come up with different interpretations of each visual argument. In fact, you can probably come up with different interpretations of each one yourself. Don't worry about finding the one and only correct interpretation. Just focus on finding a plausible interpretation—one that the creator of the visual argument might recognize as the message he or she was trying to send.

The exercises for this exercise set, including a sample exercise, can be found on the companion Web site for this book.

Need more practice? Look through a recent magazine or a Web site that includes advertisements. Analyze the visual arguments offered in each of the advertisements that you encounter.

Critical thinking activity: Found arguments

For an out-of-class activity that gives you practice in applying Rules 1 and 2, see the "Found arguments" assignment sheet (p. 441) in Part 3.

Critical thinking activity: Creating a visual argument

For an out-of-class activity that gives you practice in dealing with visual arguments, see the "Creating a visual argument" assignment sheet (p. 442) in Part 3.

Rule 3

Start from reliable premises

No matter how well you argue from premises to conclusion, your conclusion will be weak if your premises are weak.

> Nobody in the world today is really happy. Therefore, it seems that human beings are just not made for happiness. Why should we expect what we can never find?

The premise of this argument is the statement that nobody in the world today is really happy. Sometimes, on certain rainy afternoons or in certain moods, this may almost seem true. But ask yourself if this premise really is plausible. Is *nobody* in the world today really happy? Ever? At the very least, this premise needs some serious defense, and very likely it is just not true. This argument cannot show, then, that human beings are not made for happiness or that you or I should not expect to be happy.

Sometimes it is easy to start from reliable premises. You may have well-known examples at hand or reliable sources that are clearly in agreement. Other times it is harder. If you are not sure about the reliability of a premise, you may need to do some research and/or give an argument for the premise itself (see Rule 31 for more on this point). If you find you *cannot* argue adequately for your premise(s), then, of course, you need to try some other premise!

Exercise Set 1.4: Identifying reliable and unreliable premises

Objective: To give you practice recognizing reliable starting points for arguments.

Instructions: Rewrite the following arguments in premise-and-conclusion form, just as you did in Exercise Set 1.2. Then, state whether each premise is reliable and explain why or why not.

Tips for success: Arguments are both a way to convince others of something and a way to learn new things. A good argument leads you (and/or others) from premises that you already accept to conclusions that you (and/or they) did not previously accept. To do that, however, arguments need to start from premises that you or they already accept. Furthermore, when two or more people hold different views on a topic, they can't have a productive discussion unless they start from some kind of common ground. Therefore, an important part of learning to give good arguments is learning to recognize which premises are reliable and widely acceptable starting points. Deciding whether a starting point is reliable and acceptable in this way can be tricky, and can vary with the situation, but there are some rules of thumb that can guide your thinking.

First, widely accepted facts are usually reliable starting points. For instance, it's widely accepted that there is a wide variety of species on Earth and that these species resemble each other in various ways. Those facts can provide reliable starting points for an argument about evolution.

It's worth finding out how widely accepted your "facts" really are, though. Something that seems like common knowledge to you might be widely doubted in other social circles, other parts of the country, or other parts of the world. For instance, it is widely accepted in many parts of the world that the variety of species we see today evolved by natural selection, but there are also social circles and parts of the world where that is frequently denied. If you are addressing your argument to someone who denies what you regard as a widely accepted fact, you may need to find another starting point for your argument.

Second, premises that are supported by appropriate testimony or sources are usually reliable. For instance, if a trustworthy person tells you that she has been to Brazil and seen pink dolphins living in the Amazon River, you could count "There are pink dolphins living in the Amazon River" as a reliable premise.

There are also guidelines to help you spot unreliable premises. Premises that are widely known to be false or easily shown to be false are unreliable. (Again, though, remember that what's "widely known to be false" in one context may be generally accepted elsewhere. Remember your audience!) Other premises are unreliable not because we know that they're false but because we don't know, or can't know, whether they're true; such claims can't provide a solid foundation for an argument. Wild generalizations and overly vague claims fall into this category. So do controversial claims offered without support, and claims that we could not possibly verify. Remember, though, that there's a difference between claiming that a premise is unreliable and claiming that it is false. Saying that a premise is unreliable could just mean that you don't know whether it's true.

Later rules in this book, especially the rules in Chapter IV about using sources, will give you further and more developed guidelines for finding reliable starting points. Rule 31 will also invite you to offer additional reasons for seemingly unreliable premises, turning those premises into well-supported conclusions of their own arguments. But all of that is still to come. For now, just look at the premises before you, and use your common sense.

Sample

Computers will soon take over most human tasks. After all, Deep Blue, a computer, beat Garry Kasparov, the World Chess Champion, in 1997. And if computers can defeat the best human alive in an activity that symbolizes intelligence more than any other, then surely their supremacy in everything else we do is not far off.

Adapted from: Editorial, Washington Post, *May 6, 1997, http://www. washingtonpost.com/wp-srv/tech/analysis/kasparov/editorial.htm*

(1) Deep Blue, a computer, beat the World Chess Champion in 1997.

(2) If computers can beat the best human alive in chess, then their supremacy in everything else we do is not far off.

Therefore, (3) Computers will soon take over most human tasks.

Premise (1) is reliable, since it is a widely accepted fact. (If the argument were intended for an audience that didn't know about Deep Blue's victory, the author would probably want to point to news reports about the match as a way of supporting the premise with sources.)

Premise (2), however, is unreliable. It is implausible speculation to say that a victory in chess suggests that "supremacy in everything else we do" is just around the corner. After all, chess is a very different kind of activity from most things that humans do. (Think of the differences between chess and writing a novel, cooking a meal, playing basketball, or navigating the social jungles of a school or office.)

This response takes a nuanced approach to premise (1), explaining that the premise is not only widely known, but easily verified in case anyone is uncertain about it (a sad day for chess fans everywhere.) The real problem, just as this response says, is with the reliability of premise (2).

Notice that the response does not attempt to say whether the conclusion is reliable. Rule 3 is about the reliability of premises. You do not need to comment on the arguments' conclusions in this exercise set.

1. Anybody could become a zombie—a relative, a friend, or even a neighbor. Zombies are constantly looking to eat the brains of the living. This is why you should always be prepared to escape from or fight back against a zombie attack.

    Adapted from: "Zombies in Plain English," YouTube, Oct 23, 2007,
    http://www.youtube.com/watch?v=bVnfyradCPY

2. Social networking sites have revolutionized the way we interact with our friends. Such sites allow people to stay in contact with hundreds or even thousands of people. Human nature, however, prevents us from having meaningful relationships with that many people. Therefore, most of your "friends" on those sites are not people with whom you have meaningful relationships.

    Adapted from: Robin Dunbar, "You've Got to Have (150) Friends,"
    New York Times, *Dec 25, 2010, http://www.nytimes.com/2010/12/26/*
    opinion/26dunbar.html

3. Some people scoff at a liberal education as a waste of time. But a true education is not just about accumulating knowledge. It's also about educating one's emotions. A liberal arts education exposes

students not only to history, science, and math, but also to the literature and arts that speak more directly to our emotions. Thus, a liberal arts education is an essential part of any "real" education.

Adapted from: Martha Nussbaum, Not for Profit: Why Democracy Needs the Humanities *(Princeton: Princeton University Press, 2010)*

4.   There are other advanced civilizations in our galaxy. To see why this must be so, consider the following facts: There are billions of stars in our galaxy, and many of them probably have planets around them. Some planets may develop life, and some of *those* planets will probably develop intelligent life capable of producing advanced technology.

Adapted from: "Carl Sagan on Advanced Civilizations," YouTube, Feb 24, 2008, http://www.youtube.com/watch?v=i0PWOJkWgcM

5.   Radioactive materials are materials that decay into other materials. For instance, certain isotopes of carbon are radioactive; they decay into different isotopes of carbon. By looking at the ratios of radioactive materials to the products of radioactive decay in a piece of rock, we can estimate the age of the rock fairly well. This process is called "radiometric dating." Radiometric dating reveals that some large rock formations in the Earth's crust are up to four billion years old. Thus, the Earth itself is at least four billion years old.

Adapted from: G. Brent Dalrymple, The Age of the Earth *(Palo Alto: Stanford University Press, 1994), 399*

6.   Scholars have begun looking at the colonial period as a way of understanding economic development. During the colonial period, several European powers established colonies in the Americas. Some of these colonies have become economically successful, while others have not. The most striking difference between those that succeeded and those that did not is that the successful colonies had much lower levels of economic and social inequality than the unsuccessful colonies. Therefore, we suggest that inequality hinders economic development.

Adapted from: Stanley L. Engerman and Kenneth L. Sokoloff, "Colonialism, Inequality, and Long-Run Paths of Development," in Abhijit V. Banerjee, Roland Bénabou, and Dilip Mookherjee, Understanding Poverty *(New York: Oxford University Press, 2006), 37–57*

7. To date, smallpox is the only human disease that has been completely eliminated from the face of the Earth. We are getting closer to the day that polio is eliminated too. Polio used to be a serious problem in many parts of the world. As of 1988, polio remained endemic in only six countries: Niger, Egypt, India, Pakistan, Afghanistan, and Nigeria. By 2006, two of those countries—Niger and Egypt—were polio free, according to the World Health Organization.

Adapted from: Mark Prendergrast, Inside the Outbreaks: The Elite Medical Detectives of the Epidemic Intelligence Service *(New York: Houghton Mifflin Harcourt, 2010), 346*

8. Despite what the skeptics would have you believe, many people are capable of seeing ghosts. Ghosts are real, and anyone with the psychic ability known as extrasensory perception (ESP) is capable of seeing them. ESP is a real phenomenon, according to Professor Joseph Rhine of Duke University. In fact, about half of all people have ESP, although many never realize it.

Adapted from: Hans Holzer, Ghosts: True Encounters with the World Beyond *(New York: Black Dog & Leventhal Publishers, 1997), 29*

9. You should be a vegetarian. Every time you eat meat, your meal is the result of the suffering and death of an animal. Besides, it's disgusting to put a piece of a dead animal's carcass into your mouth and chew it. There is plenty of great vegetarian food, including tasty meat alternatives. Also, vegetarianism is healthier than eating meat. One more reason to be a vegetarian is that you'd be joining the company of a long list of incredible people, from Leonardo da Vinci, Isaac Newton, and Thomas Edison to Paul McCartney, Shania Twain, and Tobey Maguire.

Adapted from: Johnny Durham, "Reasons to Be Vegetarian," YouTube, Jan 7, 2009, http://www.youtube.com/watch?v=t36dufpDn9g

10. The Bureau of Justice Statistics reports that at least three hundred thousand children in the United States are forced into prostitution and other sex-trafficking crimes every year. They estimate the average age of entry into forced prostitution is twelve years old.

Forcing a child to work as a prostitute is wrong. It is a travesty that eliminating child prostitution is not a bigger priority for our country.

Adapted from: Angela Colwell, letter to the editor, Tulsa World, *Apr 23, 2010,*
http://www.tulsaworld.com/site/opinion/article
.aspx?articleid=20100423_62_A18_Acrigt552416

Model responses for odd-numbered exercises can be found on page 293.

Need more practice? Go back to the arguments presented in Exercise Sets 1.1 and 1.2 and decide which of their premises are reliable. For even more practice, go to the Web site for this book and click on the "Chapter I" link. You'll find a link to a list of Web sites that feature online debates. Find debates that interest you and read the arguments presented in those debates. Determine which premises are reliable and why.

Rule 4

Be concrete and concise

Avoid abstract, vague, and general terms. "We hiked for hours in the sun" is a hundred times better than "It was an extended period of laborious exertion." Be concise too. Airy elaboration just loses everyone in a fog of words.

NO:
For those whose roles primarily involved the performance of services, as distinguished from assumption of leadership responsibilities, the main pattern seems to have been a response to the leadership's invoking obligations that were concomitants of the status of membership in the societal community and various of its segmental units. The closest modern analogy is the military service performed by an ordinary citizen, except that the leader of the Egyptian bureaucracy did not need a special emergency to invoke legitimate obligations.[3]

YES:
In ancient Egypt the common people were liable to be conscripted for work.

3. Talcott Parsons, *Societies: Evolutionary and Comparative Perspectives* (Englewood Cliffs, NJ: Prentice Hall, 1966), p. 56. The quotation and the rewritten version that follows come from Stanislas Andreski, *Social Sciences as Sorcery* (New York: St. Martin's Press, 1972), Ch. 6.

Exercise Set 1.5: Decomplexifying artificially abstruse quotations

Objective: To help you recognize and avoid overly elaborate writing.

Instructions: Each passage in this exercise consists of a famous quote that has been rewritten using overly abstract, vague, or obscure terms. Rewrite the quote in simpler language.

Tips for success: Start by reading the passage in its entirety to get a sense for the meaning of the whole passage. Then, go back over the passage phrase by phrase, trying to figure out what each phrase means. Rewrite each phrase in the simplest language you can find, deleting words or phrases that don't add to the meaning of the sentence. Don't worry about coming up with the exact wording of the original quotation. Just try to express the ideas in the passage as simply and directly as possible.

Sample

Of this relatively limited extension of one of the ambulatory limbs of this particular male of the species *Homo sapiens*, it might also be possible to declare that a relatively much larger extension of the reach of the human species as a whole, so to speak, is also concurrently taking place at this point in time.

Adapted from: "Apollo 11 TV Broadcast—Neil Armstrong First Step on Moon,"
YouTube, Jul 20, 2009, http://www.youtube.com/watch?v=CtwSgvstl8c

This small step for a man is also a giant leap for humankind.

Neil Armstrong's original statement, which he made when he first set foot on the moon, is, "That's one small step for [a] man, one giant leap for mankind." In the "complexified" form of this quotation, the first clause ("Of this relatively limited extension of one of the ambulatory limbs of this particular male of the species Homo sapiens*") corresponds to the phrase "That's one small step for [a] man," and the rest of the quotation corresponds to "one giant leap for mankind."*

The sample response isn't exactly what Armstrong said, and that's okay. It says what Armstrong said in a clear, straightforward way. That's what matters.

1. I seem to have the distinct impression that my canine companion and I are no longer physically located within the geographical confines of the midwestern American state generally known as Kansas.

    Adapted from: The Wizard of Oz, *directed by Victor Fleming (Los Angeles: Metro-Goldwin-Mayer, 1939)*

2. Do not inquire as to what it is that your country might accomplish on your behalf, but instead inquire what actions you might take to further the interests of the country that you regard as your own.

    Adapted from: John F. Kennedy, Inaugural Address, Jan 20, 1961

3. Being able to express oneself in as concise a way as possible—that is, using the fewest, plainest words with which it is feasible to communicate the essential meaning of one's thought—is at the very core of a knack for repartee.

    Adapted from: William Shakespeare, Hamlet *2.2*

4. Putting aside all prevarication, my most beloved one, it would be utterly impossible for me, even with great effort, to care any less than I do at this precise moment.

    Adapted from: Gone with the Wind, *directed by Victor Fleming (Los Angeles: Metro-Goldwin-Mayer, 1939)*

5. We must strive to exhibit in our own persons the sorts of alterations that we most fervently desire to observe in the world that we inhabit.

    Adapted from: Mohandas Gandhi, quoted in John McCain & Mark Salter, Character Is Destiny *(New York: Random House, 2005), 14*

6. My maternal grandmother's daughter was in the frequent habit of informing me that the period between birth and death is similar to a container of cocoa-based confections.

    Adapted from: Forrest Gump, *directed by Robert Zemeckis (Los Angeles: Paramount Pictures, 1994)*

7. Regularly turning in for the night at a fairly early hour, combined with the practice of awakening at an hour that is earlier than the hour at which most others arise, will tend to the acquisition of such desirable personal features as good physical constitution, a

comfortable financial situation, and the sort of discernment and other related intellectual abilities that conduce to earning the respect of others.

Adapted from: Benjamin Franklin, Poor Richard's Almanack *(1732; repr., New York: Skyhorse Publishing, 2007), 13*

8.   It has been my constant practice to rely upon the compassionate actions of people with whom I had not yet become acquainted prior to the performance of said action.

Adapted from: A Streetcar Named Desire, *directed by Elia Kazan (Burbank, CA: Warner Bros, 1951)*

9.   A female member of the human species who finds herself without the company of a male of the species is akin to an aquatic, scale-covered vertebrate with gills and fins that has not the possession of a pedal-driven, two-wheeled vehicle that is powered by a rider sitting astride a frame to which the wheels are attached.

Adapted from: Gloria Steinem, quoted in Deborah G. Felder, The 100 Most Influential Women of All Time *(New York: Citadel Press, 2002), 258*

10. I harbor an aspiration that, at some point in the future, my four offspring, who are currently fairly young, will be assessed not according to the pigmentation of their skin but by considering the character traits that they possess.

Adapted from: Martin Luther King, Jr., speech in Washington, DC, Aug 28, 1963

Model responses for odd-numbered exercises can be found on page 297.

Need more practice? Make a list of famous quotations, well-known song lyrics, titles of famous books, etc. Have a friend or classmate do the same. Rewrite each item on the list in the overly abstract, complex style used in this exercise. Trade "complexified" lists with your friend or classmate and try to decipher the items on his or her list. For even more practice, repeat this activity with the arguments from other exercises in this book: Rewrite each premise and conclusion in an overly complex style and challenge your classmate to figure out what the argument says.

A helpful way to be concrete and concise is to define your terms carefully. For tips on giving good definitions, see Appendix II: Definitions (p. 256).

Build on substance, not overtone

Offer actual reasons; don't just play on the overtones of words.

> **NO**:
> Having so disgracefully allowed her once-proud passenger railroads to fade into obscurity, America is honor bound to restore them now!

This is supposed to be an argument for restoring (more) passenger rail service. But it offers no evidence for this conclusion whatsoever, just some emotionally loaded words—shopworn words, too, like a politician on automatic. Did passenger rail "fade" because of something "America" did or didn't do? What was "disgraceful" about this? Many "once-proud" institutions outlive their times, after all—we're not obliged to restore them all. What does it mean to say America is "honor bound" to do this? Have promises been made and broken? By whom?

Much can be said for restoring passenger rail, especially in this era when the ecological and economic costs of highways are becoming enormous. The problem is that this argument does not say it. It leaves the emotional charge of the words to do all the work, and therefore really does no work at all. We're left exactly where we started. Overtones may sometimes persuade even when they shouldn't, of course—but remember, here we are looking for actual, concrete evidence.

Likewise, do not try to make your argument look good by using emotionally loaded words to label the other side. Generally, people advocate a position for serious and sincere reasons. Try to figure out their view—try to understand their *reasons*—even if you disagree entirely. For example, people who question a new technology are probably not in favor of "going back to the caves." (What *are* they in favor of? Maybe you need to ask.) Likewise, a person who believes in evolution is not claiming that her grandparents were monkeys. (And again: what *does* she think?) In general, if you can't imagine how anyone could hold the view you are attacking, probably you just don't understand it yet.

Exercise Set 1.6: Diagnosing loaded language

Objective: To train you to recognize and avoid loaded language.

Instructions: Look for "loaded language"—that is, emotionally charged words or phrases—in each of the following arguments. If the argument contains loaded language, indicate which words or phrases are loaded and suggest a less loaded way of saying the same thing. If the passage does not contain any loaded language, say so.

Tips for success: A good argument should be able to stand on the strength of its premises and the connection between the premises and the conclusion—not on the beauty of its rhetoric or the emotional charge of the way it's presented. Learning to recognize loaded language helps you avoid being taken in by arguments that sound good but lack substance; it also helps you avoid giving arguments yourself that sound good but don't actually provide good reasons for their conclusions.

Loaded language comes in both negative and positive varieties. That is, some loaded language carries negative emotional overtones. It casts an idea, a person, or whatever in a negative light. For instance, calling bankers "corporate pirates" makes them sound bad. Other loaded language carries positive emotional overtones. For instance, calling a camp for holding prisoners of war a "pacification center" makes it sound good—almost like the kind of place you'd want to go for a relaxing vacation. Look out for both kinds of loaded language.

Some loaded language is subtle. Its emotional power may depend on the context in which it is used. For instance, the term *Ivy League school* is not necessarily emotionally charged; it refers to one of a specific group of American universities. However, imagine two politicians in a debate. If one says, "Now, I may not have gone to an Ivy League school like my opponent, but . . .", the term *Ivy League school* suddenly has an air of elitism. It can make the politician's opponent seem out of touch with ordinary people. Look out for subtle loaded language, too.

When it comes to suggesting less loaded ways of saying the same thing, look for terms that carry less—and ideally, no—emotional charge. For instance, if you're talking about doctors who perform abortions, don't call them "baby killers." A phrase like that mostly just plays on our feelings. Many people think that performing abortion and killing babies are importantly different, and so they would not accept it as a neutral description. On the other hand, you shouldn't call them "doctors who help women with medical problems" either. To people who think abortion is murder, this glosses over a tremendous moral difference between doctors who perform abortions and those who don't. Instead, just call them "doctors who perform abortions."

Sample

Certain irresponsible American politicians have been spewing lies about the latest attempts at reform. Whether these lies come from a combination of stupidity and a hysterical imagination or from cleverness and a willingness to exploit innocent Americans for personal political gain, these lies must be exposed for the damaging falsehoods that they are.

Adapted from: Keith Olbermann, Countdown with Keith Olbermann, *MSNBC, Aug 10, 2009*

This argument is full of loaded language. Calling the politicians "irresponsible" makes them sound bad without yet saying what they're doing wrong; it could be deleted without affecting the actual substance of the argument. "Spewing lies" is an emotionally evocative way of saying "making false statements." Speculating about whether the "lies" come from "stupidity and a hysterical imagination" or "a willingness to exploit innocent Americans" makes the politicians sound dumb, unstable, or evil, but it doesn't actually add any facts to support the conclusion. Even worse, it falsely suggests that stupidity and malice are the only possible motives for these politicians' statements. That whole clause can be cut, too. The argument could claim simply that some politicians are making false statements about the latest attempts at reform and that the falsehood of those statements should be made clear to the public.

This response identifies specific instances of loaded language. It explains how each instance is emotionally charged and recommends an alternative. In cases where the loaded language adds nothing substantive to the argument, this response rightly recommends that the loaded language be deleted.

Notice that in rephrasing Olbermann's statement, this response arrives at a neutral statement that may still not be true. That is, his claim *is that some politicians are making false statements about the latest attempts at reform. It remains to be seen if they are or are not; now we'd expect Olbermann to go on to offer some evidence. The point of identifying and neutralizing loaded language is simply to bring us to the point of recognizing the need for evidence in this relatively open-minded way rather than being so worked up over the alleged lie-spewing and irresponsibility that we don't have the breathing room to even notice that no evidence has yet been offered.*

1. Religious fanatics lost the battle on anti-gay discrimination in the military. This isn't the end of their dangerous influence, though. Now that they've seen that their hatemongering against

homosexuals isn't going to win elections, they may just step up their fearmongering against other groups.

Adapted from: Juan Cole, "Senate Repeal of DADT in Global Context," Informed Comment, Dec 19, 2010, http://www.juancole.com/2010/12/senate-repeal-of-dadt-in-global-context.html

2. Of course I'm going to beat Henry Cooper! He's nothing! He's a tramp! He's a bum! I'll knock him out in five rounds—no, three!

Adapted from: "Muhammad Ali Engaging in Some of His Famous Trash Talk," YouTube, Nov 11, 2010, http://www.youtube.com/watch?v=WsAC4lhbE0g

3. The dirty little secret behind factory farms' profits—namely, that there's no good reason for their monstrously cruel mistreatment of animals—is getting out. Since morally decent people abhor senseless animal cruelty, people everywhere are turning against factory farms.

Adapted from: Mylan Engel, Jr., "Animal Advocates' Successes Have Factory Farmers Running Scared," Animal Ethics, Feb 6, 2007, http://animalethics .blogspot.com/2007/02/animal-advocates-successes-have-factory.html

4. If you are trying to lose weight, it's important that you not skip meals. If you skip meals, you're likely to experience hunger and food cravings later, making it harder for you to stick to your diet. Instead of skipping meals to control your calorie intake, eat appropriately sized meals on a regular basis.

Adapted from: Kandeel Judge, Maxine Barish-Wreden, and Karen K. Brees, The Complete Idiot's Guide to the Secrets of Longevity (New York: Penguin, 2008), 80

5. We can all agree that the defendant bought the murder weapon earlier that night. The pawn shop owner saw him buy it, and his friends saw him carrying it. So how does that switchblade end up in the old man's chest if the boy didn't kill him? Remember that imaginative little fable that the boy told? He claims that the knife fell through a hole in his pocket on his way to the movie theater. You don't really believe that, do you? The boy's a murderer, plain and simple.

Adapted from: 12 Angry Men, directed by Sidney Lumet (Los Angeles: United Artist, 1957)

6.   Seriously? You're going to try to murder a sweet, gentle, leaf-eating, doe-eyed deer, and you're worried about what kind of pants you're going to wear? Imagine *you're* a deer. You're prancing around the forest. You're thirsty, so you stop at a clear, gently gurgling stream to take a nice, refreshing drink and—BAM! A bullet blows your head wide open, splattering bloodied bits of brains all over the place. Now, let me ask you: Are you going to care what kind of *pants* the jerk who shot you is wearing? No! It doesn't matter what kind of pants you wear!

Adapted from: My Cousin Vinny, *directed by Jonathan Lynn (Los Angeles: Twentieth Century Fox, 1992)*

7.   Instead of boring you with the details of the new and innovative accomplishments that I intend to achieve while I have the honor and privilege of serving as your class president, let me just say that when you vote for me, you won't just be voting for Tracy Flick. You'll be voting to make this school a better place for you, for me, and for all of our other wonderful classmates. That's why you should vote for me as your next student body president.

Adapted from: Election, *directed by Alexander Payne (Los Angeles: Paramount Pictures, 1999)*

8.   Some members of Congress don't want to raise the federal debt ceiling. They need to understand what that would mean for the economy. It would mean a bigger economic crisis than we saw in 2008. It would lead the U.S. government to default on its financial obligations—the first default anywhere to be caused purely by insanity.

Adapted from: "This Week with Christiane Amanpour," ABC, Jan 2, 2011, http:// abcnews.go.com/ThisWeek/week-transcript-white-house-adviser-austan -goolsbee/story?id=12522822

For exercises 9 and 10, find two examples of loaded language in the media, online, in conversations with friends or family, or anywhere else you can find it. Print, copy, or write down your examples. Identify the loaded words or expressions in each example, explain why they're loaded, and suggest more neutral substitutes.

Model responses for odd-numbered exercises can be found on page 299.

Need more practice? Find online news sites that allow comments on their news stories. Look for instances of loaded language in the comments on that site. See if you can tell which comments are expressing substantive arguments and which are just spouting emotionally loaded language. For the comments that are expressing arguments, try to find more neutral ways to say the same thing.

Use consistent terms

Short arguments normally have a single theme or thread. They carry one idea through several steps. Therefore, couch that idea in clear and carefully chosen terms, and mark each new step by using those very same terms again.

> **NO:**
> When you learn about other cultures, you start to realize the variety of human customs. This new understanding of the diversity of social practices may give you a new appreciation of other ways of life. Therefore, studying anthropology tends to make you more tolerant.

> **YES:**
> When you learn about other cultures, you start to realize the variety of human customs. When you start to realize the variety of human customs, you tend to become more tolerant. Therefore, when you learn about other cultures, you tend to become more tolerant.

The "Yes" version might not be stylish, but it *is* crystal clear, whereas the "No" version hardly seems like the same argument. One simple feature makes the difference: the "Yes" argument repeats its key terms, while the "No" version uses a new phrase for each key idea every time the idea recurs. For example, "learning about other cultures" is redescribed in the "No" version's conclusion as "studying anthropology." The result is that the connection between premises and conclusion is lost in the underbrush. It's interesting underbrush, maybe, but you are still liable to get stuck in it.

Re-using the same key phrases can feel repetitive, of course, so you may be tempted to reach for your thesaurus. Don't go there! The logic depends on clear connections between premises and between premises and conclusion. It remains essential to use a consistent term for each idea. If you are concerned about style—as sometimes you should be, of course—then go for the tightest argument, not the most flowery.

MOST CONCISE:
When you learn about other cultures, you start to realize the variety of human customs, a realization that in turn tends to make you more tolerant.

You can talk about studying anthropology and the like, if you wish, as you explain each premise in turn.

Be sure, of course, to use your terms in the same sense: it may be misleading or confusing to switch their meanings mid-stream! (See the fallacy of equivocation in Appendix I.)

CHAPTER EXERCISES

Exercise Set 1.7: Evaluating letters to the editor

Objective: To give you practice applying Rules 1–6.

Instructions: The following arguments are adapted from letters to the editor in various newspapers and magazines. State how well each argument follows each of the rules presented in this chapter.

Tips for success: For each argument, proceed through this chapter's rules systematically. Think of each rule as asking a question about the argument: Does the argument make clear what the conclusion of the argument is (Rule 1)? Does it present ideas in a natural order (Rule 2)? Are the premises reliable (Rule 3)? Could the argument be clearer or more concise (Rule 4)? If so, which words or expressions are unclear? What might the author have said instead? Does the argument use loaded language (Rule 5)? If so, which words or expressions are loaded? Can you suggest a more neutral substitute? Does the author confuse the argument by using more than one term for the same idea (Rule 6)? If so, identify the inconsistent terminology and suggest one term that the author might use throughout the argument.

Be as specific as possible in explaining the ways in which the argument does or does not follow each rule. If you think some of the premises are unreliable, say which premises those are. Explain why those premises are unreliable. If the argument is unclear or wordy, say which words or expressions could be improved. If the argument uses loaded language, say which terms are loaded and briefly explain why they're loaded. You might even suggest a more neutral substitute. Likewise, if the author would be better off sticking to a single, consistent term for some idea, point out exactly what terms he or she uses and suggest the best one to use.

Sample

Training poor farmers in developing countries how to use organic farming practices is an effective way to fight poverty. One organization, Harambee-Kenya, has trained hundreds of farmers to use natural farming methods, such as drip irrigation using buckets. These farmers have gone from food shortages to food security and even food surpluses. Some are using the cash they earn by selling their excess agricultural output to finance their children's medical and educational expenses.

Adapted from: Carol Carper, letter to the editor, Christian Science Monitor, *Jul 19, 2010, http://www. csmonitor.com/Commentary/Letters-to-the-Editor/2010/0728/ Letters-to-the-Editor-Weekly-Issue-of-July-19-2010*

This letter does a good job with Rule 1: The conclusion of the argument is clearly stated in the first sentence. The letter then presents the premises in a natural, understandable order (Rule 2). The premises are not yet known to be reliable, though (Rule 3). It would be better if the author cited a source where we could verify her claims about the success of Harambee-Kenya's program, since that is not part of most Americans' experience (and her audience consists of Americans). Most of the letter does a good job with Rule 4, although the last sentence could be simplified to something like: "Some are using the cash they earn by selling their extra food to pay for their children's medical and school fees." The letter does not use loaded language (Rule 5). It has a few problems following Rule 6: it uses "organic" in the first sentence and "natural" in the second, and it uses "fight poverty" in the first sentence but much more elaborate phrases and ideas in the last two.

Notice that this response addresses each rule. It also justifies most of its claims about how well the argument follows each rule. For example, instead of just saying, "The argument does not follow Rule 3," it explains why the premises are not reliable. Furthermore, it offers a nuanced evaluation with respect to various rules. For instance, instance of saying, "The argument does not follow Rule 4," this response acknowledges that the argument follows Rule 4 for the most part, but points out a specific sentence that could be more concrete and concise.

1. Marijuana edibles, like marijuana-infused gummy bears, ought to be sold and kept in childproof packaging. Adults should think of marijuana edibles as like a loaded gun: Both are dangerous to children. Just as responsible gun owners keep their guns locked away in a gun safe, responsible purchasers of marijuana edibles ought to keep them locked up where kids can't get to them.

    Adapted from: Steve Schweitzberger, letter to the editor, Denver Post, *Nov 30, 2014,*
    http://blogs.denverpost.com/eletters/2014/11/30/
    safety-marijuana-edibles-2-letters/34973/

2. The conquest of England by French-speaking Normans in 1066 completely transformed the English language. Consider *Beowulf,* written before the conquest, and Chaucer's *The Canterbury Tales,* written a few centuries after the conquest. Well-educated modern English speakers could understand *The Canterbury Tales* without too much difficulty, but they probably couldn't understand a single line of *Beowulf,* which was written in Old English.

    Adapted from: Robert Hellam, letter to the editor, The Economist, *Jun 10, 2010*

3. Politicians today are in love with 30-second sound bites. They run screaming from anything requiring thoughtful, intelligent, or honest discussion. We ought to be ashamed of the level of discourse in our politics. Instead of actual debate, we get nothing but innuendo and idiocy.

    Adapted from: Margot LeRoy, letter to the editor, USA Today, *Oct 31, 2010*

4. Science, technology, engineering, and math education in the United States is in a crisis. Incorporating engineering into the curriculum can improve learning outcomes in technical fields: Engineering makes abstract lessons about science and math more engaging. Including engineering activities also helps improve students' imaginations.

    Adapted from: Thomas Loughlin, letter to the editor, New York Times, *Oct 29,*
    2010, http://www.nytimes.com/2010/10/29/opinion/l29science.html

5. It usually takes at least 25 years for important scientific discoveries to translate into big changes in health care. This was the case

for vaccinations, antibiotics, open-heart surgery, chemotherapy, and organ transplants. Thus, it's no surprise that the Human Genome Project, which cataloged human DNA, did not immediately result in the incredible medical advances predicted by a few overly enthusiastic scientists.

Adapted from: Leon E. Rosenberg and Huntington F. Willard, letter to the editor,
New York Times, Jun 25, 2010, http://www.nytimes.com/2010/06/26/
opinion/lweb26genome.html

6. Media coverage about youth suicides usually misses the point when it comes to the real cause of suicide. The media emphasizes stress; cold, dark winters; and academic or social challenges. But most people who face those problems don't kill themselves. The real cause of suicide is mental illness. That's what makes the difference between the people who respond to those stresses by attempting suicide and those who don't. To prevent suicide, society needs to provide better access to mental health services and reduce the stigma around the use of those services. Young people are our future. When we fail to maximize their success, let alone their chances of survival, we fail ourselves and our country.

Adapted from: Maria A. Oquendo, letter to the editor, New York Times,
Mar 25, 2010, http://www.nytimes.com/2010/03/25/
opinion/lweb25cornell.html

7. Fight for your local library! Local libraries provide the public with free, equitable access to information. When you need a book for your child's school report or want to learn how to plant a garden, train a pet, or repair a dryer, the library has the information you need—and librarians to help you find it. Furthermore, libraries encourage people to read and learn for pleasure. There are limits to what you can get on the Internet.

Adapted from: Regina Powers, letter to the editor, Los Angeles Times,
Nov 17, 2010, http://articles.latimes.com/2010/nov/17/opinion/
la-le-1117-wednesday-20101117

8. Western countries claim to value justice, democracy, and egalitarianism. Yet, the United Nations Security Council's permanent members—Britain, the United States, Russia, China, and

France—have a veto over any matter before the Council. This gives each of those countries the power to overrule international consensus on important matters. That is neither just, democratic, nor egalitarian. It is only right, then, that the Security Council be reformed so that no country holds veto power.

Adapted from: Paul Khurana, letter to the editor, The Economist, *Dec 2, 2010,*
http://www.economist.com/node/17627530

9. The University of North Carolina's scandalous decision to defraud the NCAA and the people of North Carolina is a blight on American universities everywhere. By enabling so-called student-athletes to cheat their way through college so that they can focus on basketball, the university's so-called educators have engaged in a horrific and immoral abuse of their authority—one of which they ought to be deeply ashamed. Fred Snowden, the former basketball coach at the University of Arizona, was rightly praised for telling his players to put academics first. He would be appalled at this gross abnegation of the university's very *raison d'etre.*

Adapted from: Norman E. Hodges, letter to the editor, Oct 27, 2014, Daily Tar Heel,
http://www.dailytarheel.com/article/2014/10/letter-scandal-a
%20blight%20upon%20learning%20tradition

10. Some people insist that there are no well-documented instances of genuine UFO sightings or alien encounters. What these people overlook is the fact that publications that document such sightings and encounters are routinely suppressed by mainstream society. In Manhattan, the vast majority of bookstores and magazine stands refuse to stock the books and periodicals that detail sightings and encounters. Those books and periodicals are not cataloged in any of the standard reference sources. If people dig deep enough, though, they will find that publications like *UFO, UFO Universe, Fortean Times,* and *Perceptions* do document genuine UFO sightings and alien encounters.

Adapted from: Brian Camp, letter to the editor, New York Times, *Sep 1, 1996,*
http://www.nytimes.com/1996/09/01/opinion/l-teaching-science-139459.html

Model responses for odd-numbered exercises can be found on page 301.

Need more practice? Working with a friend or classmate, find the letters to the editor in your favorite magazine or newspaper. For each letter, decide whether the letter contains an argument. If so, evaluate how well the letter follows the rules from this chapter. Then, compare your evaluation with your friend's or classmate's. If you disagree about how well a letter follows any of the rules, see if you can come to an agreement by explaining how the letter does or does not follow the rule.

Critical thinking activity: Writing a letter to the editor

For an out-of-class activity that gives you practice in constructing arguments of your own, see the "Writing a letter to the editor" assignment sheet (p. 443) in Part 3.

Critical thinking activity: Analyzing unadapted arguments

For an in-class or out-of-class activity that gives you practice in applying Rules 1 and 2 to arguments in their original context, see the "Analyzing unadapted arguments" assignment sheet (p. 444) in Part 3.

Chapter II
Generalizations

Some arguments offer one or more examples in support of a generalization.

> Women in earlier times were married very young. Juliet in Shakespeare's *Romeo and Juliet* was not even fourteen years old. In the Middle Ages, thirteen was the normal age of marriage for a Jewish woman. And during the Roman Empire, many Roman women were married at age thirteen or younger.

This argument generalizes from three examples—Juliet, Jewish women in the Middle Ages, and Roman women during the Roman Empire—to "many" or *most* women in earlier times. To show the form of this argument most clearly, we can list the premises separately, with the conclusion on the "bottom line":

> Juliet in Shakespeare's play was not even fourteen years old.

> Jewish women during the Middle Ages were normally married at thirteen.

> Many Roman women during the Roman Empire were married at age thirteen or younger.

> Therefore, women in earlier times were married very young.

It is helpful to write short arguments in this way when we need to see exactly how they work.

When do premises like these adequately support a generalization?

One requirement, of course, is that the examples be accurate. Remember Rule 3: start from reliable premises! If Juliet *wasn't* around fourteen, or if most Roman or Jewish women *weren't* married at thirteen or younger, then the argument is much weaker. If none of the premises can be supported, there is no argument at all. To check an argument's examples, or to find good examples for your own arguments, you may need to do some research.

But suppose the examples *are* accurate. Even then, generalizing from them is a tricky business. The rules in this chapter offer a short checklist for assessing arguments by example.

Use more than one example

A single example can sometimes be used for the sake of *illustration*. The example of Juliet alone might illustrate early marriage. But a single example offers next to no *support* for a generalization. Juliet alone may just be an exception. One spectacularly miserable billionaire does not prove that rich people in general are unhappy. More than one example is needed.

NO:

French fries are unhealthy (high in fat).

Therefore, all fast foods are unhealthy.

YES:

French fries are unhealthy (high in fat).

Milkshakes are unhealthy (high in fat and sugar).

Deep-fried chicken and cheeseburgers are unhealthy (high in fat).

Therefore, all fast foods are unhealthy.

The "Yes" version may still be weak (Rule 11 returns to it), but it certainly gives you more to chew on, so to speak, than the "No" version.

In a generalization about a small set of things, the strongest argument should consider all, or at least many, of the examples. A generalization about your siblings should consider each of them in turn, for instance, and a generalization about all the planets in the solar system can do the same.

Generalizations about larger sets of things require picking out a *sample*. We certainly cannot list all women in earlier times who married young. Instead, our argument must offer a few women as examples of the rest. How many examples are required depends partly on how representative they are, a point the next rule takes up. It also depends partly on the size of the set being generalized about. Large sets usually require more examples. The claim that your town is full of remarkable people requires more evidence than the claim that, say, your friends are remarkable people. Depending on how many friends you have, even just two or three examples might be enough to establish that your friends are remarkable people; but, unless your town is tiny, many more examples are required to show that your town is full of remarkable people.

Exercise Set 2.1: Finding relevant examples

Objective: To give you practice finding relevant appropriate examples to support a generalization.

Rule 7

Instructions: Find two to three relevant examples to support each of the following generalizations. You may have to do a little research to find good examples in some cases.

Tips for success: A generalization is a claim about some or all things of a certain type. When thinking about generalizations, it's helpful to ask yourself two questions: First, what *type* of thing is the generalization about? Second, what does the generalization *say* about the things of that type?

Consider the fast-food example above. What type of thing is it about? It's about fast-food products. What does it say about the members of that group? It says that they're all unhealthy.

To give good examples in support of a generalization, you need to be sure that your examples are the right type of thing. If you want to support the generalization that fast foods are unhealthy, you need to give examples of things that are *both* fast foods *and* unhealthy.

Some generalizations are negative—not because they say something mean about a type of thing, but because they say that few or no things of that type are a certain way. For instance, consider the generalization "No mammals can breathe underwater." What type of thing is this generalization about? Mammals. What does it say about mammals? It says that none of them can breathe underwater. To give examples for this generalization, you'll need to find things that *are* mammals and *are not* able to breathe underwater.

Not all generalizations are expressed as clearly as the ones we've considered so far. You will sometimes need to think carefully about what a generalization means before looking for examples.

Sample

Lots of professional sports teams are named after animals.

The Chicago Bulls, the Florida Marlins, and the Philadelphia Eagles are professional sports teams that are named after animals.

To verify that these examples are appropriate, create a "mental checklist" of requirements for good examples. An example that supports this generalization must (a) be a professional sports team and (b) be named after an animal. Compare each example against your "mental checklist" of requirements. Is each example a professional sports team (as opposed to, say, a college sports team)? Is each example named after an animal? If the answer to both questions is yes, then the example is appropriate. Sometimes you'll need to think carefully about your answers, though. Is a Bruin an animal? Is a Canuck? Are the New York Red Bulls named after an animal or an energy drink?

Of course, finding three examples doesn't show that the generalization is correct. It could be that these are the only three, in which case it would be false that "lots" of professional sports teams are named after animals. The point of this exercise, however, is not to prove that the generalization is correct but only to find examples that provide evidence for the generalization.

1.   All birds can fly.

2.   Some billionaires are college dropouts.

3.   Everyone who walked on the moon in the twentieth century was American.

4.   Politicians are liars.

5.   Most fruits are sweet when they're ripe.

6.   Most of the shows on television right now are not worth watching.

7.   Developed, democratic countries no longer practice capital punishment.

8.   William Shakespeare wrote many tragedies.

9.   England has produced famous musicians.

10. The world's most populous countries are in Asia.

Model responses for odd-numbered exercises can be found on page 306.

Need more practice? Working with a friend or classmate, create a list of generalizations. Then, go down your list and try to identify at least three examples for each generalization.

Rule 8

Use representative examples

Even a large number of examples may still misrepresent the set being generalized about. A large number of ancient Roman women, for instance, might establish very little about women generally, since ancient Roman women are not necessarily representative of other women. The argument needs to consider women from other early times and from other parts of the world as well.

> Everyone in my neighborhood favors McGraw for president.
>
> Therefore, McGraw is sure to win.

This argument is weak because single neighborhoods seldom represent the voting population as a whole. A well-to-do neighborhood may favor a candidate who is unpopular with everyone else. Student wards in university towns regularly are carried by candidates who do poorly elsewhere. Besides, we seldom have good evidence even about neighborhood views. The set of people eager to display their political preferences to the world is probably not a representative cross-section of the neighborhood as a whole.

A *good* argument that "McGraw is sure to win" requires a representative sample of the entire voting population. It is not easy to construct such a sample. Public opinion polls, for instance, construct their samples very carefully. They learned the hard way. The classic example is a 1936 poll conducted by the *Literary Digest* to predict the outcome of the presidential contest between Roosevelt and Landon. Names were taken, as they are now, from telephone listings, and also from automobile registration lists. The number of people balloted was certainly not too small: more than two million "ballots" were counted. The poll predicted a wide victory for Landon. In the event, though, Roosevelt won easily. In retrospect it is easy to see what went wrong. In 1936, only a select portion of the population owned telephones and cars. The sample was sharply biased toward wealthy and urban voters, more of whom supported Landon.

Polls have improved since then. Nonetheless, there are still worries about representativeness of their samples, and they still regularly forecast elections wrong. For example, these days most of my students don't have landlines at all—only cell phones with unlisted numbers. The pollsters aren't calling *them*. Phone polls may actually be getting less representative again.

It is often an open question, then, just how representative a given sample may be. Anticipate this danger! Do some research. Juliet, for example, is just one woman. Is she representative of women in her time and place? In Shakespeare's play, Juliet's mother says to her:

> Think of marriage now; younger than you,
> Here in Verona, ladies of esteem,

Are made already mothers. By my count,
I was your mother much upon these years
That you are now a maid . . .
(1.3.69–73)

This passage suggests that Juliet's marriage at fourteen is not exceptional; in fact, fourteen seems to be a little on the old side.

In general, look for the most accurate cross-section you can find of the population being generalized about. If you want to know what students think about some subject at your university, don't just ask the people you know or generalize from what you hear in class. Unless you know quite a range of people and take quite a range of classes, your personal "sample" is not likely to mirror the whole student body. Similarly, if you want to know what people in other countries think about the United States, don't just ask tourists—for of course they are the ones who chose to come here. A careful look at a range of foreign media will give you a much more representative picture.

Exercise Set 2.2: Improving biased samples

Objective: To train you to recognize sources of sample bias in order to avoid unrepresentative examples.

Instructions: Each of the following arguments uses an unrepresentative set of examples. Suggest specific ways to improve each argument by changing the way examples are chosen. Explain why those changes would make the argument's examples more representative.

Tips for success: Many generalizations are about diverse groups. Consider, for instance, an opinion poll showing that Europeans disapprove of capital punishment. Europeans are a diverse group of people. No single individual is representative of *all* Europeans. To find representative examples, then, we need to find or assemble a group of people that is, on the whole, representative of all Europeans. That is, we need to select examples so that our group has the same characteristics as the group of all Europeans—the same mix of ages and the same proportion of men to women, of college-educated people to non-college-educated people, of native-born people to immigrants, of wealthy people to poor people, etc. A group of examples is called a *sample*. The implication of Rule 8, then, is that you want your sample to be representative of the group that you are making a generalization about. A sample that fails to represent the group accurately is called a *biased sample.*

How can we ensure that our sample is unbiased? The simplest answer is that we want our sample to be a *random sample.* A random sample of a particular group—say, Europeans—is a sample in which every member of the group has an equal chance of being included in the sample.

Collecting a random sample is not the same as choosing members of the group haphazardly or without a plan. Constructing a random sample is actually very difficult. Two rules of thumb can help you avoid the most common mistakes. You'll want to think about these rules of thumb in offering advice about the arguments in this exercise.

First, be sure that you are sampling from the *entire group* that you're making a generalization about. For instance, if you're generalizing about all North American college students, you need to be sure that students from a wide range of colleges have a proportionate probability of being included in your sample. Don't overlook students from public and private colleges, large and small colleges, and colleges in various regions of North America, etc. You also need to be sure that all *kinds* of students have an proportionate chance of being in your sample—men and women, students who live in dorms and students who commute to campus, premeds and theater majors, eighteen-year-olds who came straight from high school and fifty-year-olds who are going back for a second degree, etc.

Furthermore, Rule 8 requires choosing your examples in ways that ensure a truly proportionate sample. If you contact students at random from the college's email directory, you'll miss students who don't use their college email address. If you approach students who are on campus during the day, you'll miss students who only take evening classes. When you design your methods for choosing and contacting members of the group, think carefully about whether your methods overlook, or under- or overrepresent, any part of the group. Try to ensure that each member of the group has an equal chance of being in the sample.

If you can only sample a specific group of college students, it's best to change your generalization. For instance, if you can only manage to sample students at your school, then instead of making a claim about all North American college students, make a claim about college students at your school.

The second rule of thumb is not to let individual members of the group decide for themselves whether they want to be in the sample. For instance, if you work for a magazine and you want to know what your readers thought about last week's issue, track down a random sample of readers and ask them what they thought. Don't just email subscribers inviting them to submit their opinions. It's true that all subscribers are *invited* to join the sample, but only the ones with strong opinions will actually bother to reply. Quite likely their views will not represent the views of your readership as a whole. Instead, choose a random sample of all readers and do everything you can to get each one of your chosen readers to respond to your survey.

Sample

Derek Weatherby took a job at Schnucks, a grocery store in St. Louis, to help pay his way through college. As his student debt mounted, he took a break from school, planning to go back when his financial situation improved. But with the economy still stagnant years after the financial crisis, Derek has found that many of the other employees at Schnucks are college graduates themselves, some with degrees from prestigious schools. It seems that lots of college graduates can't find work that pays any better than the job that Derek already has.

Adapted from: Ben Cassellman and Marcus Walker, "Wanted: Jobs for the 'Lost' Generation," Wall Street Journal, *Sep 14, 2013, http://on.wsj.com/1zCAnFH*

The argument could be improved by including college graduates who work in places other than Schnucks, being sure to include students from many different parts of the country. The conclusion is supposed to be about all recent college graduates, but it only looks at those who work at Schnucks. An unbiased sample would give all recent college graduates a chance to be included in the sample, perhaps by choosing people randomly from a list of recent graduates from a broad range of colleges.

This response does three important things. First, it explains why the sample is biased: The sample consists only of recent graduates who work at Schnucks. (And of course those students don't have better paying jobs than Derek!) Second, it offers a specific, conrete suggestion about how to improve the argument: Draw names randomly from lists of recent graduates of a broad range of colleges. Third, it explains why that would make the sample less biased: It would give all recent college graduates an equal chance to be in the sample. (Since the conclusion is about all recent college graduates, that's the group whose members each need an equal chance to be included.)

---

1. Republican voters are starting to lean more libertarian. An extreme libertarian candidate easily won the most votes in a mock election held at the Republican Leadership Conference. The conference, held just outside the libertarian candidate's home state,

drew busloads of libertarian supporters, as well as political junkies from further afield who wanted to hear from early contenders for the Republican presidential nomination.

Adapted from: Reuters, "Ron Paul Wins 2012 Republican Straw Poll in New Orleans," Reuters.com, Jun 18, 2011, http://www.reuters.com/article/2011/06/18/ us-usa-campaign-poll-idUSTRE75H1YX20110618

2. Not all doctors are rolling in money. By the time they finish their education, most would-be doctors are buried under a mountain of debt. At Michigan State University's medical school, average student debt at graduation is $160,937. That kind of debt discourages students from going into much-needed but lower-paying medical careers, including primary care.

Adapted from: Editorial, "Defer student medical debt," Grand Rapids Press, Apr 3, 2009, http://www.mlive.com/opinion/grand-rapids/index.ssf/ 2009/04/editorial_defer_medical_school.html

3. The University of St. Andrews in Scotland now has over twelve hundred Americans among its roughly seven thousand students. That's up from about two hundred American students a decade earlier. The University of Edinburgh, also in Scotland, enrolls about the same number of Americans as St. Andrews. Trinity College and the University of Limerick, both in Ireland, are also attracting more American students. The students cite lots of reasons for going—to see a different part of the world, to experience a different educational system, and to avoid the hefty price tags at top-notch private universities at home. Whatever the students' reasons, though, foreign universities are enrolling more and more American students.

Adapted from: Tamar Lewin, "Going Off to College For Less (Passport Required)," New York Times, Nov 30, 2008, http://www.nytimes.com/2008/12/01/ education/01scotland.html

4. Women have long been underrepresented and underfunded in the sciences and mathematics. In recent years, though, women have made significant and visible progress in academia. At MIT, female scientists' salaries and lab spaces are now equal to those of their male colleagues. Female scientists now head MIT, the

University of Michigan, Princeton University, and four campuses of the University of California.

Adapted from: Sara Rimer, "For Women in Sciences, Slow Progress in Academia," New York Times, Apr 15, 2005, http://www.nytimes.com/2005/04/15/ education/15women.html

5. Drivers who switched to Allstate saved an average of $396 a year on their car insurance. Those who switched from GEICO saved even more, knocking an average of $473 off their bill. Therefore, most drivers can save money by switching to Allstate.

Adapted from: Bob Trebilcock, "Car Insurance: Save Money by Switching?" CBS News, May 4, 2010, http://www.cbsnews.com/news/ car-insurance-save-money-by-switching/

6. Each package of Nestle Foods' new line of high-quality, freeze-dried soup products contained a postage-paid survey form. The package encouraged customers to complete the survey and mail it back to Nestle Foods. Over ten thousand survey responses flooded the Nestle offices, and they were all extremely positive. Everybody loved it! Nestle had hit upon a winning product line.

Adapted from: Anthony G. Bennett, The Big Book of Marketing *(Columbus, OH: McGraw-Hill), 102*

7. Parenting can't be that hard to figure out. After all, every single one of my ancestors over billions of years has successfully managed to raise at least one child to adulthood. So have the ancestors of every other living thing on this planet. And most of those ancestors didn't even have language or culture to teach them what to do, much less parenting books and Internet forums; they just did what came naturally. Thus, parenting well comes naturally to most living things.

Adapted from: Randall Munroe, "Natural Parenting," xkcd, Dec 11, 2009, http://xkcd.com/674

8. There are over 450 species of sharks—for now, at least. Sharks have been subjected to serious overfishing, both for food and for the use of their cartilage, which allegedly has therapeutic powers. Beyond overfishing, the shark population is threatened by human encroachment on the mangroves that serve as nurseries for baby

sharks. Great white sharks, hammerheads, and oceanic whitetip sharks, to name just a few, have seen population declines of 90 percent or more in the last few decades alone. Clearly, the word "biodiversity" has become nothing but a joke, and people don't really care about endangered species at all.

Adapted from: Abhijit Naik, "Endangered Sharks," Buzzle.com, May 10, 2010,
http://www.buzzle.com/articles/endangered-sharks-species-of-endangered
-sharks.html

9.   The American justice system is so dysfunctional that it puts lots of people behind bars for crimes they didn't commit. The Innocence Project at Cardozo Law School uses DNA testing to investigate the cases of people who were convicted of serious crimes prior to the widespread use of DNA evidence. In the first decade of its existence, the project exonerated nearly two-thirds of the inmates whose cases they investigated. That's over one hundred people wrongly convicted of serious crimes!

Adapted from: Donald E. Campbell, Incentives, *2nd ed. (Cambridge: Cambridge*
University Press, 2003), 14

10.   Over seven hundred scientists from around the world have gone to dissentfromdarwin.org to register their skepticism about the theory of evolution. These scientists include members of the national academies of science in their home countries and faculty from prestigious institutions in a range of scientific disciplines. Thus, many scientists are skeptical about the theory of evolution.

Adapted from: "Ranks of Scientists Doubting Darwin's Theory on the Rise,"
Discovery Institute, Feb 8, 2007, http://www.discovery.org/a/2732

Model responses for odd-numbered exercises can be found on page 308.

Need more practice? Work with one or more classmates. Have each person create hypothetical scenarios in which someone tries unsuccessfully to create a representative sample to support a particular conclusion. Make them amusing too—mistakes in reasoning often are! These scenarios should take the form, "Suppose that someone tried to prove that all cars are made in America by driving around the parking lot of a Ford factory counting the different makes of cars"—or more generally, "Suppose that someone tried to prove X by doing Y to find examples." (Be sure that X is a generalization and that Y is a faulty method for finding a representative sample.) Then, trade scenarios with your classmates and suggest improvements to the methods for finding representative samples.

Background rates may be crucial

To persuade you that I am a first-rate archer, it is not enough to show you a bull's-eye I have made. You should ask (politely, to be sure), "Yes, but how many times did you *miss*?" Getting a bull's-eye in one shot tells quite a different story than getting a bull's-eye in, say, a thousand, even though in both cases I genuinely do have a bull's-eye to my name. You need a little more data.

Or again:

> Leon's horoscope told him that he would meet a vivacious new stranger, and lo and behold he did! Therefore, horoscopes are reliable.

Dramatic as such examples may be, the problem is that we are only looking at the cases in which horoscopes came true. To properly evaluate this evidence, we need to know something else as well: how many horoscopes *didn't* come true. When I survey my classes we can usually find a few Leons out of twenty or thirty students. The other nineteen or twenty-nine horoscopes go nowhere. But a kind of prediction that comes true only once out of twenty or thirty tries is hardly reliable—it's just lucky once in a while. It may have some dramatic successes, like my archery, but its success *rate* may still be abysmal.

To evaluate the reliability of an argument featuring a few vivid examples, then, we need to know the ratio between the number of "hits," so to speak, and the number of *tries*. It's a question of representativeness again. Are the featured examples the only ones there are? Is the rate impressively high or low?

Another case in point:

> The "Bermuda Triangle" area off Bermuda is famous as a place where many ships and planes have mysteriously disappeared. Avoid it at all costs! There have been several dozen disappearances in the past decade alone.

No doubt. But several dozen out of how many ships and planes that *passed through* the area? Several dozen, or several hundred thousand? If only twenty, say, have disappeared out of maybe two hundred thousand, then the disappearance *rate* in the Bermuda Triangle may well be normal, or even unusually low—certainly not mysterious.

Exercise Set 2.3: Identifying relevant background rates

Objective: To give you practice identifying relevant background rates when dealing with generalizations and statistics.

Instructions: Each of the following arguments jumps to a conclusion on the basis of dramatic statistics or a few vivid examples. In order to justify each conclusion, you would need to know more about relevant background rates. State what additional information you would need to know to calculate the relevant background rates. (This will require you to figure out which background rates are relevant.)

Tips for success: Arguments from a few vivid examples work because we naturally tend to pay more attention to dramatic and vivid events or examples than to the relatively boring "background" where nothing happens, like horoscopes that didn't work out or ships and planes that didn't disappear in the Bermuda Triangle. But non-events or non-examples are actually just as important as examples in evaluating the generalization we might make from them. That is what the occurrence *rate* tells you: how significant the examples really are against the relevant background.

When dealing with an argument for a generalization, think about which background rates are relevant for deciding how well the particular examples or statistics in the argument support the argument's conclusion. In the Bermuda Triangle example above, for instance, the relevant rate is the rate at which planes disappear in the Bermuda Triangle. Likewise, learning that a dozen famous models have lost weight following a particular diet plan doesn't tell you much about the effectiveness of that plan. For one thing, the models constitute a biased sample. (Remember Rule 8!) But even more importantly, learning about those dozen models doesn't tell you the relevant background rate, which is the percentage of people on this diet plan—models or not—who lose weight. In both cases, we also need to know another rate to evaluate the argument: the rate at which planes disappear in the rest of the world and the percentage of people on any diet plan—and on none—who lose weight.

Once you know what rate you're looking for, ask yourself what further information you would need to calculate that rate. In the Bermuda Triangle example, you would need to know how many planes pass through that area. In the diet example, you would need to know (roughly) how many people are on this diet plan and how many of them have lost weight. Often, this information is the information you would be looking for if you responded to an argument for a generalization with the snide, but still appropriate, comment, "Oh, yeah—out of how many?"

Sometimes background rates matter in a more subtle way. Consider this little puzzle:

> Tanya is a talented card player with the most impassive poker face you've ever seen. Which is she more likely to be: a high school teacher or a professional poker player?

Tanya sounds a great deal like a professional poker player, and since this doesn't appear to be an argument by generalization, you might not think to consider background rates. If you do consider background rates, though, you'll realize that there are a very large number of high school teachers—many of whom could be excellent poker players—and almost no professional poker players at all. Thus, regardless of Tanya's penchant for poker and the impassiveness of her face, she's much more likely to be a high school teacher. The lesson here is to think about background rates even when the argument does not obviously invoke any generalizations.

Sample

In a recent experiment, some students used a studying technique called "retrieval practice essays." After reading a passage, the students wrote down what they remembered from it, without the passage in front of them. A week later, these students answered about two out of three questions about the passage correctly. Therefore, writing retrieval practice essays is a good way to study.

Adapted from: Pam Belluck, "To Really Learn, Quit Studying and Take a Test," New York Times, Jan 20, 2010, http://www.nytimes.com/2011/01/21/science/21memory.html

We need to know how well students did if they studied using different techniques—or even if they didn't study at all. That is, we need to know the proportion of questions that students got right if they used other forms of studying besides the "retrieval practice essay."

You might think that this argument gives the only background rate that you need. However, in claiming that retrieval practice essays are a good way to study, the argument is implicitly comparing retrieval practice essays to other forms of studying. So, we need to be able to compare the rates for the various alternatives, including the rate for students who don't study at all.

---

1.   In the second half of 2010, the University of Western Ontario did not have a single car stolen on campus. The campus police must be doing an outstanding job protecting the university.

      Adapted from: Jonathan Tieu, "Campus Police Report Zero Car Thefts," Gazette *(University of Western Ontario), Jan 18, 2011, http://www .westerngazette.ca/2011/01/18/campus-police-report-zero-car-thefts/*

2.   Despite historic gains in the 114th U.S. Congress, women are vastly underrepresented, just as they were in all previous Congresses. The Senate has twenty women, while the House of Representatives has just over 100 women.

      Adapted from: Lauren French, "Women Leaders Meet after Historic Year at Polls," Politico, *Dec 9, 2014, http://www.politico.com/story/2014/12/ women-congress-sexism-113429.html*

3.   Being highly paid goes hand in hand with loving your job. Across a range of professions, two out of three highly paid professionals say they love their job. This figure goes up to 75 percent for highly paid top executives in multinational corporations.

      Adapted from: Marilyn Gardner, "'Extreme' Jobs on the Rise," Christian Science Monitor, *Dec 4, 2006, http://www.csmonitor.com/2006/1204/p14s01-wmgn.html*

4.   Mercury is "retrograde" three times a year, meaning that it appears to move backward in the sky. As everyone knows, when Mercury is retrograde, it causes all kinds of miscommunication and confusion here on Earth. This year's first occurrence of Mercury retrograde is especially troublesome, since Mercury will appear under the sign of Aquarius this time. The last time it happened was in 2008—the year of the major financial meltdown that ruined the world economy. Before that, it happened twice in 2001. During the first occurrence, the "dot com" bubble burst, plunging the economy into recession. The second included September 11, 2001, when terrorists struck the World Trade Center and the Pentagon. Clearly, whenever Mercury is retrograde in Aquarius, there are many catastrophes here on Earth.

      Adapted from: Larry Schwimmer, "Mercury Retrograde: Jan 21–Feb 11th—It's Groundhog Day All Over Again," Huffington Post, *Jan 20, 2015, http://www.huffingtonpost. com/larry-schwimmer/mercury-retrograde-jan-21_b_6508342.html*

5. Jennifer's financial troubles began when she lost her job. After ordering supplies online to perform some hoodoo rituals, her financial situation has turned around. Tammie and Angela have similar stories: When they fell on hard times, they turned to hoodoo rituals and found their financial problems disappearing. Therefore, people in financial trouble who perform hoodoo rituals are likely to recover from their financial problems.

    Adapted from: Cameron McWhirter, "Need a Job? Losing Your House? Who Says Hoodoo Can't Help?" Wall Street Journal, *Dec 28, 2010, http://on.wsj.com/1w7s985*

6. The death of the Ultimate Warrior, just days after his induction into the wrestling hall of fame, illustrates an often overlooked problem: Professional wrestling is a grueling sport that poses a serious long-term risk to wrestlers' health. Consider the wrestlers who participated in Wrestlemania VI in 1990, which was the pinnacle of the Ultimate Warrior's career. Those wrestlers are only in their fifties or sixties now, but already twelve of them have died.

    Adapted from: "Ultimate Warrior: One-Third of WrestleMania VI Competitors Now Dead," ThePostGame, *Apr 9, 2014, http://www.thepostgame.com/blog/list/201404/ ultimate-warrior-dead-wrestlers-wrestlemania-vi-andre-savage-rude-hennig*

7. New York's "Take 5" lotto game sells one hundred thousand winning tickets every single day. Therefore, buying a "Take 5" ticket gives you a good shot at winning too.

    Adapted from: "NY Lotto Commercial Take 5," YouTube, Feb 2, 2008, http://www.youtube.com/watch?v=_fMxRH2YQPo

8. Digital downloads and rampant piracy have greatly reduced the record labels' main source of revenue: album sales. The best selling CD in 2007, for instance, sold only 3.7 million copies, according to Nielsen SoundScan.

    Adapted from: Jeff Leeds, "In Rapper's Deal, a New Model for Music Business," New York Times, *Apr 3, 2008, http://www.nytimes.com/2008/04/03/arts/ music/03jayz.html*

9. Exactly zero children died from measles in the United States between 2004 and 2015. But in that same time period, 106 infants

died after exhibiting reactions to measles vaccines. Obviously, the real danger here is not measles; it's the measles vaccine.

Adapted from: Brian Shilhavy, "ZERO U.S. Measles Deaths in 10 Years, but Over 100 Measles Vaccines Deaths Reported," Health Impact News, *Jan 30, 2015, http://healthimpactnews.com/2015/zero-u-s-measles-deaths-in-10-years-but-over-100-measles-vaccine-deaths-reported*

10. David Arroyo's shooting spree in Tyler, Texas, left two people dead and wounded four others. Among the wounded were Arroyo's son and several police officers. Among the dead were Arroyo's ex-wife and a bystander, Mark Wilson, whose heroism prevented Arroyo's rampage from becoming an even bigger tragedy. Wilson, who owns a handgun, heard Arroyo's shots from his nearby apartment. He ran outside and started shooting at Arroyo, who was about to kill another victim. Arroyo turned to face Wilson instead. While the ensuing gun battle left Wilson fatally wounded, it bought enough time for more police to arrive. Those police officers managed to take Arroyo down. The lesson here is that if more law-abiding citizens carried guns, more deaths could be averted.

Adapted from: John Lott, Jr., "Good Samaritan Gun Use," FOX News, Mar 8, 2005, http://www.foxnews.com/story/0,2933,149250,00.html

Model responses for odd-numbered exercises can be found on page 311.

Need more practice? Make a list of ten stereotypes. These could be stereotypes about types of people (e.g., scientists or musicians), types of events (e.g., baseball games, political elections, royal weddings), etc. Give one or two examples from real life or fiction that support the stereotype. Then ask yourself what background rate(s) you would need to know to determine whether the stereotype is true and what information you would need to calculate the relevant background rate(s).

Rule 10

Statistics need a critical eye

Some people see numbers—*any* numbers—in an argument and conclude from that fact alone that it must be a good argument. Statistics seem to have an aura of authority and definiteness (and did you know that 88 percent of doctors agree?). In fact, though, numbers take as much critical thinking as any other kind of evidence. Don't turn off your brain!

> After an era when some athletic powerhouse universities were accused of exploiting student athletes, leaving them to flunk out once their eligibility expired, college athletes are now graduating at higher rates. Many schools are now graduating more than 50 percent of their athletes.

Fifty percent, eh? Pretty impressive! But this figure, at first so persuasive, does not really do the job it claims to do.

First, though "many" schools graduate more than 50 percent of their athletes, it appears that some do not—so this figure may well exclude the most exploitative schools that really concerned people in the first place.

The argument does offer graduation rates. But it would be useful to know how a "more than 50 percent" graduation rate compares with the graduation rate for *all* students at the same institutions. If it is significantly lower, athletes may still be getting the shaft.

Most importantly, this argument offers no reason to believe that college athletes' graduation rates are actually *improving*, because no comparison to any previous rate is offered! The conclusion claims that the graduation rate is now "higher," but without knowing the previous rates it is impossible to tell.

Numbers may offer incomplete evidence in other ways too. Rule 9, for example, tells us that knowing background rates may be crucial. Correspondingly, when an argument offers rates or percentages, the relevant background information usually must include the *number* of examples. Car thefts on campus may have doubled, but if this means that two cars were stolen rather than one, there's not much to worry about.

Another statistical pitfall is *overprecision*:

> Every year this campus wastes 412,067 paper and plastic cups. It's time to switch to reusable cups!

No doubt the amount of campus waste is huge. But no one really knows the precise number of cups wasted—and it's extremely unlikely to be exactly the same every year. Here the appearance of exactness makes the evidence seem more authoritative than it really is.

Be wary, also, of numbers that are easily manipulated. Pollsters know very well that how a question is asked can shape how it is answered. These days we are even seeing "polls" that try to change people's minds, about, say, a political candidate, just by asking loaded questions ("If you were to discover that she is a liar and a cheat, how would that change your vote?"). Then too, many apparently "hard" statistics are actually based on guesswork or extrapolation, such as data about semilegal or illegal activities. Since people have a major motive not to reveal or report things like drug use, under-the-counter transactions, hiring illegal aliens, and the like, beware of any confident generalizations about how widespread they are.

Yet again:

> If kids keep watching more TV at current rates, by 2025 they'll have no time left to sleep!

Right, and by 2040 they'll be watching thirty-six hours a day. Extrapolation in such cases is perfectly possible mathematically, but after a certain point it tells you nothing.

There's much more to be said about statistics and probability than we could possibly say in this book. You might consider taking a course in statistics in order to understand these topics more deeply. We think everyone who aspires to be an educated person should take at least one such course! In the meantime, take a look at the "Resources" section on this book's companion Web site for links to helpful books and online resources about statistics and probability. Perusing those resources might even help you complete the following exercises.

Exercise Set 2.4: Evaluating simple arguments that use numbers

Objective: To develop a critical eye for arguments using simple statistics.

Instructions: Each of the following arguments uses numbers in a misleading way. Explain why each argument's use of numbers does not adequately support the argument's conclusions.

Tips for success: Many misleading uses of statistics can be detected with three simple questions: What *exactly* are these statistics saying? Are these statistics believable? Do these statistics really show what the argument claims they show? Be sure to ask yourself each of these questions when evaluating the following arguments—or any arguments that use statistics.

In addition, Rule 10 introduces some specific pitfalls in arguments that use simple statistics: rates or percentages offered without relevant background information; statistics, often surprisingly precise, that no one is likely to know with any confidence; results of manipulative surveys or opinion polls; thoughtless extrapolations; and in general, the sloppy use of numbers to try to justify conclusions that the statistics just don't support. Look out for all of these pitfalls in the arguments below.

Whereas Rule 9 urged you to include background rates when giving examples, the use of rates or percentages without background information is just as problematic. If you see an argument that *only* gives rates or percentages, ask yourself whether those rates might be misleading. Do you know enough background information to figure out whether, say a 10 percent decline is significant? If not, the argument's author may be trying to mislead you into thinking that something is a big deal, even when it's not.

Another question to ask yourself when dealing with statistics is how someone would or could have learned that particular statistic—and how reliable that method is. Suppose you are told that 68 percent of people floss daily. How would anyone know that? Most likely, a pollster asks people whether they floss daily. People sometimes lie (or, let's just say, shade the truth) for pollsters, though—especially when they are embarrassed about the true answer, don't quite want to face it themselves, or otherwise fear that the true answer is not "socially desirable." So, that figure of 68 percent probably overestimates the percentage of people who floss daily.

In general, the harder it would be to figure out a statistic, the more skeptical you should be that a statistic is accurate. (But don't go overboard with this, either. Statisticians have developed very clever techniques to get around these kinds of problems. You'll need to consider whether a particular argument was written by someone with the ability and motivation to use those techniques.)

Even with statistics that *could* be determined with some accuracy, some organizations might be more interested in getting a particular result than learning the truth. Pollsters can skew the results by using biased samples or asking loaded questions. Running tests over and over again until you get the desired result is another way to manipulate statistics. A toothpaste company can keep asking groups of ten dentists which toothpaste they recommend until they find a group where nine out of ten recommend the company's brand. If a statistic comes from a source that is more interested in getting their preferred result than in getting the truth, you should be skeptical of the statistic.

Sample

According to *U.S. News & World Report*'s compilation of statistics provided by law schools, 93 percent of law school graduates have a job nine months after finishing law school. That's up nearly ten percentage points from 1997, when law schools reported an average employment rate of 84 percent. The employment picture for law school graduates is better than ever!

Adapted from: David Segal, "Is Law School a Losing Game?" New York Times, *Jan 8, 2011, http://www.nytimes.com/2011/01/09/business/09law.html*

This argument cites two "employment rates" for recent law school graduates to show that the employment picture for law school graduates is "better than ever." There are several reasons to be skeptical of this argument. First of all, it's worth noting that these statistics come from the law schools themselves, who have an incentive to inflate employment rates. Second, the argument doesn't specify that 93 percent of graduates are employed as <u>lawyers</u>, which is what we really want to know about. It could be that half are employed as lawyers and 43 percent are flipping burgers and making cappuccinos. Third, the argument claims that the employment picture is "better than ever," but it offers only one point of comparison: 1997. It could be that 1997 was a particularly bad year for law school graduates. We would need more background information to evaluate the relevance of that statistic.

This response starts by explaining what the argument attempts to do with statistics. It then cites three reasons, related to those statistics, to be skeptical of the argument. Notice that the response doesn't give us a strong reason to think the conclusion itself is false. The upshot is that we just don't know. We would need to do more research to know whether law school graduates really do have good prospects. The point is that thinking critically about statistics can help prevent you from being taken in by misleading arguments.

1. A burglary occurs every fifteen seconds in the United States. Up to 80 percent of forced entries occur through a front door or a window. That's why it's essential to invest in a product like the OnGARD Security Door Brace, which helps prevent would-be burglars from breaking through your front door.

    Adapted from: "Stop a Home Invasion with the Strongest Door Brace in the World. OnGARD Brace," YouTube, Dec 20, 2010, http://www.youtube.com/watch?v=kFRbYO503og

2. A recent survey by British researchers found that heterosexual men have an average of 12.7 sexual partners over the course of their lives. The same study found that heterosexual women average 6.5 sexual partners. An American survey, recently reported by the U.S. government, found a similar discrepancy: heterosexual men averaged seven sexual partners, while heterosexual women averaged four. Men must be more promiscuous than women.

    Adapted from: Gina Kolata, "The Myth, the Math, the Sex," New York Times, Aug 12, 2007, http://www.nytimes.com/2007/08/12/weekinreview/12kolata.html

3. Beef is not high in cholesterol. Three ounces of cooked lean beef contain 73 milligrams of cholesterol. By comparison, the same amount of roast chicken contains 76 mg; fried chicken, 74 mg; pork, 77 mg; shrimp, 130 mg; cheddar cheese, 90 mg.

    Adapted from: "12 Myths about Beef," a flyer distributed at the North Carolina State Fair on behalf of the National Cattleman's Association, n.d.

4. Cigarettes contain 101 different kinds of poison. That's one hundred more poisons than rat poison. Therefore, smoking cigarettes is even more foolish than eating rat poison.

    Adapted from: "The Truth.com—Rat Poison," YouTube, Oct 14, 2007, http://www.youtube.com/watch?v=vyxxub_2n6Y

5. Environmentalists warn that humans' carbon dioxide emissions are endangering the planet. But the Earth naturally emits far more carbon dioxide than we do. In fact, humans' cumulative carbon dioxide emissions over the whole of human history are just 0.00022 percent of the total amount that has been emitted by volcanoes over geological history. Given that our emissions are such a tiny fraction of natural emissions, there's no need to worry that our emissions will change the climate.

    Adapted from: Charlotte Meredith, "100 Reasons Why Climate Change Is Natural," Daily Express (London), Nov 20, 2012, http://express.co.uk/news/uk/146138/100-reasons-why-climate-change-is-natural

6. Our psychics are supernaturally accurate. Our Psychic Managers thoroughly test every psychic who applies to work for us, screening them for accuracy, professionalism, and compassion. Only two out of every hundred psychics who apply make the cut.

    Adapted from: "How Accurate Are Your Psychics?" California Psychics, n.d., http://www.californiapsychics.com/help/category.aspx?contentid=4226#4226

7. During a typical week, the average person lies to 34 percent of the people whom he or she encounters during that week. This includes both altruistic lies (i.e., lies told to avoid hurting someone's feelings) and selfish lies (i.e., lies told to gain some advantage), as

well as lies to both close friends and casual acquaintances. Clearly, you can't believe much of anything that anyone says.

Adapted from: B. D. DePaulo & D. A. Kashy, "Everyday Lies in Close and Casual Relationships," Journal of Personality and Social Psychology *74 (1998), 63–79*

8. Israel's military is supposed to be the world's leader in gender equality. Israel has opened 92 percent of the jobs in its military to women, including many combat roles. Yet, only 3 percent of women actually serve in combat roles. Clearly, women are not actually treated equally in the Israeli military.

Adapted from: Jodi Rudoren, "Looking to Israel for Clues on Women in Combat," New York Times, *Jan 25, 2013, http://www.nytimes.com/2013/01/26/world/middleeast/ looking-to-israel-for-clues-on-women-in-combat.html?hp*

9. In 1996, the Australian government banned most guns. They forced gun owners to surrender 640,381 guns to the government. Guess what happened? In the following year, homicides increased 3.2 percent across the country; assaults were up 8.6 percent; armed robberies rose 43.2 percent; and most amazingly, gun homicides in the Australian state of Victoria soared 171 percent! There's no doubt that crime has gotten much worse since the government banned guns.

Adapted from: Jon E. Dougherty, "Crime Up Down Under," WorldNet Daily, *Mar 3, 2000, http://www.wnd.com/news/article.asp?article_id=15304*

10. Hydraulic fracturing—or "fracking," as it's commonly known—involves pumping special fluids into rocks at very high pressure to fracture the rock. This makes it easier to extract gas and oil from the rock. But those fracking fluids are nasty stuff. They contain 208 different kinds of chemicals. And 96.6 percent of those chemicals are known to cause serious health problems, including birth defects and cancer. That's why fracking should be banned.

Adapted from: Shaleshock, "Drilling 101," shaleshock.org, n.d., *http://shaleshock.org/drilling-101/*

Model responses for odd-numbered exercises can be found on page 314.

Need more practice? Get together with a few classmates. Have each person pick a specific Web site, newspaper, or magazine and look for arguments that use statistics. Try to estimate how many arguments from your chosen site, newspaper, or magazine use statistics in relatively good versus relatively poor ways. As a group, rank the various sources in terms of the reliability of their use of statistics. Alternatively, each person could review a specific section from the same Web site, newspaper, or magazine.

Critical thinking activity: Finding misleading statistics

For an out-of-class activity that gives you practice in applying Rule 10, see the "Finding misleading statistics" assignment sheet (p. 449) in Part 3. This activity has an optional, in-class extension.

Consider counterexamples

Counterexamples are examples that contradict your generalization. No fun—maybe. But counterexamples actually can be a generalizer's best friends, if you use them early and use them well. Look for them on purpose and systematically. It is the best way to sharpen your own generalizations and to probe more deeply into your theme.

Consider this argument once again:

French fries are unhealthy (high in fat).

Milkshakes are unhealthy (high in fat and sugar).

Deep-fried chicken and cheeseburgers are unhealthy (high in fat).

Therefore, all fast foods are unhealthy.

This argument offers multiple and apparently representative examples. However, as soon as you start thinking about counterexamples instead of just more examples, you will find that the argument overgeneralizes. Subway sandwiches, for example, are "fast food" as well, but vegetables and buns are the primary ingredients, meats and cheeses are add-ons, and nothing is deep-fried. So it turns out that not *all* fast foods are unhealthy.

If you can think of counterexamples to a generalization that you want to defend, then you need to adjust your generalization. If the last argument were yours, for instance, you might change the conclusion to "*Many* fast foods are unhealthy."

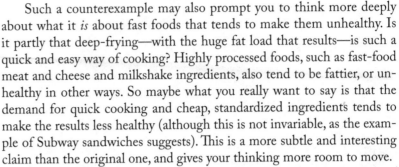

Such a counterexample may also prompt you to think more deeply about what it *is* about fast foods that tends to make them unhealthy. Is it partly that deep-frying—with the huge fat load that results—is such a quick and easy way of cooking? Highly processed foods, such as fast-food meat and cheese and milkshake ingredients, also tend to be fattier, or unhealthy in other ways. So maybe what you really want to say is that the demand for quick cooking and cheap, standardized ingredients tends to make the results less healthy (although this is not invariable, as the example of Subway sandwiches suggests). This is a more subtle and interesting claim than the original one, and gives your thinking more room to move.

Ask yourself about counterexamples when you are assessing others' arguments as well as evaluating your own. Ask whether *their* conclusions might have to be revised and limited, or rethought in more subtle and complex directions. The same rules apply both to others' arguments and to yours. The only difference is that you have a chance to correct your overgeneralizations yourself.

Exercise Set 2.5: Finding counterexamples

Objective: To give you practice identifying counterexamples to generalizations.

Instructions: Try to find a counterexample to each of the generalizations below. If there are no counterexamples, say so.

Tips for success: Remember that a counterexample is an *example* that *counts against* a generalization. Consider the generalization "All birds can fly." It's a generalization about birds. It says that all members of that group (i.e., birds) can fly. A counterexample to that generalization would be a bird that cannot fly. Penguins are counterexamples to the generalization. So are ostriches, and so (unfortunately for them) were dodo birds.

In order to decide whether something is a counterexample to a particular generalization, you'll need to think about the same questions you asked yourself in Exercise Sets 2.1 and 2.2: What type of thing is the generalization about? What does the generalization say about this type of thing? A counterexample must be the right type of thing. If your generalization is about birds, your counterexample must be a bird. Furthermore, your counterexample must contradict the generalization. If the generalization says that birds can fly, your counterexample must be a bird that is *not* able to fly.

Many logicians, philosophers, and mathematicians use the word *counterexample* to refer specifically to an example that disproves a "universal" generalization—that is, a generalization that says something about *all* members of a group (e.g., "All birds can fly"). You might also think of counterexamples in a less technical sense as "exceptions" to a generalization, even non-universal generalizations. In this weaker sense of *counterexample*, the rainforests of Norway and Alaska are counterexamples to the generalization that most rainforests are in the tropics. While this exercise focuses exclusively on universal generalizations, it will be important to keep this weaker sense of *counterexample* in mind for later exercises.

Remember that not all counterarguments count as counterexamples. A counterargument to a generalization is just any argument for thinking that the generalization is false. A counterexample has to be an *example* of a member of the relevant group that is an exception to the generalization. For instance, "My history teacher told me that there was a U.S. president who never married" is a counterargument to the generalization that all U.S. presidents have been married, but it's not a counterexample. The only counterexample to that generalization is James Buchanan—the fifteenth president of the United States and the only one who never married.

Sample

All major world leaders have been men.

Margaret Thatcher, prime minister of Great Britain from 1979 to 1990, was a major world leader, and she was not a man.

The generalization here is about major world leaders. It says that all of them have been men. Thus, a counterexample must be a major world leader who is not (or was not) a man. There are plenty of others besides Thatcher, of course: Historical figures include Queen Elizabeth I (England), Catherine the Great (Russia), the Dowager Empress Cixi (China), and somewhat more recently, Indira Gandhi (India) and Golda Meir (Israel). More contemporary figures include Angela Merkel (Germany), Park Geun-hye (South Korea), and Dilma Rousseff (Brazil), among others.

As usual, there may be some interpretive questions about the generalization. Cleopatra was the last pharaoh of ancient Egypt. She governed an important country and played an important role in the politics of the ancient Mediterranean world. Does that make her a "major world leader"? The American secretary of state plays an important role in world politics. Does that mean that Madeline Albright and Condoleezza Rice were major world leaders when they were secretary of state? Do major world leaders even have to be in politics? What about female leaders of major multinational organizations, such as Indra Nooyi, CEO of PepsiCo, or Christine Lagarde, managing director of the International Monetary Fund?

1.   All Hollywood movie stars are native English speakers.

2.   College textbooks are deathly boring.

3.   Every country in the world belongs to the United Nations.

4.   No women have won the Nobel Prize in chemistry.

5.   No mammals lay eggs.

6.   Baseball players make too much money.

7.   Salads are made of vegetables.

8.   Spanish is the official language of all South American countries.

9.   Mammals have hair.

10.   Everything in the room you're in right now was made outside the United States.

Model responses for odd-numbered exercises can be found on page 318.

Need more practice? See if you can find counterexamples to the generalizations in Exercise Sets 2.1 and 2.2. For even more practice, work with a friend or classmate to create a list of generalizations, and then look for counterexamples to each one.

CHAPTER EXERCISES

Exercise Set 2.6: Evaluating arguments for generalizations

Objective: To give you practice using Rules 7–11 to evaluate arguments for generalizations.

Instructions: Evaluate how well each of the following arguments follows the rules from this chapter.

Tips for success: To evaluate an argument is to decide how strong the argument is. When you encounter an argument in which someone tries to support a generalization by giving examples, ask yourself how well it follows Rules 7–11. The better it does, the stronger the argument is. To be sure that you've done a thorough job in evaluating an argument, it's best to take a systematic approach. Go through Rules 7–11 one by one, asking yourself how well the argument follows each one.

There are some things to keep in mind when applying these rules.

In general, the more examples an argument gives, the better it does in following Rule 7. Although Rule 7 literally says that an argument should "use more than one example," two examples usually aren't much better than one. The real question is whether the argument gives *enough* examples. How many is "enough?" That's a tough question. When an argument is generalizing about a small number of things, it's best to look at every one of those things. When there are too many examples to consider all of them, you need to take a sample. Knowing how big a sample needs to be to count as "enough" examples is tough, since it varies from case to case. But you should know that it's possible to support generalizations about really large groups, like the entire population of the United States, based on surprisingly small samples—sometimes only one or two thousand people, provided that the samples are truly representative.

In deciding how well an argument follows Rule 8, keep in mind what you learned from Exercise Set 2.2. Ask yourself how many of the examples are representative or whether the sample is unbiased. If most or all of them are representative or if the sample is reasonably unbiased, the argument does a good job following Rule 8.

To decide whether an argument follows Rule 9, ask yourself whether you need to know any background rates. Often background rates are expressed in terms of percentages. Suppose someone tells you that faulty ignition switches made by General Motors have caused thirty-one car crashes. In order to conclude that General Motors' cars are notably unsafe, you'd need to know what *percentage* of General Motors cars have crashed because of defective ignition switches. Does the argument provide that percentage—or at least the information you'd need to calculate that percentage? Or can the arguer reasonably assume that you know the background rates (in this case, actually very low)? If not, the argument does a poor job following Rule 9.

Deciding whether an argument follows Rule 10 is more difficult because there are so many ways that statistics can be abused. When you encounter statistics in an argument, think carefully about what the statistics mean, where they came from, and whether they really support the generalization that they're meant to support.

When it comes to Rule 11, ask yourself first whether the conclusion is a universal generalization—that is, a generalization that says something about *all* members of a group, such as "Everyone in Portland, Oregon, is a vegetarian." If it is a universal generalization, see if you can find a counterexample. If there are any counterexamples at all, then the argument's conclusion is false, and the argument needs to be revised.

What about conclusions that are not universal generalizations? You can't prove such conclusions wrong by finding just a few exceptions to them. In the "Tips for success" for Exercise Set 2.5 though, we suggested a looser sense of "counterexample," in which any exception to a generalization is a counterexample to that generalization. Thus, if you can find so many exceptions to a generalization that you think the generalization is false, then the argument is not following Rule 11. In most cases where the argument overlooks that many exceptions, however, the argument also violates Rule 8. If the argument had used a genuinely representative sample, it probably would have found many of the counterexamples.

Sample

Nothing on television is worth watching. News shows mostly feature sensationalized crime stories and public figures' peccadilloes. Just about everything else is a "reality" TV show—actually about as far from reality as you can get—or a show that revels in over-the-top materialism and celebrities' problems.

Adapted from: Deanna McLaffert, "Edit Desk: The Trash on TV," The Brown & White, Nov 16, 2010, http://media.www.thebrownandwhite.com/media/storage/paper1233/news/ 2010/11/16/Opinion/Edit-Desk.The.Trash.On.Tv-3958966.shtml

This is a weak argument. It gives only a few examples, described in vague and loaded generalities. Although those examples cover a lot of what's on TV, it's still not enough to generalize about everything on TV (Rule 7). What about dramas, sitcoms, movies, educational programming, children's programming, etc.? Thus, the argument doesn't do a good job with Rule 8. The author of the argument is probably relying on the reader to know what percentage of TV is devoted to news and reality TV, so it does okay with Rule 9. The argument doesn't misuse any statistics (Rule 10), but that's only because it doesn't use any statistics. The biggest problem with the argument is that it ignores counterexamples (Rule 11): some dramas, movies, and educational programming are definitely worth watching. Other shows are at least possible counterexamples: Some people think that cooking shows are worth watching, for instance.

Notice that this response addresses each rule in turn. It states how well the argument follows the rule, and then it justifies those claims by explaining how the argument does or does not follow the rule.

A good explanation of how a particular argument follows a given rule should mention the details of that specific argument. For instance, saying that some movies and dramas are worth watching is better than just saying that the author ignores some counterexamples. Giving specific examples of worthwhile movies or dramas would be even better.

1. Voters spend far too much time in the voting booth. I saw one person take eleven minutes to fill out her ballot.

   Adapted from: Anne Kreutzer, letter to the editor, Washington Post, *Nov. 9, 2006*

2. Eight members of Congress resigned during 2012. More than half of those who resigned did so because of bad or bizarre behavior, such as having extramarital affairs or tweeting mostly naked selfies. The American public is clearly in no mood to tolerate politicians' personal failings. Unlike in past decades, we're now in an age where any politician who misbehaves will be forced from office.

   Adapted from: Susan Davis, "Public Shows Little Tolerance for Lawmakers' Bad Behavior," USA Today, *Jul 16, 2012, http://usatoday30.usatoday.com/news/washington/story/2012-07-14/antics-prompt-resignations-from-congress/56205160/1*

3. No empire lasts very long. Just look at the empires that collapsed in the twentieth century. The Soviet Union was going to last forever, but it collapsed after seventy years. Hitler's and Mussolini's

regimes were supposed to last for thousands of years. You know what happened to them. Even the British Empire came to an end!

Adapted from: Associated Press, "Doris Lessing Wins 2007 Nobel Literature Prize," FOXNews.com, Oct 11, 2007, http://www.foxnews.com/story/ 0,2933,301073,00.html

4.   When public health experts try to help Americans become healthier, Americans just get fatter. When the government encouraged Americans to quit smoking, ex-smokers gained an estimated fifteen pounds on average. Take another example: When the public health experts said to switch to a low-fat diet, Americans switched. But they replaced their high-fat foods with sugary drinks and low-fat snacks devoured by the fistful. What happened? Americans got so much fatter that the experts rescinded their low-fat advice.

Adapted from: John Tierney, "When It Comes to Salt, No Rights or Wrongs. Yet," New York Times, Feb 22, 2010, http://www.nytimes.com/2010/02/23/ science/23tier.html

5.   Of the 3,141 counties in the United States, the 314 counties with the lowest rates of kidney cancer per year are almost all very rural counties. Furthermore, based on data from 2004, the only counties in which no one developed kidney cancer all had populations of less than 100,000. Thus, the counties where people have the lowest risk of kidney cancer are sparsely populated, rural counties.

Adapted from: Howard Wainer, "The Most Dangerous Equation," American Scientist, May–June 2007, 251–52

6.   Most major news outlets do not provide much coverage of defensive gun uses. There are more than two million defensive gun uses in the United States each year. But in 2001, the three major television news networks did not run a single story about someone who used a gun to stop a crime. The newspaper *USA Today* didn't print a single story on defensive gun use either. The *New York Times* did publish one article on defensive gun use—but it was only 163 words long, compared to a combined 50,745 words that year on crimes committed with guns.

Adapted from: John R. Lott Jr., "Why People Fear Guns," FOXNews.com, Jan 3, 2004, http://www.foxnews.com/story/0,2933,107274,00.html

7. A power company in the state of Georgia is trying to build a new nuclear power plant. They plan to use a safer, more efficient nuclear reactor design from Westinghouse, called the AP1000. China started building a power plant with an AP1000 reactor last year, and the construction costs there have skyrocketed. So far, they're already more than three times higher than expected. Therefore, building power plants with AP1000 reactors will usually lead to cost overruns.

Adapted from: Editorial, "Nuclear Reaction," Sarasota Herald-Tribune, *Feb 22, 2010*

8. Themistocles was a virtuous man, and though he taught his son many things, he could not teach his son to be virtuous. Likewise, Aristides was a virtuous man, but his son was not, even though Aristides had his son trained in many things. Pericles, too, was a virtuous man whose son was not virtuous. Thucydides, another virtuous man, had two sons, to whom he gave a good education, but he did not succeed in making them virtuous. So, we can see that even a good man cannot teach his children to be virtuous.

Adapted from: Plato, "Meno," in Five Dialogues, *2nd ed., translated by G. M. A. Grube (Indianapolis: Hackett Publishing Company, 2002), 85–86*

9. In the 1920s, Dr. Harrison Matland was investigating whether boxing caused brain damage. A fight promoter gave him a list of twenty-three former boxers whom the promoter regarded as "punch drunk." Though he sought all twenty-three of them, Matland only located ten. Of those ten, all suffered clear signs of brain damage: Four had dementia. Two had difficulty speaking coherently. Two had trouble walking. One was blind. One had the symptoms like those of Parkinson's disease. This proved that many former boxers have brain damage.

Adapted from: Deborah Blum, "Will Science Take the Field?" New York Times, *Feb 4, 2010, http://www.nytimes.com/2010/02/05/opinion/05blum.html*

10. We asked 599 first-year undergraduates at a selective Northeastern public university how much money they had borrowed in student loans during the previous academic year. When we compared those results to the university's financial aid records, we found that only 228 of the students had answered within $1,000 of the

actual amount they had borrowed. Therefore, most American college students do not know how much money they are borrowing to pay for college.

Adapted from: Elizabeth J. Akers and Matthew W. Chingos, "Are College Students Borrowing Blindly?" (Washington, DC: Brookings Institution, 2014), 3–5

Model responses for odd-numbered exercises can be found on page 320.

Need more practice? For more practice evaluating arguments for generalizations, look and listen for generalizations in newspapers, in conversations with your friends or family, on television, or online. Ask yourself what arguments people give for those generalizations—if any!—and see how well those arguments measure up against the rules from this chapter.

Exercise Set 2.7: Arguing for and against generalizations

Objective: To give you practice supporting generalizations by constructing arguments that follow Rules 7–11.

Instructions: Consider the following generalizations. Are they true or false? Support your answer with an argument that follows Rules 7–11. You may need to do a little bit of research to complete this exercise. If you can't find the examples to support your initial answer, even after doing some research, you may need to change your answer!

Tips for success: If you're not sure whether a generalization is true or false, look for examples and counterexamples before you begin constructing your argument. Examples count in favor of the generalization; counterexamples count against it.

If you think that a generalization is true, give examples to support it, keeping in mind Rules 7, 8, 9, and 11 in particular. If you think that a generalization is false, give examples that support the *opposite* claim. For instance, if you think the generalization "Most reptiles are dangerous" is false, construct an argument to support a generalization like "Many reptiles are not dangerous."

It's natural to focus on examples that support whatever it is we believe (or want to believe). Rule 11, in particular, provides a helpful check on this tendency. No matter what generalization you're considering, actively look for exceptions to that generalization.

Sample

Illegal drugs are safer than alcohol.

This generalization is false. While it's arguable that some drugs, such as marijuana and certain hallucinogens, are safer than alcohol, most illegal drugs are more dangerous than alcohol. Cocaine, crack, methamphetamines, opium, and heroin are particularly dangerous because they are all highly addictive, they do serious damage to the body, and it's easy to overdose on them. Ecstasy can cause brain damage, and impure ecstasy can be lethal. While alcohol is addictive and can damage your body or kill you, it is not as addictive or damaging as these drugs. Thus, in general, illegal drugs are not safer than alcohol.

This response does two things. First, it states whether the generalization is true or false. Then, it gives an argument to support that claim. The argument does a reasonably good job following each of the rules from this chapter: It gives many examples (Rule 7), which are representative of the most widely used illegal drugs (Rule 8). While it doesn't say how many kinds of illegal drugs there are (Rule 9), we can probably rely on the reader to know roughly how many kinds of drugs are left out. The argument does not give any statistics to support its claim, which means that it doesn't give any misleading statistics (Rule 10), although well-chosen statistics could have strengthened the argument. The argument does mention some specific counterexamples (Rule 11), but only to point out that there are only a few of them.

---

1. Most U.S. presidents were born in Ohio or Virginia.

2. The Japanese make the best cars.

3. Classical music is boring.

4. Your classes this term are interesting.

5. Skydiving is dangerous.

6. Anything that can go wrong, will. (Murphy's Law)

7. All generalizations have exceptions.

8.   Cat owners are more neurotic than dog owners.

For exercises 9 and 10, write your own generalization and then support your generalization with an argument that follows Rules 7–11.

Model responses for odd-numbered exercises can be found on page 324.

Need more practice? Look and listen for generalizations in newspapers, in conversations with your friends or family, on television, or online. Ask yourself whether those generalizations are true or false, and then try to support your answer with arguments that follow the rules in this chapter.

Critical thinking activity: Generalizations about your classroom

For an in-class or out-of-class activity that gives you practice in applying all of these rules, see the "Generalizations about your classroom" assignment sheet (p. 450) in Part 3.

There is an exception to Rule 7 ("Use more than one example"). *Arguments by analogy*, rather than multiplying examples to support a generalization, argue from *one* specific example to another, reasoning that because the two examples are alike in many ways they are also alike in one further specific way.

For example, here is how a doctor argues that everyone should have a regular physical checkup:

> People take in their car for servicing and checkups every few months without complaint. Why shouldn't they take similar care of their bodies?[1]

This argument suggests that getting a regular physical checkup is *like* taking your car in for regular servicing. Cars need that kind of attention—otherwise, major problems may develop. Aren't our bodies like that too?

> People should take their cars in for regular service and checkups (otherwise major problems may develop).

> People's bodies are *like* cars (because human bodies, too, are complex systems that can develop problems if not regularly checked up).

> Therefore, people should take themselves in for regular "service" and checkups too.

Notice the italicized word "like" in the second premise. When an argument stresses the likeness between two cases, it is very probably an argument from analogy.

Here is another striking example.

> An interesting switch was pulled in Rome yesterday by Adam Nordwell, an American Chippewa chief. As he descended his plane from California dressed in full tribal regalia, Nordwell announced in the name of the American Indian people that he was taking possession of Italy "by right of discovery" in the same way that Christopher Columbus did in America. "I

---

1. Dr. John Beary III, quoted in "News You Can Use," *U.S. News and World Report*, Aug 11, 1986, p. 61.

proclaim this day the day of the discovery of Italy," said Nordwell. "What right did Columbus have to discover America when it had already been inhabited for thousands of years? The same right I now have to come to Italy and proclaim the discovery of your country."[2]

Nordwell is suggesting that his "discovery" of Italy is *like* Columbus' "discovery" of America in at least one important way: both Nordwell and Columbus claimed a country that already had been inhabited by its own people for centuries. Thus Nordwell insists that he has as much "right" to claim Italy as Columbus had to claim America. But, of course, Nordwell has no right at all to claim Italy. It follows that Columbus had no right at all to claim America.

> Nordwell has no right to claim Italy for another people, let alone "by right of discovery" (because Italy has been inhabited by its own people for centuries).

> Columbus' claim to America "by right of discovery" is *like* Nordwell's claim to Italy (America, too, had been inhabited by its own people for centuries).

> Therefore, Columbus had no right to claim America for another people, let alone "by right of discovery."

How do we evaluate arguments by analogy?

The first premise of an argument by analogy makes a claim about the example used as an analogy. Remember Rule 3: make sure this premise is true. It's true that cars need regular service and checkups to keep major problems from developing, for instance, and it's true that Adam Nordwell could not claim Italy for the Chippewa.

The second premise in arguments by analogy claims that the example in the first premise is *like* the example about which the argument draws a conclusion. Evaluating this premise is harder, and needs a rule of its own.

Analogies require relevantly similar examples

Arguments by analogy do not require that the example used as an analogy be *exactly* like the example in the conclusion. Our bodies are not just like cars, after all. We are flesh and bone, not metal; we don't have wheels or

---

2. *Miami News,* Sep 23, 1973.

seats or windshield wipers. Analogies require *relevant* similarities. What cars are made of or exactly what their parts are is irrelevant to the doctor's point. The argument is about the upkeep of complex systems.

One relevant difference between our bodies and our cars is that our bodies do not need regular "service" in the way our cars do. Cars regularly need oil changes, new pumps or transmissions, and the like. Replacing body parts or fluids is much rarer: think organ transplants or blood transfusions. On the other hand, it's true that we need regular checkups—otherwise problems can develop undetected—and older and strenuously used bodies, like older and higher mileage cars, may need checkups more often. So the doctor's analogy is partly successful. The "service" part is somewhat weak, in our view, but the checkup part is persuasive.

Likewise, twentieth-century Italy is not just like fifteenth-century America. Italy is known to every twentieth-century schoolchild, whereas America was unknown to much of the world in the fifteenth century. Nordwell is not an explorer, and a commercial jet is not the *Santa Maria*. But these differences are not relevant to Nordwell's analogy. Nordwell simply means to remind us that it is senseless to claim a country already inhabited by its own people. Whether that land is known to the world's schoolchildren, or how the "discoverer" arrived there, is not important. The more appropriate reaction might have been to try to establish diplomatic relations, as we would try to do today if somehow the land and people of Italy had just been discovered. *That's* Nordwell's point, and taken in that way his analogy makes a good (and unsettling) argument.

One famous argument uses an analogy to try to establish the existence of a Creator of the world. We can infer the existence of a Creator from the order and beauty of the world, this argument claims, just as we can infer the existence of an architect or carpenter when we see a beautiful and well-built house. Spelled out in premise-and-conclusion form:

> Beautiful and well-built houses must have "makers": designers and builders.

> The world is *like* a beautiful and well-built house.

> Therefore, the world also must have a "maker": a Designer and Builder, God.

Again, more examples are not necessarily needed here. The argument turns on the similarity of the world to *one* well-understood example, a house.

Whether the world really *is* relevantly similar to a house, though, is not so clear. We know quite a bit about the causes of houses. But houses are *parts* of the world. We know very little, actually, about the structure of the world (the universe) as a *whole* or about what sort of causes it might be expected to have. The philosopher David Hume discussed this argument in his *Dialogues Concerning Natural Religion* and asked:

> Is part of nature a rule for the whole? . . . Think [of how] wide a step you have taken when you compared houses . . . to the universe, and from their similarity in some circumstances inferred a similarity in their causes. . . . Does not the great disproportion bar all comparison and inference?[3]

Hume therefore suggests that the universe is *not* relevantly similar to a house. Houses indeed imply "makers" beyond themselves, but for all we know the universe as a whole may contain its cause within itself, or perhaps has some kind of cause unique to universes. This analogy, then, makes a poor argument. Some other kind of argument is probably needed if the existence of God is to be inferred from the nature of the world.

Exercise Set 3.1: Identifying important similarities

Objective: To give you practice identifying the kinds of similarities needed to support an argument by analogy.

Instructions: For each of the following pairs of things, come up with one to three important ways in which the things are similar.

Tips for success: There are lots of different answers you could give to all of these questions. What matters is that you come up with important similarities between two things that might initially seem quite different. Roughly, a similarity is "important" if noticing that two things are similar in that way gives you a reason to think that the things might be similar in some other way. For instance, noticing that Belize and New Zealand both have English as an official language is a reason to think that they were both British colonies. Noticing that they both have the letter *e* in their name doesn't allow you to draw many inferences about one country based on what you know about the other.

---

3. David Hume, *Dialogues Concerning Natural Religion* (1779; repr., Indianapolis: Hackett Publishing Company, 1980), p. 19.

Sample

Adopting a dog and having a child

Adopting a dog is like having a child in that both require taking responsibility for another living being. Also, they can both turn your home into a big mess!

---

1.   Being a student and having a job

2.   Your brain and a computer

3.   First-degree murder and euthanasia (physician-assisted death)

4.   Butterflies and children

5.   Planet Earth and a globe

6.   Planet Earth and a living organism

7.   Planet Earth and a watch

8.   A cow and a six-foot diameter, 1,500-pound metal sphere

9.   A mouse and an adult human

10. Cooking a meal and living a life

Model responses for odd-numbered exercises can be found on page 327.

Need more practice? Find a short list of recent or classic movies, like "Best Films of 2015" (or 1955). Many Web sites that compile information about movies will have such lists. Try to find at least one important way in which each movie on the list is like each other movie on the list.

Exercise Set 3.2: Identifying important differences

Objective: To give you practice identifying the kinds of differences that you will need to consider in evaluating an argument by analogy.

Instructions: Go back to the pairs of things listed in Exercise Set 3.1. For each pair, identify one to three important ways in which the things differ.

Tips for success: As in Exercise Set 3.1, there are lots of different answers you could give for each pair. Your criterion for "important" differences should be similar to the criterion you used for important similarities in the previous exercise: A difference is important if noticing the difference makes it harder to draw conclusions about one thing from characteristics of the first. For instance, New Zealand and Belize are both former British colonies. Thus, you might expect them to be culturally similar. An important difference, however, is that Belize is in Latin America, whereas New Zealand is not. This makes it less likely that they are culturally similar. An unimportant difference for just about all purposes is that New Zealand's capital is by the water, whereas Belize's is not.

Sample

Adopting a dog and having a child

Adopting a dog differs from having a child in that having a child involves taking on a lot more responsibility, creates a much longer commitment, and eventually leads to there being another adult human being in the world.

Model responses for odd-numbered exercises can be found on page 330.

Need more practice? To get more practice, pair up with a friend or classmate. Have each partner fill in one blank in the sentence "_____ is like _____." See how many important similarities and differences you can find between the things in the blanks. Vary this activity by restricting the words you put in the blanks to specific categories (e.g., celebrities, historical figures, people you know, paintings, video games, animals, etc.).

CHAPTER EXERCISES

Exercise Set 3.3: Evaluating arguments by analogy

Objective: To give you practice evaluating arguments by analogy.

Instructions: Evaluate how well each of the following arguments follows Rule 12.

Tips for success: Every argument by analogy compares two things. To make a judgment about how well an argument by analogy follows Rule 12, you need to think systematically about how similar those two things are. To do that, it helps to structure your thinking in terms of four questions:

1. In what ways are the two things similar?

2. How is each of these similarities relevant to the conclusion?

3. In what ways are the two things different?

4. How is each of these differences relevant to the conclusion?

The author of an argument by analogy is likely to list some of the ways in which the two things are similar. You might be able to think of some more. The author probably will not point out the differences between the two things. It's essential that you think carefully about what those differences are. If you don't have a list of both similarities and differences, you can't make an informed judgment about the argument.

You practiced coming up with answers to the first and third questions in Exercise Sets 3.1 and 3.2. In this Exercise Set, you're more likely to have to do a little bit of research to find the important differences. The argument is likely to list the important similarities, although you can usually dig up more of them.

What about the other two questions? To explain how a similarity is relevant to the conclusion, you'll need to argue that the similarity gives you a reason to think that the conclusion is true. Likewise, to explain how the differences are relevant, you'll need to argue that the differences give you a reason to doubt that the conclusion follows. It can often be hard to articulate why a similarity or difference is relevant. If you find yourself at a loss for words, imagine that you are explaining the similarity to a child: Start from the very beginning and state all of your assumptions as plainly as you can.

You might find it helpful to proceed systematically through these questions. First, generate a list of important similarities. Then, go through each similarity on the list and construct a brief argument to show that the similarity gives you a reason to think the conclusion is true. Third, generate a list of important differences. Then, go through each difference on your list and explain why the difference gives you a reason to doubt that the conclusion is well established by this analogy.

Once you've compiled your list of the important similarities and differences and you understand why the similarities and differences are relevant, you need to make a judgment call about whether the similarities outweigh the differences or vice versa. Other people might not always agree with your judgment call. In that case, there's sometimes nothing you can do to convince those people except try to come up with a different argument. This is one of the great weaknesses of arguments by analogy.

Sample

A store owner in Colorado had an unusual way of deterring shoplifters. When he caught one, the shop owner threatened to call the police unless the shoplifter turned over a shoe. He found that shoplifters were too embarrassed to come back to the store after having surrendered their shoe. The police used the following argument to stop this practice: Demanding a shoe in return for leniency is like demanding twenty dollars in return for leniency. Both involve threatening someone to get them to give up something of value. It would be a form of robbery to demand twenty dollars in return for leniency. Thus, it's a form of robbery to demand a shoe in return for leniency.

Adapted from: Associated Press, "Liquor Store Owner Told to Stop Confiscating Shoplifters' Shoes or Face Felony Charges," FOXNews.com, May 27, 2008, http://www.foxnews.com/story/ 0,2933,358702,00.html

This is a fairly strong argument because demanding twenty dollars and demanding a shoe are relevantly similar. Both involve threatening the shoplifter with harm (in this case, arrest) unless they surrender something of value. Since threatening someone to give you money is what makes, say, mugging a form of robbery, this similarity is relevant to the conclusion that demanding a shoe is robbery. There is one relevant difference. The store owner could spend the twenty dollars, but he can't do anything with one shoe. This is relevant because it makes it clear that the owner's goal is really to deter theft, not personal gain, which is the goal of robbery. But on balance, that difference doesn't change the fact that demanding a shoe is still relevantly like robbery, since giving up the shoe is still a loss for the shoplifter. (Taking money by force is still robbery even if the robber gives the money to the poor or uses it to mulch his garden.)

This response does more than list similarities and differences. After identifying an important similarity, it explains why that similarity gives us a reason to accept the conclusion: demanding a shoe in return for leniency shares the special feature that would make demanding money a form of robbery. After identifying an important difference—namely, that a single shoe is not valuable to the shop owner—the argument explains why this difference is relevant: It demonstrates that the shop owner is trying to deter theft, rather than seeking personal gain.

Having explained the relevance of the similarities and differences, the response makes a final judgment about whether the analogy works: It does. The two things are relevantly similar, and so the analogy does a good job supporting its conclusion. The response even says a little bit about why the similarity outweighs the difference.

You might make a different final judgment about the success of this argument, even if you agree about what the important similarities and differences are.

1. The Earth supports living organisms. Europa, one of the moons of Jupiter, is like Earth in that both have large oceans of liquid water. Therefore, Europa supports living organisms.

    Adapted from: Larry Palkovic, "An Ocean Discovered: Europa Surrenders Her Secrets," The Galileo Messenger *43, May 1997, http://www2 .jpl.nasa.gov/galileo/mess43/ocndscvd.html*

2. The mugger who forces me to give him my wallet is not entitled to my money. A nation that conquers another nation in an unjust war is like a mugger: both use violence to take what they want. Therefore, a nation that conquers another nation in an unjust war is not entitled to that nation's resources.

    Adapted from: John Locke, Second Treatise of Government *(1689; repr., Indianapolis: Hackett Publishing Company, 1980), 91*

3. We all know that people should not drive while they are drunk. Texting while driving is like driving while drunk in that both make people react more slowly to road hazards. Therefore, people should not text while driving.

    Adapted from: Nicole Arce, "Texting Is More Dangerous Than Drugs, Alcohol While Driving: Study," Tech Times, Jun 9, 2014, http://www.techtimes.com/articles/8185/20140609/texting-is-more-dangerous-than-drugs-alcohol-while-driving-study

4. Religion is like opium in that both give people an illusory sense of happiness or hope, even if their lives are not going well. But people shouldn't have anything to do with opium. Therefore, people shouldn't have anything to do with religion.

    Adapted from: Karl Marx, "Toward a Critique of Hegel's Philosophy of Right," in Selected Writings, ed. Lawrence H. Simon (Indianapolis: Hackett Publising Company, 1994), 28

5. A geneticist named Robert Naviaux injected pregnant mice with genes from a virus. As a result, the offsprings' brain cells reacted differently to purines, which are naturally occurring chemicals in the body. When exposed to purines, the cells—including brain cells—would activate a "stress response" that made it harder for them to communicate with one another. These chronically stressed mice exhibited symptoms that are similar to those exhibited by autistic humans, such as avoiding strangers and novel situations. Thus, autism in humans might be caused by a hyperactive stress response by brain cells.

    Adapted from: Elizabeth Norton, "Century-Old Drug Reverses Signs of Autism in Mice," Science News, Jun 17, 2014, http://news.sciencemag.org/biology/2014/06/century-old-drug-reverses-signs-autism-mice

6. The First Amendment does not protect the right to shout "Fire!" in a crowded theater when there is no fire. During a war, distributing pamphlets that encourage people to resist a military draft is like shouting "Fire!" in a crowded theater in that both present a danger to the public. Therefore, the First Amendment does not protect the right to distribute anti-draft pamphlets.

    Adapted from: Schenck v. United States, 249 U.S. 47 (1919)

7. Some people insist that students should learn how to do advanced math by hand, not just on a calculator. Some of these people argue that students need to know how to do advanced math by hand because they may not always have calculators available to them. But this is like arguing that farmers should learn how to do everything without tractors or other equipment because their equipment might break down. That's a ridiculous argument; when a farmer's equipment does break down, he or she gets it repaired rather than finishing the job by hand. Thus, the argument that students need to learn to do math by hand because they might not have a calculator is also ridiculous.

   Adapted from: Carmen M. Latterell, Math Wars: A Guide for Parents and Teachers *(Santa Barbara, CA: Greenwood Publishing Group, 2005), 93*

8. Imagine that a department store offered a storewide shopping spree for five thousand dollars. After paying your fee, you could take anything that you could carry out of the store, including designer clothes, expensive jewelry, and other luxury goods. Someone who paid the fee and walked out with a piece of bubble gum would be acting foolishly. Students who choose their college courses based on which courses are easiest or the most entertaining are like someone who picks up a piece of bubble gum in that imaginary department store shopping spree: After paying tuition, university students can learn things that the world's greatest scientists and thinkers spent years discovering; they can have their pick of the world's most valuable intellectual treasures. Instead of looking for the most valuable learning experiences they can, they go for the "mental bubble gum" offered by the easiest courses. Thus, students who choose easy courses instead of the most stimulating and edifying courses are acting foolishly.

   Adapted from: Ronald Munson, The Way of Words: An Informal Logic *(Boston: Houghton Mifflin, 1976), 357*

9. Lei Zhang, a Chinese businessman educated at the Yale School of Management, recently donated $8,888,888 to Yale University. He said that Yale had changed his life. Some Chinese argue that it was wrong for Zhang to donate to a foreign school when Chinese schools need his help. They say that he has betrayed his country. But consider the similar case of John Leighton Stuart, an

American who raised over $2.5 million between 1919 and 1937 for Yenching University in China. Stuart's fundraising was a generous act, even though he wasn't raising money for an American school. Stuart did nothing wrong in raising money for a foreign school; he did not betray his country. Neither did Zhang.

Adapted from: Wu Zhong, "Yale Donation Sets Tongues Wagging," Asia Times, Jan 14, 2010, http://www.atimes.com/atimes/China/LA14Ad01.html

10.   Imagine that you are walking by a shallow pond and you see a young child drowning in the pond. You know that you can wade into the pond and save the child at no risk to yourself, but you would ruin your shoes in the process. If you don't do anything, the child will die. It would be wrong of you to let the child drown in order to avoid ruining your shoes. But we all do something like this every day. We could save the lives of children in developing countries by donating relatively small amounts of money to international relief organizations like Oxfam or CARE. Not donating money to international relief organizations is like letting a child drown in a shallow pond. Therefore, it's wrong not to donate money to international relief organizations.

Adapted from: Peter Singer, "Famine, Affluence, and Morality," Philosophy and Public Affairs *1 (1972), 229–43*

Model responses for odd-numbered exercises can be found on page 333.

Need more practice? Arguments by analogy are common in public debates. Watch your favorite news shows or look at editorials, op-eds, and letters to the editor in your favorite newspaper. When you hear or read an argument by analogy, assess how well it follows Rule 12.

Exercise Set 3.4: Constructing arguments by analogy

Objective: To give you practice constructing good arguments by analogy.

Instructions: Construct an argument by analogy as prompted in each scenario below. Be sure that your argument follows Rule 12.

Tips for success: Start by figuring out exactly what you want your conclusion to be. Your conclusion should have the form "**X** is/was **F**." For instance, the conclusion of Adam Nordwell's argument, discussed above, is that Christopher Columbus was unjustified in claiming land for his own people. In that case, **X** stands for "Christopher Columbus" and **F** stands for "unjustified in claiming land for his own people."

The next step in constructing your argument is to find something to compare to **X**. This thing—call it **Y**—should also be **F**. Thus, the first premise of your argument should have the form "**Y** is/was **F**." For instance, the first premise of Nordwell's argument is that he, Adam Nordwell, is unjustified in claiming land for his own people. In that case, **Y** stands for "Adam Nordwell" and **F**, again, stands for "unjustified in claiming land for his own people." To make your argument work, you need to be sure that this first premise is fairly uncontroversial: Everyone should agree that **Y** is **F**, just as everyone would agree that Nordwell didn't really have the right to claim Italy for the Chippewa.

The key step is to argue that **X** is *relevantly like* **Y**. The similarity that Nordwell uses is that he and Columbus were both claiming lands that were already inhabited. This is relevant to the claim that Columbus was unjustified in claiming lands for his own people because, other things being equal, claiming lands that are already inhabited amounts to stealing the land from its current inhabitants.

Be sure to consider relevant differences between **X** and **Y**. If the differences outweigh the similarities, you'll either need to find something else to compare **X to** or you'll need to give up your conclusion that **X** is **F**.

Sample

Imagine that you are a movie producer. You are trying to produce a new movie based on *Arthur*, the popular children's television series about Arthur, the anthropomorphic aardvark. You have already lined up the original voice actors from the TV show, a great team of animators, and a well-known director of children's movies. Construct an argument by analogy to convince executives at a major movie studio to back your movie.

The SpongeBob SquarePants movie was quite successful, bringing in over $140 million worldwide. An Arthur movie would be like the SpongeBob SquarePants movie in that it is based on a long-running animated children's television series, so we know that lots of people like it. Like SpongeBob SquarePants, the television series on which the movie was based spawned a profitable line of toys and other merchandise, so we know that people are willing to spend money on <u>Arthur</u>. And like <u>SpongeBob</u> <u>SquarePants</u>, the <u>Arthur</u> movie would feature the original voice actors, which is important for winning over fans of the television series. Therefore, the <u>Arthur</u> movie would also be extremely successful.

This argument begins by identifying the thing to which the Arthur *movie is going to be compared: the* SpongeBob SquarePants *movie. It then explains how the two things are similar and why those similarities are important. Finally, it clearly states the point of the comparison: the* Arthur *movie would be extremely successful.*

1. Suppose that a friend of yours has downloaded dozens of movies from the Internet without paying for them. Has your friend done something wrong? Or is it okay to download movies without paying for them? Construct an argument by analogy to support your position.

2. Textbook publishers often provide instructors with "test banks" that contain questions the instructors can use on exams. These test banks are not supposed to be available to students, but some students gain access to them and review them before exams. Professors generally regard this as a form of cheating, but some students say that it's just another way of studying. Is it cheating to use such test banks to prepare for an exam? Construct an argument by analogy to support your position.

3. Many states or countries have laws requiring people to wear helmets while riding motorcycles. Should it be illegal to ride a motorcycle without a helmet? Construct an argument by analogy to support your position.

4. Imagine that your best friend is in a romantic relationship that has become destructive. When you encourage your best friend to get out of the relationship, your friend tells you to mind your own business. Do you think it's appropriate for you to continue to encourage your friend to get out of the relationship? Construct an argument by analogy to support your position.

5. Over three thousand years ago, a people called the Olmecs dominated what is now southern Mexico. Today, the Olmecs are most famous for the stone heads that they carved out of enormous boulders. Each head, as tall as a grown man and weighing up to 40 tons, has a unique and expressive face. Archaeologists suspect that the heads depicted powerful Olmec rulers. The ancient Olmec city of San Lorenzo boasted ten of these colossal heads, but when the city collapsed, the heads were mutilated and buried. No one knows exactly why. Come up with your own guess about why the heads were mutilated and buried. No one knows why. Come up with your own guess about why the heads were mutilated and buried. Construct an argument by analogy to support your position. (Want a hint? Think about other instances in which a culture's political or religious monuments have been destroyed.)

6. Some politicians insist that the children of undocumented immigrants should not be allowed to attend public schools in the United States. Do you agree with this suggestion? Construct an argument by analogy to support your answer.

7. People frequently argue that some activity should be avoided because it is "unnatural." For instance, some people argue that people should not be vegetarians because humans "naturally" eat an omnivorous diet. Construct an argument by analogy to show that this argument is flawed.

8. Is it reasonable to believe that the different species on Earth evolved by natural selection? Construct an argument by analogy to support your position.

For exercises 9 and 10, pick a conclusion of your own and construct an argument by analogy to support it. You may need to consider several different conclusions before you find one that can be supported with an argument by analogy.

Model responses for odd-numbered exercises can be found on page 338.

Need more practice? Go to the companion Web site for this book and click on the link for "Chapter III." You'll find links to Web sites that enable users to participate in structured debates on a wide range of topics. Browse the debates until you find one to which you could contribute a good argument by analogy. (If you want to participate in the debate, you can post your argument, but just thinking about what argument you *would* contribute can be good practice too.) For even more practice, see whether you can come up with a good argument by analogy for the other side of the same debate. While you're there, of course, you can always contribute other kinds of arguments as well.

Critical thinking activity: Using analogies to understand unusual objects

For an out-of-class activity with an in-class component, see the "Using analogies to understand unusual objects" assignment sheet (p. 452) in Part 3.

Critical thinking activity: Using analogies in ethical reasoning

For an out-of-class activity with an optional in-class component, see the "Using analogies in ethical reasoning" assignment sheet (p. 453) in Part 3.

No one can be an expert through direct experience on everything there is to know. We do not live in ancient times ourselves and therefore cannot know first-hand at what age women tended to marry back then. Few of us have enough experience to judge which kinds of cars are safest in a crash. We do not know first-hand what is really happening in Sri Lanka or the state legislature or even the average American classroom or street corner. Instead, we must rely on others—better-situated people, organizations, surveys or reference works—to tell us much of what we need to know about the world. We argue like this:

> X (a source that ought to know) says that Y.
>
> Therefore, Y is true.

For instance:

> Carl Sagan says that there could be life on Mars.
>
> Therefore, there could be life on Mars.

It's a risky business, though. Supposedly expert sources may be over-confident, or may be misled, or may not even be reliable. And everyone has biases, after all, even innocent ones. Once again we must consider a checklist of standards that truly reliable sources need to meet.

Cite your sources

Some factual assertions, of course, are so obvious or well known that they do not need support at all. It is usually not necessary to *prove* that the United States has fifty states or that Juliet loved Romeo. However, a precise figure for the current population of the United States does need a citation. Likewise, the claim that Juliet was only fourteen should cite a few Shakespearean lines in support.

NO:
> I once read that there are cultures in which makeup and clothes are mostly men's business, not women's.

If you're arguing about whether men and women everywhere follow the gender roles familiar to us, this is a relevant example—a striking case of

Rule 13

different gender roles. But few of us know anything about this sort of difference first-hand. To nail down the argument, you need to call upon a fully cited source.

YES:

Carol Beckwith, in "Niger's Wodaabe" (*National Geographic* 164, no. 4 [October 1983], 483–509), reports that among the West African Fulani peoples such as the Wodaabe, makeup and clothes are mostly men's business.

Citation styles vary—you may need a handbook of style to find the appropriate style for your purposes—but all include the same basic information: enough so that others can easily find the source on their own.

The "Resources" section on this book's companion Web site has links to instructions and advice for different styles for citing sources. Your school's library or writing center may also have resources for you. (If you don't know whether your school *has* a writing center, find out! Writing centers usually offer help on papers and other writing assignments.)

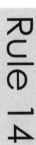

Rule 14

Seek informed sources

Sources must be qualified to make the statements they make. Honda mechanics are qualified to discuss the merits of different Hondas, midwives and obstetricians are qualified to discuss pregnancy and childbirth, teachers are qualified to discuss the state of their schools, and so on. These sources are qualified because they have the appropriate background and information. For the best information about global climate change, go to climatologists, not politicians.

Where a source's qualifications are not immediately clear, an argument must explain them briefly. Carl Sagan says that there could be life on Mars, eh? But who is Carl Sagan? Here is the answer: Sagan was an astronomer and astrobiologist, a leader in the space program, and among the designers of the first Mars landers. (And, in the spirit of citing sources, I will add that you can find out more about him in William Poundstone's biography, *Carl Sagan: A Life in the Cosmos* [New York: Holt and Company, 1999].) When someone with a background like *that* says that there could be life on Mars, we should listen.

As you explain your source's qualifications, you can also add more evidence to your argument.

Carol Beckwith, in "Niger's Wodaabe" (*National Geographic* 164, no. 4 [October 1983], 483–509), reports that among the West African Fulani peoples such as the Wodaabe, makeup and clothes are mostly men's business. Beckwith and an anthropologist colleague lived with the Wodaabe for two years and observed many dances for which the men prepared by lengthy preening, face-painting, and teeth-whitening. (Her article includes many pictures too.) Wodaabe women watch, comment, and choose mates for their beauty—which the men say is the natural way. "Our beauty makes the women want us," one says.

Note that an informed source need not fit our general stereotype of an "authority"—and a person who fits our stereotype of an authority may not even be an informed source. If you're checking out colleges, for instance, students are the best authorities, not administrators or recruiters, because it's the students who know what student life is really like. (Just be sure to find yourself a representative sample.)

Note also that authorities on one subject are not necessarily informed about every subject on which they offer opinions.

Einstein was a pacifist. Therefore, pacifism must be right.

Einstein's genius in physics does not establish him as a genius in political philosophy. Likewise, just because someone can put the title "Doctor" before their name—that is, they have a PhD or MD in some field—does not mean that they are qualified to deliver opinions on any subject whatsoever. (Not to name any names or anything, but there are some quite prominently cited "Doctors" these days whose doctorates actually have nothing to do with the fields in which they make very self-assured and widely publicized pronouncements.)

Sometimes we must rely on sources whose knowledge is better than ours but still limited in various ways. On occasion the best information we can get about what is happening in a war zone or a political trial or inside a business or bureaucracy is fragmentary and filtered through journalists, international human rights organizations, corporate watchdogs, and so on. If you must rely on a source that may have limited knowledge in this way, acknowledge the problem. Let your readers or hearers decide whether imperfect authority is better than none at all.

Truly informed sources rarely expect others to accept their conclusions simply because they assert them. Most good sources will offer at least some reasons or evidence as well—examples, facts, analogies, other kinds of arguments—to help explain and defend their conclusions. Beckwith, for example, offers photographs and stories from the years she lived with the Wodaabe. Sagan wrote whole books explaining space exploration and what we might find beyond Earth. Thus, while we might need to take some of their *specific* claims on authority alone (for instance, we must take Beckwith at her word that she had certain experiences), we can expect even the best sources to offer arguments as well as their own judgments in support of their general conclusions. Look for those arguments too, then, and look at them critically as well.

Seek impartial sources

People who have the most at stake in a dispute are usually not the best sources of information about the issues involved. Sometimes they may not even tell the truth. People accused in criminal trials are presumed innocent until proven guilty, but we seldom completely believe their claims of innocence without confirmation from impartial witnesses. Readiness to tell the truth as one sees it, though, is not always enough. The truth as one honestly sees it can still be biased. We tend to see what we expect to see. We notice, remember, and pass on information that supports our point of view, but we may not be quite so motivated when the evidence points the other way.

Therefore, look for *impartial* sources: people or organizations who do not have a stake in the immediate issue, and who have a prior and primary interest in accuracy, such as (some) university scientists or statistical databases. Don't just rely on interest groups on *one* side of a major public question for the most accurate information on the issues at stake. Don't just rely on manufacturers' advertisements for reliable information concerning that product.

NO:
My car dealer recommends that I pay $300 to rustproof my car. He should know; I guess I'd better do it.

He probably *does* know, but he might not be entirely reliable, either. The best information on consumer products and services comes from independent consumer testing agencies, agencies not affiliated with any manufacturer or provider but answering to consumers who want the most accurate information they can get. Do some research!

YES:
Consumer Reports says that rust problems have almost disappeared in modern cars due to better manufacturing, and

advises that dealer rustproofing is not needed (see "Don't Waste Money on Unnecessary Extras," *Consumer Reports Buying Guide 2006*, 153). Therefore, I don't need it!

Likewise, independent service professionals and mechanics are relatively impartial sources of information. On political matters, especially when the disagreements are basically over statistics, look to independent government agencies, such as the Census Bureau, or to university studies or other independent sources. Organizations like Doctors Without Borders are relatively impartial sources on the human rights situation in other countries because they practice medicine, not politics: they are not trying to support or oppose any specific government.

Of course, independence and impartiality are not always easy to judge, either. Be sure that your sources are *genuinely* independent and not just interest groups masquerading under an independent-sounding name. Check who funds them; check their other publications; look for their track record; watch the tone of their statements. Sources that make extreme or simplistic claims, or spend most of their time attacking and demeaning the other side, weaken their own claims. Again, seek out sources that offer constructive arguments and responsibly acknowledge and thoroughly engage the arguments and evidence on the other side. At the very least, try to confirm for yourself any factual claim quoted from a potentially biased source. Good arguments cite their sources (Rule 13); look them up. Make sure the evidence is quoted correctly and not pulled out of context, and check for further information that might be helpful.

Exercise Set 4.1: Identifying biased sources

Objective: To help you guard against biased sources.

Instructions: For each of the questions below, think of one source that would *not* be impartial. Explain why that source would not be impartial. You do not need to name a specific person; you can simply describe what kind of person you have in mind.

Tips for success: An impartial source is an unbiased source. This exercise asks you to find *biased* sources—sources that you would *not* want to use in your arguments because they are *not* impartial.

Here's one way to come up with biased sources: Ask yourself what answers different people might give to each question in this exercise. Then, for each answer, ask yourself whether there is someone who would benefit from convincing you of that answer.

People can benefit in various ways from convincing you of a particular answer. Sometimes people benefit financially. For instance, a sales clerk at a store gains financially by convincing you that the jeans you're considering look great on you. Sometimes people stand to gain in other ways. For instance, a candidate for political office can get extra votes by convincing voters that his or her opponent is corrupt. Thus, the sales clerk is a biased source about the jeans you're considering and the politician is a biased source about his or her opponent.

Remember, though, that sources can be biased even if they don't stand to benefit from pushing a particular answer. Sources who are likely to reach a particular answer regardless of the truth are also biased. For instance, suppose you asked the parents of the players on a high school basketball team whether their children are better than the average player on the team. A significant majority of parents would probably say that their child is above average, even though it's unlikely that a significant majority of the players really are better than average. The parents don't stand to gain anything by convincing you that their child is better, but they're still biased. This extends more generally to individuals' beliefs about how they compare to others: individuals are frequently biased when it comes to rating their own abilities. For example, a study published in 1981 by Ola Svenson, of the University of Stockholm, found that 93 percent of Americans rated themselves as better drivers than the median driver. A similar study published in 1986 by Iain McCormick and his colleagues at Victoria University of Wellington found that up to 80 percent of drivers consider themselves above average.

Sample

How much does smoking increase your chances of getting cancer?

An executive at a tobacco company is a biased source. The executive has a strong financial incentive to convince people that smoking does not increase your chances of getting cancer very much. If people believe that smoking doesn't increase your chance of getting cancer, more people will smoke and the company will do better. The executive may also prefer not to think that his company's product causes suffering and death.

1.   Is it worthwhile to buy an extended warranty on a new appliance?

2.   Are Macs better than PCs?

3.   What is the best university in the United States?

4.   Is Andrew Luck, who plays for the Indianapolis Colts, a better quarterback than the New England Patriots' Tom Brady?

5.   Do vaccines weaken children's immune systems?

6.   Is it better to save for retirement by putting your money in a savings account or by investing it through a stockbroker?

7.   How often do women suffer dangerous complications from an abortion?

8.   Do laws requiring background checks at gun stores reduce crime?

9.   Would vouchers for private schools improve education in the United States?

10.   Is there life after death?

Model responses for odd-numbered exercises can be found on page 340.

Need more practice? To get more practice in brainstorming biased sources, go to the Web site of your favorite newspaper and find an article that interests you. Imagine that you were a reporter assigned to write that article. Make a list of people or organizations that you think would be biased sources of information about the topic of that article. For each person or organization, explain why you suspect they might be biased. Are there steps you could take to compensate for that bias?

Cross-check sources

Consult and compare a variety of sources to see if other, equally good authorities agree. Are the experts sharply divided or in agreement? If they're pretty much in agreement, theirs is the safe view to take. (At the very least, if you propose to take a different view, you have some serious explaining to do.) Where even the experts disagree, though, it's best to reserve judgment yourself too. Don't jump in with two feet where truly informed people tread with care. See if you can argue on some other grounds—or rethink your conclusions.

Authorities are most likely to agree about specific factual matters. That Wodaabe men spend a great deal of time on clothes and makeup is a specific factual claim, for instance, and in principle not hard to verify. On larger and less tangible issues, it is harder to find authorities who agree. Can or should the U.S. Constitution be read in terms of the Founders' "original intent"? Do we have free will? Distinguished jurists disagree with each other; great philosophers have held opposing views. You can still quote some of them as authorities if you know that your audience already agrees with them and respects them (but then again there's always that question: should *you*?). In general, though, do not expect their mere assertions to carry authority. Once again, look to the arguments behind the assertions.

Remember, though: mere disagreement does not automatically disqualify a source. A few people may still disagree that the Earth is round, but it is not a genuinely open question. Likewise, although there was a time when experts disagreed about global climate change, the world scientific community is now nearly unanimous that it is occurring and needs to be addressed.[1] Sure, there's still controversy, but not among the experts. You may need to look into disagreements such as these to decide how seriously to take them.

Exercise Set 4.2: Identifying independent sources

Objective: To give you practice identifying independent sources.

---

1. Still the best source is the Intergovernmental Panel on Climate Change, a global scientific effort established by the United Nations Environmental Program and the World Meteorological Organization, on the Web at http://www.ipcc.ch/. If you are interested in this issue, a good project would be to apply the points in this chapter to the controversy, such as it is, over the IPCC and its reports.

Instructions: For each of the following questions, think of two informed, impartial sources that you might cite in an argument. You do not need to find or cite specific sources; you can just describe the kind of source you have in mind. Be sure your two sources are genuinely independent—that is, that neither gets its information from the other and that the two are not relying on the same source for their information.

Tips for success: Rules 14, 15, and 16 deal with three important features of arguments that use sources. Rule 14 requires that sources know what they're talking about. Rule 15 requires that sources be unbiased.

What about Rule 16? Rule 16 requires more than just checking multiple sources. When you are using multiple sources, it's important that your sources are *independent* of one another. Two sources are independent of one another when neither one is getting its information from the other.

The idea of independent sources is best illustrated by an example. Suppose that, days before a mayoral election, a polling organization announces that the incumbent candidate is well ahead in the polls. On the basis of this announcement, the local newspaper runs the headline, "Mayor on Track to Win Second Term." If you cite both the polling organization and the local newspaper, have you cross checked your sources? No. Since the local paper got its information from the polling organization, it is not an independent source. Citing the newspaper does not strengthen your argument. You would need to cite another source that did its own, independent polling.

Sample

Is peanut oil bad for your health?

1. A scientific paper published in a reputable medical journal.
2. A professional dietitian (a specialist in the science of nutrition) other than the one(s) who wrote or were cited in the scientific paper used for source 1.

Notice that both of these answers could be more specific. For instance, you might identify a specific reputable journal that is likely to publish papers on the health effects of peanut oil. Notice also that you'd want to find out where the dietitian was getting his or her information about peanut oil, in order to make sure that it wasn't just coming from the paper that you used for source 1.

---

1. What is the best way to get from Vancouver to the popular ski resort in Whistler, British Columbia?

2. Do students do better in class if they take notes with a pen and paper instead of a computer?

3. How do I write a good paper for a philosophy class?

4. What are the best restaurants in Miami?

5. Is it possible for deadly viruses like Ebola to become "airborne," meaning that they could spread from person to person without direct contact?

6. Is being a lawyer a rewarding career?

7. Where was your great-grandmother born?

8. How does religion affect contemporary Egyptian politics?

9. Does the death penalty deter crime?

10. What caused the collapse of the Soviet Union?

Model responses for odd-numbered exercises can be found on page 343.

Need more practice? Go to the Web site of your favorite newspaper and find an article that interests you. Check to see if the article attributes any claims to a specific source. If so, try to think of an additional, independent source that the article's author could have used as well.

Use the Web with care

Enter a few keywords and the Web will give you truckloads of information on almost any question or issue. All manner of views and topics are available, almost instantly, that would take forever to turn up if we had to search painstakingly and by hand in libraries or by correspondence.

Reliability, though, is quite another matter. Libraries have at least some checks on the reliability of the books and other materials they collect. Reputable publishers consult the community of experts before presenting any views as expert. Some publishers are even renowned for employing offices of fact-checkers of their own. But on the Web anyone can say anything whatsoever, and with a little skill or money even the flimsiest opinion site can be dressed up to look sober-minded and professional. There are very few checks on the content of Web sites—often no checks at all.

Only rely on Web sources, then, if you are dealing with an identifiable and independently reputable source. Don't rely on a Web site at all unless you have some idea of its source. Key questions are: Who created this site? Why did they create it? What are their qualifications? What does it mean if they don't tell you? How can you double-check and cross-check its claims?

Be aware also that Web search engines do not search "everything"— far from it. They search only what is indexed, which is only 10 to 20 percent of the available Web, and heavily weighted toward merchandising and "hot" sites. Especially on controversial issues where evidence and conclusions are in dispute, the sites that come up first (and are often *designed* to come up first) are likely to be opinionated bluster from non-experts with agendas. In fact, the best information is often in databases or other academic resources that standard search engines cannot enter at all. Normally you have to search *within* these databases to find the most reliable articles or information on any given topic.

When you really need to know something, then, dig deeper than the standard Web search. What you'll get usually will require harder and more careful reading and thinking—which is what you want, of course—and sometimes a password (hopefully available to you as a student or library patron) in turn. If you are preparing a research project for a class, your teacher should be able to guide you to appropriate Web resources. If not, ask your librarian!

Critical thinking activity: Recognizing reliable Web sources

For an out-of-class activity that helps you apply Rule 17, see the "Recognizing reliable Web sources" assignment sheet (p. 454) in Part 3.

CHAPTER EXERCISES

Exercise Set 4.3: Evaluating arguments that use sources

Objective: To give you practice evaluating the use of sources in arguments.

Instructions: Evaluate how well each of the following arguments obeys Rules 13–17.

Tips for success: You can divide your evaluation of these arguments into two steps.

First, ask yourself how well the argument cites its source (Rule 13). This is not an all-or-nothing affair. A newspaper, for instance, might report that "researchers from the University of Alberta" published a paper on polar bear fossils "in this week's issue of the journal *Science*," without giving the exact names of the researchers or title of the paper. This isn't a full citation, but as long as you know the date that the news story was published, you'll probably be able to find the original source. To determine how well an argument follows Rule 13, ask yourself how easy it would be for you to find the source, given what the argument tells you. The easier it is, the better the argument does.

Second, ask yourself whether the sources are good—that is, whether they are informed (Rule 14), impartial (Rule 15), and independent (Rule 16). If the source's qualifications are not widely known, you might also consider whether the argument establishes that the source is a good one.

If an argument only cites one source, of course, then it does not follow Rule 16. This is a bigger problem in some cases than in others. It's a big problem in cases where the conclusion of the argument is controversial or disputed—that is, where the relevant experts disagree. The point of Rule 16 is that even an informed, impartial source provides relatively little support if there are other, equally informed and impartial sources that say the opposite. Cross-checking sources is a way to ensure that there is consensus, or at least fairly widespread agreement, among the experts.

A failure to cross-check sources might not be much of a problem in cases where facts are well established and widely known. When the source is extremely reputable, and the claim is not particularly controversial, you might not need to cross-check your source. For instance, if the U.S. Geological Survey announces that an earthquake measured 7.4 on the Richter scale, you probably wouldn't need to check that claim against another source. Barring special circumstances, there is little reason to think that the

U.S. Geological Survey would lie about or err in measuring the magnitude of an earthquake.

There's one further kind of case to keep in mind. Some facts are very hard or very expensive to discover. In cases like these, there may be only one source for a particular claim. (Of course, other sources might repeat the claim, but they don't count as independent sources.) The best an argument can do, then, is rely on the single source. For instance, it would be very difficult to figure out exactly how many people of Chinese origin are currently living in Canada. Statistics Canada, the Canadian government agency that conducts the Canadian census, is the only organization likely to obtain an accurate count. Thus, it would be reasonable for an argument to cite only the Canadian census to support a claim about the number of Chinese people in Canada.

In most cases where you are evaluating someone else's argument, violations of Rule 17 will probably show up as violations of other rules too. If the argument has failed to use the Web with care, its sources are likely to be improperly cited, uninformed, or biased. Keep in mind that there are three ways for a Web site to be untrustworthy. Some Web sites present original research—that is, information that they have discovered themselves. In that case, you should treat the Web site as the source for the argument and evaluate whether *it* is informed and impartial. Some Web sites merely cite other sources. In that case, you will need to determine whether you should trust the site's sources. Finally, sometimes it's simply unclear whether a Web site is informed, impartial, and independent. In that case, you should say that the argument fails Rule 17 by relying on a Web source whose credentials are hard to verify. After all, if you can't tell where the information on a site comes from, you can't tell whether the argument follows Rules 14, 15, and 16.

Sample

According to a recent study published online by the scientific journal *Alcoholism: Clinical & Experimental Research*, somewhere between 10 percent and 20 percent of the population carries a gene that makes them less likely to develop an addiction to alcohol. The lead author of the study, Dr. Kirk Wilhelmsen, is a professor of genetics at the University of North Carolina, Chapel Hill.

Adapted from: Shari Roan, "Gene May Protect Against Alcoholism," Los Angeles Times, *Oct 20, 2010,*
http://articles.latimes.com/2010/oct/20/news/la-heb-alcohol-gene-20101020

This argument does a decent job citing its sources (Rule 13). It clearly identifies the author of the study and the journal that published the study. Since we know when the LA Times ran this article, we know roughly when the study was published. So, we could find the study with a little bit of work. The argument could do better by giving us the study's exact title and publication date. The argument does a good job finding an informed and impartial source (Rules 14 and 15). As a geneticist at a good university, Dr. Wilhelmsen is presumably well informed about genetics, and we have no reason to think that he has ulterior motives in claiming that a certain gene protects against alcoholism. The argument does not do a good job cross-checking sources (Rule 16). There may not be other studies on this exact gene, but it might help to know what other geneticists think of the study. Cross-checking sources would also help show that geneticists who have read Dr. Wilhelmsen's paper agree with the way the newspaper has represented the study's conclusions. The argument cites the online version of a scientific journal, which is a good Web source (Rule 17).

This response proceeds methodically through the rules from Chapter IV. It addresses Rules 14 and 15 together, which is appropriate when your reason for thinking that a source is well informed is the same as your reason for thinking that the source is impartial. Notice that the response gives brief but detailed explanations for its judgments about how well the argument follows each rule.

1. Massimiliano Vasile, an aerospace engineer at the University of Glasgow, spent two years comparing nine different technologies that could be used if an asteroid were on a collision course with Earth. Dr. Vasile's study revealed that it would be a bad idea to blow up an incoming asteroid with nuclear weapons. Thus, blowing up Earth-bound asteroids with nuclear weapons is a bad idea.

    Adapted from: Lia Miller, "The Best Way to Deflect an Asteroid," New York Times Magazine, *December 9, 2007, http://www.nytimes.com/2007/12/09/magazine/09_5_asteroid.html*

2. It is possible to develop reliable, effective, data-driven measurements of teacher effectiveness in primary and secondary schools. Dr. William Sanders, a senior director of research for a company that helps school districts measure teacher performance, says that

by using "rigorous, robust methods" of data analysis and adding "safeguards" to protect against error, school districts can reliably distinguish excellent teachers from average and poor teachers.

Adapted from: Sam Dillon, "Method to Grade Teachers' Skills Gains Acceptance, and Critics," New York Times, Aug 31, 2010, http://www.nytimes.com/ 2010/09/01/education/01teacher.html

3.   A very enthusiastic man on a late night infomercial confirms that the exciting new product he's about to show you can do the job of more than a dozen other items. What's more, the new product costs half as much and requires half the time of those other items, according to the highly animated spokesman. And as the spokesman demonstrates, the new product fits easily in your kitchen cupboard while you're not using it! Therefore, the new product really can take the place of a dozen other appliances, saving you time, money, and counter space.

Adapted from: "New Product Can Do All That, More," The Onion, Dec 10, 2007, http://www.theonion.com/content/news_briefs/new_product_can_do_all_that

4.   Prince Andrew, the younger son of the Queen of England, has been accused of having sex with a 17-year-old girl. According to a spokesman for the royal family, the charges filed against Prince Andrew are completely untrue. Therefore, Prince Andrew is innocent.

Adapted from: Robert Booth, Jon Swaine, and Paul Lewis, "Palace Digs in over Prince Andrew's Links to Sex Offender Jeffrey Epstein," The Guardian, Jan 6, 2015, http://www.theguardian.com/uk-news/2015/jan/06/ palace-prince-andrew-links-jeffrey-epstein

5.   The world-famous physicist Stephen Hawking addressed the seventeenth International Conference on General Relativity and Gravitation at Oxford University in July 2004. In front of seven hundred people, Professor Hawking admitted that he had been wrong about black holes. The physicist had long held that the extreme gravitational fields of black holes somehow destroyed all of the information that entered the black holes. Professor Hawking now says that black holes never completely destroy the

information that falls in. Instead, they continue to emit radiation for extended periods and eventually reveal the information within them.

Adapted from: Carolyn Johnson, "A Black Hole Theory Zapped," The Boston Globe, July 22, 2004

6.   Eighty-seven (or is it 116?) studies have shown that making up numbers is just as good as using accurate numbers. Thus, it doesn't matter whether you use accurate numbers or just make numbers up.

Adapted from: Scott Adams, Dilbert, May 8, 2008, http://dilbert.com/strips/comic/2008-05-08/

7.   It turns out that being overweight won't kill you. In fact, it may help you live longer. Federal researchers from the Centers for Disease Control and Prevention and the National Cancer Institute report that overweight people have a lower death rate than people categorized as "obese," "normal weight," or "underweight." Their study was published in the prestigious *Journal of the American Medical Association* on November 7, 2007. Dr. Elizabeth Barrett-Connor, a professor in the University of California, San Diego School of Medicine, agrees with the study. Being overweight, she says, may be optimal in some respects.

Adapted from: Gina Kolata, "Causes of Death Are Linked to a Person's Weight," New York Times, Nov 7, 2007, http://www.nytimes.com/2007/11/07/health/07fat.html

8.   Fox Glacier and Franz Josef Glacier in New Zealand both attract thousands of tourists each year. According to companies that run glacier tours there, both glaciers have retreated so quickly over the last few years that once-popular hiking trips have become impossible. The only way to access the glaciers now is by taking a (much more expensive) helicopter ride.

Adapted from: Mike Ives, "New Zealand Glaciers Ebb and Tour Guides Play Catch-Up," New York Times, Jan 2, 2015, http://www.nytimes. com/2015/01/03/business/international/new-zealand-glaciers-ebb-and-tour-guides-play-catch-up.html

9.   The National Center for Health Statistics, part of the United States government's Centers for Disease Control and Prevention, runs a program called the National Health and Nutrition Examination System (NHANES). NHANES collects data on the health and

nutrition of a representative cross-section of the American public. According to NHANES data for 2007/2008, about 33.8 percent of Americans over the age of twenty are obese. Thus, roughly one in every three American adults is obese.

Adapted from: Katherine M. Flegal, Margaret D. Carroll, Cynthia L. Ogden, and Lester R. Curtin, "Prevalence and Trends in Obesity Among U.S. Adults, 1999–2008," Journal of the American Medical Association *303 (2010), 235–41*

10. Many Muslims object to images of Mohammed, even though Islam does not strictly prohibit them. Religious studies scholar Reza Aslan explains that the Quran does not specifically prohibit such images, and the history of Islamic art is full of images of Mohammed; but Islam does prohibit portraying God as a human being. According to Dalia Mogahed, Director of Research at a non-partisan think tank studying Muslim-American life, even though the Quran itself does not prohibit depictions of Mohammed, Islamic scholars have gradually extended the prohibition on depictions of God to include a prohibition on images of Mohammed. This has created a strong cultural norm against such images, even though there is technically no religious law against them.

Adapted from: Amanda Taub, "What Everyone Gets Wrong about Islam and Cartoons of Mohammed," Vox, Jan 9, 2015, http://www.vox.com/ 2015/1/9/7517221/charlie-hebdo-blasphemy

Model responses for odd-numbered exercises can be found on page 344.

Need more practice? For more practice evaluating arguments that use sources, browse the editorials, op-eds, and letters to the editor in some of your favorite newspaper or magazines. When you find a piece in which the author uses sources to support his or her claims, evaluate how well the author has followed Rules 13–17. Alternatively, go to the companion Web site for this book and click on the link for "Chapter IV." You'll find links to Web sites that allow users to post questions for other people to answer. Many of these sites encourage people to identify the sources on which they base their answers. Using the rules in this chapter, evaluate how well the people on those sites have used sources to support their claims.

Exercise Set 4.4: Using sources in arguments

Objective: To give you practice using sources in arguments.

Instructions: In this exercise, you will use sources to construct arguments for or against specific claims. First, you will need to decide whether each claim below is true or false. This may require some research. Once you have decided whether each claim is true, do your best to construct arguments that follow this chapter's rules for using sources. After each argument, briefly explain why you think your sources are good sources.

Tips for success: This exercise set is a lot like Exercise Set 4.2. The biggest difference is that in this exercise, you'll need to find specific sources so you can cite them in your argument. As in Exercise Set 4.2, be sure that your sources are informed, impartial, and independent.

Sample

The Chinese philosopher Confucius was born in 551 BCE.

This claim is true. According to the historian of philosophy Fung Yu-Lan (A Short History of Chinese Philosophy, ed. Derk Bodde [1948; repr., New York: Free Press, 1997], 4), Confucius was born in 551 BCE. This is the same date given by the Stanford Encyclopedia of Philosophy entry on Confucius.

This response begins by stating clearly whether the response is true or false. It then identifies two independent, reliable sources that support the claim (although it could do even better by making sure that the Stanford Encyclopedia *doesn't rely on Fung's book). It gives a detailed citation for* A Short History of Chinese Philosophy, *including a page number. It gives enough information about the other source (the* Stanford Encyclopedia of Philosophy*) that you could find the reference with a little bit of online research. (As it happens, the* Stanford Encyclopedia of Philosophy *is an online encyclopedia, so it would be easy to find it online.)*

---

1.   The United States produces more wine per year than any other country.

2.   Plutonium is the heaviest naturally occurring element.

3. Worldwide, more than one million children die from diarrhea every year.

4. There are more than one thousand known exoplanets (i.e., planets outside our solar system).

5. Humans first came to the Americas more than 13,000 years ago.

6. Given their limited technology, it would have been impossible for the ancient Egyptians to build the pyramids without help from aliens.

7. The safest minivans are built by Japanese companies.

8. The U.S. Constitution guarantees the separation of church and state.

For exercises 9 and 10, pick any claim you want. Support that claim with sources, following this chapter's rules for using sources.

> Model responses for odd-numbered exercises can be found on page 347.

Need more practice? Go to the companion Web site for this book and click on the link for "Chapter IV." You'll find links to Web sites that allow users to post questions for other people to answer. Using the rules in this chapter, you should be able to construct convincing answers to many questions on those site.

Critical thinking activity: Finding good sources

For an out-of-class activity that gives you practice finding good sources to support claims, see the "Finding good sources" assignment sheet (p. 455) in Part 3. This activity could also be done during class time in a library or computer lab.

Critical thinking activity: Thinking critically about Wikipedia

For several out-of-class activities that give you practice applying the rules from this chapter, go to the companion Web site for this book, click on the link for "Part 3," and then click on the link for "Thinking critically about Wikipedia."

Chapter V
Arguments about Causes

Did you know that students who sit at the front of the classroom tend to get better grades? And that people who are married are, on average, happier than people who aren't? Wealth, by contrast, doesn't seem to correlate with happiness at all—so maybe it is true after all that "the best things in life are free." If you'd rather have the money anyway, you might be interested to know that people with "can-do" attitudes tend to be wealthier. So you'd better work on your attitude, eh?

Here we come to arguments about causes and their effects—about what causes what. Sometimes they are vital. Good effects we want to increase, bad effects we want to prevent, and we often want to give appropriate credit or blame for both. It won't surprise you, though, that reasoning about causes also takes care and critical thinking.

Causal arguments start with correlations

The evidence for a claim about causes is usually a *correlation*—a regular association—between two events or kinds of events: between your grades in a class and where you sit in the classroom; between being married and being happy; between the unemployment rate and the crime rate, etc. The general form of the argument therefore is:

> Event or condition E_1 is *regularly associated* with event or condition E_2.
>
> Therefore, event or condition E_1 *causes* event or condition E_2

That is, *because* E_1 is regularly associated with E_2 in this way, we conclude that E_1 causes E_2. For example:

> People who meditate tend to be calmer.
>
> Therefore, meditation calms you down.

Trends may also be correlated, as when we note that increasing violence on television correlates with increasing violence in the real world.

Shows on television portray more and more violence, callousness, and depravity—and society is becoming more and more violent, callous, and depraved.

Therefore, television is ruining our morals.

Inverse correlations (that is, where an increase in one factor correlates to a *decrease* in another) may suggest causality too. For example, some studies correlate increased vitamin use with decreased health, suggesting that vitamins may (sometimes) be harmful. In the same way, *non*-correlation may imply *lack* of cause, as when we discover that happiness and wealth are not correlated and therefore conclude that money does not bring happiness.

Exploring correlations is also a scientific research strategy. What causes lightning? Why do some people become insomniacs, or geniuses, or Republicans? And isn't there *some* way (please?) to prevent colds? Researchers look for correlates to these conditions of interest: that is, for other conditions or events that are regularly associated with lightning or genius or colds, for example, but without which lightning or genius or colds don't tend to happen. These correlates may be subtle and complex, but finding them is often possible nonetheless—and then (hopefully) we have a handle on causes.

Correlations may have alternative explanations

Arguments from correlation to cause are often compelling. However, there is also a systematic difficulty with any such claim. The problem is simply that *any correlation may be explained in multiple ways*. It's often not clear from the correlation itself how best to interpret the underlying causes.

First, some correlations may simply be just coincidental. It's not likely that the expanding universe is driving, say, the rise in the price of tomatoes or textbooks. Both the universe and consumer prices continue to inflate, but there is no causal connection.

Second, even when there really is a connection, correlation by itself does not establish the *direction* of the connection. If E_1 is correlated with E_2, E_1 may cause E_2—but E_2 may instead cause E_1. For example, while it is true (on average) that people with "can-do" attitudes tend to be wealthier, it's not at all clear that the attitude leads to the wealth. Surely it is more plausible the other way around: that the wealth causes the attitude. You're more apt to believe in the possibility of success when you've already been successful. Wealth and attitude may correlate, then, but if you want to get wealthier, just working on your attitude is not likely to get you very far.

Rule 19

Likewise, it's entirely possible that calmer people tend to be drawn to meditation, rather than becoming calmer *because* they meditate. And the very same correlation that suggests that television is "ruining our morals" could instead suggest that our morals are ruining television (that is, that rising real-world violence is leading to an increase in the portrayal of violence on television).

Third, some other cause may underlie and explain both of the correlates. Again E_1 may be correlated with E_2, but rather than E_1 causing E_2 *or* E_2 causing E_1, something else—some E_3—may cause both E_1 and E_2. For example, the fact that students who sit in the front of the classroom tend to get better grades may not imply *either* that sitting in the front leads to better grades *or* that getting better grades leads to sitting in the front of the class. More likely, some students' special commitment to making the most of their schooling leads *both* to sitting in the front of the classroom *and* to better grades.

Finally, multiple or complex causes may be at work, and they may move in many directions at the same time. Violence on television, for example, surely reflects a more violent state of society, but also, to some degree, it surely helps to worsen that violence. Quite likely there are other underlying causes as well, such as the breakup of traditional value systems and the absence of constructive pastimes.

Exercise Set 5.1: Brainstorming explanations for correlations

Objective: To give you practice brainstorming possible explanations for a correlation.

Instructions: For each of the correlations below, list at least two possible explanations for the correlation. The correlations do not need to be equally likely, but try to avoid explanations that are clearly outlandish. You do not need to decide which is most likely. The goal is to practice brainstorming alternative explanations for a correlation.

Tips for success: In the discussion of Rules 18 and 19, we identified four possible explanations for a correlation: E_1 may be correlated with E_2 because E_1 causes E_2. E_1 may be correlated with E_2 because E_2 causes E_1. E_1 may be correlated with E_2 because E_1 and E_2 are both caused by or correlated with some third thing, E_3. Finally, the correlation between E_1 and E_2 might just be a coincidence, with no causal connection between them. Keep all of these possibilities in mind when doing this exercise.

Sample

There is a correlation between being bitten by a specific kind of tropical mosquito called *Aedes aegypti* and developing yellow fever.

One possible explanation is that A. aegypti carries a virus that causes yellow fever. Another possibility is that A. aegypti likes to bite people who are carrying the virus for yellow fever, and the mosquito can detect the virus before people show symptoms of the illness. A third possibility is that yellow fever is caused by something else that is common in the tropics; being in tropics makes you more likely both to get yellow fever and (independently) to get bitten by A. aegypti.

This response gives three possible explanations for the stated correlation. It does not attempt to establish whether the correlation is true or figure out which explanation is most likely. While some of the proposed explanations are more likely than others, none are totally outlandish.

---

1. The GRE is an exam used for graduate school admissions. Philosophy students tend to do extremely well on all sections of the test—especially the verbal reasoning and analytical writing sections. That is, there is a correlation between studying philosophy and doing well on the GRE.

   Adapted from: Justin Weinberg, "Philosophy Majors and the GRE 2011–2014," Daily Nous, *Aug 12, 2014, http://dailynous.com/2014/08/12/ philosophy-majors-and-the-gre-2011-2014/*

2. There is an inverse correlation between the unemployment rate and the chance of a U.S. president being reelected for a second term. That is, when the unemployment rate is high at the end of a president's first term, that president is less likely to be reelected.

   Adapted from: Nate Silver, "On the Maddeningly Inexact Relationship between Unemployment and Re-Election," New York Times, *Jun 2, 2011, http://fivethirtyeight.blogs.nytimes.com/2011/06/02/ on-the-maddeningly-inexact-relationship-between-unemployment-and-re-election/*

3. When the leaves on the trees turn colors, geese always fly south. That is, there's a correlation between the leaves turning colors and geese flying south.

   Adapted from: Ramzi Nasser, "Deciding Whether There Is Statistical Independence or Not?" Journal of Mathematics and Statistics *3 (2007), 151*

4. In Washington State, judges are elected by the public rather than appointed by experts or politicians. When a judge in Washington is facing reelection, he or she tends to issue harsher sentences for people convicted of violent crimes.

    Adapted from: Sara Grossman, "Elected Judges Rule More Harshly on Violent Crime When Up for Re-election, Study Shows," The Daily Californian, Nov 25, 2012, http://www.dailycal.org/2012/11/25/elected-judges-rule-hrasher-on-violent-crime-when-up-for-re-election-study-shows/

5. People who graduated from college tend to make more money than those who never attended or never graduated from college.

    Adapted from: Mary C. Daly and Leila Bengali, "Is It Still Worth It to Go to College?" Federal Reserve Bank of San Fransisco Economic Letters, *May 5, 2014, http://www.frbsf.org/economic-research/publications/economic-letter/2014/may/is-college-worth-it-education-tuition-wages/*

6. The Dow Jones index of the stock market correlates with the hemlines of women's skirts and dresses. When the stock market goes up, so do hemlines: women tend to wear shorter skirts. When the stock market goes down, hemlines drop too.

    Adapted from: John L. Casti, Mood Matters: From Rising Skirt Lengths to the Collapse of World Powers *(New York: Springer, 2010), 65–66*

7. Indians, who eat foods containing a lot of turmeric, have a much lower incidence of Alzheimer's disease than do Americans. Most Americans do not eat much turmeric. That is, there is an inverse correlation between developing Alzheimer's and eating turmeric.

    Adapted from: Hilary E. MacGregor, "Out of the Spice Box, Into the Lab," Los Angeles Times, *Feb 6, 2006, http://articles.latimes.com/2006/feb/06/health/he-turmeric6*

8. People are slightly more likely to work at a business where the first three letters of the business's name match the first three letters in the worker's name, as opposed to businesses where the first three letters do not match. That is, there is a definite but weak

correlation between a person's name and the name of the business where he or she works.

Adapted from: Joe Brownstein, "Does Your Name Determine Your Destiny?"
LiveScience, *Mar 30, 2011, http://www.livescience.com/13477-*
names-life-decisions-career-choices.html

9.   After future U.S. president William Harrison attacked the village of a Shawnee chief named Tecumseh, Tecumseh's brother supposedly set a curse on Harrison. Harrison was elected president in 1840; he died in office in 1841. For the next 120 years, every U.S. president who was elected in a year ending in zero also died in office. That is, there is (or, at least, was) a correlation between being elected president in a year ending in zero and dying in office.

Adapted from: "The Curse of Tecumseh," Snopes.com, Feb 12, 2009,
http://www.snopes.com/history/american/curse.asp

10.   The amount of artificial colors in children's foods has increased significantly over the last several decades. So has the proportion of children diagnosed with attention deficit hyperactivity disorder (ADHD).

Adapted from: Steven Reinberg, "Food Additives Could Fuel Hyperactivity
in Kids," U.S. News & World Report, Sep 6, 2007, http://health
.usnews.com/usnews/health/healthday/070906/food-additives
-could-fuel-hyperactivity-in-kids.htm

Model responses for odd-numbered exercises can be found on page 349.

Need more practice? Go to science journalism Web sites like LiveScience, *Scientific American*, or the science section of your favorite newspaper. Look for articles that mention correlations or causal connections. You can also find articles about correlation by entering the search term "correlation" in the Google News search engine at http://news.google.com. Brainstorm possible explanations for the correlations reported in those articles.

Rule 20

Work toward the most likely explanation

Since a variety of explanations for a correlation are usually possible, the challenge for a good correlation-based argument is to find the most *likely* explanation.

First, fill in the connections. That is, spell out how each possible explanation could make sense.

> **NO:**
> Most of my open-minded friends are well read; most of my less open-minded friends are not. I conclude that reading leads to open-mindedness.

> **YES:**
> Most of my open-minded friends are well read; most of my less open-minded friends are not. It makes sense that the more you read, the more you encounter challenging new ideas, ideas that make you less insistent on your own. Reading also lifts you out of your daily world and shows you how different and many-sided life can be. Reading, therefore, leads to open-mindedness.

Try to fill in the connections in this way not just for the explanation you favor, but also for alternative explanations. Consider for example the studies that correlate increased vitamin use with decreased health. One possible explanation is that vitamins actually worsen health, or anyway that some vitamins (or taking a lot of them) are bad for some people. It is also possible, though, that people who are already in bad or worsening health may be using more vitamins to try to get better. In fact, this alternative explanation seems, at least at first glance, equally or even more plausible.

To decide which is the most likely explanation for this correlation, you need more information. In particular, is there other evidence that (some?) vitamins can sometimes be harmful? If so, how widespread might these harms be? If there is little direct and specific evidence of harm to be found, especially when vitamins are taken in appropriate dosages, then it's more likely that poorer health leads to more vitamin use than that more vitamin use leads to poorer health.

Or again: Marriage and happiness correlate (again, on average), but is it because marriage makes you happier or because happier people tend to be more successful at getting and staying married? Fill in the connections for both explanations and then step back to think. Marriage clearly offers companionship and support, which could explain how marriage might make you happier. Conversely, it may be that happy people are better at getting and staying married. To me, though, this second explanation seems less likely. Happiness may make you a more appealing partner, but then again it may not—it could instead make you more self-absorbed—and it is not clear that happiness by itself makes you any more committed or responsive a partner. We'd prefer the first explanation.

Note that the most likely explanation is very seldom some sort of conspiracy or supernatural intervention. It is *possible*, of course, that the Bermuda Triangle really is spooked and that is why ships and planes disappear there. But that explanation is far less likely than another simple and natural explanation: that the Bermuda Triangle is one of the world's heaviest-traveled shipping and sailing areas, with tropical weather that is unpredictable and sometimes severe. Besides, people do tend to embellish spooky stories, so some of the more lurid accounts, after having passed through countless retellings, aren't (let's just say) the most reliable. Good fodder for the movies, maybe, but hardly reliable premises for an argument.

Likewise, although people fasten onto inconsistencies and oddities in dramatic events (the JFK assassination, 9/11, etc.) to justify conspiracy theories, such explanations usually leave a great deal more *un*explained than the usual explanations, however incomplete. (For instance, why would any plausible conspiracy take *this particular form?*) Don't assume that every little oddity must have some nefarious explanation. It's hard enough to get the basics right. Neither you nor anyone else needs to have an answer for everything.

Exercise Set 5.2: Identifying the most likely explanation

Objective: To give you practice working toward the most likely explanation of a correlation.

Instructions: Go back to your answers to the exercises in Exercise Set 5.1. (If you haven't done Exercise Set 5.1 yet, complete it before doing these exercises.) For each of the exercises in Exercise Set 5.1, state which of your three possible explanations you think is most likely. Give reasons to support your claim.

Tips for success: There is no magic formula for identifying the most likely explanation. If E_1 is correlated with E_2, and you think this is because E_1 causes E_2, do your best to tell as convincing and detailed a story as possible about *how* E_1 causes E_2. Even better, see if you can come up with ways that someone could test your story about how E_1 causes E_2. For instance, how could someone test the idea that the leaves' changing colors causes geese to fly south in the autumn? (See the model response to exercise 3 for a hint!) Likewise, if you think E_2 causes E_1, tell as convincing and detailed a story as you can about how that happens. The more you know about E_1 and E_2, the easier this process will be. If you can't come up with any convincing accounts of how one thing could cause the other, then the most likely explanation may be that the correlation is just a coincidence. Note that in scientific studies, it's usually possible to say how likely or unlikely it is for the correlation to be a coincidence. If the study shows that the chance of a pure coincidence is 1 in 10,000, you may want to look harder for other explanations (besides a coincidence) than if the chance of a coincidence is 1 in 20.

Sample

There is a correlation between being bitten by a specific kind of tropical mosquito called *Aedes aegypti* and developing yellow fever.

The most likely explanation of this correlation is that A. aegypti causes yellow fever. According to the Centers for Disease Control, yellow fever is caused by a virus that is "transmitted to humans through the bite of a mosquito." The World Health Organization's online fact sheet about yellow fever states that A. aegypti is a "yellow fever vector," meaning that it transmits yellow fever. Presumably, it works like this: The bite of A. aegypti injects the virus into the human bloodstream. The virus then causes yellow fever.

This response builds on the sample response in Exercise Set 5.1, which gave three possible explanations of the correlation between being bitten by A. aegypti *and getting yellow fever. This response does two things. First, it cites an authoritative source to establish which of those three explanations is correct. This is only one of many ways to argue that one explanation is most likely, and it's one that may not be available in all cases. Second, this response explains how the causal connection is supposed to work. If you want to claim that a correlation is best explained by a causal connection, it's usually important to be able to say something about how one thing causes the other.*

Model responses for odd-numbered exercises can be found on page 351.

Need more practice? Go to science journalism Web sites or the science section of your favorite newspaper. Look for stories about causal connections; most of them will tell you about a correlation, which someone has explained as a causal connection. Ask yourself what the best explanation of that correlation is. Do you agree with the article's claim that the connection is causal? Why or why not?

Expect complexity

Plenty of happy people are not married, of course, and plenty of married people are unhappy. It does not follow that marriage has no effect on happiness *on average*. It's just that happiness and unhappiness (and, for that matter, being married or unmarried) have a myriad of other causes too. One correlation is not the whole story. The question in such cases is about the *relative weight* of different causes.

If you or someone else has argued that some E_1 causes some E_2, it is not necessarily a counterexample to show that occasionally E_1 doesn't produce E_2, or that another cause entirely may also sometimes produce E_2. The claim is just that E_1 *often* or *usually* produces E_2, and that other causes less commonly do, or that E_1 is among the *major contributors* to E_2, though the full story may involve multiple causes and there may be other major contributors too. There are people who never smoke cigarettes at all and still get lung cancer, and also people who smoke three packs of cigarettes a day and never get it. Both effects are medically intriguing and important, but the fact remains that smoking is the prime cause of lung cancer.

Many different causes may contribute to an overall effect. Though the causes of global climate change are many and varied, for instance, the fact that some of them are natural, like changes in the sun's brightness, does not show that human contributions therefore have no effect. Once again, the causal story is complex. Many factors are at work. (Indeed, if the sun is *also* contributing to global warming, there's even more reason to try to decrease our contribution.)

Causes and effects may interpenetrate as well. Reading, for instance, surely does lead to open-mindedness. But open-mindedness also leads to reading . . . which then creates more open-mindedness in turn. Meanwhile, certain other factors promote both reading *and* open-mindedness, such as going to college, family environment, certain enthusiastic friends always pressing some new book on us, and so on . . . but then again, more open-minded people are more likely to go to college and sustain open-minded families and friendships in the first place. Often the most interesting causal stories are *loops!*

CHAPTER EXERCISES

Exercise Set 5.3: Evaluating arguments about causes

Objective: To give you practice evaluating arguments about causes.

Instructions: Evaluate how well each of the following arguments obeys Rules 18–21.

Tips for success: A good argument about causes should do two things.

First, a good argument about causes should convince you that there really is a correlation between two things (Rule 18). Remember that a correlation is a *systematic* relationship between two things. Giving a few examples of one thing following another, for instance, does not prove that there is a correlation between the two things.

There are two main ways for an argument to establish a correlation. It might do this by citing sources that establish the correlation. Alternatively, it might give an argument by example or a statistical argument. When a claim about correlation relies on either of these techniques, you'll need to apply the rules from Chapter IV or Chapter II to decide how well it does in establishing a correlation.

Second, a good argument about causes should convince you that the best explanation for that correlation is that one thing causes the other. To decide whether an argument does this, you'll need to brainstorm alternative explanations of the correlation, as you did in Exercise Set 5.1. Then, use the skills you developed in Exercise Set 5.2 to figure out whether you think the best explanation of the correlation really is the one claimed in the argument. If you think there are better explanations for the correlation, then the argument has failed Rule 19, Rule 20, or both.

Rule 21 comes into play in two ways. First, some arguments will overstate the strength of their conclusions. If an argument seems to suggest that it has explained the *entire* cause of some effect, be suspicious that it's ignoring complexity. On the other hand, just because an argument doesn't address the full range of causes for an effect does not mean that the argument has failed to identify a genuine causal connection. For instance, when public health experts publish a study claiming that eating fast food causes obesity, the fast-food industry sometimes retorts, "Our products don't cause obesity. Obesity is caused by a combination of genetics, diet, exercise, and other factors." They're right: diet isn't the *only* cause of obesity. Still, this retort violates Rule 21 when (if) it moves from the claim that diet isn't the only cause of obesity to the suggestion that eating fast foods does not contribute to obesity at all. Don't make the same mistake when you are evaluating arguments.

Sample

Physical exercise improves people's "executive function"—the set of psychological abilities involved in planning and executing a task. People who get regular exercise have better executive function than their age peers who don't. This isn't because people with better executive function exercise more. When inactive people begin exercising, their executive function improves.

Adapted from: Sandra Aamodt and Sam Wang, "Exercise on the Brain," New York Times, Nov 8, 2007, http://www.nytimes.com/2007/11/08/opinion/08aamodt.html

This is a decent causal argument. It clearly states that there is a correlation between exercise and executive function (Rule 18), although it doesn't say anything to support that claim. It proposes that exercise is the cause and improved executive function is the effect. To deal with the alternative possibility (Rule 19) that better executive function leads to more exercising, the argument gives a reason to think that the proposed explanation of the correlation is the most likely (Rule 20): inactive people's executive function improves when they begin exercising. Furthermore, since we know that exercise affects your body and mind in many different ways, it's not totally implausible to think that it could improve executive function, although this argument does not propose any specific mechanism by which exercise does so. The argument leaves room for complexity (Rule 21) by making the modest claim that exercise "improves" executive function, rather than making a less nuanced claim like, "Executive function is determined by exercise." Thus, the argument is fairly good, despite the flaw that it offers no account of <u>how</u> exercise does what it's claimed to do.

This response addresses each of the rules from Chapter V in a systematic way, citing specific details from the argument to support its claims about how well the argument follows each rule. In thinking about how well an argument follows the rules from Chapter V, it's important to do your own thinking about alternative explanations of correlations. In weaker arguments especially, the most important alternative explanations might not be explicitly mentioned, leaving you to come up with them on your own.

1. Watching television will kill you. A study of 11,000 Australian adults found that people who watch an average of six hours of television per day die about five years younger than those who watch no television. More generally, the study found that each hour of television that you watch as an adult chops about 22 minutes off your lifespan. This is partly because people tend to eat junk food while watching television, partly because time spent in front of the television is time away from healthy activities like exercising, and partly because people tend to be driven to watch a lot of television when they are lonely, isolated, or depressed, all of which can lead to worse health outcomes.

   Adapted from: Steven Reinberg, "Too Much TV May Take Years Off Your Life," HealthDay, Aug 15, 2011, http://consumer.healthday.com/senior-citizen-information-31/misc-death-and-dying-news-172/too-much-tv-may-take-years-off-your-life-655869.html

2. Based on a study of 26,069 Canadian adolescents, researchers at McGill University found that eating dinner together as a family promotes better emotional health among teenagers. Teenagers' emotional well-being, trust in others, and overall life satisfaction improved with each additional dinner they ate with their families during the week.

   Adapted from: Sharon Jayson, "Each Family Dinner Adds Up to Benefits for Adolescents," USA Today, Mar 24, 2013, http://www.usatoday.com/story/news/nation/2013/03/24/family-dinner-adolescent-benefits/2010731/

3. Want your state's football team to go to the Super Bowl? Legalize marijuana! In 2012, both Washington state and Colorado legalized marijuana. The Seattle Seahawks (from Washington) and the Denver Broncos (from Colorado) played in the Super Bowl the following football season. Thus, football teams from states that legalize marijuana go to the Super Bowl!

   Adapted from: Anne Howeth, Twitter post, Jan 20, 2014, 7:38 pm, https://twitter.com/AnneOfGreenMtns/

4. Eating a "Mediterranean diet" and getting regular exercise lowers your chances of developing or dying from heart disease or cancer. American doctors first encouraged the Mediterranean diet when they noticed how healthy the people were in countries that eat such

a diet, including southern Italy, Greece, and Crete. Since then, several carefully designed studies have confirmed the correlation between eating a Mediterranean diet and lower incidence of heart disease and cancer. These studies reveal that the correlation is not the result of coincidence or of other aspects of life in Mediterranean countries.

Adapted from: Francesco Sofi, Francesca Cesari, Rosanna Abbate, Gian Franco Gensini, and Alessandro Casini, "Adherence to Mediterranean Diet and Health Status: Meta-analysis," British Medical Journal *337 (2008) a1344*

5. Serving in the military causes people to earn less money later in life. A decade after their military service, men who were drafted into the Vietnam War in the early 1970s earned about 85 percent as much as similar men who had not been drafted. Since people were chosen randomly for the draft, it can't be that (future) income caused people to be drafted or that some other factor caused both being drafted and lower incomes.

Adapted from: Peter Dizikes, "The Natural Experiment," MIT Technology Review, *Jan 2, 2013, http://www.technologyreview.com/article/508381/the-natural-experimenter/*

6. In researching best practices for Twitter users, Buddy Media found that tweets of between 71 and 100 characters get retweeted far more than either shorter or longer tweets. Therefore, keeping your tweets between 71 and 100 characters will boost the number of retweets you get.

Adapted from: Kevan Lee, "The Ideal Length of Everything Online, Backed by Research," Buffer, *Mar 31, 2014, https://blog.bufferapp.com/ the-ideal-length-of-everything-online-according-to-science*

7. Depression causes brittle bones, according to a recent study by researchers at the Hebrew University of Jerusalem. The scientists drugged mice to induce behavior similar to that found in depressed humans. The "depressed" mice lost bone mass, especially in their hips and vertebrae. When given antidepressants, the mice recovered—both in terms of their behavior and their bone density.

Adapted from: "Connection Between Depression and Osteoporosis Shown by Hebrew University Researchers," ScienceDaily, *Oct 31, 2006, http://www.sciencedaily.com/ releases/2006/10/061030183243.htm*

8. Some hockey sticks are made for left-handed players. Others are made for right-handed players. This wasn't always the case. Left- and right-handed sticks were only introduced in the 1960s. Since that time, though, around two thirds of Canadians have used left-handed sticks and two thirds of Americans have used right-handed sticks. This is true even though most Canadians, like most Americans, are naturally right-handed. The only reasonable explanation is that being Canadian causes people to prefer left-handed hockey sticks.

    Adapted from: Jeff Z. Klein, "It's Not Political, but More Canadians Are Lefties,"
    New York Times, *Feb 15, 2010, http://www.nytimes.com/2010/02/16/*
    sports/olympics/16lefty.html

9. Among British people born around 1970, there is a correlation between IQ as a child and vegetarianism as an adult. Those with higher childhood IQs were more likely to be vegetarians as an adult. Researchers considered the possibility that vegetarianism causes a higher IQ, but this would require the vegetarians to have become vegetarians when they were quite young. They found that this was not the case. The vast majority of vegetarians became vegetarians as teenagers or adults, not as children. It's more likely that some other mechanisms are at work. For instance, higher IQ was correlated with greater educational attainment, which is correlated with vegetarianism. Perhaps having a higher IQ causes more education, which causes an increased likelihood of becoming a vegetarian. Even when researchers factored out education, however, they still saw a significant link between IQ and vegetarianism. More directly, then, maybe higher IQs increase the likelihood that one will respond to evidence about the health and other benefits of vegetarianism. There is presumably some mix of various mechanisms at work here.

    Adapted from: Catharine R. Gale, Ian J. Deary, Ingrid Schoon, and
    G. David Batty, "IQ in Childhood and Vegetarianism in Adulthood:
    1970 British Cohort Study," British Medical Journal *334 (2006), 245*

10. People read for fun much less often than they used to. The decline in recreational reading occurred at the same time as a decline in reading abilities in Americans, as measured by test scores and employers' reports about employees' reading skills. The correlation

shows up on the individual level too. Individuals who read for fun more often score better on tests of reading abilities. Thus, reading for fun causes people to become better readers.

Adapted from: Motoko Rich, "Study Links Drop in Test Scores to a Decline in Time Spent Reading," New York Times, Nov 19, 2007, http://www.nytimes. com/2007/11/19/arts/19nea.html

---

Model responses for odd-numbered exercises can be found on page 354.

Need more practice? Return to the science journalism articles that you found in doing more practice for Exercise Set 5.2. Even better, use your library to find scientific papers on a topic that interests you. (If you're not sure how to do this, ask your librarians. Librarians are experts in finding information!) How well do the arguments in those articles or papers follow Rules 18–21?

Exercise Set 5.4: Constructing arguments about causes

Objective: To give you practice constructing arguments about causes that follow Rules 18–21.

Instructions: Each question below asks whether one thing causes another. Use the rules in this chapter to settle on an answer to each question. Construct an argument to defend your answer.

Tips for success: Begin by establishing that there is a correlation between the alleged cause and effect. (None of the questions below are trick questions. In every case there really is a correlation.) You might establish a correlation by citing sources, in which case you should be sure to follow Rules 13–17. Alternatively, you might do this by giving examples, in which case you should be sure to follow Rules 7–11.

Once you've established that a correlation exists, follow the steps you took in exercises 5.1 and 5.2 to identify the most likely explanation for that correlation. You may need to do some research to answer these questions. Then, explain why you think your chosen explanation is the most likely one.

Sample

Do economic downturns cause anti-immigrant sentiments in the United States?

As Harvard economist Benjamin Friedman documents in his book The Moral Conse-quences of Economic Growth, anti-immigrant sentiment tends to rise in the United States during economic downturns. Friedman's book shows that this correlation has held since at least the nineteenth century. This is because economic downturns cause anti-immigrant sentiment. During economic downturns, many people face very difficult circumstances, often for reasons beyond their control. In trying to cope with and understand those challenges, people look for obvious changes in their environ-ment. Recent immigrants, by definition, bring change to their new country. Thus, it is easy for people to make an erroneous connection between the arrival of the most recent immigrants and the economic downturn. Because people blame immigrants for their economic hardships, anti-immigrant sentiments increase. This is more plausible than claiming that the correlation is a pure coincidence, given how long it has gone on, or that anti-immigrant sentiment causes an economic downturn, since the anti-immigrant sentiment usually increases after the economy deteriorates.

This response begins by citing a source to establish that there is a correlation between eco-nomic downturns and anti-immigrant sentiment. If there were no correlation, there would be no argument for a causal connection. The response then argues that the most likely ex-planation for the correlation is that an economic downturn causes an increase in anti-immigrant sentiment. At the very end, it employs a useful tactic in arguing that causation must go in one direction rather than another: If one thing happens before another, the second cannot be the cause of the first.

1. Does smoking cigarettes cause lung cancer?

2. Does being president of the United States make you left handed?

3. Do earthquakes cause volcanic eruptions?

4. Does watching conservative news channels make people vote for conservative political candidates?

5. Does sleeping with the light on as a baby cause myopia (near-sightedness)?

6.   Does having good public schools cause a neighborhood to be wealthy?

7.   Does attending religious services on a regular basis cause people to be happier?

For exercises 8, 9, and 10, construct arguments about a causal connection of your choice. Be sure to establish a correlation between two things (Rule 18), and then follows Rules 19–21 to show that the best explanation of the correlation is that one thing causes the other.

Model responses for odd-numbered exercises can be found on page 359.

Need more practice? Make a list of questions of the form "What causes X?" Do some research to see whether you can identify possible answers to each of those questions. Using Rules 17–21, try to identify the best answers.

Critical thinking activity: Bluffing about causal explanations

For an in-class activity that gives you practice brainstorming alternative explanations of a correlation and working toward the best explanation, see the "Bluffing about causal explanations" assignment sheet (p. 456) in Part 3.

Critical thinking activity: Reconstructing scientific reasoning

For an in-class or out-of-class activity that gives you practice thinking about scientific reasoning, which frequently involves causal arguments, see the "Reconstructing scientific reasoning" assignment sheet (p. 457) in Part 3.

Critical thinking activity: Analyzing arguments in scientific reasoning

For an in-class or out-of-class activity that gives you practice analyzing causal arguments and other kinds of scientific reasoning, see the "Analyzing arguments in scientific reasoning" assignment sheet (p. 458) in Part 3.

Chapter VI
Deductive Arguments

Consider this argument:

> If there are no chance factors in chess, then chess is a game of pure skill.
>
> There are no chance factors in chess.
>
> Therefore, chess is a game of pure skill.

Suppose that the premises of this argument are true. In other words, suppose it's true that *if* there are no chance factors in chess, then chess is a game of pure skill—and suppose there *are* no chance factors in chess. You can therefore conclude with perfect assurance that chess is a game of pure skill. There is no way to admit the truth of these premises but deny the conclusion.

Arguments of this type are called *deductive arguments*. That is, a (properly formed) deductive argument is an argument of such a form that if its premises are true, the conclusion must be true too. Properly formed deductive arguments are called *valid* arguments.

Deductive arguments differ from the sorts of arguments so far considered, in which even a large number of true premises does not guarantee the truth of the conclusion (though sometimes they may make it very likely). In non-deductive arguments, the conclusion unavoidably goes beyond the premises—that's the very point of arguing by example, authority, and so on—whereas the conclusion of a valid deductive argument only makes explicit what is already contained in the premises.

In real life, of course, we can't always be sure of our premises either, so the conclusions of real-life deductive arguments still have to be taken with a few (sometimes many) grains of salt. Still, when strong premises can be found, deductive forms are very useful. And even when the premises are uncertain, deductive forms offer an effective way to organize arguments.

This chapter provides a brief introduction to the much larger topic of deductive logic. The "Resources" section on this book's companion Web site has links to books and online resources for those who would like to explore deductive logic in more depth. Many of these resources are free, and some are interactive.

Modus ponens

Using the letters **p** and **q** to stand for declarative sentences, the simplest valid deductive form is

> If [sentence **p**] then [sentence **q**].
> [Sentence **p**].
> Therefore, [sentence **q**].

Or, more briefly:

> If **p** then **q**.
> **p**.
> Therefore, **q**.

This form is called *modus ponens* ("the mode of putting": put **p**, get **q**). Taking **p** to stand for "There are no chance factors in chess" and **q** to stand for "Chess is a game of pure skill," our introductory example follows *modus ponens* (check it out). Here is another:

> If drivers on cell phones have more accidents, then drivers should be prohibited from using them.
>
> Drivers on cell phones *do* have more accidents.
>
> Therefore, drivers should be prohibited from using cell phones.

To develop this argument, you must explain and defend both of its premises, and they require quite different arguments (go back and look). *Modus ponens* gives you a way to lay them out clearly and separately from the start.

Modus tollens

A second valid deductive form is *modus tollens* ("the mode of taking": take **q**, take **p**).

> If **p** then **q**.
> Not-**q**.
> Therefore, not-**p**.

Here "Not-**q**" simply stands for the denial of **q**, that is, for the sentence "It is not true that **q**." Similarly for "not-**p**."

Remember Sherlock Holmes' argument, discussed under Rule 1:

> A dog was kept in the stables, and yet, though someone had been in and fetched out a horse, [the dog] had not barked. . . .

> Obviously the . . . visitor was someone whom the dog knew well.

Holmes' argument can be put as a *modus tollens:*

> If the visitor was a stranger, then the dog would have barked.
>
> The dog did not bark.
>
> Therefore, the visitor was not a stranger.

To write this argument in symbols, you could use **s** for "The visitor was a stranger" and **b** for "The dog barked."

> If **s** then **b**.
> Not-**b**.
> Therefore, not-**s**.

"Not-**b**" stands for "The dog did not bark," and "not-**s**" stands for "The visitor was not a stranger." As Holmes puts it, the visitor was someone whom the dog knew well.

Be careful not to confuse *modus ponens* and *modus tollens* with their evil twins, "affirming the consequent" and "denying the antecedent." For details on those two invalid argument forms, see page 249 in Appendix I: Fallacies.

Rule 24

Hypothetical syllogism

A third valid deductive form is "hypothetical syllogism."

> If **p** then **q**.
> If **q** then **r**.
> Therefore, if **p** then **r**.

For instance:

> If you **s**tudy other cultures, then you start to realize the **v**ariety of human customs.
>
> If you start to realize the **v**ariety of human customs, then you become more **t**olerant.
>
> Therefore, if you **s**tudy other cultures, then you become more **t**olerant.

Using the letters in boldface to stand for the component sentences in this statement, we have:

If **s** then **v**.
If **v** then **t**.
Therefore, if **s** then **t**.

Hypothetical syllogisms are valid for any number of premises as long as each premise has the form "If **p** then **q**" and the **q** (called the "consequent") of one premise becomes the **p** (the "antecedent") of the next.

Disjunctive syllogism

A fourth valid deductive form is "disjunctive syllogism."

p or **q**.
Not-**p**.
Therefore, **q**.

Consider, for instance, Bertrand Russell's argument discussed under Rule 2:

Either we hope for progress by improving **m**orals, or we hope for progress by improving **i**ntelligence.

We can't hope for progress by improving **m**orals.

Therefore, we must hope for progress by improving **i**ntelligence.

Again using the boldface letters as symbols, this argument goes

m or **i**.
Not-**m**.
Therefore, **i**.

There is one complication. In English the word "or" can have two different meanings. Usually "**p** or **q**" means that at least one of **p** or **q** is true and possibly both. This is called an "inclusive" sense of the word "or" and is the sense normally assumed in logic. Sometimes, though, we use "or" in an "exclusive" sense, in which "**p** or **q**" means that either **p** or **q** is true but *not* both. "Either they'll come by land or they'll come by sea," for example, suggests that they won't come both ways at once. In that case you might be able to infer that if they come one way, then they're *not* coming the other way (better be sure!).

Disjunctive syllogisms are valid regardless of which sense of "or" is used (check it out). But what *else*, if anything, you may be able to infer from a statement like "**p** or **q**"—in particular, whether you can conclude not-**q** if you also know **p**—depends on the meaning of "or" in the specific "**p or q**" premise you are considering. Take care!

Dilemma

A fifth valid deductive form is the "dilemma."

> **p** or **q**.
> If **p** then **r**.
> If **q** then **s**.
> Therefore, **r** or **s**.

Rhetorically, a "dilemma" is a choice between two options both of which have unappealing consequences. The pessimist philosopher Arthur Schopenhauer, for example, formulated what is sometimes called the "Hedgehog's dilemma," which we could paraphrase like this:

> The closer two hedgehogs get, the more likely they are to poke each other with their spikes; but if they remain apart, they will be lonely. So it is with people: being close to someone inevitably creates conflicts and provocations and opens us to a lot of pain; but on the other hand, we're lonely when we stand apart.

In outline this argument might be put:

> Either we become **c**lose to others or we stand **a**part.
>
> If we become **c**lose to others, we **s**uffer conflict and pain.
>
> If we stand **a**part, we'll be **l**onely.
>
> Therefore, either we **s**uffer conflict and pain or we'll be **l**onely.

And in symbols:

> Either **c** or **a**.
> If **c** then **s**.
> If **a** then **l**.
> Therefore, either **s** or **l**.

A further argument in dilemma form could conclude, even more simply, something like "Either way we'll be unhappy." I'll leave this one to you to write out formally.

Since this is such a jolly little conclusion, maybe we should add that hedgehogs are actually quite able to get close without poking each other. They can be together and comfortable too. Schopenhauer's second premise turns out to be false—at least for hedgehogs.

Exercise Set 6.1: Identifying deductive argument forms

Objective: To give you practice recognizing uses of Rules 22–26 in plain English.

Instructions: State which of the preceding rules each of the following arguments follows.

Tips for success: It's easier to recognize which rule a deductive argument uses if you use letters to abbreviate the different parts of the argument. For instance, recall how we used the letters **s** and **b** to stand for different independent clauses in discussing *modus tollens* (Rule 23). We used **s** to abbreviate "The visitor is a stranger" and **b** to stand for "The dog barked."

How do you figure out which parts of the argument to abbreviate? The first step is to look for uses of "if," "and," and "or." When these words are used to connect two independent clauses, they are called "logical connectives." (An independent clause is a part of a sentence that could be a sentence on its own. For instance, the sentence "If there are no chance factors in chess, then chess is a game of pure skill" has two independent clauses: "There are no chance factors in chess" and "Chess is a game of pure skill.")

When you find one of these logical connectives, circle it. Then, underline the independent clauses that it connects. Assign a letter to each of those clauses; write the letter underneath or beside the clause. Logicians often use the letters **p** and **q**, but you can use any letters you want.

Remember that "if," "and," and "or" are not always used as logical connectives. For instance, the word "and" appears in lists of two or more things (e.g., "Lions and tigers and bears!"). Look for sentences that use these words to connect two independent clauses. Those are the most likely to be genuine logical connectives.

Once you've found all of the logical connectives in an argument and assigned letters to the independent clauses that they connect, see if any of those clauses appear elsewhere in the argument. If so, underline the clause and write the letter for it underneath or beside it. Again, you can use any letters you want, but you must be consistent. If you used **p** to stand for "There are no chance factors in chess" once, you must use **p** for all and only instances of "There are no chance factors in chess" in that argument.

Finally, check for sentences that say the *opposite* of one of the clauses that you've symbolized. Put a "not" in front of the letter for that clause. For instance, if you're using **b** to stand for "The dog barked," look for sentences that say that the dog did not bark. Underline that sentence and write "not-**b**" underneath or beside it.

Once you have done this, you will probably notice that there are phrases, clauses, or entire sentences that you have not yet symbolized. This is perfectly normal. You will usually find arguments embedded in larger passages. The passage might include background information or commentary on the premises of the argument. You do not need to symbolize these. They are probably not premises of the argument.

Note that the arguments you encounter in your daily life may not always express one idea in the same way every time. If you're confident that two different clauses express the same idea, you can use the same letter to symbolize them, even if they don't use exactly the same words. For instance, consider the argument:

> Either the dog knew the visitor or the dog barked. The dog did not bark. Therefore, the visitor was not a stranger.

The first clause and the last sentence express the same idea—namely, that the dog knew the visitor—in different words. It makes sense to symbolize them with the same letter.

Once you've assigned letters to the clauses in your argument, compare the symbolized version of the argument to each of the preceding rules. If the symbolized version matches the form given by one of the rules, then the argument follows that rule. If not, it doesn't. Note that the order of the premises doesn't matter, though of course it does matter which sentence is the conclusion and which are the premises.

Sample

If money is the most important thing in life, then we will pursue it for its own sake. We do not pursue money for its own sake, but rather as a means to achieving something else. Thus, money is not the most important thing in life.

Adapted from: Aristotle, Nicomachean Ethics, *2nd ed., trans. Terence Irwin (Indianapolis: Hackett Publishing Company, 2000), 5*

Modus tollens.

To see why the answer is modus tollens, *let p stand for "money is the most important thing in life" and q stand for "we will pursue money for its own sake." We could symbolize the first sentence as "If p then q." The third sentence is not-q and the fourth sentence is not-p. This fits the form of* modus tollens. *Notice that the phrase "but rather as a means to achieving something else" is not part of the argument itself.*

1. If I am thinking, then I exist. I am thinking. Therefore, I exist.

    Adapted from: René Descartes, Discourse on Method, *4th ed., trans. Donald A. Cress (Indianapolis: Hackett Publishing Company, 1998), 18*

2. Determinism is the view that everything that happens is fully determined by the laws of nature and the way the world was long before we were born. Either determinism is false or humans have no free will. Humans do have free will. Thus, determinism is false.

    Adapted from: Peter van Inwagen, "The Incompatibility of Free Will and Determinism," Philosophical Studies *27 (1975), 185–99*

3. If the Great Spirit had desired me to be a white man, he would have made me a white man. He did not make me a white man. Hence, he did not desire me to be a white man.

    Adapted from: Chief Sitting Bull, quoted in David Ross, 1,001 Pearls of Wisdom *(San Francisco: Chronicle Books, 2006), 21*

4. I'm offering you two pills: one red, one blue. You can take the red pill or you can take the blue pill. It's up to you. But once you've made your choice, there's no turning back. If you take the blue pill, you'll forget this ever happened and you'll go on living your life in blissful ignorance. If you take the red pill, your life will be changed forever by what I am about to show you. Thus, your choice is really between the life you know now and a totally different life that you cannot begin to imagine.

    Adapted from: The Matrix, *directed by Andy Wachowski and Lana Wachowski (Burbank, CA: Warner Bros., 1999)*

5. Many medical texts suggest that the best way to treat bee stings is by scraping the stinger without squeezing or pulling the stinger. In 1996, some researchers tested this by allowing honeybees to sting them repeatedly. They scraped some stingers out and pulled the others out. They said that if scraping worked better than pulling, then scraping the stingers should leave a smaller welt. They found

that scraping the stingers did not leave a smaller welt. Therefore, scraping the stingers out did not work better than pulling them out.

Adapted from: Anahad O'Connor, "The Claim: Bee Stings Can Be Treated by Scraping out Stingers," New York Times, May 30, 2006, http://www .nytimes.com/2006/05/30/health/30real.html

6.   The prosecution has presented a lot of evidence to show that the defendant killed her husband. But if my client *had* killed her husband, then she wouldn't want to get caught, would she? And if she didn't want to get caught, then she wouldn't have left all that evidence behind. So, you see, if my client were guilty, then she wouldn't have left behind all of the evidence that the prosecution has presented!

Adapted from: Zach Weinersmith, "Comic for February 26, 2007," Saturday Morning Breakfast Comics, Feb 26, 2007, http://www.smbc-comics.com/index.php?id=743

7.   Steve Salerno, a former self-help book editor for Rodale Press, said, "If the self-help books we sold worked, then one would not expect people to need further help from us on the same topic." But he found that most of his company's customers did need further help from them—on the same topic—after reading their self-help books. This implies that the self-help books he sold did not work.

Adapted from: Michael Shermer, "SHAM Scam," Scientific American, May 2006, http://www.scientificamerican.com/article.cfm?id=sham-scam

8.   If all the other Baratheon children have dark hair, then it is unlikely that the king's son would be blond. And if it is unlikely that the king's son would be blond, then the prince probably isn't the king's child! Thus, if all the other Baratheon children have dark hair, the prince probably isn't the king's child.

Adapted from: George R. R. Martin, A Game of Thrones (New York: Bantam Spectra, 1996), 486

9.   You say I'm some kind of demon. Well, either you're right about that, and I really am a demon, or you're wrong about me, and I'm just a poor old country boy. Now, if I'm just a poor old country boy, you'd better be nice to me. But if I'm actually a demon, then you had really better be nice to me, because I could cause you all kinds of trouble. So either way, you'd better be nice to me!

Adapted from: Montgomery Pittman, "The Last Rites of Jeff Myrtlebank," The Twilight Zone video, 24:55, Feb 23, 1962, http://www.hulu.com/watch/440889

10. After drinking a potion labeled "DRINK ME," which had made
     her smaller, Alice found herself trapped. There was only one door
     out of the room, but it was locked. The key sat on top of the table,
     far out of her reach. Looking about for a solution to her problem,
     she discovered a tiny little cake labeled "EAT ME." She surmised
     that the cake might change her size too, although she wasn't sure in
     what way. It might make her grow back to her original size, or it
     might make her shrink even further. If it made her grow, then she
     would be able to reach the key and unlock the door. If it made her
     shrink, then she would be able to slip under the door. Therefore, she
     reasoned, she would be able to unlock the door or she would be able
     to slip under the door. Either way, she could escape from the room!

Adapted from: Lewis Carroll, Martin Gardner, and John Tenniel, The Annotated
Alice: The Definitive Edition *(New York: W. W. Norton, 1999), 18*

Model responses for odd-numbered exercises can be found on page 362.

Exercise Set 6.2: Identifying deductive arguments in more complex passages

Objective: To give you practice recognizing deductive argument forms
when they are expressed in more complicated ways.

Instructions: State which of the preceding rules each of the following
arguments follows.

Tips for success: Most of the deductive arguments you encounter won't
come as neatly packaged as those in Exercise Set 6.1. Most will be embedded in longer passages. Some will make their logical moves in ways that are
less obvious than in the arguments above.

Still, the basic technique for recognizing deductive argument forms in
more complex passages is the same as in Exercise Set 6.1. Look for logical
connectives. Assign letters to the independent clauses joined by the logical
connectives. Look for other occurrences of those clauses elsewhere in the
passage. Remember that you may find arguments embedded in larger passages. Some of the phrases, clauses, or sentences in the larger passage will
not be premises of the argument. You do not need to symbolize everything
in the passage. Symbolize only those clauses or sentences that express the
premises or conclusion of the argument.

One big difference between this exercise and the last one is that you will need to know about alternative ways of expressing "if **p** then **q**." Three of the most common are:

p if **q**	*means*	if **q** then **p**
p only if **q**	*means*	if **p** then **q**
p unless **q**	*means*	if not-**q** then **p**

Another problem that sometimes arises has to do with the little word "not." Consider, for example, the following argument:

(1) If the murder was committed at noon, then the butler did not do it.
(2) If the butler did not do it, then the maid must have done it.
Therefore, (3) if the murder was committed at noon, then the maid must have done it.

It would be natural to symbolize the argument as follows:

(1) If **a** then not-**b**.
(2) If not-**b** then **c**.
Therefore, (3) if **a** then **c**.

On the face of it, this may not look like a hypothetical syllogism (Rule 24), since the discussion of hypothetical syllogism makes no mention of "nots" (check it out). If you look just a little more carefully, though, you will see that this arguments does exactly what any good hypothetical syllogism does: it makes a tight link between **a** and **c** by means of an intermediate term, which happens to be not-**b** in this case. To see this clearly, try using a new symbol for not-**b**, like **d**. Then the argument reads:

(1) If **a** then **d**.
(2) If **d** then **c**.
Therefore, (3) if **a** then **c**.

and you can see that this argument forms just the sort of "chain" that makes hypothetical syllogisms valid. (Can you figure out what **not-d** means in English?)

By the same token, an argument like

(1) If not-**m** then not-**j**.
(2) Not-**m**.
Therefore, (3) not-**j**.

is a straightforward *modus ponens*, despite all the "nots." As long as the *antecedent* (i.e., the first part) of premise (1) exactly matches what's in premise (2), then the *consequent* (i.e., the second part) of premise (1) follows. What matters is the relation between the premises.

Sample

Scientists have known for some time now that Mars has water on it, but they have been unsure about whether that water ever flowed across the surface in streams or rivers. In 2012, NASA's Curiosity rover found rocks on Mars that have smooth, rounded pebbles embedded in them. Pebbles have that shape only if they have been in a stream or river that was flowing for a long time. Thus, the pebbles must have been in a stream or river. This confirms that Mars had flowing water at some point in the past.

Adapted from: NASA, "Pebbly Rocks Testify to Old Streambed on Mars," nasa.gov, May 30, 2013, http://www.nasa.gov/mission_pages/msl/news/msl20130530f.html

Modus ponens.

The key connective here is the word if *in the third sentence. If we use* **p** *to stand for "the Martian pebbles have a smooth, rounded shape" and* **q** *to stand for "the pebbles were in a stream or river," then the third sentence reads "**p** only if **q**." We know that this means "if **p** then **q**." So, once we notice that the second sentence asserts* **p** *and the fourth sentence asserts* **q***, we know that we're looking at an instance of* modus ponens. *Notice that the first sentence is just background information, and the last sentence tells us why the conclusion of our* modus ponens *argument is important. We don't need to symbolize either sentence. Notice also that the "or" in "streams or rivers" isn't a logical connective because it's not connecting two independent clauses.*

1. In January 1610, Galileo pointed a new telescope at Jupiter. He noticed three points of light beside Jupiter that weren't visible with his other, weaker telescopes. At first, he thought they were stars. But, as he wrote in his notes, he reasoned that if they were stars, then they should be about as bright as the other stars, and arranged randomly like the other stars. But they were brighter than the other stars and arranged in a straight line next to Jupiter. Thus, he concluded, they were not stars. This was his first step in discovering the moons of Jupiter.

    Adapted from: Robert J. Sternberg and Jacqueline P. Leighton, The Nature of Reasoning (Cambridge University Press, 2004), 30–35

2. All of our actions are motivated either by respect for duty or by something else. They will never treat others as means to an end if

they are motivated by respect for duty, and they will never have moral worth if they are not motivated by respect for duty. Thus, either our actions do not treat others as means to an end or they have no moral worth.

Adapted from: Immanuel Kant, Grounding for the Metaphysics of Morals, *3rd ed., trans. James W. Ellington (Indianapolis: Hackett Publishing Company, 1993), 11, 36*

3.   Without a government, people would have so little security that they would choose to steal from others—even killing others if they must—rather than try to produce and protect their own goods or food. If people living without a government are prone to steal from and kill one another, then life would be so terrible without a government that the only rational thing to do is to set up a government to force everyone to behave. Hence, we ought to set up a government to force everyone to behave.

Adapted from: Thomas Hobbes, Leviathan, *ed. Edwin Curley (Indianapolis: Hackett Publishing Company, 1994), 74–80*

4.   When federal prosecutors accused Ross Ulbricht of running the Silk Road, an online marketplace for illegal goods, Ulbricht said he'd been framed. He said he had no connection to the computers that hosted the Silk Road. Furthermore, his lawyers argued, the FBI had hacked into that server illegally, and so it could not use evidence from that server in court. But a judge countered that Ulbricht couldn't have it both ways. Either he had some connection to the Silk Road server or he didn't. If he did, then he couldn't claim that he'd been framed. On the other hand, he had no grounds for objecting to the FBI's methods of accessing the server unless he *did* have such a connection. So, either he had to give up his claim that he'd been framed or give up his claim that the government's evidence was inadmissible in court.

Adapted from: "The Silk Road Trial: Bitcoin Buccaneers," The Economist, Jan 17, 2015, http://www.economist.com/news/united-states/21639525-one-dread-pirate-trial-what-about-others-bitcoin-buccaneers

5.   In the 1700s, before the invention of modern chemistry, scientists believed that flammable materials contained a substance called "phlogiston." When something burned, it was thought to lose

phlogiston. This "phlogiston theory" of combustion explained many scientific observations, but it also raised some puzzles. One puzzle was that certain metals gained weight when they burned. But burning metals would cause them to *lose* weight if burning was the release of phlogiston. Thus, the puzzle led some scientists to suspect that the phlogiston theory was incorrect.

Adapted from: Thomas Kuhn, The Structure of Scientific Revolutions: 50th Anniversary Edition *(Chicago: University of Chicago Press), 71–72*

6. As surprising as it may seem, I am now prepared to share with you something that philosophers have sought for centuries: a proof that the external world really exists. Observe: my right hand exists. My left hand, you will notice, also exists. Thus, there exist at least two hands. Notice, however, that if there exist at least two hands, as these two hands here exist, then the external world exists.

Adapted from: G. E. Moore, "Proof of an External World," in Classics of Analytic Philosophy, *edited by Robert Ammerman (Indianapolis: Hackett Publishing Company, 1990), 81*

7. Part of an economist's job is to figure out why people do stupid things—or at least, why they do things that *appear* stupid. Take celebrity endorsements of consumer goods, for instance. Companies hire celebrities to endorse their products even though the celebrities have no expertise related to the product. For some reason, consumers respond to these endorsements. That is, celebrity endorsements cause consumers to buy more of a product. Some people might think this is just stupidity. But economists assume it's not. They reason that consumers wouldn't respond to celebrity endorsements if celebrity endorsements didn't signal a better product or a more trustworthy company. Thus, celebrity endorsements must signal a better product or a more trustworthy company. The puzzle for the economist is to figure out *how* celebrity endorsements do this.

Adapted from: Steven E. Landsburg, The Armchair Economist *(New York: Free Press, 1993), 14*

8. If a man is truly good, then he will recognize the difficulty of everything he does. Furthermore, he will be hesitant to speak if he recognizes the difficulty of everything he does. Thus, a man is truly good only if he is hesitant to speak.

    Adapted from: Confucius, Analects, *tr. Edward Slingerland (Indianapolis: Hackett Publishing Company, 2003), 126*

9. To call oneself a Christian, one must believe in certain things. At the very least, one must believe in God and immortality. If someone does not believe in those two things, that person is not truly a Christian. Bertrand Russell did not believe in God or immortality. Thus, Bertrand Russell was not a Christian.

    Adapted from: Bertrand Russell, Why I Am Not a Christian *(London: George Allen & Unwin, 1957; repr., London: Routledge, 2004), 2*

10. This man just told us that he's going to steal a ship, pick up a pirate crew in Tortuga, and raid, pillage, and pilfer his way around the Caribbean. If he were telling the truth, he wouldn't have told us all that. So he can't be telling the truth!

    Adapted from: Pirates of the Caribbean: The Curse of the Black Pearl, *directed by Gore Verbinski (Burbank, CA: Walt Disney Pictures, 2003)*

Model responses for odd-numbered exercises can be found on page 364.

Exercise Set 6.3: Drawing conclusions with deductive arguments

Objective: To train you to draw conclusions using deductive argument forms.

Instructions: Each of the following sets of premises enables you to draw a specific conclusion using a deductive argument. State the conclusion that you can draw from each set of premises and the deductive argument form(s) that you used to draw the conclusion.

Tips for success: As in Exercise Sets 6.1 and 6.2, it will help to start by symbolizing each statement. Look for statements containing logical connectives first. Once you've symbolized everything you can, see whether the statements you've symbolized match the premises of any argument forms. If so, use that argument form to draw a conclusion.

Sample

If dolphins act similarly to us under similar circumstances, the psychology behind their behavior is probably similar to ours. Dolphins do act similarly to us
under similar circumstances.

Adapted from: Franz de Waal, "Looking at Flipper, Seeing Ourselves," New York Times, Oct 9, 2006,
http://www.nytimes.com/2006/10/09/opinion/09dewaal.html

Using modus ponens, we can conclude that the psychology behind dolphins' behavior
is probably similar to ours.

Using p to stand for "dolphins act similarly to us under similar circumstances" and q to stand
for "the psychology behind dolphins' behavior is probably similar to ours," we can symbolize
the premises as:

(1) If p then q.
(2) p.

These are the premises needed for modus ponens, *which allows us to conclude that q is true—*
that is, that the psychology behind dolphins' behavior is probably similar to ours.

1.   If the SAT were a useful test, then it would test skills like research
     and critical analysis. It does not test those skills.

     Adapted from: Jeanne Heifetz, letter to the editor, New York Times, Sep 22, 2006,
     http://www.nytimes.com/2006/09/22/opinion/l22test.html

2.   Either moral judgments are derived from reason or they are
     caused by emotion. Moral judgments are not derived from reason.

     Adapted from: David Hume, A Treatise of Human Nature: Two-Volume Set,
     edited by David Fate Norton and Mary J. Norton (Oxford: Clarendon Press,
     2007), 293–301

3.   I believe that South America and Africa used to be joined to-
     gether into a single supercontinent, but that they have since
     drifted apart. If this "continental drift" hypothesis is correct, then
     there would have been animals that lived nowhere but near the
     place where the old supercontinent split apart. And if there were

such animals, then there will be fossils in eastern South America that can be found nowhere else but in western Africa.

Adapted from: Alfred Wegener, The Origin of Continents and Oceans, *translated by John Biram (Mineola, NY: Dover, 1966), 70*

4. Unless we can be sure of the existence of objects, we cannot be sure that other people's bodies exist. If we cannot be sure that other people's bodies exist, then we cannot be sure that other people's minds exist.

    Adapted from: Bertrand Russell, The Problems of Philosophy *(1912; repr., New York: Barnes & Noble, 2004), 9*

5. Either light consists of tiny particles or it consists of waves. Light does not consist of tiny particles.

    Adapted from: M. Shamos, Great Experiments in Physics *(New York: Holt, Rinehart and Winston, 1959), 93–107*

6. If the rich countries had become rich purely by stealing from the rest of the world, then the rest of the world would be poorer now than it used to be. But the rest of the world is richer now than it used to be, even though it is not nearly as wealthy as the rich countries.

    Adapted from: Jeffrey D. Sachs, The End of Poverty *(New York: Penguin, 2005), 31*

7. We've become slaves to our smartphones, constantly connected to each other and to a barrage of information. For many busy professionals, this has become a real problem, with work texts and emails interrupting their personal lives. Individuals could try to cut back their use on their own, or they could do it in cooperation with their colleagues. If they try to cut back on their own, however, then their colleagues may resent their time offline. Their colleagues will appreciate their time offline, however, if workers cut back in cooperation with everyone else.

    Adapted from: "Slaves to the Smartphone," The Economist, *Mar 10, 2012, http://www.economist.com/node/21549904*

8.   The nametag on your mattress says "J. Watson." If your nametag says "J. Watson," then your first name is probably James.

Adapted from: Young Sherlock Homes, *directed by Barry Levinson (Hollywood, CA: Paramount Pictures, 1985)*

9.   In 2012, a Turkish court convicted 330 military officers guilty of plotting a coup back in 2003. The court's main evidence came from computer files allegedly created in 2003. But computer experts who examined the files found that they had been created using Microsoft Office 2007, which didn't exist in 2003. Obviously, the files couldn't have been created in 2003 if they had been created using Office 2007.

Adapted from: Dani Rodrik, "Turkish Court Provides (Lack of) Reasoning Behind Sledgehammer Verdict," Dani Rodrik's Weblog, *Jan 8, 2013, http://rodrik.typepad.com/dani_rodriks_weblog/2013/01/turkish-court-provides-lack-of-reasoning-behind-sledgehammer-verdict.html*

10. You can either measure the position of a subatomic particle or you can measure its momentum. A law of physics known as the Heisenberg uncertainty principle entails that if you measure its position, then you cannot know its momentum precisely, but if you measure its momentum, then you cannot know its position precisely.

Adapted from: George Gamow, Mr. Tompkins in Paperback *(1965; repr., Cambridge University Press, 1993), 65–80*

Model responses for odd-numbered exercises can be found on page 366.

Reductio ad absurdum

One traditional deductive strategy deserves special mention even though, strictly speaking, it is only a version of *modus tollens*. This is the *reductio ad absurdum*, that is, a "reduction to absurdity." Arguments by *reductio* (or "indirect proof," as they're sometimes called) establish their conclusions by showing that assuming the opposite leads to absurdity: to a contradictory or silly result. Nothing is left to do, the argument suggests, but to accept the conclusion.

To prove: **p.**

Assume the opposite: Not-**p.**

Rule 27

Argue that from the assumption we'd have to conclude: **q**.

Show that **q** *is false (contradictory, "absurd," morally or practically unacceptable . . .).*

Conclude: **p** *must be true after all.*

Rule 12 discussed an argument for the existence of a Creator. Houses have creators, the argument goes, and the world is *like* a house—it too is ordered and beautiful. Thus, the analogy suggests, the world must have a Creator too. Rule 12 also cited David Hume's argument that the world is not relevantly similar enough to a house for this analogy to succeed. In Part V of his *Dialogues*, Hume also suggested a *reductio ad absurdum* of the analogy.[1] Developed, it goes something like this:

> Suppose the world has a Creator like a house does. Now, when houses are not perfect, we know who to blame: the carpenters and masons who created them. But the world is also not wholly perfect. Therefore, it would seem to follow that the Creator of the world is not perfect either. But you would consider this conclusion absurd. The only way to avoid the absurdity, however, is to reject the supposition that leads to it. Therefore, the world does not have a Creator in the way a house does.

Spelled out in *reductio* form, the argument is:

> *To prove:* The world does not have a Creator in the way a house does.
>
> *Assume the opposite:* The world does have a Creator in the way a house does.
>
> *Argue that from the assumption we'd have to conclude:* The Creator is imperfect (because the world is imperfect).
>
> *But:* God cannot be imperfect.
>
> *Conclude:* The world does not have a Creator in the way a house does.

Not everyone would find the idea of an imperfect God "absurd," but Hume knew that the Christians with whom he was arguing would not accept it.

---

1. David Hume, *Dialogues Concerning Natural Religion*, pp. 34–37.

Exercise Set 6.4: Working with *reductio ad absurdum*

Objective: To give you practice recognizing instances of *reductio ad absurdum* and to help you understand how *reductio* works.

Instructions: Identify the *reductio ad absurdum* argument pattern in each of the passages below. That is, specify the claim to be proven, the assumption that is made, the conclusion that one is supposed to have to draw from that assumption, the reason for thinking that conclusion to be implausible, and the final conclusion of the *reductio* argument.

Tips for success: As we noted above, *reductio ad absurdum* is closely related to *modus tollens*. Both argument forms work by arguing that one claim leads to another claim and that the second claim is false. That is, they work by arguing that "if **p** then **q**" and that **q** is false. This allows us to infer that **p** is false.

One difference between *modus tollens* and *reductio ad absurdum* is that *reductio ad absurdum* involves a claim that is not just false, but absurd or ridiculous, whereas *modus tollens* only involves a claim that's false.

What's the difference between being false and being ridiculous? The claim that every king of England was born in England is false—William III, for instance, was born in what is now the Netherlands—but you might have to look it up to find out whether it's false. The claim that every king of England was born on Jupiter is ridiculous. You don't need to look it up to know whether it's true.

The other difference between *modus tollens* and *reductio ad absurdum* is that *modus tollens* simply asserts that **p** leads to **q**. In a *reductio ad absurdum*, you'll often find a lengthy argument showing that **p** leads to **q**.

Your task in each of these exercises is to figure out what **p** and **q** are, as well as the reason that the author of the argument thinks that **q** is "absurd." To do this, look to see what the argument asks you to assume or suppose to be true. That will be **p**. The conclusion of the argument—the claim that the author wants to prove—will be not-**p**. Then, look to see what ridiculous implication that assumption would force us to accept. That will be **q**. Finally, check what, if anything, the author says about why **q** is hard to believe. (If it's obviously ridiculous, of course, the author might not need to say anything about why it's hard to believe!) You don't need to symbolize or say anything more about the argument that the author uses to get from **p** to **q**.

Once you have all of these pieces, you can insert them into the template above, as follows:

To prove: Not-**p**
Assume the opposite: **p**
Argue that from the assumption we'd have to conclude: **q**
But: **q** is absurd (or obviously false)
Conclude: Not-**p**

Sample

Some people insist that Americans never really landed on the moon. They say that the moon landings were an elaborate hoax. NASA employed thousands of people to (allegedly) put astronauts on the moon, but in the decades since the first landing, no one involved in the project has claimed that the landings were staged. Suppose for a moment that the landings *were* a hoax. It's ridiculous to think that NASA could have kept all of those people silent. Thus, the only reasonable thing to believe is that the landings were not a hoax.

Adapted from: Brent Silby, "Of Course We Went to the Moon: A Defense of the Lunar Landings," 2001, http://www.def-logic.com/articles/lunarlanding.html

To prove: The American moon landings were not a hoax.
Assume the opposite: The landings were a hoax (i.e., astronauts never walked on the moon).
Argue that from the assumption we'd have to conclude: NASA has kept thousands of people silent about the hoax for decades.
But: There's no way NASA could have kept that many people silent for so long.
Conclude: The American moon landings were not a hoax.

*In terms of the symbolization recommended in the "Tips for success" above, the main conclusion of this argument—which we suggested you symbolize as not-**p**—is "The American moon landings were not a hoax." This goes on the first and last lines of the reductio "template." The argument assumes the opposite of this conclusion—**p**—which is that the landings were a hoax. It then argues that the assumption would lead us to **q**, which stands for "NASA has kept thousands of people silent about the hoax for decades." Since it's practically impossible for NASA to have done that, we're entitled to reject the assumption that **p**. This leaves us with the main conclusion of the reductio: not-**p**. The American moon landings were not a hoax.*

Notice that strictly speaking, it's not impossible that NASA kept thousands of people silent. The claim that NASA kept so many silent after a hoax, however, is sufficiently incredible that we should reject any assumption that would require us to believe that the claim is true.

1.   No man has yet had sex in space. It's well known that no one who's been in space has admitted to it. But suppose, just for the sake of argument, that one of the men who's been to space had sex there. That would mean that there's some guy out there who had sex *in space* and didn't tell anyone about it. That's really hard to believe. No guy could keep that to himself.

Adapted from: Mike Wall, "No Sex in Space, Yet, Official Says," Space.com,
Apr 22, 2011, http://www.space.com/11473-astronauts-sex-space-rumors.html

2.   Some people believe that ordinary citizens should be allowed to own any weapons that they want. Suppose that this were true. That would mean that ordinary citizens could own tanks, large stock-piles of explosives, fighter jets—even nuclear bombs! Clearly, ordinary citizens shouldn't be allowed to own nuclear bombs. Thus, it's false that ordinary citizens should be allowed to own any weapons they want.

Adapted from: "Reductio Ad Absurdum—Use With Caution," IncreaseBrainPower
.com, n.d., http://www.increasebrainpower.com/reductio-ad-absurdum.html

3.   My psychiatrist is trying to convince me that my college room-mate, whom I've known for years, is just a hallucination. Could he be right? Suppose that my roommate is real. He's looked exactly the same for as long as I've known him. In all this time, he hasn't aged a day. That means that my roommate doesn't age. But it's absurd to think that my roommate doesn't age. My psychiatrist is right! My roommate *isn't* real!

Adapted from: A Beautiful Mind, directed by Ron Howard (Universal City, CA:
Universal Pictures, 2001)

4.   There's a popular myth out there that aliens were somehow in-volved in building the pyramids of Egypt. Assume, just for the sake of argument, that aliens really did build the pyramids. As anyone who's been to the pyramids can tell you, the stones used in building the pyramids were clearly shaped by simple hand tools. You can see the chisel marks on the stones. This would mean that despite having the ability to reach Earth from some distant planet, the aliens would have had to rely on the Egyptians' basic hand tools to shape the rocks. It's ridiculous to think that any civiliza-tion with the technology for interplanetary travel wouldn't have

used something like a laser—or at least a high-powered, precision saw—to carve the stones used in the pyramids. That's why I don't believe that aliens were involved in building the pyramids.

Adapted from: "Do You Think the Great Pyramids Were Built By Aliens?" Yahoo! Answers, May 2010, http://answers.yahoo.com/question/ index?qid=20100518111720AAVHT6k

5.   It is impossible to accelerate something to the speed of light. To see this, suppose that you *could* accelerate a space ship to the speed of light. The theory of relativity says that as the space ship gets faster and faster, it will get shorter and shorter. If you were to accelerate the space ship to the speed of light, its length would become zero. But the idea of an object with a length of zero is absurd. Thus, it's impossible to accelerate the space ship—or anything else—to the speed of light.

Adapted from: Albert Einstein, Relativity, *trans. Robert W. Lawson (New York: Pi Press, 2005), 47–48*

6.   The police claim that the defendants were using an elaborate code to arrange drug deals. The police also claim that they didn't know about this code before they arrested the defendants a few hours ago. Suppose they're telling the truth. That would mean that the police cracked this elaborate code within a matter of hours. There's simply no way they could have pulled that off. It's impossible for the cops to have cracked such a sophisticated code so quickly. Thus, the police must have known about the code before the arrests.

Adapted from: David Simon, "–30–," The Wire, HBO, March 9, 2008

7.   Some people hold that Earth may be the only planet with life in our Milky Way galaxy. But astronomers now say that there could be up to thirty billion potentially habitable planets in the Milky Way. If we really were the only planet with life in the whole galaxy, then the probability of life arising on any potentially habitable planet would be so tiny as to basically be zero. But if the probability of life arising on any potentially habitable planet is basically zero, there should not be life on Earth either! Since there

obviously is life on Earth, the supposition is absurd. There must be life elsewhere!

Adapted from: Stephen Webb, If the Universe Is Teeming with Aliens . . . Where Is Everybody? Fifty Solutions to the Fermi Paradox and the Problem of Extraterrestrial Life *(New York: Copernicus Books, 2002), 235*

8.　Physicists have proven that many features of our universe are "fine-tuned" for the existence of life as we know it. That is, things like the strength of the force of gravity are *just right* to make life possible. If they were very slightly different, there would be no life at all. If we assume that the universe is not designed by an intelligent creator, then this "fine-tuning" is just a freak accident. It is wildly improbable that the physics of our universe would be so perfectly adjusted for life by accident. Thus, the universe must be designed by an intelligent creator.

Adapted from: "Precise Fine-Tuning of the Universe Suggests Design," YouTube, Dec 3, 2006, http://www.youtube.com/watch?v=KM7Q43KspuY

9.　A prime number is a number that can only be divided by one and itself (without leaving a remainder). There is no largest prime number. To see why, assume that there is some largest prime number. Call that largest prime number N. Now, consider another number, M, which we get by multiplying all of the prime numbers that are less than N and then adding one. M is definitely larger than N, but it is not divisible by any prime number less than N. Thus, either M is a prime number that is larger than N, or it is divisible by a prime number that is larger than N (because every non-prime number is divisible by some prime number, and M is not divisible by any prime number less than N). Either way, there is some prime number that is larger than N. This contradicts our claim that N is the largest prime number. Therefore, our initial assumption that there is a largest prime number must be false.

Adapted from: Euclid, Elements *9.20*

10.　God is the greatest being that you can possibly imagine. This implies that you cannot imagine a being that is greater than God. Now, suppose that God did not exist. Then you could imagine a being that is exactly like God except that it exists. Since it is better to exist than not to exist, such a being would be even better than

God. Thus, you would be imagining a being that is greater than God—even though you cannot imagine a being that is greater than God. So, God must exist.

Adapted from: St. Anselm, Proslogion, *in* Philosophy in the Middle Ages: The Christian, Islamic, and Jewish Traditions, *3rd ed., edited by Arthur Hyman and James J. Walsh (Indianapolis: Hackett Publishing Company, 2010), 162–63*

Model responses for odd-numbered exercises can be found on page 368.

Need more practice? Make a list of claims that are false. For each claim, can you show that you would be forced to accept an absurd conclusion if you assumed that the claim were true? Alternatively, work with a group of friends or classmates and see who can derive the most absurd conclusion from each false claim.

Deductive arguments in several steps

Rule 28

Many valid deductive arguments are combinations of the basic forms introduced in Rules 22–27. Here, for example, is Sherlock Holmes performing a simple deduction for Doctor Watson's edification, meanwhile commenting on the relative roles of observation and deduction. Holmes has casually remarked that Watson visited a certain post office that morning, and furthermore that he sent off a telegram while there. "Right!" replies Watson, amazed, "Right on both points! But I confess that I don't see how you arrived at it." Holmes replies:

> "It is simplicity itself. . . . Observation tells me that you have a little reddish mold adhering to your instep. Just opposite the Wigmore Street Post Office they have taken up the pavement and thrown up some earth, which lies in such a way that it is difficult to avoid treading in it in entering. The earth is of this peculiar reddish tint which is found, as far as I know, nowhere else in the neighborhood. So much is observation. The rest is deduction."
>
> [Watson]: "How, then, did you deduce the telegram?"
>
> [Holmes]: "Why, of course I knew that you had not written a letter, since I sat opposite you all morning. I see also in your open desk there that you have a sheet of stamps and a thick bundle of postcards. What could you go to the post office for,

then, but to send a wire? Eliminate all the other factors, and the one which remains must be the truth."[2]

Putting Holmes' deduction into explicit premises, we might have:

1. Watson has a little reddish mold on his boots.

2. If Watson has a little reddish mold on his boots, then he has been to the Wigmore Street Post Office this morning (because there and only there is reddish dirt of that sort thrown up, and in a way difficult to avoid stepping in).

3. If Watson has been to the Wigmore Street Post Office this morning, he either mailed a letter, bought stamps or cards, or sent a wire.

4. If Watson had mailed a letter, he would have written the letter this morning.

5. Watson wrote no letter this morning.

6. If Watson had bought stamps or cards, he would not already have a drawer full of stamps and cards.

7. Watson already has a drawer full of stamps and cards.

8. Therefore, Watson sent a wire at the Wigmore Street Post Office this morning.

We now need to break the argument down into a series of valid arguments in the simple forms presented in Rules 22–27. We might start with a *modus ponens*:

2. If Watson has a little reddish mold on his boots, then he has been to the Wigmore Street Post Office this morning.

1. Watson has a little reddish mold on his boots.

I. Therefore, Watson has been to Wigmore Street Post Office this morning.

(We will use I, II, etc. to stand for the conclusions of simple arguments, which then can be used as premises to draw further conclusions.)

Another *modus ponens* follows:

---

2. Sir Arthur Conan Doyle, "The Sign of Four," in *The Complete Sherlock Holmes*, pp. 91–92.

3. If Watson has been to the Wigmore Street Post Office this morning, he either mailed a letter, bought stamps or cards, or sent a wire.

I. Watson has been to the Wigmore Street Post Office this morning.

II. Therefore, Watson either mailed a letter, bought stamps or cards, or sent a wire.

Two of these three possibilities now can be ruled out, both by *modus tollens*.

4. If Watson had gone to the post office to mail a letter, he would have written the letter this morning.

5. Watson wrote no letter this morning.

III. Therefore, Watson did not go to the post office to mail a letter.

and:

6. If Watson had gone to the post office to buy stamps or cards, he would not already have a drawer full of stamps and cards.

7. Watson already has a drawer full of stamps and cards.

IV. Therefore, Watson did not go to the post office to buy stamps or cards.

Finally we can put it all together:

II. Watson either mailed a letter, bought stamps or cards, or sent a wire at the Wigmore Street Post Office this morning.

III. Watson did not mail a letter.

IV. Watson did not buy stamps or cards.

8. Therefore, Watson sent a wire at the Wigmore Street Post Office this morning.

This last inference is an extended disjunctive syllogism. "Eliminate all the other factors, and the one which remains must be the truth."

Exercise Set 6.5: Identifying deductive arguments in several steps

Objective: To give you practice recognizing deductive arguments in several steps.

Instructions: Each of the following arguments uses two or more forms of deductive argument. For each argument, list all of the argument forms used in the argument.

Tips for success: This exercise set builds on Exercise Sets 6.1 and 6.2. You should approach it in the same way: Look for logical connectives. Then, look for other occurrences of the independent clauses that are joined by logical connectives.

The twist here is that the conclusion of one (short) argument will appear as a premise in the next (short) argument. It might help to think of the arguments as being "chained" together, with one claim serving as the link between one argument and the next. For instance, you might have a hypothetical syllogism (Rule 24) "chained" to a use of *modus ponens* (Rule 22), as follows:

> If **p** then **q**.
> If **q** then **r**.   } hypothetical syllogism
> Therefore, if **p** then **r**.
> **p**.   } *modus ponens*
> Therefore, **r**.

In this case, the claim "if **p** then **r**" is both the conclusion of the hypothetical syllogism and a premise in *modus ponens*. In general, keep an eye out for claims that function in this double way—that is, as both premises and conclusions. Those are likely to be the links between arguments that are "chained" together.

In particularly difficult cases, the premises may appear out of order. When that happens, you should treat the argument like a jigsaw puzzle. Try rearranging the pieces to get them to fit together in a sensible or meaningful way. For instance, after you've symbolized the argument, you may find yourself with the following five statements:

> (1) If **q** then **r**.
> (2) **p**.
> (3) If **p** then **q**.
> Therefore, (4) If **p** then **r**.
> Therefore, (5) **r**.

You would need to rearrange these to see that (3), (1), and (4) constitute a hypothetical syllogism, while (2), (4), and (5) fit the form of *modus ponens*.

Since (4) is both the conclusion of one argument *and* a premise in a second argument, we call (4) a "subconclusion." Since (5) is not used as a premise in any further argument, we call it the "main conclusion" of the whole argument.

Sample

Uranium emits rays similar to X-rays. These rays arise either from an interaction between the uranium and its surroundings or from the uranium itself. If the rays arise from an interaction between the uranium and its surroundings, then the amount of radiation should vary with temperature, illumination, or other factors. The radiation, however, is constant: it does not vary with temperature, illumination, or other factors. Thus, the radiation does not arise from an interaction between the uranium and its surroundings. The radiation, therefore, comes from the uranium itself.

Adapted from: Marie Skłodowska Curie, "Radium and Radioactivity," Century Magazine
(Jan 1904), 461–66

Modus tollens and disjunctive syllogism.

To see how this argument uses modus tollens *and disjunctive syllogism, let* ***p*** *stand for "The rays arise from an interaction between the uranium and its surroundings,"* ***q*** *stand for "The amount of radiation should vary with temperature, illumination, or other factors," and* ***r*** *stand for "The radiation arises from the uranium itself." We can symbolize the argument as follows:*

> *(1)* ***p*** *or* ***r****.*
> *(2) If* ***p*** *then* ***q****.*
> *(3) Not-****q****.*
> *Therefore, (4) Not-****p****.*
> *Therefore, (5)* ***r****.*

Notice that we did not symbolize the first sentence. Premises (2) and (3) lead to (4) by modus tollens. *Premises (1) and (4) lead to the main conclusion, (5), by disjunctive syllogism. (Check out the sample in Exercise Set 12.2 in Appendix III to see how you can represent this argument with argument maps.)*

1. Either God is able to prevent evil or He is not. If God is unable to prevent evil, then God is not all powerful. After all, saying that God is unable to prevent evil is admitting that there is something that God does not have the power to do. On the other hand, if God is able to prevent evil and chooses not to do so, then God is not perfectly good. This is because a perfectly good being would not willingly permit evil to occur. So, either God is not all powerful or God is not all good. Let us accept that God is perfectly good. Then we must admit that God is not all powerful.

    Adapted from: John Stuart Mill, "Nature," in Three Essays on Religion
    (Amherst, NY: Prometheus Books, 1998), 36–40

2. If we were supposed to live forever, then we would live forever. Since we don't live forever, it's clear that we're not supposed to live forever. If we're not supposed to live forever, then I would not choose to live forever. Therefore, I would not choose to live forever.

    Adapted from: "Miss Alabama Quotes Blooper," The Slip-Up Archive,
    Apr 4, 2000, http://www.slipups.com/items/2868.html

3. Miss Windham, you claim that your father was shot sometime after you arrived home from getting a perm. You say that you did not hear the gunshot because you were in the shower. Now, you also claim that you have had a perm every six months or so for the last fifteen years. But isn't it the first rule of perm maintenance that you are not allowed to wet your hair for twenty-four hours after getting a perm, so as to avoid deactivating the ammonium thioglycolate? And if, as you claim, you've had thirty perms in your life, wouldn't you know that? And if you knew not to wet your hair, you wouldn't have gotten in the shower when you came home, would you? And if you wouldn't have gotten in the shower, aren't you lying about not hearing the gunshot? I think you are! You heard the gunshot, Miss Windham! Admit it!

    Adapted from: Legally Blonde, *directed by Robert Luketic (Los Angeles:*
    Metro-Goldwyn-Mayer, 2001)

4. Don't worry about being a loser! You won't be a loser! Look, when you enter that contest tomorrow, maybe you'll win, maybe you'll

lose. If you win, then you're not a loser, right? But did you know that if you lose, you won't be a loser, either? See, if you compete and you lose, you still competed. And if you competed, then you're not a loser, because a real loser is someone who's so afraid of losing that she doesn't even compete.

Adapted from: Little Miss Sunshine, *directed by Jonathan Dayton and Valerie Faris (Los Angeles, CA: Fox Searchlight Pictures, 2006)*

5.   Geologists have long known that the Earth's core has two layers: an "outer core" of molten iron surrounds an "inner core" of solid iron crystals. Seismologists—scientists who study earthquakes—have noticed that the seismic waves generated by earthquakes move faster when they're traveling between the north and south pole, rather than between points on the equator. This shows that the crystals in the inner core are aligned in a north-south direction. More recently, however, several seismologists discovered that when seismic waves travel close to the very center of the inner core, they move fastest when traveling between Central America and Southeast Asia, nearly perpendicular to the north-south direction of the crystals of the inner core. The seismologists did not observe the same effect for waves that only travel through the edge of the inner core. If the speed of north-south seismic waves indicates that most crystals in the inner core are aligned north-south, then the speed of seismic waves traveling through the center of the inner core indicates that most crystals in the center inner corse are aligned east-west. And if the speed of seismic waves traveling through the center of the inner core indicates that the crystals there are aligned east-west, then the inner core has its own "inner inner core." Thus, these researchers conclude, the Earth's core has three layers: an outer core, an outer inner core, and an inner inner core.

Adapted from: Tao Wang, Xiaodong Song, and Han H. Xia, "Equatorial Anistropy in the Inner Part of Earth's Inner Core from Autocorrelation of Earthquake Code," Nature Geoscience 8 (2015): 224–27

6.   If the borogroves are all mimsy and the slithy toves are gimbling in the wabe, then my beamish boy has come galumphing back. My boy, being beamish, would come galumphing back only if he

has snicker-snacked the manxome foe with his vorpal blade. So, you see, my boy must have snicker-snacked the manxome foe at last if the borogroves are all mimsy and the slithy toves are gimbling in the wabe. O frabjous day!

Adapted from: Lewis Carroll, Martin Gardner, and John Tenniel, The Annotated Alice: The Definitive Edition *(New York: W. W. Norton, 1999), 148–50*

7.   It seems like I have awakened in my own apartment. But it's also possible that I'm still asleep and still dreaming. If I am actually awake, then everything in my apartment will look and feel like it does in real life. If everything in my apartment looks and feels like it does in real life, then this carpet will feel like wool. But the carpet definitely feels like it is made of polyester. Thus, I can't be awake. I must still be dreaming!

Adapted from: Inception, *directed by Christopher Nolan (Burbank, CA: Warner Bros., 2010)*

8.   The worst is when you know that something is going to happen but you don't know whether it's going to be a good thing or a bad thing. Whenever you know that something is going to happen, either you'll know whether it's going to be good or bad or you won't. If you know that it's going to be a good thing, then you don't need to worry because it's a good thing. But you don't need to worry as much if you know it's going to be a bad thing either because you can get yourself used to the idea. So as long as you know whether it will be good or bad, you don't need to worry so much. The trouble is that if you don't know whether it will be good or bad you can make yourself sick with worrying. So, when you know that something is going to happen, there's no in between. Either you don't worry much at all or you worry yourself sick.

Adapted from: Mark Haddon, The Curious Incident of the Dog in the Night-Time *(New York: Random House, 2004), 214–15*

9.   A law either fits with the moral law or it is unjust. Laws requiring or promoting racial segregation conflict with the moral law. If a law is unjust, then one has a moral responsibility to disobey it. Thus, one has a moral responsibility to disobey segregation laws.

Adapted from: Martin Luther King, Jr., "Letter from a Birmingham Jail,"
Liberation: An Independent Monthly, *Jun 1963*

10. In war, as in life, either you know the facts or you don't. If you know the facts, you're dealing with a known fact. If you don't know the facts, then either you know you don't know them or you don't know that you don't know them. If you know you don't know the facts, you've got a known unknown. If you don't know that you don't know the facts, you've got an unknown unknown. So if you don't know the facts, then you've got either a known unknown or an unknown unknown. Thus, either you've got a known fact or a known unknown fact or an unknown unknown fact.

Adapted from: Donald Rumsfeld, "Department of Defense News Briefing,"
Feb 12, 2002, http://www.defense.gov/transcripts/transcript
.aspx?transcriptid=2636

Model responses for odd-numbered exercises can be found on page 372.

Critical thinking activity: Recognizing deductive argument forms

For an in-class activity that gives you practice in recognizing deductive argument forms in difficult contexts, see the assignment sheet for "Recognizing deductive argument forms" (p. 466) in Part 3.

Now suppose that you have picked, or been assigned, an issue or question on which to work out an argumentative essay or oral presentation. Maybe you're writing for a class; maybe you're about to speak at a public forum or write a letter to the editor; maybe you're just fascinated by the issue and want to figure out what you think.

To do this you need to go beyond the short arguments we have so far considered. You must work out a more detailed line of thought, in which the main ideas are laid out clearly and their own premises in turn are spelled out and defended. Anything you say requires evidence and reasons, which in turn may take some research; and you will need to weigh arguments for opposing views as well. All of this is hard work, but it is also good work. For many people, in fact, it is one of the most rewarding and enjoyable kinds of thinking there is!

Explore the issue

You begin with an issue but not necessarily a position. Do not feel that you must immediately embrace some position and then try to shore it up with arguments. Likewise, even if you have a position, do not just dash off the first argument that occurs to you. You are not being asked for the first opinion that occurs to you. You are being asked to *arrive* at a well-informed opinion that can be defended with solid arguments.

Is life likely on other planets? Carl Sagan says that it is—but why? How could he, or we, argue the point? Here is one line of thought that some astronomers suggest. There are billions of stars in our galaxy alone—and billions of galaxies in the universe. If even a tiny fraction of all these stars have solar systems of their own, and even a tiny fraction of those have planets suitable for life, and even a tiny fraction of *those* actually *have* life, still there must be a myriad of planets with life. The number of chances is still unimaginably huge.[1]

Rule 29

---

1. For a contemporary presentation of this argument, see Donald Goldsmith and Tobias Owen, *The Search of Life in the Universe,* 3rd ed. (Sausalito, CA: University Science Books, 2002), Ch. 17.

Then again, why do some people have doubts? Find out. Some scientists point out that we really have no idea how common habitable planets might be, or how likely life is to develop on them. It's all guesswork.[2] Other critics argue that life elsewhere (or rather, intelligent life) by now should have announced itself, which (they say) hasn't happened.

All of these arguments carry some weight, and clearly much more must be said. You already see, then, that unexpected facts or perspectives may well turn up as you research and develop your argument. Be ready to be surprised. Be ready to hear evidence and arguments for positions you may not like. Be ready, even, to let yourself be swayed. True thinking is an open-ended process. The whole point is that you don't know when you start where you'll find yourself in the end.

Even if you have been assigned not just a topic but a position on that topic, you still need to look at arguments for a variety of other views—if only to be prepared to respond to them—and very likely you still have a lot of leeway about how to develop and defend the view you're given. On the most contentious issues, for example, you do not need to roll out the same arguments that everyone has heard a thousand times already. In fact, please don't! Look for creative new approaches. You could even try to find common ground with the other side. In short, take the time to choose your direction carefully, and aim to make some real progress on the issue, even (if you must) from within "given" positions.

Exercise Set 7.1: Identifying possible positions

Objective: To give you practice identifying a variety of positions on any topic.

Instructions: For each of the following questions, list at least three answers that you think are important enough to be worth considering.

Tips for success: When you are considering what position to take on an issue, it's often helpful to think about the issue in the form of a question. This both helps you focus on a specific aspect of the issue and identify a range of positions that you might consider. To take a position on an issue, after all, is just to adopt a specific answer to a question about that issue.

---

2. You can find a thorough and historical summary of many sides of this discussion in Steven J. Dick, *Life on Other Worlds: The 20th-Century Extraterrestrial Life Debate* (New York: Cambridge University Press, 1998), Chs. 3 and 6.

For instance, suppose you are considering the issue of global poverty. Exactly what question are you trying to answer about global poverty? Do you want to know what life is like for the global poor? Do you want to know how the current disparity between developed countries and developing countries came to be? Are you trying to figure out whether people in developed countries have a moral obligation to help the global poor, or what they (we) could do to help? Or are you trying to answer some other question about global poverty?

Once you have a specific question in mind, try to identify potential answers to that question. You don't have to include every possible answer, of course. Focus on the answers that are either plausible or popular: if you think there's a significant chance that some answer is correct, include it; if you know that many other people (or at least a few well-informed, thoughtful people) endorse a particular answer, include that one too. Even if you think that some popular answer is dead wrong, it's worth including here because you'll want to understand *why* people believe it. Besides, once you see the arguments for that answer, you may find it more plausible yourself.

Don't forget to include nuanced answers. Even if the question you're considering is phrased as a "yes or no" question, think about answers that start with "Yes, but . . .", "No, but . . .", "No, unless . . .", or similar qualifications. For instance, if you are considering whether to go to medical school, don't just list "Yes" and "No." Consider more nuanced answers, as well, such as "Yes, but only if I get a good financial aid package."

Sample

Should college students be required to learn a foreign language?

(1) Yes.

(2) No.

(3) No, except for students pursuing certain majors.

(4) Yes, but they need only learn to read and write the language, not necessarily speak it.

This response doesn't just list the simple answers of "Yes" and "No." It identifies some more nuanced possibilities. Of course, there are indefinitely many other answers you could give too. You might consider nuanced answers that begin with "Yes, except . . .", "Sometimes . . .", etc.

Notice that these answers do not contain reasons for the answers; they simply give a direct answer to the question. We will consider reasons for each answer later.

Some of the answers are a bit vague. For instance, answer (3) does not specify which majors should be required to learn a foreign language. When you're just starting to explore an issue, such vagueness is okay. You may not know which majors you want to include. As you do more research, you'll be able to refine your answers.

1. Should marijuana be legalized?

2. Should we increase taxes on the richest 1 percent of Americans to fund government programs to help middle-class households?

3. Should developers be allowed to destroy the habitats of endangered species in order to build new housing developments?

4. Should colleges require students to get regular exercise?

5. How should schools measure how well teachers are doing their job?

6. Is there life on other planets?

7. How should someone in his or her twenties save for retirement?

8. Is it wrong to download copyrighted media (e.g., music, movies, and television shows) without paying for it?

For exercises 9 and 10, pick questions (on any topic) to which you would like to know the answer and identify at least three answers to each question.

Model responses for odd-numbered exercises can be found on page 376.

Exercise Set 7.2: Exploring issues of your choice

Objective: To get you started thinking about possible issues for your own argumentative essay.

Instructions: Pick three specific questions that you need to ask or would like to ask about the topic you have picked or been assigned. Then, identify at least three answers to each question.

Tips for success: These exercises extend Exercise Set 7.1 to cover your assigned topic, if you have one, or a topic of your own choosing that is of particular interest to you. Later exercises will build on this set, culminating in an argumentative essay, so choose your questions carefully!

The questions you choose should be neither too narrow nor too broad. If your questions are too narrow, they will be too easy to answer. That won't make for a very interesting argumentative essay. (Only specialists want to read five pages about when the War of 1812 began.) If your questions are too broad, they will be too difficult to answer. That won't make for a very convincing argumentative essay.

Above all, be sure to pick questions that are interesting enough that you want to spend a lot of time thinking about them!

See the Model Responses for Exercise Set 7.1 for models of good responses to these exercises.

Need more practice? Find the opinion section in your favorite newspaper and look for editorials or op-eds on topics that interest you. Figure out exactly what issue the editorial or op-ed is addressing and what position it takes on that issue. Identify at least two other positions on that issue that are worth considering.

Spell out basic ideas as arguments

Now remember that you are constructing *arguments*: that is, specific conclusions backed by evidence and reasons. As you begin to formulate a position, then, take its basic idea and frame it as an argument. Get out a large sheet of scratch paper and literally draft your premises and conclusion in outline.

Aim first for a relatively short argument—say, three to five premises—using the forms offered in this book. The basic argument just introduced in Rule 29 for life on other planets, for example, might be put into premises-and-conclusion form in this way:

> Other planets and solar systems are being discovered beyond our own.

> If there are other solar systems beyond our own, then it is very probable that there are other planets like Earth.

> If there are other planets like Earth, then it is very probable that some of them have life.

> Therefore, it is very probable that there is life on some other planets.

For practice, work this argument out as a deductive argument using *modus ponens* and hypothetical syllogism.

For a second example, consider a quite different topic. Some people have recently proposed a major expansion of student exchange programs. Many more young Americans should have the chance to go abroad, they say, and many more young people from other parts of the world should have the chance to come here. It would cost money, of course, and would take some adjustment all around, but a more cooperative and peaceful world might result.

Suppose you want to develop and defend this proposal. First, again, sketch out the main argument for it—the basic idea. Why would people propose (and be so passionate about) expanding student exchange programs?

FIRST TRY:

Students who travel abroad learn to appreciate different countries.

More appreciation between different countries would be good.

Therefore, we should send more students abroad.

This outline does capture a basic idea, but in truth it is a little *too* basic. It hardly says enough to be much more than a simple assertion. Why, for example, would more appreciation between different countries be good? And how does sending students abroad produce it? Even a basic argument can be worked out a little further.

BETTER:

Students who travel abroad learn to appreciate other countries.

Students who travel abroad become person-to-person ambassadors who help their hosts appreciate the students' home countries.

More appreciation both ways will help us better coexist and cooperate in our interdependent world.

Therefore, we should send more students abroad.

You may have to try several different conclusions—even quite varied conclusions—before you find your best basic argument on a topic. Even after you have settled on the conclusion you want to defend, you may have to try several forms of argument before you find a form that really works well. (We are serious about that *large* sheet of scratch paper!) Again, use the rules in the earlier chapters of this book. Take your time—and give yourself time to take.

Exercise Set 7.3: Sketching arguments for and against positions

Objective: To give you practice formulating basic arguments for and against a position.

Instructions: For each of the following positions, construct one basic argument *for* the position and one basic argument *against* the position.

Tips for success: An argument for a particular position is just an argument that has the position itself as the conclusion of the argument. You can construct a basic argument for a position by providing some basic reasons that someone might give to support that position. If you are unsure about the appropriate level of detail, use the examples just presented in the discussion of Rule 30 as a guide.

Remember that it is usually possible to find *some* arguments in favor of a position, even if you think the position is clearly false. Thus, by constructing arguments for a position, you are not committing yourself to thinking that the position is true. There might be more powerful arguments on the other side. This is why it's important to look at arguments both for and against each position.

In constructing arguments against each position, use the *denial* of that position as the conclusion of your argument. Though it's not necessarily the most stylish way, you can express the denial of any claim by adding "It's false that" to the front of it. So, if you were developing an argument against the position that judges should be forced to retire at age seventy, the conclusion of your argument could be put as: "It's false that judges should be forced to retire at age seventy." (Logicians often call the denial of a claim its *negation*.)

Sample

College students should be required to learn to read and write a foreign language, but not necessarily speak it.

An argument for the position:

(1) Being able to communicate with people in other countries is increasingly important for participating in exciting career and personal opportunities.

(2) Most communication with people in other countries occurs in writing.

Therefore, (3) College students should be required to learn to read and write a foreign language but not necessarily speak it.

An argument against the position:

(1) Traveling or living in a very foreign country is a valuable, mind-opening experience.

(2) Colleges should equip students to have such valuable experiences.

(3) To travel or live in a very foreign country, you need to be able to speak the language.

Therefore, (4) College students should be required to learn to read, write, and speak a foreign language.

Therefore, (5) It's false that college students should be required to learn to read and write a foreign language but not necessarily speak it.

These arguments contain only the basic premises needed to argue for or against the position. There's still a lot to be said about each premise, including why anyone should think that the premises are true. There are also objections to be considered. As it is, though, the first argument conveys a reason for thinking that students should be required to learn to read and write but not necessarily speak a foreign language. The second argument conveys a reason for thinking that this position is false.

Remember that when you are dealing with nuanced answers like this one, there are often many ways to argue against the answer. For instance, you could argue that students shouldn't be required to learn a foreign language at all, that they shouldn't be required to learn to read and write a foreign language, or that they should be required to do more than just read and write—as the second sample argument does.

1. National service ought to be required of every American eighteen-year-old.

2. Everyone should contribute the same proportion of their income in taxes—that is, pay a "flat tax" on their income.

3. The extinction of an endangered species is a serious problem.

4. The Founding Fathers considered the United States a Christian country.

5. Autism is becoming more common.

6. Genetically modified animals, such as GMO salmon, should not be sold as food for humans.

7. Alcohol is more dangerous than marijuana.

8. If public school teachers should be encouraged to be critical of scientific theories such as evolution, then they should be encouraged to be critical of religious doctrines as well.

9. All college students should be required to take at least one course in _____. [Fill in the blank with a subject of your choice.]

10. The health care system in _____ serves most of that country's citizens well. [Fill in the blank with the country of your choice.]

Model responses for odd-numbered exercises can be found on page 378.

Exercise Set 7.4: Sketching arguments about your own topic

Objective: To help you construct or discover arguments about the topic of your own argumentative essay.

Instructions: Complete Exercise Set 7.2 before beginning this one. Pick one of the three questions that you wrote down for Exercise Set 7.2. For each answer to that question that you wrote down for Exercise Set 7.2, construct two basic arguments *for* that answer and two basic arguments *against* that answer.

Tips for success: Pick the question from Exercise Set 7.2 about which you would most like to write an argumentative essay. You should have identified at least three distinct answers to that question. Your job now is to find or come up with two arguments for each of those answers and two arguments against each of those answers, much as you did in Exercise Set 7.3. You will end up with twelve arguments—four arguments concerning each of the three answers that you wrote down for Exercise Set 7.2. See Model Responses for Exercise Set 7.3 for further models of good responses.

Need more practice? Find the results of some recent opinion polls by searching for "opinion polls" on the Internet. Each poll will report several different positions that respondents adopted. Identify or come up with one argument for each position reported in the polls. For instance, suppose that pollsters asked people which city should host the summer Olympics. The poll might report the top five choices. In that case, you could give an argument for holding the Olympics in each of those five cities.

Rule 31

Defend basic premises with arguments of their own

Once you have spelled out your basic idea as an argument, it will need defense and development. For anyone who disagrees—in fact, for anyone who doesn't know much about the question in the first place—most of the basic premises will need supporting arguments of their own. Each premise therefore becomes the conclusion of a further argument that you need to work out.

Look back, for example, at the argument about life on other planets. The argument begins with the premise that solar systems are already being discovered beyond our solar system. This you can show by citing the scientific literature and news reports.

> As of 8 August 2011, the Paris Observatory's "Extrasolar Planet Encyclopaedia" (http://exoplanet.eu/) lists 573 known planets of other stars, including over fifty in multi-planet systems. And the number is constantly rising![3]

> Therefore, other solar systems are being discovered beyond our own.

The second premise of the basic argument for life on other planets is that *if* there are other solar systems beyond our own, then it is very probable that some of them include planets like Earth. Well, how do we know this? What's the supporting argument? Here you probably need to draw on factual knowledge and/or research. If you've paid attention to those same news reports, you have some good reasons to offer. The usual argument is an analogy:

> Our own solar system has a variety of kinds of planets, from gas giants to smaller rocky and watery planets suitable for life.

> As far as we know, other solar systems will be *like* ours.

> Therefore, it is very probable that other solar systems also contain a variety of planets, including some suitable for life.

Continue in this way for all the premises of your basic argument. Once again, it may take some work to find appropriate evidence for each premise that needs defense, and you may even find yourself changing some premises, and therefore the basic argument itself, so that they can be adequately supported by the kinds of evidence you end up finding. This is as it should be! Good arguments are usually in "flow," and each part depends on the others. It's a learning experience.

You'd need to approach the basic argument for student exchange programs in the same way. Why do you think, for instance—and how will you persuade others—that students who go abroad learn to appreciate other cultures? Examples would help; maybe the results of surveys or studies you can find through research or consulting the experts (people who actually run student exchange programs, or social scientists). Again, in some way or other, you need to fill in the argument. The same goes for the second basic

---

3. As of January 21, 2015, this number has risen to nearly 2,000 planets, including nearly 500 multi-planet systems!

premise: how do we know that students abroad really do become "person-to-person ambassadors"?

The third basic premise (the value of mutual appreciation) may be more obvious, and in some quick arguments you could reasonably leave it undeveloped. (A point to remember: not *every* premise of your basic argument necessarily needs development and defense.) However, it is also a fine occasion to make the force of the argument—the expected benefits—more vivid. Maybe this way:

> Appreciation leads us to see virtues in others' ways, and to expect virtues even when we don't see them yet.

> Appreciation is also a form of enjoyment: it enriches our own experience.

> When we see or expect virtues in others' ways, and find that they enrich our own experience, we are less tempted to make harsh or single-minded judgments about them, and we can work with them more readily.

> Therefore, mutual appreciation will help us better coexist and cooperate in our interdependent world.

Add some concrete examples to fill out these premises in turn, and you'll have yourself a fine argument overall.

Exercise Set 7.5: Developing arguments in more detail

Objective: To give you practice developing basic arguments.

Instructions: Identify one premise in each of the following arguments that is controversial but defensible—that is, a premise that might be reasonably doubted but for which a good argument could be given. Construct an argument for that premise.

Tips for success: "Developing" an argument involves doing three things. First, it involves stating any assumptions that you have left unsaid. Second, it involves explaining any premises that your audience might not understand. Third, it involves defending, or giving arguments for, any premises that might be considered controversial. This exercise focuses on the third aspect of developing an argument.

To develop the arguments below, begin by deciding which premise you want to defend. (It will be easier to do that if you rewrite the argument in premise-and-conclusion form first.) On the one hand, you should pick a premise that is at least somewhat controversial. There's no point in defending a premise that everybody already accepts. On the other hand, you should pick a premise that is defensible. If there are no good arguments for a premise, then you can't defend it!

Once you have chosen a premise to defend, construct a simple argument that has that premise as its conclusion, much as you did in Exercise Set 7.3. You may find it helpful to think about what kind of argument would best support the premise that you have decided to defend. Is the premise a generalization? Then give an argument that follows the rules from Chapter II. Can you think of an analogy that you could use to support the premise? If so, construct an argument by analogy using the techniques you learned in Chapter III. Is the premise the kind of thing that you could support by finding appropriate sources? Look to Chapter IV. Is the premise about a causal relationship? Follow the rules in Chapter V to construct a good causal argument. If you can think of a deductive argument to support the conclusion, be sure that it follows one of the rules from Chapter VI.

Ideally, of course, developing an argument involves defending *every* controversial premise. For the purposes of this exercise, however, you only need to choose one.

Sample

This response offers an argument for the second premise of the second sample argument in Exercise Set 7.3, which is that "Colleges should equip students to have valuable experiences, such as traveling or living in a foreign country." (Go back to p. 166 to check out the whole argument.)

(1) One major purpose of college is to prepare students to live richer, more interesting lives.

(2) Equipping students to have valuable experiences that they could not otherwise have is one way for colleges to prepare students to live richer, more interesting lives. Therefore, (3) Colleges should equip students to have valuable experiences, such as traveling or living in a foreign country.

The premises in this response would benefit from further defense in turn. For instance, why should we think that preparing students to live richer, more interesting lives is a "major purpose" of college? By asking questions like these, you can develop an argument even further. Ideally, as Rule 3 points out, you would stop only when you reach premises that everyone in your audience finds reliable.

When you're developing an argument, it's worthwhile to think about why someone would disagree with the argument's premises and/or its conclusion. See if you can anticipate and address some of those concerns in the way that you support the premises in the argument you're developing.

1. Concussions are common in many high-impact sports, such as football and hockey. Concussions—especially repeated concussions—are also very dangerous. By encouraging their kids to play high-impact sports, parents are putting their kids at serious risk. Parents ought not to put their kids at serous risk. Therefore, parents ought not to encourage their kids to play high-impact sports.

    Adapted from: Joshua Shepherd, "Is It Morally Permissible for Parents to Encourage Their Children to Play High-Impact Sports?" Practical Ethics, Dec 12, 2013, http://blog.practicalethics.ox.ac.uk/2013/12/is-it-morally-permissible-for-parents-to-encourage-their-children-to-play-high-impact-sports/

2. Most Americans support capital punishment. Politicians are unlikely to ban a practice that most of their constituents support. Therefore, American politicians are unlikely to ban capital punishment.

    Adapted from: Rabah Ghezali, "When Capital Punishment Is a Crime: The Atlantic Divide Over the Death Penalty," The Huffington Post, Oct 18, 2010, http://www.huffingtonpost.com/rabah-ghezali/when-capital-punishment-i_b_765638.html

3. It is cruel to force pigs to live on factory farms. It is wrong to be cruel. Therefore, it is wrong to force pigs to live on factory farms.

    Adapted from: Natalie Angier, "Pigs Prove to Be Smart, if Not Vain," New York Times, Nov 9, 2009, http://www.nytimes.com/2009/11/10/science/10angier.html

4. Our financial success is not always under our control. That's why defining success in terms of money is risky. We do control whether we try to make a positive difference in the world. And trying to make a positive difference is something we can be proud of. That's why it's better to define success in terms of trying to make a positive difference in the world rather than in terms of money.

    Adapted from: Peter Buffett, "How Should College Graduates Define Success?" USA Today, May 25, 2011, http://usatoday30.usatoday.com/news/opinion/forum/2011-05-25-Defining-success-for-college-grads_n.htm

5.   If there is no government, then people will constantly be afraid of everyone else. If people are constantly afraid of everyone else, then there will be no industry or business. Thus, if there is no government, then there will be no industry or business.

> *Adapted from: Thomas Hobbes,* Leviathan, *ed. Edwin Curley (Indianapolis: Hackett Publishing Company, 1994), 76*

6.   Either God exists or he doesn't. If God exists, then it is in your interest to believe in God. If God does not exist, then you do not lose anything significant by believing in God. Therefore, either it is in your interest to believe in God or you do not lose anything significant by believing in God.

> *Adapted from: Blaise Pascal,* Pensées, *tr. Roger Ariew (Indianapolis: Hackett Publishing Company, 2005), 212–13*

7.   Doctors have a responsibility to report parents who are seriously harming their children. A pregnant woman who uses cocaine or other hard drugs during the third trimester of pregnancy is seriously harming a child. Therefore, doctors have a responsibility to report women who use hard drugs during the third trimester of pregnancy.

> *Adapted from: Mark Helm, "Justices Debate Drug Testing for Pregnant Women,"* Pittsburgh Post-Gazette, *Oct 5, 2000*

8.   Carbon dioxide emissions from the burning of fossil fuels have caused a dramatic increase in the amount of carbon dioxide in Earth's atmosphere. Some of this carbon dioxide is absorbed by the oceans. This increases the acidity of the ocean water. This "ocean acidification," in turn, causes problems for plankton. Since plankton are essential parts of the marine ecosystem, the burning of fossil fuels is damaging the marine ecosystem.

> *Adapted from: Brian Dawson and Matt Spannagle,* The Complete Guide to Climate Change *(Abingdon, UK: Routledge, 2009), 258–59*

9.   Imagine that a mad scientist has developed a way to remove people's brains from their bodies, keep them alive in a vat of nutrients, and stimulate the brain to mimic any experience that the scientist chooses. For instance, the scientist could mimic the

experience of reading a good book about arguments [this one for example!]. If you were such a brain-in-a-vat, you would not be able to tell that you were a brain-in-a-vat; you would think that you were a "normal" person having normal experiences. Thus, you cannot use your current experiences to rule out the possibility that you are a brain-in-a-vat. But you have no other way to rule out the possibility that you are a brain-in-a-vat. If you have no way to rule out the possibility that you are a brain-in-a vat, then you cannot know that you *aren't* a brain-in-a-vat. Therefore, you cannot know that you aren't a brain-in-a-vat.

Adapted from: Anthony Brueckner, "Skepticism and Closure," in Companion to Epistemology, edited by Jonathan Dancy, Ernest Sosa, and Matthias Steup (Oxford: Oxford University Press, 2010), 14–15

10.   College students don't like writing papers for required courses. Professors teaching those courses don't like grading the enormous stacks of mostly uninspired essays that students turn in. Furthermore, those classes are too large for professors to give students the help they need to become better writers. If students aren't interested in writing a paper and doing it isn't going to help them become better writers, then there's no good reason to ask students to write that paper. Therefore, professors should stop assigning papers in required college courses.

Adapted from: Rebecca Schuman, "The End of the College Essay," Slate, Dec 13, 2013, http://www.slate.com/articles/life/education/2013/12/college_papers_students_hate_writing_them_professors_hate_grading_them_let.html

Model responses for odd-numbered exercises can be found on page 381.

Exercise Set 7.6: Developing your own arguments

Objective: To help you develop your own arguments for your own argumentative essay.

Instructions: Complete Exercise Set 7.4 before beginning this one. Develop each of your arguments from Exercise Set 7.4 by working out an argument for every controversial premise in each of those arguments.

Tips for success: The first step to completing this exercise set is to identify the controversial premises in each of your arguments from Exercise Set 7.4. If you haven't completed Exercise Set 7.5, read the "Tips for success" section of that exercise for advice on identifying controversial premises.

Once you've identified the controversial premises, try to find or write good arguments for each of those premises, much as in Exercise Set 7.5. In some cases, you will find that there is no good argument for a premise. You might even discover that the premise is false. In that case, you have learned something valuable: The argument in which that premise appears will need to be revised or abandoned.

See the Model Responses for Exercise Set 7.5 for models of good responses. One big difference between this exercise set and Exercise Set 7.5, however, is that this exercise set asks you to defend *every* controversial premise in your arguments, not just one. Another big difference, of course, is that this time the argument is your own.

Need more practice? If you want still more practice, look for controversial premises in the arguments presented throughout this book. Construct arguments for any controversial premise that you find. (This will keep you busy for a while!)

Consider objections

Too often when we make arguments we concern ourselves only with the *pro* side: what can be said in support. Objections tend to come as a shock. We realize, maybe a little late, that we didn't think enough about possible problems. It's better to do it yourself, and hone your argument—maybe even make fundamental changes—in advance. In this way you will also make it clear to your eventual audience that you have done your homework, that you have explored the issue thoroughly and (hopefully!) with a somewhat open mind. So consider: what are the best arguments *against* the conclusion you are working on?

Most actions have *many* effects, not just one. Maybe some of the other effects—ones you haven't looked at yet—are less desirable. Thoughtful and well-meaning people may oppose even such obviously good ideas ("obvious" to us, anyway) as taking ourselves in for regular checkups or getting married in order to be happy or sending more students abroad. Try to anticipate and honestly consider their concerns.

Rule 32

Students abroad, for example, may also end up in dangerous situations, and bringing large numbers of new foreign students here might raise national security risks. And all of it might cost a lot of money. These are important objections. On the other hand, perhaps they can also be answered. Maybe you'll argue that the costs are worth it, for example, in part because there are also costs of *not* reaching out to other cultures. After all, we are already sending large numbers of young people—in the military—into extreme danger abroad. You could argue that giving ourselves another and different face abroad might be a very good investment.

Other objections may lead you to rethink your proposal or argument. In this case, for example, worries about national security might require us to be careful about who is invited to come here. Clearly they need to come—how else are we going to correct false impressions?—but (you could argue) it may be fair to impose certain restrictions too.

Maybe you are making some general or philosophical claim: that humans have (or don't have) free will, say, or that war is (or isn't) inherent in human nature, or that there is (or isn't) life on other planets. Here too, anticipate objections. If you are writing an academic paper, look for criticisms of your claim or interpretation in the class readings or in secondary texts or (good) online sources. Talk to people who have different views. Sift through the concerns and objections that come up, pick the strongest and most common ones, and try to answer them. And don't forget to re-evaluate your own argument. Do your premises or conclusion need to be changed or developed to take account of the objections?

Exercise Set 7.7: Working out objections

Objective: To give you practice working out objections to arguments.

Instructions: Go back to the arguments listed in Exercise Set 7.5. Work out one objection to each argument.

Tips for success: Two kinds of objection are possible to any argument. One kind of objection seeks to prove that the conclusion of the argument is false. Another kind of objection seeks to prove only that the argument is flawed, without necessarily proving that the conclusion of the argument is false.

Consider a lawyer who is defending someone accused of murder. The prosecution will, of course, present arguments designed to show that the defendant committed the murder. The defense could counter this argument in two ways, corresponding to the two kinds of objections. The defense could attempt to prove that the defendant did not commit the murder. (Maybe there's a solid argument that the defendant was out of the country at the time of the murder.) Alternatively, the defense could simply try to prove that the prosecution's argument is inconclusive—that the prosecution has not presented a strong enough case to convince the jury that the defendant is guilty. (Maybe the prosecution's argument relies on unreliable witnesses.)

There are several common strategies for showing that a particular argument doesn't work. First, you can argue that one or more of the premises is false or unreliable. Second, you can argue that the argument has a flaw in its logic. (One great way to do that is to explain how the argument violates one of the rules in this book.) Third, you can argue that while the argument gives *some* reason to accept the conclusion, it does not give *enough* reason. If you take this third approach, though, be prepared to say what more you would need. Would confirmation from additional sources do the trick? More or better examples? Does the argument overlook alternatives that need to be ruled out? The more specific you can be about what the argument lacks, the better.

Sample

This objection raises a specific objection to premise 3 of the "yes" argument we developed as a sample for Exercise Set 7.3, which is that "To travel or live in a very foreign country, you need to be able to speak the language." (Go back to p. 166 to check out the whole argument.)

Many foreigners already speak English. And rapidly improving smartphone apps enable people to interact with one another even if they don't speak a common language. Therefore, English speakers don't need to speak a foreign language to travel in a foreign country.

If this objection holds up, then it may not be true that to travel or live in a very foreign country, you need to be able to speak the language, and the argument sketched in Exercise Set 7.3 fails as a whole.

Notice that this objection is an argument in its own right. You could make this objection more convincing by developing it in more detail, just as you developed your arguments in Exercise Set 7.3. For instance, it would be helpful to find a good source to back up the claim that many foreigners can already speak English.

Model responses for odd-numbered exercises can be found on page 384.

Exercise Set 7.8: Working out objections to your own arguments

Objective: To help you identify objections to the arguments about the topic of your own argumentative essay.

Instructions: Complete Exercise Set 7.6 before beginning this one. Work out one objection to each of the arguments that you developed in Exercise Set 7.6.

Tips for success: If you haven't completed Exercise Set 7.7, review the "Tips for success" section for that exercise. All of that advice applies here, too.

In addition to objections that point out genuine weaknesses and flaws in your arguments, consider objections that are popular but, in your view, misguided. For instance, if you are arguing that high school teachers should be paid higher salaries, you might consider the objection that teachers are overpaid because they only work during school hours. This popular objection is misguided because schoolteachers spend considerable time after school preparing lesson plans, grading students' homework, etc. Many people reading or listening to your argument will raise such objections. It's important to be prepared to respond to them.

See the Model Responses for Exercise Set 7.7 for further models of good responses.

Need more practice? For a particularly challenging form of practice, make a list of some of your strong convictions, for example on moral or political questions, along with a brief argument for each of those convictions. Can you come up with objections to those arguments?

Consider alternatives

If you are defending a proposal, it is not enough to show that your proposal will solve a problem. You must also show that it is better than other plausible ways of solving that same problem.

> Durham's swimming pools are overcrowded, especially on weekends. Therefore, Durham needs to build more pools.

This argument is weak in several ways. "Overcrowded" is vague, for one thing: who decides when there are too many people in a pool? But remedying this weakness still will not justify the conclusion. There may be other and more reasonable ways to address the (possible) problem. Maybe the existing pools could have more open-swim hours so that swimmers can spread themselves over more available times. Maybe the typically lighter-use times could be more widely publicized. Maybe swim meets and other closed-pool activities could be moved to the weekdays. Or maybe Durham should do nothing at all and let users adjust their swim schedules for themselves. If you still want to argue that Durham should build more pools, you must show that your proposal is better than any of these (far less expensive) alternatives.

Considering alternatives is not just a formality. The point is not just to quickly survey a few boringly obvious, easily-countered alternatives and then (big surprise!) to re-embrace your original proposal. Look for serious alternatives, and get creative. You might even come up with something quite new. How about . . . maybe keeping the pools open around the clock? How about putting in an evening smoothie bar or the like and enticing some of the day swimmers to come at odd hours instead?

If you come up with something really good, you might even need to change your conclusion. Are there possibly much better ways to organize foreign exchange programs, for instance? Maybe we should extend such opportunities to all sorts of people, not just students. How about exchange programs for *elders*? Why not for families, congregations, work groups? Then it's not just about "sending students abroad" anymore . . . so it's back to your scratch paper to recast the basic argument. This is how real thinking works.

Even general or philosophical claims have alternatives. Some people argue, for instance, that there are not likely to be other civilizations elsewhere in the universe, because if there were, we'd surely have heard from them by now. But is the premise true? Aren't there other possibilities? Maybe they *are* out there but are just listening. Maybe they choose to keep still, or just aren't interested, or are "civilized" in some other direction and do not have the technology. Maybe they are trying to communicate but

not in the ways we are listening for. It's a very speculative question, but the existence of alternative possibilities like these does weaken the objection.

Many scientists also think, by the way, that life could arise on planets very different from Earth—it would just be a very different form of life. This is an alternative possibility too, and also difficult to judge, but one that you could use to support and even extend the basic argument. Suppose life could be even more widespread than the basic argument suggests?

Exercise Set 7.9: Brainstorming alternatives

Objective: To give you practice brainstorming alternative solutions to problems.

Instructions: Each problem in this exercise identifies a proposal designed to solve a specific problem. Suggest two plausible alternative ways to solve the problem. Then, state which of the three proposals is best and briefly explain why.

Tips for success: It's easy to come up with alternatives by making small changes to existing proposals, but you're more likely to hit upon an innovative idea if you look for genuinely different alternatives. If your friends suggested getting pizza at Gino's, don't just propose pizza at Giordano's as an alternative. You might also consider a totally different type of food, such as falafel and hummus, Mongolian stir-fry, or Kenyan peanut soup; cooking dinner at home with your friends instead of going out to eat at all; or fasting (that is, not eating at all) and donating the food you'd otherwise have eaten, or the money you'd otherwise have spent, to a soup kitchen.

One way to generate more interesting alternatives is to imagine a perfect solution to a problem and work backward to something practical. Are leftover fast-food wrappers a problem? What if they were edible, so that you could eat them for dessert? (Ice cream cones are, in a sense, edible wrappers for ice cream.) Even if edible wrappers aren't on the menu in the near future, approaching the problem in this way might open your mind to genuine alternatives, as opposed to more trash cans or bigger fines for littering.

Another way to find creative ideas is to consider how the problem has been addressed or viewed in other places or at different times. For example, if traffic is a problem in your community, do some research to find out how other communities have approached the problem or how they avoided the problem altogether. Building more and bigger roads isn't the only solution.

Finally, consider some ways of reframing the problem. Try thinking about the problem as a symptom of a deeper problem. If Americans are overweight, should we frame the problem in terms of Americans' unhealthy diet choices? Or is the problem that junk food is cheaper than healthier alternatives? The first way of framing the problem suggests that a public health campaign might help. The second way suggests that subsidizing fresh fruits and vegetables might help more. Alternatively, try thinking of a problem as an opportunity. The summer sun heats rooftops, requiring building owners to spend more money on air conditioning. Instead of seeing that heat as a problem, maybe we can see it as a resource. If the building's owners use the heat from the roof to heat water, they save money on air conditioners and water heaters. Problems are only problems from a certain point of view. Try switching perspectives!

Sample

All college students should be required to study abroad in a non-English-speaking country in order to learn a foreign language.

Alternative 1: All college students should be required to pass an intermediate foreign language course.

Alternative 2: All college students should be required to download a translation app for their phone.

Alternative 1 is the best proposal for learning a foreign language. While it may not be 100 percent effective—since it's possible to pass an intermediate language course without truly mastering the language—it has distinct advantages over the other proposals. Alternative 1 is better than the original proposal because it is less burdensome. While studying abroad might be a valuable experience, not everyone is able to do so. For instance, students with children or spouses may not be able to spend time abroad. Besides, some people might prefer to study abroad in an English-speaking country. Alternative 1 is better than Alternative 2 because Alternative 2 doesn't actually accomplish what it's supposed to accomplish. Just because you have a translation app doesn't mean that you've learned a language. In fact, it doesn't mean that you've learned anything about the language! Furthermore, it would be awkward and maybe insulting to try to interact with someone in a foreign language through your electronic translator. And anyway, not everyone has a smartphone, so this alternative would be unfair to some people.

Notice first that both alternatives are presented as ways to ensure that students master a foreign language, but while Alternative 2 is creative and may seem tempting, one big problem with it is that it doesn't actually achieve the stated goal. (That's not always a problem. Reframing a problem may lead you to pursue a different goal. Alternative 2 has other problems, as noted above.) Alternative 1 and the original proposal are both reasonably effective means of achieving the goal. In deciding between them, you'll need to balance effectiveness with cost. The original proposal is more effective but more costly—in terms of time, money, potential strains on one's family and friends, missed opportunities elsewhere, etc.

It's also worth noticing that you could create new alternatives by combining these proposals. For instance, a college could require students to pass an exam, study abroad in a non-English-speaking country, or pass an intermediate foreign language class in order to demonstrate mastery of a foreign language. Combining proposals is a great way to come up with new alternatives.

1.   To discourage texting while driving, states should pass laws completely prohibiting the use of any handheld electronic device while driving.

Adapted from: Nancy Bean Foster, "Police: Texting While Driving Tough to Prove," New Hampshire Union Leader, Jan 14, 2014, http://www.unionleader.com/article/20140115/NEWS07/140119601

2.   Handguns should be banned in order to decrease the number of crimes committed with handguns.

Adapted from: Royson James, "Petition Worthy of Our Names," Toronto Star, Apr 8, 2008, http://www.thestar.com/article/411252

3.   Space exploration should be carried out by private companies in order to expand the number and scope of missions to space.

Adapted from: "Space: Roles Exist for Both Public, Private Sectors," Editorial, Sioux City Journal, Oct 14, 2009, http://www.siouxcityjournal.com/news/opinion/editorial/article_2ad01fe6-92fe-5406-a3cc-15c9719f45d7.html

4.   The U.S. government should encourage more nuclear power plants in order to reduce America's dependence on foreign oil.

> *Adapted from: Heritage Foundation, "Meeting America's Energy and Environmental Needs," Aug 17, 2010, http://www.heritage.org/research/ reports/2010/08/meeting-america-s-energy-and-environmental-needs*

5.   Newspapers should charge readers to access articles online in order to generate enough money to pay for quality news reporting.

> *Adapted from: James Rainey, "On the Media: 'Old Media's' Dilemma of Charging for Online Content," Los Angeles Times, Nov 6, 2010, http://articles.latimes.com/ 2010/nov/06/entertainment/la-et-onthemedia-20101106*

6.   Universities should pay upperclassmen to tutor freshmen in difficult classes in order to help students make it through their first year of college.

> *Adapted from: Miranda Sain, "Georgia State Strives to Improve Graduation Rates and Help Student Keep HOPE," The Signal (Georgia State University), Jun 8, 2010, http://www.gsusignal.com/news/georgia-state-strives-to-improve-graduation -rates-and-help-student-keep-hope-1.2273024*

7.   Governments should tax unhealthy products, such as fast food and sugary soft drinks, in order to encourage people to make healthier choices.

> *Adapted from: Derrick Z. Jackson, "Soda Tax: It's the Real Thing," Boston Globe, Sep 19, 2009, http://www.boston.com/bostonglobe/editorial_opinion/ oped/articles/2009/09/19/soda_tax_its_the_real_thing/*

8.   Governments should decriminalize prostitution in order to protect sex workers from sexually transmitted diseases.

> *Adapted from: Jeffrey D. Klausner, "Decriminalize Prostitution—Vote Yes on Prop K," San Francisco Chronicle, Sep 8, 2008, http://articles.sfgate.com/ 2008-09-08/opinion/17156632_1_prostitution-decriminalization -san-francisco-task-force*

9.   High schools should require students to wear uniforms in order to improve discipline in schools.

> *Adapted from: Tracy Gordon Fox, "In Hartford Schools, Uniforms for All," New York Times, Oct 3, 2008, http://www.nytimes.com/2008/10/05/ nyregion/connecticut/05uniformct.html*

10. In order to deter locally elected prosecutors from seeking unreasonably harsh prison sentences, each county should have to pay the costs of imprisoning the people that it sends to jail.

Adapted from: Leon Neyfakh, "How to Stop Overzealous Prosecutors," Slate, Feb 25, 2015, http://www.slate.com/articles/news_and_politics/crime/2015/02/overzealous_ prosecutors_hold_them_accountable_by_defunding_state_prisons.html

---

Model responses for odd-numbered exercises can be found on page 385.

Exercise Set 7.10: Considering alternatives to your own conclusions

Objective: To help you identify possible alternatives to the conclusions that you have considered so far for your own argumentative essay.

Instructions: Complete Exercise Sets 7.2, 7.4, 7.6, and 7.8 before beginning this one. In light of what you have learned from Exercise Sets 7.4, 7.6, and 7.8, identify at least three alternative answers to your chosen question from Exercise Set 7.2. Then, state which answer you currently find most plausible and explain why.

Tips for success: If you haven't completed Exercise Set 7.9, review the "Tips for success" section for that exercise. All of that advice applies here too.

In Exercise Sets 7.4, 7.6, and 7.8, you have devised and developed arguments about answers to a specific question from Exercise Set 7.2. For this exercise set, you are asked to identify three alternative answers to that same question. These alternatives could be slight modifications of the original answers, or they could be entirely different answers that you discovered in the course of your research for the other exercise sets.

The purpose of devising alternatives at this stage of the process is that you now know a lot more about your topic than you did when you began. You might be able to recognize better, more nuanced, or more creative answers than you could initially. You might also be able to see problems with your original answers, which can be avoided or overcome by choosing slightly different answers.

See the sample response and the Model Responses for Exercise Set 7.9 for models of good responses.

Need more practice? Find out about recent laws enacted by your local or state government. Identify the problems that those laws were designed to address and then identify alternatives that lawmakers might have considered instead. Alternatively, working on your own or with a classmate, brainstorm a list of problems at your school, in your town, etc., and then identify several options for addressing each of those problems.

Critical thinking activity: Compiling your research into an extended outline

For an activity that gives you practice putting all of your work together to create an extended argument, see the "Compiling your research into an extended outline" assignment sheet (p. 470) in Part 3. This is part of a series of activities that builds up to writing and presenting an argumentative essay.

Chapter VIII
Argumentative Essays

Suppose now that you have explored your issue, outlined a basic argument and defended its premises. You are ready to go public—maybe by writing an argumentative essay.

Remember that actually writing an argumentative essay is the *last* stage! If you have just picked up this book and opened it to this chapter, reflect: there is a reason that this is the last chapter and not the first. As the proverbial country Irishman said when a tourist asked him how to get to Dublin: if you want to get to Dublin, don't start here.

Remember too that the rules in Chapters I–VI apply to writing an essay as well as to writing short arguments. Review the rules in Chapter I in particular. Be concrete and concise, build on substance and not overtone, and so forth. What follow are some additional rules specific to writing argumentative essays.

Rule 34

Jump right in

Launch straight into the real work. No windy windups or rhetorical padding.

NO:
For centuries philosophers have debated the best way to be happy . . .

We knew that already. Get to *your* point.

YES:
In this essay I will try to show that the best things in life really *are* free.

Exercise Set 8.1: Writing good leads

Objective: To give you practice writing good *leads* for argumentative essays.

Instructions: Each question in this exercise set provides a summary of an argumentative essay. Write one to three sentences that you could use to begin each essay.

Tips for success: Journalists excel at writing good opening sentences. In journalism, the beginning of a news story is called the *lead* (sometimes spelled "lede"). The lead is a journalist's chance to get readers interested in his or her article. The same is true for the first few sentences of your argumentative essays, and you should take as much care in crafting those first sentences as journalists do in crafting theirs.

Journalists distinguish between *hard* and *soft* leads. A hard lead communicates the main point of the story in one short sentence. A soft lead uses an indirect approach to catch the reader's interest; if an article opens with a soft lead, the main point of the article may not appear for a few sentences.

You can adapt this journalistic approach to writing your own essays. Especially when you're writing an essay that's only a few pages long, start with a hard lead—a strong sentence that communicates the main topic or main point of the essay. If you have more space, you can start with a soft lead, such as an anecdote about a recent event, a description of an imaginary example, or an interesting fact that illustrates or relates to the main point of the paper.

For the purposes of this exercise, you can write a hard lead or a soft lead for each question. If you take the direct, hard lead approach, write one sentence that states the main point of the essay. If you take the indirect, soft lead approach, write a two- to three-sentence anecdote or story that illustrates the main topic or point of the paper in an interesting way. Since this is a written presentation of your ideas, however, even a soft lead should be presented more formally than if you were relating a story to your friends.

You might find it helpful to browse through your favorite news source to see how its writers start their articles. If you are writing an essay in a particular discipline, such as history or philosophy, looking at essays or book chapters by professionals in that discipline can help give you ideas too.

Sample

The U.S. Congress passed a new rule allowing members to bring smartphones, tablet computers, and other electronic devices into the House of Representatives. When they are in the House chambers, Representatives should be devoting their full attention to the business at hand, not to checking their email, reading un-related news, or booking their next plane ticket home. Thus, it is a bad idea to allow electronic devices, such as smartphones, into the House of Representatives.

Adapted from: Editorial, Los Angeles Times, *Jan 3, 2011, http://articles.latimes.com/2011/jan/03/ opinion/la-ed-devices-20110103*

Most people have grown accustomed to others constantly tapping away at handheld electronics, but you might hope that the hallowed halls of Congress would be a differ-ent story. A recent change in Congressional rules, however, means that the glow of smartphones and the tap-tap of keyboards may soon fill the House of Representatives.

This soft lead begins with a comment about a common experience in modern life—people glued to the screens of their electronic devices. It immediately moves on to the main topic of the argument, which is the new rule that allows electronic devices into the House of Rep-resentatives. The tone of these sentences already suggests the conclusion of the argument too: Allowing these devices into Congress is a mistake.

A hard lead response to this question, by contrast, would get straight to the point: "Con-gress has made a mistake in allowing its members to bring smartphones and other electronic devices into the House of Representatives." This opening sentence identifies the issue and it indicates what position the essay will take on that issue. If you have trouble writing a hard lead for your own arguments, try writing a summary first and then condensing that sum-mary even further to create a hard lead.

1. When deciding what kinds of foods to eat, we should choose a diet that causes the least amount of unnecessary suffering to ani-mals. While it might seem intuitive that this would be a vegetar-ian diet, it turns out that's not the case. Planting crops requires clearing native vegetation, which kills many sentient animals and deprives others of necessary habitat. Range-fed cattle, on the other hand, coexist with the natural vegetation, enabling other animals to continue to survive. (This isn't true for cattle raised in

feedlots.) Therefore, adding beef from range-fed cattle to your diet actually leads to less animal suffering than an entirely vegetarian diet.

Adapted from: Mike Archer, "Ordering the Vegetarian Meal? There's More Animal Blood on Your Hands," The Conversation, Dec 15, 2011, http://theconversation.com/ ordering-the-vegetarian-meal-theres-more-animal-blood-on-your-hands-4659

2.   If you think that buying lots of stuff will make you happy, you'll always be disappointed. No matter what you buy, you'll quickly become used to having it, and then you'll move on to wanting something else. Therefore, it's foolish to think that you can buy your way to happiness.

Adapted from: Elizabeth Kolbert, "No Time," New Yorker, May 26, 2014, http://www.newyorker.com/magazine/2014/05/26/no-time

3.   The encryption software on your smartphone helps keep your data private. But until recently, Apple and Google could break into your phone if law enforcement needed access to that data. In 2014, they changed the software so that no one—including Apple, Google, or the government—can access the data on your phone without your password. This creates a big problem for law enforcement, which can often use the data on encrypted phones to solve crimes. It is irresponsible for Apple and Google to hamper law enforcement. Therefore, Apple and Google ought to reverse the change.

Adapted from: Craig Timbert, "The Toughest Case: What if Osama Bin Laden Had an iPhone?" Washington Post, Sep 26, 2014, http://www.washingtonpost.com/blogs/ the-switch/wp/2014/09/26/the-toughest-case-what-if-osama-bin-laden-had-an-iphone

4.   Gun control laws don't work. They're meant to prevent criminals from using guns to commit crimes. Since criminals don't care about obeying the law, though, they'll get guns even if we impose gun control laws. The only thing gun control laws do is make it harder for law-abiding citizens to get the guns that they need to protect themselves.

Adapted from: Erich Pratt, "Opposing View: Firearms Control Doesn't Work," USA Today, Jan 10, 2011, http://www.usatoday.com/news/opinion/editorials/ 2011-01-11-editorial11_ST1_N.htm

5. With college getting ever more expensive, many college students choose to major in something that has a clear financial reward or provides a clear career path, such as accounting or engineering. The number of students who enter subjects like history and English continues to decline. Students should consider studying the humanities for several reasons. First, humanities courses improve your ability to read and write, which you will need to do in just about any career you choose. Second, the humanities teach you "the language of emotion." Third, the humanities enable you to think analytically and to draw lessons from the past for your own future.

    Adapted from: David Brooks, "History for Dollars," New York Times, Jun 7, 2010, http://www.nytimes.com/2010/06/08/opinion/08brooks.html

6. There are two questions to ask about the estate tax. The first is whether it promotes economic growth, provides meaningful government revenue, or provides some other financial benefit to the country, and the second is whether it is morally right. It does not promote economic growth, does not provide a meaningful amount of revenue, or provide any other financial benefit to the country. In fact, it often destroys or damages small businesses by forcing the children of entrepreneurs to dismantle the family business to pay the estate tax. The tax is not morally right, either, since the government has no right to tax money that was already taxed once. Thus, the estate tax ought to be abolished.

    Adapted from: Chris Chocola, "Opposing Views on Inheritances: 'Death Tax' Is Unfair," USA Today, Dec 15, 2010, http://www.usatoday.com/news/ opinion/editorials/2010-12-16-editorial16_ST1_N.htm

7. Mark Twain's *Huckleberry Finn* always stirs up controversy. The latest hubbub over the book involves a new edition that substitutes the word *slave* for the racial slur that Huck uses in the novel to describe Jim. The editor of this new edition has good intentions: He hopes that more people will read Twain's masterpiece if it's less offensive. But the bottom line is that other people's literary works—especially masterpieces like *Huckleberry Finn*—should be left just as they are. The "n-word" is an integral part of Twain's book. Instructors ought to confront the work as it is and use the opportunity to explore Twain's and society's use of the word.

    Adapted from: Kathleen Parker, "Leave Twain Alone," Washington Post, Jan 9, 2011, http://www.washingtonpost.com/wp-dyn/content/article/ 2011/01/07/AR2011010704451.html

8. Presentation software, such as Microsoft PowerPoint, is often used badly. PowerPoint's pre-built templates, cheesy clip art, and time-wasting animated transitions encourage people to create bad presentations. The result is that people come to hate PowerPoint because they hate the presentations that people make with PowerPoint. Well-done PowerPoint presentations, however, can be an effective communications tool. People should learn to use PowerPoint well, rather than dismissing it outright.

Adapted from: Farhad Manjoo, "No More Bullet Points, No More Clip Art," Slate, May 5, 2010, http://www.slate.com/id/2253050/

9. A recent study by two scholars at the University of Southern California found that films aimed at families with young children typically have far more male characters than female characters. Furthermore, the female characters are typically scantily clad and sexy. Many are ditzy, and very few do much that is heroic. Therefore, these films, which are aimed squarely at young boys and girls, reinforce negative gender stereotypes about women.

Adapted from: Julia Baird, "Why Family Films Are So Sexist," Newsweek, Sep 22, 2010, http://www.newsweek.com/2010/09/22/why-family -films-are-so-sexist.html

10. Assume for the moment that everything that happens is completely determined by the laws of nature and the state of the world at some time in the past. Assume also that we cannot be responsible for something if we could not have prevented it from happening. Given these assumptions, it follows that none of us are responsible for anything we have ever done. For our assumptions entail that everything that we do is completely determined by the laws of nature and the state of the world before we were born. Since we can't change either the laws of nature or the way the world was before we were born, we couldn't have prevented ourselves from doing anything that we've actually done.

Adapted from: Peter van Inwagen, "The Incompatibility of Free Will and Determinism," Philosophical Studies 27 (1975): 185–99

Model responses for odd-numbered exercises can be found on page 388.

Need more practice? Working with two or three other classmates, collect a dozen editorials and op-eds from your favorite newspapers. Have each person in your group write a new lead for each piece. Then, share your leads with one another and vote on which lead is the best. For practice writing leads for academic essays, find a professional journal in your preferred discipline. If you can, find one that includes abstracts, or short summaries, at the beginning of each paper. (You may need to ask your instructor for help.) Based on the abstracts, write a lead for each paper in the journal.

Make a definite claim or proposal

If you are making a proposal, be specific. "Something should be done" is not a real proposal. You need not be elaborate. "Cell phones should be banned while driving" is a specific proposal but also a very simple one. If you want to argue that the United States should expand study-abroad programs, though, the idea is more complex and therefore needs some elaboration.

Similarly, if you are making a philosophical claim, or defending your interpretation of a text or event, begin by stating your claim or interpretation *simply*.

Very probably there is life on other planets.

That's forthright and clear!

Academic essays may aim simply to assess some of the arguments for or against a claim or proposal. You may not be making a claim or proposal of your own or even arriving at a specific decision. For example, you may be able to examine only one line of argument in a controversy. If so, make it clear immediately that this is what you are doing. Sometimes your conclusion may be simply that the arguments for or against some position or proposal are inconclusive. Fine—but make that conclusion clear immediately. You don't want your own essay to seem inconclusive!

Rule 35

Exercise Set 8.2: Making definite claims and proposals

Objective: To give you practice making vague claims and proposals more definite.

Instructions: Each statement below makes a vague claim or proposal. Write two more definite claims or proposals that sharpen the general idea of the vague statements in different ways.

Tips for success: The main problem with vague claims or proposals is that your readers will not know exactly what you're trying to say. (You might not know either!) One way to see that is to recognize that a vague statement can be made precise in more than one way. For instance, consider the claim, "Countries should use military force only in extreme circumstances." The phrase "in extreme circumstances" is vague. Thus, the claim might mean that countries should use military force only when they or their allies are being attacked. Alternatively, it might mean that countries should use military force only when they have tried every other way of getting what they want. This exercise asks you to find two alternative ways of making each claim more precise.

To get started, determine which parts of the claim or proposal are vague or ambiguous. For instance, there might be a word or phrase that could mean many different things. Then, think about different possible interpretations of that vague or ambiguous part of the claim—that is, different ways of making it more precise. Pick your favorite two interpretations and use them to generate two more definite claims.

Sample

Marijuana should be legal in some circumstances.

Version 1: Marijuana should be legal for people suffering from terminal cancer or other painful, fatal illnesses.

Version 2: Marijuana should be legal for people over twenty-one.

The phrase "in some circumstances" is vague. The two versions offered here make the claim more precise by citing the specific circumstances under which marijuana should be legal.

What should you do if you have a long list of conditions under which marijuana should be legal? Listing them all in a single sentence may make your proposal awkward to read. The best thing to do is to try to find a way to describe the various circumstances in a more general way. Ask yourself, "What ties these circumstances together?" Another alternative is to say something like, "Marijuana should be legal in four circumstances," and then describe those four circumstances in separate sentences.

Note that there is another source of vagueness in the original claim too. What does it mean for marijuana to be legal? Does it mean that it is legal to possess it? Or does it mean that it is legal to grow, sell, and buy it? In many cases, you will have more than one option for making your claims more precise. You could even combine them. For instance, another response to this question would be, "It should be legal for anyone over twenty-one to grow, sell, buy, possess, and use marijuana."

1. Schools should evaluate teachers by looking at how well they're teaching their students.

2. People should eat better.

3. Important endangered species should be protected.

4. Taxes are too high.

5. Rich people are more likely to use drugs than poor people are.

6. Companies should not be able to tell their employees how to vote.

7. America is a Christian nation.

8. People who download music without paying for it should be punished.

9. There is life on other planets.

10. God cares about what happens on Earth.

Model responses for odd-numbered exercises can be found on page 390.

Need more practice? Work with a group of friends or classmates to generate a list of vague proposals or claims. Then, have each person in the group come up with more definite versions of each proposal or claim. See how many different versions of each proposal or claim your group can generate.

Your argument is your outline

You now move to the main body of your essay: your argument. First, just summarize it. Take the basic argument you've outlined and put it into a concise paragraph.

> Many solar systems are now being discovered beyond our own. I will argue that many of them are likely to include planets like Earth. Many of these planets in turn are likely to have life. Very probably, then, there is life on other planets.

Here your aim is just to give the reader the big picture: a clear overview of where you are going and how you propose to get there.

An argumentative essay should now advance each of the premises of this basic argument in turn, each with a paragraph that begins with a restatement of the premise and continues by developing and defending it.

> Consider first the remarkable fact that many other solar systems are being discovered beyond our own. As of 8 August 2011, the Paris Observatory's "Extrasolar Planet Encyclopaedia" (http://exoplanet.eu/) lists 573 known planets of other stars, including over fifty in multi-planet systems. . . .

You might go on to discuss a few examples—say, the most recent and intriguing discoveries. In a somewhat longer essay, you might cite other lists too, and/or explain the methods being used to discover these planets—it depends on how much room you have and the level of detail and support your readers need or expect. Then go on to explain and defend your other basic premises in the same way.

Some premises in your basic argument may need fairly involved defenses. Treat them exactly the same way. First state the premise you are defending and remind your readers of its role in your main argument. Then summarize your argument for that premise in turn (that is, treating it now as the conclusion of a further argument). Then spell out that argument, giving a paragraph or so, in order, to each of *its* premises.

Rule 36

For instance, in the last chapter (Rule 31) we developed a defense of the second premise of the basic argument for life on other planets. You could insert it now in paragraph form and with a little more style.

> Why might we think that other solar systems include planets like Earth? Astronomers propose an intriguing argument by analogy. They point out that our own solar system has a variety of kinds of planets—some huge gas giants, some others rocky and well-suited for liquid water and life. As far as we know, they continue, other solar systems will be *like* ours. Therefore, they conclude, other solar systems very probably contain a variety of planets, including some that are rocky and well-suited for liquid water and life.

Now you may need to explain and defend these points in turn, maybe even giving some of them their own paragraph or two each. You could try to awaken your readers' appreciation for the diversity of planets right here in our solar system, for example, or describe some of the variety of extra-solar planets already known.

Depending on how long and involved all of this gets, you may need to reorient your reader to the basic argument when you return to it. Pull out the road map, as it were, and remind your readers—and yourself—where you are in your journey toward the main conclusion.

> We have seen, then, that solar systems are already being discovered beyond our own, and that it seems very probable that there are other planets like Earth. The last main premise of the argument then is this: if there are other planets like Earth, then very probably some of them have life.

In your outline you will have worked out the argument for this premise too, and you can now bring it smoothly up to bat.

Notice, in all of these arguments, the importance of using consistent terms (Rule 6). Clearly connected premises such as these become the parallel sentences or phrases that hold the whole essay together.

Exercise Set 8.3: Writing out your arguments

Objective: To help you convert premise-and-conclusion outlines of your arguments into stylish prose.

Instructions: Write out each of the arguments that you developed in Exercise Set 7.6 in a few stylish paragraphs. (You'll need to have completed Exercise Sets 7.2, 7.4, and 7.6 before beginning this one.)

Tips for success: The final product of Exercise Set 7.6 should be a set of arguments—most likely in the form of a premise-and-conclusion outline. (If you've studied Appendix III on argument mapping, you might have maps of your arguments too.) Your goal here is to convert those premise-and-conclusion outlines into the kind of stylish prose that you would see in a newspaper editorial or (occasionally) in an academic paper. Depending on the complexity of your argument, this may take one paragraph or it may take several.

Remembering a few rules from Chapter I will help with this task. Use premise- and conclusion-indicators—but not too many of them—to distinguish premises from conclusions (Rule 1). Present your ideas in a natural order (Rule 2), so that someone who has never thought about your topic could follow along easily. Be concrete and concise (Rule 4), using consistent terms (Rule 6). Avoid loaded language (Rule 5). At this point, your arguments will be strong enough to stand on their own two feet, as it were, without the crutch of loaded language.

Be sure to use a word processor to write out your arguments. You will need to revise them several times to get them into really good shape.

Sample

Suppose that you are writing a paper in which you argue that the dinosaurs were killed by a meteor impact. You might have an argument that looked, in outline, like this:

(1) The dinosaurs, along with many other kinds of plants and animals, went extinct approximately 65.5 million years ago.

(2) There is a 110-mile-wide impact crater near the Mexican town of Chicxulub that dates to roughly sixty-five million years ago.

(3) A 110-mile-wide impact crater must have been created by a huge meteor.

Therefore, (4) A huge meteor must have struck Earth roughly sixty-five million years ago.

(5) The impact of a huge meteor would have thrown enough dust into the atmosphere to change the climate and reduce sunlight for a long time.

(6) Many species and ecosystems would not survive such a sudden, dramatic change in the climate.

Therefore, (7) The impact of a meteor near Chicxulub, Mexico, roughly sixty-five million years ago caused the extinction of the dinosaurs.

Buried beneath the Mexican town of Chicxulub is a sixty-five-million-year-old impact crater. The crater is over a hundred miles across. A crater that big could only have been caused by the impact of a huge meteor. An impact like that would have thrown enough dust into the atmosphere to cloud the sun and change the climate for years. Such a sudden, dramatic change in the climate would have been too much for many plants and animals. Entire ecosystems would have collapsed. And indeed, dinosaurs—along with many other plants and animals—disappear from the fossil record approximately 65.5 million years ago, right about the time of the Chicxulub impact. It stands to reason that the meteor that created the Chicxulub crater also caused the extinction of the dinosaurs.

This response draws very heavily on the premise-and-conclusion outline above, as it should. It repeats the main ideas of each premise, even using a lot of the same words. However, it does reorder the premises to add some drama to the passage. After all, everyone knows that the dinosaurs went extinct. That's not exciting (except to dinosaurs). But a hundred-mile-wide impact crater "buried" beneath a Mexican town? That's a bit more intriguing. As long as you present your premises in a natural order (Rule 2), you don't have to follow the order from your premise-and-conclusion outline.

Need more practice? Get together with several classmates and exchange arguments from Exercise Set 7.6. Write each of your classmates' arguments in stylish prose. For even more practice, work from the premise-and-conclusion outlines that you developed in Exercise Set 7.5 to write stylish prose arguments.

Detail objections and meet them

Rule 32 asks you to think about and rework your argument in light of possible objections. Detailing them and responding to them in your essay helps to make your views more persuasive to your readers, and attests that you have thought carefully about the issue.

NO:

Someone might object that expanded student exchange programs will create too many risks for students. But *I* think that . . .

Well, what kinds of risks? Why would such risks arise? Spell out the *reasons* behind the objection. Take the time to sketch the whole counterargument, not just to mention its conclusion as you rush by to defend *your* argument.

YES:

Someone might object that expanded student exchange programs will create too many risks for students. The concern is partly, I think, that students abroad, who are mostly young people after all and not so worldly, may be more easily taken advantage of or hurt, especially in places where life is more desperate and there are fewer safeguards and protections.

In this time of rising fear and mistrust of foreigners, coupled with fears of terrorism, the concern may also take on more of an edge: students' lives may be at stake. We would certainly not want exchange students to become hostages in desperate local power games. Western tourists abroad are already sometimes targeted by terrorists: we could justifiably fear that the same might happen to exchange students.

These are serious concerns. Still, equally serious responses are also possible. . . .

Now it is clear exactly what the objections are, and you can try to respond to them effectively. You might point out, for instance, that risks don't just start at the border. Many foreign countries are actually safer than American cities. A more complex response might be that it is also risky, at least to our society as a whole, *not* to send more cultural ambassadors abroad, since international misunderstandings and the hatreds they fuel are

making the world more risky for all of us. And surely there are creative ways to design exchange programs to reduce some of the risks? You might not even have thought of these possibilities, though, if you had not detailed the arguments behind the objection, and your readers would probably not have seen the point even if you had mentioned them. Detailing the objections enriches *your* argument in the end.

Exercise Set 8.4: Detailing and meeting objections

Objective: To give you practice writing detailed discussions of objections.

Instructions: Each of the following passages sketches an argument and mentions an objection to that argument. Develop the objection in detail by providing a short argument for it, and then offer a brief response on behalf of the author of the original argument.

Tips for success: As we noted in the "Tips for success" for Exercise Set 7.7, an objection is a kind of argument. Since all arguments have both premises and a conclusion, every objection therefore has both premises and a conclusion. Detailing an objection, like developing any other kind of argument, involves stating its premises explicitly.

In each of the following arguments, the gist of an objection is given for you. Even if you think the objection is misguided, do your best to figure out how someone might develop that basic idea into a full-fledged objection. This may require a little research on your part. It's important that you confront the strongest version of the objection that you can come up with. Spell out the objection just as you spell out your own arguments. (Again, think back to Exercise Sets 7.2, 7.3, and 7.4.)

Once you have stated the objection in detail, you need to meet it. That is, you need to explain why, in your view, the objection doesn't undermine the main argument. There are two main ways to do this. First, if you can find an argumentative flaw in the objection, explain why the objection doesn't work. Since an objection is just a kind of argument, all of the rules that apply to arguments also apply to objections.

Second, even if there is no argumentative flaw in the objection, you might still be able to explain why the main argument is stronger than the objection. There are good arguments on both sides of many important issues; sometimes the only thing to do is to admit that an objection is a good one and then explain why the arguments on the other side are even better.

Sometimes, of course, you'll discover an objection that turns out to be decisive. In that case, the only thing to do is to admit that the objection undermines the original argument. In that case, you can either fall back on other arguments for the same conclusion or give up that conclusion altogether.

When detailing an objection to your argument, it's important to differentiate the objection from your own views. You don't want your reader to think that you are *endorsing* the objection. Phrases like "It might be objected that . . ." can help you do this.

Sample

Electric cars will never be more than a niche product. They may become popular in dense urban areas, but never outside of big cities. The biggest reason for this is "range anxiety," the fear of not being able to go far enough before you run out of electricity. Green-technology enthusiasts dismiss range anxiety as a temporary problem, but it will be a long time before you can recharge your all-electric car on the side of the highway.

Adapted from: Peter M. DeLorenzo, "'Range Anxiety' Remains," New York Times, Oct 7, 2010, http://www.nytimes.com/roomfordebate/2010/10/07/will-electric-cars-finally-succeed/ electrics-as-part-of-the-mix

Green-technology enthusiasts dismiss "range anxiety" as only a temporary problem. As more people buy electric cars, they claim, entrepreneurs will build recharging stations that allow owners to recharge their cars, just as gas stations allow drivers of gasoline-powered cars to refuel along the way. Over time, running out of battery power in your car will be no bigger a fear than running out of gas. Once this happens, the objection goes, there will be no major obstacles to using electric cars outside of big cities.

This argument, however, faces a chicken-and-egg problem. Until there are enough recharging stations outside of big cities, people who live outside of big cities won't buy electric cars, and people with electric cars won't travel outside big cities. But until people are buying or driving electric cars outside of big cities, people won't build recharging stations. Thus, range anxiety is likely to remain a problem for the foreseeable future.

This response does not restate the main argument. It jumps right in with a detailed version of the objection. There are two things to notice about this response's discussion of the objection.

First and most importantly, the response treats the objection as a full-fledged argument. The response clearly states the conclusion of the objection, which is that range anxiety is a temporary problem. (Note that the conclusion of the objection is, in effect, that the main premise of the original argument is false. That is, the conclusion of the objection is that "range anxiety" is not just a temporary problem.) The response then gives premises for that conclusion: More people buying electric cars will lead to people building recharging stations. Recharging stations will make range anxiety a thing of the past, just as gas stations ease anxiety about running out of gas.

Second, the response makes it clear which views are the author's and which are someone else's. It even attributes the objection to a specific kind of critic—a "green-technology enthusiast." The response uses the phrases "they claim" and "the objection goes" to remind the reader that it is considering an objection.

After stating the objection in detail, the response gives a clear rebuttal that explains why the objection fails. This, too, is an argument—an objection to the objection—and the response treats it as one, clearly presenting premises and a conclusion.

1. Russian scientists are excited about exploring Mars. Sending humans to Mars and getting them back safely is difficult and expensive. Therefore, some scientists have proposed that the first non-robotic mission to Mars should involve a monkey rather than a human. Animal rights activists will object that this is extremely cruel, but the benefit to the Russian space program is worth it.

    Adapted from: Urmee Khan, "Monkey to Be Sent to Mars," Telegraph (London), Dec 22, 2009, http://www.telegraph.co.uk/science/space/6864142/ Monkey-to-be-sent-to-Mars.html

2. The government should not be allowed to ban hate speech in newspapers or magazines. To grant government that power would be to give them too much power to decide what gets published in the press. Supporters of a hate-speech ban might object that allowing the government to ban hate speech is not granting them any additional power. After all, the government is already allowed to censor speech that incites violence, and hate speech does incite violence. This objection fails, though, because there's an important difference between saying something hateful and actively encouraging people to commit violence.

    Adapted from: Adam Liptak, "Unlike Others, U.S. Defends Freedom to Offend in Speech," New York Times, Jun 12, 2008, http://www.nytimes.com/ 2008/06/12/us/12hate.html

3.   Euthanasia is going to happen whether it's legal or not. It's better to legalize it so that it's done in the open. That will make it harder to misuse or abuse euthanasia. Critics of euthanasia might object that legalizing it will make people more likely to abuse it, but that's not very plausible.

Adapted from: Noelle Knox, "An Agonizing Debate about Euthanasia," USA Today, Nov 22, 2005, http://www.usatoday.com/news/world/2005-11-22 -euthanasia_x.htm

4.   Classes in music and arts keep young students engaged and interested. It also offers them a creative outlet. Therefore, elementary schools should provide music and arts classes for all students. Some people might object that music and arts classes should be cut because of tight budgets and the need to focus on testing, but we need to keep our priorities straight.

Adapted from: Kathy Bushouse, "Broward Elementary Schools to Consider Cuts to Arts, Music, Physical Education Classes," Sun Sentinel (Ft. Lauderdale, FL), Mar 9, 2010, http://articles.sun-sentinel.com/2010-03-09/news/fl-broward -elementary-specials-030910.doc20100308_1_elementary-schools -electives-broward-teachers-union

5.   The percentage of children born to unwed mothers has increased significantly over the last few decades. This is nothing to worry about. Women should be free to have children whenever they feel they are ready to do so, whether they are married or not. Some people will object that women's rights aren't the issue here—that the real problem is that children who grow up outside of a traditional, husband-and-wife household do not turn out as well. That old wives' tale, however, just isn't true.

Adapted from: "Room for Debate: A New Trend in Motherhood," New York Times, May 17, 2009, http://roomfordebate.blogs.nytimes.com/2009/05/17/ a-new-trend-in-motherhood/

6.   Some states have begun to legalize marijuana. Supporters say that legalization will bring many advantages. Critics, however, worry that legalizing marijuana will cause more and younger teenagers to experiment with marijuana. Perhaps this is true, but advocates claim that the other benefits probably outweigh the costs.

Adapted from: Adam Nagourney and Rick Lyman, "Few Problems with Cannabis in California," New York Times, Oct 26, 2013, http://www.nytimes.com/2013/10/27/us/ few-problems-with-cannabis-for-california.htm

7.   For better or for worse, students who attend elite colleges reap substantial benefits compared to students who go to less prestigious schools. Elite colleges spend far more money per student on education, providing all kinds of free perks that are not included elsewhere. Students at elite colleges are far more likely to graduate from college than students of similar ability who attend less prestigious schools. Students of similar ability, as measured by SAT scores, are also much more likely to go on to graduate or professional school if they attend an elite school. Some might insist that what really matters here is what you do with your time in college, not where you go. I wish that were true, but the facts simply don't bear it out.

Adapted from: "Room for Debate: Does It Matter Where You Go to College?"
New York Times, Nov 30, 2010, http://www.nytimes.com/roomfordebate/
2010/11/29/does-it-matter-where-you-go-to-college

8.   Airport security has become a major hassle in the United States, leading to long waits, restrictive regulations, and invasive searches. All of this is done to prevent terrorists from hijacking airplanes. The United States should do what Israel does: it should use profiling to target people for additional screening, leaving everyone else alone. With the proper training, professionals can use identity and behavioral profiling to target people for extra screening while still treating people respectfully. The defenders of political correctness will object that this will lead to harassment or discrimination, but profiling has worked well for Israel, and it would work well in the United States.

Adapted from: Asra Q. Nomani, "Opposing View on Airport Screening: Follow the
Israeli Model," USA Today, Dec 21, 2010, http://www.usatoday.com/news/
opinion/editorials/2010-12-22-editorial22_ST1_N.htm

9.   Upon entering college, many freshmen remain in close contact with their parents, even if they have traveled far from home to attend school. They call, text, and email parents about everything from choosing classes to writing papers to the grades they received on their latest exam. This constant contact has serious negative effects on the students. They don't learn the independence, self-control, and perseverance necessary to succeed in life. Furthermore, if they resent their parents' intrusions, they may suffer emotional problems. That's why parents need to learn to let their

children manage their own lives once they get to college. Especially with rising tuition costs, however, many parents will object that they are merely "protecting their investment." It's not protecting your investment, though, if you're preventing your child from transitioning into adulthood.

Adapted from: "Room for Debate: Have College Freshmen Changed?" New York Times, Oct 11, 2010, http://www.nytimes.com/roomfordebate/ 2010/10/11/have-college-freshmen-changed

10. One in five American teenagers has already suffered some degree of hearing loss. That's a 30 percent increase since shortly before the introduction of MP3 players. We can infer that teenagers' constant use of MP3 players, often at extremely high volume for extended periods of time, is damaging their hearing. I can hear teenagers objecting already: People are exposed to loud noises all the time anyway, from subway trains to highway traffic. MP3 players couldn't possibly make the difference. In fact, though, loud noises in the environment only make matters worse, because it causes people to turn their MP3 players up even further.

Adapted from: "Room for Debate: Why Teenagers Can't Hear You," New York Times, Aug 18, 2010, http://www.nytimes.com/roomfordebate/ 2010/08/18/how-dangerous-are-ipods-for-teenage-ears

> Model responses for odd-numbered exercises can be found on page 393.

Exercise Set 8.5: Considering objections to your own arguments

Objective: To help you develop discussions of objections for your own argumentative essay.

Instructions: Complete Exercise Sets 7.2, 7.4, 7.6, and 7.8 before beginning this one. Write the objections that you worked out in Exercise Set 7.8 in stylish paragraphs. Then, write a response to each objection, also in a stylish paragraph.

Tips for success: If you haven't completed Exercise Set 8.4, review the "Tips for success" section for that exercise set. Much of that advice applies here too.

You might find that some of the objections you worked out in Exercise Set 7.8 are truly devastating: There is no way to respond to the objection except to admit that the argument doesn't work. If that's the case, don't be afraid to admit it—even if it was an argument that you initially thought was a good one or an argument for a conclusion that you believe or used to believe. Some people think that it shows some kind of personal flaw to admit that one of their arguments doesn't work. Having to abandon an argument because you've discovered that it's flawed is much less embarrassing, however, than clinging stubbornly to it even after you've seen that it's flawed!

Use the sample objection and the Model Responses for Exercise Set 8.4 for models of good responses.

Need more practice? Go to the companion Web site for this book. Click on the "Chapter VIII" link to find links to Web sites on which users can engage in debates. Find debates that interest you, and identify objections that debaters raise against one another. Notice how the debaters detail and meet the objections. Then, using the main point of each objection as a starting point, write out your own version of the objection and a response that the other debater(s) might offer to your objection.

Rule 38

Get feedback and use it

Maybe you know exactly what you mean. Everything seems clear to you. However, it may be far from clear to anyone else! Points that seem connected to you may seem completely unrelated to someone reading your essay. Students may hand in an essay that they think is sharp and clear only to find, when they get it back, that they themselves can barely understand what they were thinking when they wrote it. Their grades usually aren't too encouraging either.

Writers—at all levels—need *feedback*. It is through others' eyes that you can see best where you are unclear or hasty or just plain implausible. Feedback improves your logic too. Objections may come up that you hadn't expected. Premises you thought were secure may turn out to need defending, while other premises may turn out to be more secure than they seemed. You may even pick up a few new facts or examples. Feedback is a "reality check" all the way around—welcome it.

Some teachers build student feedback on paper drafts right into the timetable of their classes. If your teacher does not, arrange it yourself. Find willing fellow students and exchange drafts. Go to your campus writing center (yes, you do have one—you may just need to look). Encourage your readers to be critical, and commit yourself to being a critical reader for them in turn. If need be, you might even assign your readers a quota of specific criticisms and suggestions they have to make, so they don't fear hurting your feelings by suggesting some. It may be polite but it really does *not* do you a favor if your would-be critics just glance over your writing and reassure you that it is lovely, whatever it says. Your teacher and eventual audience will not give you such a free pass.

We may underrate feedback partly because we typically don't see it at work. When we only read finished pieces of writing—essays, books, magazines—it can be easy to miss the fact that writing is essentially a *process*. The truth is that every single piece of writing you read—certainly this book, for one—is put together by people who start from scratch and make thousands of choices, and multiple revisions, along the way. Development, criticism, clarification, and change are the keys. Feedback is what makes them go.

Modesty, please!

Don't claim more than you've shown.

> **NO:**
> In sum, every reason favors sending more students abroad, and none of the objections stands up at all. What are we waiting for?

> **YES:**
> In sum, there is an appealing case for sending more students abroad. Although uncertainties may remain, on the whole it seems to be a promising step. It's worth a try.

Maybe the second version overdoes it in the other direction, but you see the point. Very seldom will you put all the objections to rest, and anyway the world is an uncertain place. We're not experts, most of us, and even the experts can be wrong. "It's worth a try" is the best attitude.

Rule 39

Critical thinking activity: Improving a sample paper

For an activity that gives you practice applying many of these rules, see the "Improving a sample paper" assignment sheet (p. 471) in Part 3.

Critical thinking activity: Compiling a draft of an argumentative essay

For an out-of-class activity that helps you combine your work from Exercises Sets 8.3 and 8.5 into a draft of an argumentative essay, see the "Compiling a draft of an argumentative essay" assignment sheet (p. 474) in Part 3.

Critical thinking activity: Peer-review workshop

For an activity that gives you practice applying Rule 38—along with all of these rules in this chapter—see the "Peer-review workshop" assignment sheet (p. 475) in Part 3.

Sometimes you will find yourself arguing in face-to-face public settings: debating in front of a class; arguing for a bigger share of the student government budget or speaking for your neighborhood at City Council; invited to make a presentation on a subject of your interest or expertise by a group that is interested. Sometimes your audience will be friendly, sometimes they will be neutral but willing to listen, and sometimes they will really need to be won over. At all times, you'll want to present good arguments effectively.

All of the rules in the earlier chapters of this book apply to oral arguments as well as argumentative essays. Here are a few further rules for oral arguments in particular.

Reach out to your audience

Rule 40

In making an oral argument you are quite literally asking for a *hearing*. You want to be heard: to be listened to with respect and at least some degree of open-mindedness. But your hearers may or may not start out respectful or open-minded, and may not even bring a genuine interest in your topic. You need to reach out to them to create the kind of hearing you want to have.

One way to reach out is through your own enthusiasm. Bring some of your own interest and energy for the topic into your talk early on. It personalizes you and notches up the energy in the room.

> I appreciate the chance to speak to you today. In this talk, I want to put forward a new idea on the subject of student exchange programs. It's a proposal I find exciting and inspiring, and I'm hoping that, by the end, you will too.

Notice also that this way of talking itself displays the respectful and inviting attitude toward your hearers that you'd like them to take toward you. You may not get it back from them, even so—but you certainly won't get it from them if you don't bring it to them in the first place. Arguing face-to-face can be a powerful thing, and done deftly and persistently, it can reinforce and build respect itself, even across major differences.

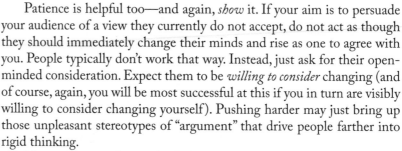

Patience is helpful too—and again, *show* it. If your aim is to persuade your audience of a view they currently do not accept, do not act as though they should immediately change their minds and rise as one to agree with you. People typically don't work that way. Instead, just ask for their open-minded consideration. Expect them to be *willing to consider* changing (and of course, again, you will be most successful at this if you in turn are visibly willing to consider changing yourself). Pushing harder may just bring up those unpleasant stereotypes of "argument" that drive people farther into rigid thinking.

Never give an audience the feeling that you are talking down to them. They may know less than you do about the subject, but they can certainly learn, and it is pretty likely you have some learning to do too. You're not there to rescue them from their ignorance, but rather to share some new information or ideas that you hope they'll find as intriguing and suggestive as you do. Again, approach your audience from *enthusiasm*, not some sort of superiority.

Respect your audience, then, and also respect yourself. You are there because you have something to offer, and they are there because either they want to hear it or because it is required by their jobs or studies. You do not need to apologize for taking their time. Just thank them for listening, and use the time well.

Exercise Set 9.1: Reaching out to your audience

Objective: To give you practice reaching out to the audience during an oral presentation.

Instructions: Each exercise in Exercise Set 8.1 (p. 186) contains a summary of an argument. Read each summary and write a brief opening for an oral presentation of each argument that would engage the attention of a live audience. Assume that you would be presenting the argument to your classmates.

Tips for success: Engaging a live audience in your presentation often requires a different approach than engaging someone through the written word. In many contexts, the opening of an oral presentation can be much less formal and more conversational than the opening lines of a written essay—less formal, even, than a "soft lead" for a written essay. You have a chance to make a personal connection with the audience that you don't have in a written essay.

The goal of your opening line is to engage your audience's interest. There are lots of ways to do this. You might tell a story, raise a puzzle, or cite some surprising statistic that will make audience members want to hear about your topic. You might explain how your topic relates to their lives or have them recall an experience of their own that relates to your topic. You could ask the audience to imagine themselves in an interesting situation that relates to your topic. You might even ask a few audience members to tell you what they would do in that situation. Getting audience members actively engaged in your presentation, however briefly, is a good way to turn them from passive listeners into active listeners.

Unless you are giving a very long presentation, aim for three to five sentences worth of introductory material. By the end of that paragraph, you should be ready to transition smoothly into the main topic of your presentation.

When writing your opening, remember who your audience is. You wouldn't want to use the same opening when presenting something to your classmates as you would when presenting the same material to, say, a group of bankers from whom you hope to get a loan.

Sample

The U.S. Congress passed a new rule allowing members to bring smartphones, tablet computers, and other electronic devices into the House of Representatives. When they are in the House chambers, Representatives should be devoting their full attention to the business at hand, not to checking their email, reading unrelated news, or booking their next plane ticket home. Thus, it is a bad idea to allow electronic devices, such as smartphones, into the House of Representatives.

Adapted from: Editorial, Los Angeles Times, Jan 3, 2011, http://articles.latimes.com/2011/jan/03/opinion/la-ed-devices-20110103

Some instructors, as you know, prohibit cell phones and laptops in the classroom—and with good reason. As students, we get a better view of what our fellow students are doing than instructors do. We know that the person in front of us is on Instagram, not taking notes. We see that the person next to us is texting, not looking for a new pen in her backpack. Computers, phones, and similar devices can be very distracting. That's why Congress's new rule allowing elected officials to bring electronic devices into the House of Representatives is a mistake.

This opening begins with two topics that are likely to grab your classmates' interests: instructors' annoying rules and their classmates' amusing (or annoying) misbehavior. It uses specific details—a student on Instagram and a student trying to hide her texting inside her backpack—to get students to recall things that they have most likely seen for themselves. These details connect those everyday experiences to the lives of the politicians that the argument is about. The response then transitions smoothly and quickly to the main topic of the presentation.

Compare this sample to the sample lead for Exercise Set 8.1, which called for an opening for a written essay on the same topic. This opening is slightly longer and more personal and engaging than either the hard or soft lead for the written essay.

Notice that this response is carefully tailored to a specific audience—namely, a group of students. How would you change this opening if you were giving this presentation to a group of instructors or business executives—or, for that matter, to the House of Representatives?

Model responses for odd-numbered exercises can be found on page 397.

Need more practice? Working with two or three other classmates, collect a dozen editorials and op-eds from your favorite newspapers. Have each person in your group write an opening for an oral presentation of the argument in each editorial or op-ed. Then, share your openings with one another and vote on which opening is the best. For more practice, go to the companion Web site for this book and click on the link for "Chapter IX." You'll find links to other Web sites containing videos of oral presentations on interesting topics. Watch videos on topics of interest to you and write new openings for each presentation.

Critical thinking activity: Writing opening lines

For an activity that gives you practice applying Rules 34 and 40, see the "Writing opening lines" assignment sheet (p. 478) in Part 3.

Be fully present

A public talk or speech is a face-to-face occasion. It is not simply a public version of what we do privately when we read. After all, if people just wanted your words, reading would be much more efficient. They are there partly for your *presence*.

So be present! For starters, look at your audience. Take the time to connect. Meet people's eyes and hold them. People who get nervous speaking to groups are sometimes advised to just talk to one person in the group, as if one to one. Do so, if you need to, but then go a step farther: talk to your whole audience one to one, one person at a time.

Speak with expression. Do not read your pre-prepared words as if it were a chore. Remember, you're *talking* to people here! Imagine that you are having an animated conversation with a friend (OK, maybe a little one-sided . . .). Now speak to your audience in the same spirit.

Writers seldom get to see their readers. When speaking in public, though, your hearers are right there in front of you, and you have constant feedback from them. Use it. Do people meet your eyes with interest? What is the feeling in the audience as a whole? Are people leaning forward to hear better . . . or not? If not, can you pick up the energy? Even if you have a presentation to get through, you can still adjust your style, or stop to explain or review a key point if necessary. When you are not sure of your audience, plan in advance to be able to adjust to different responses. Have an extra story or illustration ready to go, just in case.

By the way, you are not glued to the floor behind the podium (should you have one) either. You can walk around or at least come out from behind the lectern. Depending on your own comfort level and the occasion, you can establish a much more engaged feeling in the room by visibly engaging with your audience yourself.

Signpost your argument

Readers can take in an argument selectively. They can stop and think, double back, or choose to drop it entirely and move on to something else. Your hearers can't do any of these things. You set the pace for everyone.

So be considerate. On the whole, oral arguments need to offer more "signposting" and repetition than written arguments. At the beginning you may need to summarize the argument more fully, and then you need to refer more regularly back to the summary, or what Rule 36 called the "road

map." For your summary, use labels like "Here is my basic argument." For your premises, as the argument turns, say something like "We come now to the second [third, fourth, etc.] basic premise of my argument. . . ." Summarize again at the end. Pause to mark important transitions and to give people time to think.

In debate training, students are often taught to literally repeat their key claims word for word—that's right, to literally repeat their key claims word for word—mainly because other people will be writing them down. Teachers sometimes do this as well: it shows that they know that students are listening hard, and may want and need the key points signposted. In other settings this might seem odd. Even if you don't repeat the key points word for word, though, at least mark them out in some way, and make it clear that—and why—you are doing so.

Be especially alert to your audience at important transitions. Look around and make sure that most of your hearers are ready to move with you. You'll communicate better and show your audience that you actually care that they take in and understand what you are saying.

Exercise Set 9.2: Signposting your own arguments

Objective: To help you develop transitions for oral presentations of your own arguments.

Instructions: Complete Exercise Set 8.3 (p. 196) before beginning this one. Rewrite each of the arguments from Exercise Set 8.3, adding "signposts" to make it easier to follow an oral presentation of the argument. Assume that you have already engaged the audience's attention and told them what your main conclusion is.

Tips for success: In Exercise Set 8.3, you worked your arguments into stylish paragraphs. If you were going to present any of those arguments orally, however, the paragraphs that you wrote for Exercise Set 8.3 would probably be too dense. Your listeners might have a hard time following your train of thought.

For this exercise set, you'll need to introduce phrases that remind your listeners—sometimes more than once—where they are in the argument, how your various points fit together, and what the main point is.

You will want to offer different kinds of signposts for different kinds of transitions. For instance, you may be transitioning between two premises that give examples. In that case, your signpost could be as simple as saying, "Another example is . . ." If your examples are complicated, you might want to remind your audience what the examples are examples *of*—that is, what the *point* of the examples is. Alternatively, you might be offering a complicated deductive argument. In that case, it might be helpful to provide a lengthier transition that reminds your reader of the steps that have come before and how the next step fits into the overall structure of the argument.

The bottom line, though, is that your signposts have to work in an oral presentation. Be sure to read your arguments out loud to yourself—or better yet, to a friend or classmate—in order to be sure that they help your listener follow the argument.

Sample

The sample argument from Exercise Set 8.3 was written out as follows: Buried beneath the Mexican town of Chicxulub is a sixty-five-million-year-old impact crater. The crater is over 100 miles across. A crater that big must have been caused by the impact of a huge meteor. An impact like that would have thrown enough dust into the atmosphere to cloud the sun and change the climate for years. Such a sudden, dramatic change in the climate would have been too much for many plants and animals. Entire ecosystems would have collapsed. And indeed, dinosaurs—along with many other plants and animals—disappear from the fossil record approximately 65.5 million years ago, right about the time of the Chicxulub impact. It stands to reason that the meteor that created the Chicxulub crater also caused the extinction of the dinosaurs.

The central argument for my claim that the dinosaurs were killed by a meteor begins beneath the Mexican town of Chicxulub. Buried beneath Chicxulub is an impact crater over 100 miles across. A crater that big could only have been caused by a truly huge meteor. What would the impact of such a large meteor do to the Earth? For starters, it would throw so much dust into the atmosphere that the sun would be clouded for a very long time. This would cause major changes in the climate and create problems for plants that rely on the sun for food. As a result, many plants and animals would have died, and entire ecosystems would have collapsed, which brings me to the dinosaurs. The Chicxulub crater dates to about sixty-five million years ago, right around the time that the dinosaurs went extinct. Since the impact of the Chicxulub meteor would have caused an ecological catastrophe and mass extinctions, and the dinosaurs, along with many other plants and animals, died at just about that time, it stands to reason that the Chicxulub meteor killed the dinosaurs.

This passage begins by alerting the listeners that they are about to hear the central argument of the presentation. Sometimes listeners need to be reminded to listen especially closely! The passage also moves more slowly through the premises. It doesn't quite repeat its main claims word for word, but it does restate them in slightly different forms. Two major signposts help listeners follow along with the argument: The rhetorical question, "What would the impact of such a large meteor do to the Earth?" makes it clear that the speaker is moving from a discussion of the meteor to a discussion of its effects. The phrase "which brings me to the dinosaurs" signals that the speaker is moving from the general effects to a discussion of the presentation's main topic—the dinosaurs. The passage ends with a clear statement of the argument's conclusion.

There is a more subtle difference in this version of the argument too. The written version from Exercise Set 8.3 states the age of the Chicxulub crater right away. This version waits until the listener really needs to know that information—when the speaker is comparing the age of the crater to the date of the dinosaurs' extinction. Readers can always go back and look at information you presented earlier. Listeners can't. So while it's not quite a matter of signposting, your listeners will follow more easily if you give them information on an as-needed basis.

Need more practice? Write oral presentations for each of the arguments in Exercise Set 7.6, being sure to include adequate signposting. For even more practice, find editorials or op-eds in your favorite newspaper and rewrite them for oral presentations.

Rule 43

Offer something positive

Offer your audience something to do, something to hope for, some sense of possibility—at least some kind of positive spin.

> **NO:**
> This city stinks at conserving water! Even with the reservoirs down to a month's supply, we've only been able to cut back consumption by 25 percent, and people still don't get it about not washing their cars or leaving their sprinklers going forever. . . .

Maybe, maybe . . . But when we focus on the severity of a problem, we also run the risk of making people feel like nothing can be done about it. Couldn't the same issue be framed in more empowering ways?

YES:

This city needs to do better at conserving water. We've been able to cut back consumption by 25 percent so far, but with the reservoirs down to a month's supply, people should really start seeing the need to stop washing their cars or leaving their sprinklers going. . . .

These are exactly the same facts, even similar phrases and sentences, but the overall feeling is sharply different.

The point is not to be mindlessly optimistic. We should not ignore what is negative. But when we let it fill the screen entirely, it becomes the only reality. We create more of it, we preoccupy ourselves with it, and it gets our energy and attention, even if we wish to resist it.

Instead, give your audience some direction forward, some way to respond, something to do, not just something to resist or avoid or lament. Part of the power of Martin Luther King, Jr.'s famous "I Have a Dream" speech is that it is, after all, about *dreams*: about positive visions for a shared and just future. "I have a dream that the children of former slaves and the children of former slave-owners will be able to sit down together at the table of brotherhood. . . ." Imagine if he'd spoken only about nightmares instead: "I have a *nightmare* that the children of former slaves and the children of former slave-owners will *never* be able to sit down together at the table of brotherhood. . . ." In one way this is exactly the same idea—but if King had put it this way, would his great speech live on today?

All arguments—not just oral arguments—should try to offer something positive. Again, though, there is a special energy in oral arguments, which is why this rule belongs in this chapter. An audience's optimism and excitement can be infectious, and can become a power of its own, as can a sense of gloom and disempowerment. Which will you choose to create?

Exercise Set 9.3: Reframing arguments in a positive way

Objective: To give you practice presenting ideas in a positive light for an oral presentation.

Instructions: Rewrite each of the following passages in a positive way without changing the overall meaning of the passage.

Tips for success: Negative presentations tend to focus on problems rather than solutions—things that people are doing wrong or things that are going badly. Offering something positive involves emphasizing the people who are doing the right thing and focusing on solutions. This gives your audience something motivating to carry away.

In each of the following passages, look for an emphasis on people who are behaving badly or things that are going badly. Often, these are implicitly contrasted with people who are behaving well or things that are going well. For instance, a passage that emphasizes how many criminals are repeat offenders implicitly contrasts repeat offenders with people who abandon their criminal activity after being released from prison. To put a positive ending on a presentation about repeat offenders, emphasize the people who have reformed themselves or the programs or policies that have helped them do so.

If the passage emphasizes a problem, see if you can frame your ending in terms of a potential solution to the problem. Often the statement of a problem contains hints of its solution. Focusing on the solution, not just on the problem, may help you transform those vague hints into a more concrete plan—or at least put you on the right track.

Sample

If a plane catches on fire during a crash, passengers can have as little as ninety seconds to escape before the temperature inside the cabin becomes lethally hot. That leaves virtually no room for error. And yet the Federal Aviation Authority (FAA) estimates that up to 61 percent of passengers tune out during the safety announcements at the beginning of every flight. During FAA evacuation drills, many passengers didn't follow proper procedures. Thus, one reason that plane crashes are so dangerous is that so many passengers don't know what to do.

Adapted from: "Room for Debate: Miracles and Plane Crashes," New York Times, Jan 16, 2009, http://roomfordebate.blogs.nytimes.com/2009/01/16/miracles-and-plane-crashes/

Everyone knows that plane crashes are dangerous. If a plane catches on fire during a crash, passengers need to be able to evacuate in ninety seconds or less. The FAA requires safety announcements at the beginning of each flight, but only about 40 percent of passengers listen, and only some of the passengers follow proper procedure during FAA evacuation drills. If more people paid attention during safety announcements and knew what to do in an emergency, or if the airlines found more attention-grabbing ways to present that safety information, more lives could be saved.

These two passages convey almost all of the same information, but they do so in very different ways. Whereas the original passage focuses on what people do wrong and on how dangerous it is, the response emphasizes the things that people do right—providing safety announcements, paying attention to those announcements, and following proper procedure during drills—and the fact that doing these things can save lives.

1. If you've been trying to lose weight, I've got bad news for you. Those diet sodas you've probably been drinking are actually making it *harder* for you to lose weight. It turns out that the artificial sweeteners in diet sodas change the kinds of bacteria that live in your intestines. This change makes it harder for your body to metabolize sugars. This can lead to obesity and diabetes.

   Adapted from: Anna Almendrala, "This Might Explain Why Diet Soda Drinkers Are Often Overweight," Huffington Post, *Sep 18, 2014, http:/www.huffingtonpost. com/2014/09/18/artifical-sweeteners-gut-bacteria_n_5837646.html*

2. Students in other countries routinely outperform American students on standardized tests in math, science, and reading. This is because students in those countries know that success requires hard work, whereas Americans are trapped in the belief that success depends on innate ability. We talk about being "good at math" or "good at reading," suggesting that those of us who are lucky enough to be good don't need to work hard, and that those of us who aren't good can't get better by trying. This attitude is holding America back.

   Adapted from: Jonathan Zimmerman, "Why Shanghai Schooled the U.S.: Americans Think We're Too Smart to Work Hard," Christian Science Monitor, *Dec 14, 2010, http://www.csmonitor.com/Commentary/Opinion/ 2010/1214/Why-Shanghai-schooled-the-US-Americans -think-they-re-too-smart-to-work-hard*

3. It's hard for museums to acquire archaeological artifacts in a legitimate way. Most artifacts were either stolen from their host countries long ago or were smuggled out more recently. The problem is that no one with a legitimate interest in protecting artifacts, including museums, is doing very much to excavate new artifacts.

   Adapted from: Bernard Frischer, "Museums Should Dig In," New York Times, *Dec 22, 2010, http://www.nytimes.com/2010/12/23/opinion/23frischer.html*

4. Environmentalists oppose nuclear energy, despite its very low carbon emissions and the high efficiency of nuclear power plants, so it's unlikely that we'll build more nuclear plants anytime soon. Instead, environmentalists are looking at things like solar power, wind farms, and biofuels. Neither solar nor wind, however, provides a steady source of electricity. Besides, solar farms and wind

farms take up an unrealistic amount of space. Unfortunately, then, it looks like we're going to have to keep building traditional power plants with the same old huge carbon footprints.

Adapted from: Stewart Brand, "Debate: Does the World Need Nuclear Energy," TED, Jun 2010, http://www.ted.com/talks/debate_does_the_world _need_nuclear_energy.html

5. Everyone knows that good posture is important. So why are so many people careless about their posture? People sleep twisted on their sides or stomachs, which is terrible for your back, neck, and posture. They slouch over their desks because they don't have the lighting or eyeglasses needed to see their computer screens without hunching over their desks. They go through workouts at the gym with hunched shoulders and rounded backs. If people want good posture, they have to shape up!

Adapted from: "How to Get Good Posture," YouTube, Jun 20, 2008, http:// www.youtube.com/watch?v=qOOFjMyWqyQ

6. The threat of medical malpractice lawsuits drives medical costs through the roof. Doctors order unnecessary but expensive tests in order to avoid appearing negligent. They prescribe multiple treatments to avoid the suggestion that they failed to address a treatable problem. The result is that patients pay much more than they would if their doctors weren't afraid of being sued.

Adapted from: Peter Orszag, "Malpractice Methodology," New York Times, Oct 20, 2010, http://www.nytimes.com/2010/10/21/opinion/21orszag.html

7. Despite the introduction of new programs to improve their academic performance, about one out of every two Hispanic students was unprepared for college-level English courses, and two out of three were unprepared for college-level math. And that doesn't even include students who don't graduate from high school. This probably explains why, even though Hispanics are enrolling in college at a higher rate than black and non-Hispanic white students, the college graduation rate for Hispanics remains low.

Adapted from: Delece Smith-Barrow, "National Initiatives Help Minorities Prepare for College Course Work," U.S. News & World Report, Sep 8, 2014, http://www.usnews.com/education/best-colleges/articles/2014/09/08/ resources-minorities-can-use-to-ensure-college-readiness

8. People used to need a prescription to buy pseudoephedrine, one of the main ingredients in methamphetamines. In 1976, though, the FDA made pseudoephedrine-based cold medicines available over the counter. In the decades since, methamphetamine use has become a major problem in the United States. Most efforts to stop meth labs from acquiring pseudoephedrine, such as prohibiting people from purchasing large amounts of cold medicine at once, have failed. As long as pseudoephedrine is available without a prescription, methamphetamine use will continue to ruin lives and destroy families.

    Adapted from: Rob Bovett, "How to Kill the Meth Monster," New York Times, *Nov 15, 2010, http://www.nytimes.com/2010/11/16/opinion/16bovett.html*

9. Eleven thousand volunteers turned out in November 2013 to help make a wish come true for a seriously ill five-year-old: They turned San Francisco into Gotham City, and the boy spent a day fighting supervillains while dressed as "Batkid." It was a genuinely heartwarming event put on by the Make-a-Wish Foundation, but it was also a waste of money. The Make-a-Wish Foundation spends an average of $7,500 per "wish." These wishes bring joy to children who really need it. But donating that money to more effective charities, such as the Against Malaria Foundation, would literally save lives. That same $7,500 would pay for enough anti-mosquito bed nets to save at least two to three children's lives. And no matter how valuable it is to brighten the day of a seriously ill child, it's surely more valuable to save the lives of two or three others. That's why donating to the Make-a-Wish Foundation is a poor use of money.

    Adapted from: Peter Singer, "Heartwarming Causes Are Nice, but Let's Give to Charity with Our Heads," Washington Post, *Dec 19, 2013, http://www.washingtonpost.com/ opinions/heartwarming-causes-are-nice-but-lets-give-to-charity-with-our-heads/2013/12/19/43469ae0-6731-11e3-a0b9-249bbb34602c_story.html*

10. Some statistics are too shocking to ignore—even if they aren't true. For instance, the U.S. attorney general once claimed that "intimate partner homicide" was the leading cause of death for African-American women aged eighteen to forty-five. That's just not true. Similarly, activists used to claim that domestic abuse skyrocketed on Super Bowl Sunday. Until a journalist did some fact-checking, this hoax popped up again every year. It even reappeared in

a different guise during the World Cup, with British officials warning of domestic abuse after soccer matches. That myth also persisted until some journalists actually bothered to check their facts. As you can see, misinformation is everywhere, and it leads to bad policy decisions and unfair mistreatment of innocent people.

Adapted from: Christina Hoff Sommers, "Domestic Violence Myths Help No One," USA Today, Feb 4, 2011, http://www.usatoday.com/news/opinion/forum/2011-02-03-sommers04_st_N.htm

Model responses for odd-numbered exercises can be found on page 400.

Need more practice? One good place to get more practice with this skill is by looking at your own arguments, such as those developed in the exercise sets in Chapter VI or those developed in papers for other courses. For even more practice, work with two or three other classmates and have each person in your group write a negative ending to several imaginary presentations on topics of interest to the group. Feel free to exaggerate the negativity in your endings, as this will make the process of rewriting them more challenging. Then, have each member of the group rewrite each ending in a positive way. Vote on the best positive ending to each imaginary presentation.

Use visual aids sparingly

Rule 44

PowerPoint has become a familiar accompaniment to visual presentations. Some people even expect to read presentations off computer projectors as a matter of course.

Nonetheless, audiences may quickly tire of seeing totally different subjects all presented in the same way, often using the very same backgrounds and formats. Then too, PowerPoint can make it too easy to think that you've got "content" when mostly what you have is just a nicely decorated presentation. Critics have also pointed out that PowerPoint formats tend to oversimplify. The writing on slides is typically very clipped; charts and graphs can display little detail. And computer glitches inevitably lead to distractions and total disasters.

So think carefully about what kinds of visual aids you really need—if any. Learn PowerPoint if you have to (students going into business may need it), but do not assume that it is the only way to make a presentation. Try for something more engaging and fully focused. Perhaps you can ask for a

show of hands on some subject, or solicit some structured audience participation. Read briefly from a book or article. Put up a short video clip or some
graphs or data, if needed, but then turn the screen off to continue talking.
At the very least, don't let your presentation be reduced to a tour through
some slides—for that can be done just as well, or better, without *you*.

If you do really want or need to use visual aids, consider paper handouts. You can include far more information—more complex words and
pictures; graphs, data, references, links—including much that can be left
for people to read before or after the presentation if they choose. Distribute your handouts in advance, or only when you are ready to use them, or
for reference at the end, and encourage people to take it with them when
they go.

The "Resources" section on this book's companion Web site has links to advice on creating
good visual aids and avoiding bad ones.

Critical thinking activity: Creating a visual aid

For an out-of-class activity that gives you practice in applying Rule 44, see the "Creating a
visual aid" assignment sheet (p. 479) in Part 3.

End in style

First, end on time. Find out how long you are supposed to speak, and don't
go over. You know from your own experiences as a listener that nothing
irritates an audience more than a speaker going on too long.

Second, don't just peter out.

NO:
Well, I guess that's about all the time I have. Why don't we
stop and chat a bit if any of these ideas have interested you?

Come to a rousing end. End in style, with flair or a flourish.

YES:
In this talk I have tried to suggest that real happiness is at-
tainable after all, and by everyone; that it takes no special luck
or wealth; indeed that its preconditions lie within easy reach,
all around us. I thank you for your attention, my friends, and
naturally wish you all the greatest happiness yourselves!

Rule 45

Exercise Set 9.4: Ending in style

Objective: To give you practice signaling important transitions and endings in oral arguments.

Instructions: Each exercise in Exercise Set 8.1 (p. 186) contains a summary of an argument. In Exercise Set 9.1 you wrote an opening for an oral presentation of that argument. Now write a good ending for an oral presentation of the argument.

Tips for success: Your last few sentences are your best chance to remind your audience exactly what you want them to take away from your presentation. Reiterate your most important points, and do it in a way that will make your ideas stick in their head—but remember your modesty (Rule 39)!

Of course, the way in which you end your arguments is a matter of style, and styles differ from person to person. Just as there is no single right way to reach out to your audience, there is no single right way to end a presentation. Find something that suits your personal voice and style and figure out how to make it work.

Sample

The U.S. Congress passed a new rule allowing members to bring smartphones, tablet computers, and other electronic devices into the House of Representatives. When they are in the House chambers, Representatives should be devoting their full attention to the business at hand, not to checking their email, reading unrelated news, or booking their next plane ticket home. Thus, it is a bad idea to allow electronic devices, such as smartphones, into the House of Representatives.

The main point is that electronic gadgets are distracting, and we don't want our congressional representatives distracted when they're supposed to be focused on governing. Thus, the recent move to allow electronic devices into the House chambers is a terrible idea. For those who have been looking at your phones the entire time, this is the point in the presentation where you nod in agreement and clap politely. Thank you.

This response ends the presentation with a self-effacing if slightly snappy joke that not only relates to the topic of the presentation, but also clearly signals that the presentation is over. If ending with a joke is not your style (or if your joke falls flat), a firm, well-timed, "Thank you for your attention" will do the trick.

Model responses for odd-numbered exercises can be found on page 405.

Need more practice? Write endings for oral presentations based on other arguments from this book. Alternatively, find a letter to the editor or an editorial in your favorite newspaper and write endings for an oral presentation of the arguments in those letters or editorials.

CHAPTER EXERCISES

Exercise Set 9.5: Evaluating oral presentations

Objective: To give you practice evaluating oral presentations of arguments.

Instructions: Go to the companion Web site for this book. Click on the link for "Chapter IX" and then click on the link for "Exercise Set 9.5." You will get a list of links to online videos of oral presentations. Watch each video and evaluate how well the presenter in the video follows each of the rules from Chapter IX.

Tips for success: Your focus here should be evaluating the oral presentation of the arguments, not the quality of the arguments themselves. Proceed through the rules from Chapter IX systematically, being sure to address each one in detail.

In thinking about Rule 40 ("Reach out to your audience"), ask yourself both how well the presenter engages your attention at the beginning and how well he or she continues to reach out to the audience throughout the presentation. Identify specific things that the presenter does or says that increase or decrease your engagement with the presentation.

Keep Rule 41 ("Be fully present") in mind throughout the entire presentation. If the presenter is speaking to the camera, does it feel like he or she is making eye contact with you through the screen? If the presenter is speaking to a live audience, does he or she engage with the audience? Identify specific things that the presenter does to make you feel connected or disconnected from him or her during the presentation.

Another thing to watch for throughout the entire video is the presenter's use of "signposting" (Rule 42). Try pausing the video periodically and asking yourself if you can explain the main point of the presentation and say how the previous sentence in the presentation—right before you paused the video—relates to that main point. If you can do that, then think about the specific signposts that the presenter used to enable you to do that. If you can't, then ask yourself what the presenter might have done differently to clarify the presentation.

Overall, has the presenter offered something positive (Rule 43)? If so, say what it is. If not, suggest a more positive version of the presenter's overall message, as you did in Exercise Set 9.3.

Be sure to say something about the presenter's use of visual aids (Rule 44). Did the presenter use visual aids? Were the visual aids helpful? (If the presenter is talking to a live audience, the visual aids might have been helpful to the live audience but not to those of us watching the video.) What changes would you recommend to improve the presenter's use of visual aids?

Finally, did the presenter end in style (Rule 45)? Cite specific things that you liked or disliked about the way the presenter ended the presentation.

The exercises for this set, including a sample evaluation of an oral presentation, can be found on the companion Web site for this book.

Model responses for odd-numbered exercises can be found on page 406.

Need more practice? Explore the Web sites that host the videos for this exercise. Find videos of other presentations and evaluate those presentations.

The "Resources" section on this book's companion Web site has links to resources for improving your public speaking.

Critical thinking activity: Oral presentations

For an in-class or out-of-class activity that gives you practice in applying Rules 40–45, see the "Oral presentations" assignment sheet (p. 480) in Part 3.

Critical thinking activity: In-class debates

For an in-class activity that gives you practice in applying all of the rules in this book, see the "In-class debates" assignment sheet (p. 481) in Part 3.

Critical thinking activity: Extended in-class group debates

For an extended in-class activity that gives you practice in applying all of the rules in this book, see the "Extended in-class group debates" assignment sheet (p. 483) in Part 3.

Appendix I
Some Common Fallacies

Fallacies are misleading types of arguments. Many of them are so tempting, and therefore so common, that they even have their own names. This may make them seem like a separate and new topic. Actually, though, to call something a fallacy is usually only another way of saying that it violates one of the rules for *good* arguments. The fallacy of "false cause," for example, is a questionable conclusion about causes, and you can look to Chapter V for an explanation of how to find better ones.

Here is a short list and explanation of some of the classical fallacies, including their Latin names when frequently used.

ad hominem (literally, "to the man"): attacking the *person* of a source rather than his or her qualifications or reliability or the actual argument he or she makes. You know from Chapter IV that supposed authorities may be disqualified if they are not informed, impartial, or largely in agreement. But other sorts of attacks on supposed authorities are typically not legitimate.

> It's no surprise that Carl Sagan argues for life on Mars—after all, he was a well-known atheist. I don't believe it for a minute.

Although Sagan did take part in the public discussion about religion and science, there is no reason to think that his views about religion colored his scientific judgment about Martian life. Look to the argument, not "the man."

ad ignorantiam (appeal to ignorance): arguing that a claim is true just because it has not been shown to be false. A classic example is this statement by Senator Joseph McCarthy when he was asked for evidence to back up his accusation that a certain person was a Communist:

> I do not have much information on this except the general statement of the agency that there is nothing in the files to disprove his Communist connections.

ad misericordiam (appeal to pity): appealing to pity as an argument for special treatment.

> I know I flunked every exam, but if I don't pass this course, I'll have to retake it in summer school. You *have* to let me pass!

Pity is sometimes a good reason to help, but it is certainly inappropriate when objective evaluation is called for.

ad populum: appealing to the emotions of a crowd; also, appealing to a person to go along with the crowd ("Everyone's doing it!"). Arguments *ad populum* are good examples of *bad* arguments from authority. No reasons are offered to show that "everybody" is any kind of knowledgeable or reliable source.

affirming the consequent: a deductive mistake of the form

> If **p** then **q**.
> **q**.
> Therefore, **p**.

Remember that in the statement "if **p** then **q**," **p** is called the "antecedent" and **q** the "consequent." The second premise of *modus ponens*—a valid form—affirms (asserts) the antecedent, **p** (go back to Rule 22 and check). Affirming the *consequent* (**q**), though, yields quite a different—and invalid—form. A true conclusion is not guaranteed even if the premises are true. For example:

> When the roads are icy, the mail is late.
> The mail is late.
> Therefore, the roads are icy.

Although the mail would be late if the roads were icy, it also may be late for other reasons too. This argument **overlooks alternatives**.

begging the question: implicitly using your conclusion as a premise.

> God exists because it says so in the Bible, which I know is true because God wrote it, after all!

To put this argument in premise-and-conclusion form, you'd have to write:

> The Bible is true, because God wrote it.
> The Bible says that God exists.
> Therefore, God exists.

To defend the claim that the Bible is true, the arguer claims that God wrote it. But, obviously, if God wrote the Bible, then God exists. Thus the argument assumes just what it is trying to prove.

circular argument: same as **begging the question**.

> You can count on WARP News for the facts, because they constantly say on the air that "we just give you the facts," so that must be a fact too!

Real-life circular arguments often follow a bigger circle, but they all eventually end up starting in the same place they want to end.

complex question: posing a question or issue in such a way that people cannot agree *or* disagree with you without committing themselves to some other claim you wish to promote. A simple example: "Are you still as self-centered as you used to be?" Answering either "yes" or "no" commits you to agreeing that you used to be self-centered. More subtle example: "Will you follow your conscience instead of your pocketbook and donate to the cause?" Saying "no," regardless of their real reasons for not donating, makes people feel guilty. Saying "yes," regardless of their real reasons for donating, makes them noble. If you want a donation, just ask for it.

denying the antecedent: a deductive mistake of the form

> If **p** then **q**.
> Not-**p**.
> Therefore, not-**q**.

Remember that in the statement "If **p** then **q**," **p** is called the "antecedent" and **q** the "consequent." The second premise of a *modus tollens*—a valid form—denies the consequent, **q** (go back to Rule 23 and check). Denying the antecedent (**p**), though, yields quite a different—and invalid—form. A true conclusion is not guaranteed even if the premises are true. For example:

> When the roads are icy, the mail is late.
> The roads are not icy.
> Therefore, the mail is not late.

Although the mail would be late if the roads were icy, it may be late for other reasons too. This argument **overlooks alternatives**.

equivocation: sliding from one meaning of a term in the middle of an argument.

> Women and men are physically and emotionally different. The sexes are *not* "equal," then, and therefore the law should not pretend that we are.

Between premise and conclusion this argument shifts the meaning of the term "equal." The sexes are not physically and emotionally "equal" in the sense in which "equal" means simply "identical." Equality before the law, however, does not mean "physically and emotionally identical" but "entitled to the same rights and opportunities." Rephrased with the two different senses of "equal" made clear, the argument goes:

> Women and men are not physically and emotionally identical. Therefore, women and men are not entitled to the same rights and opportunities.

Once the equivocation is removed, it is clear that the argument's conclusion is neither supported by nor even related to the premise. No reason is offered to show that physical and emotional differences imply different rights and opportunities.

false cause: generic term for any questionable conclusion about cause and effect. To figure out specifically *why* the conclusion is (said to be) questionable, go back to Chapter V.

false dilemma: reducing the options you consider to just two, often diametrically opposed and unfair to the people against whom the dilemma is posed. For example, "America: Love It or Leave It." A more subtle example from a student paper: "Since the universe could not have been created out of nothingness, it must have been created by an intelligent life force. . . ." Well, maybe, but is creation by an intelligent life force the *only* other possibility? This argument **overlooks alternatives**.

Ethical arguments seem especially prone to false dilemmas. Either the fetus is a human being with all the rights that adults have, some say, or else it is a lump of tissue with no moral significance at all. Either every use of animal products is wrong or all of the current uses are acceptable. In fact, usually, other possibilities exist. Try to increase the number of options you consider, not narrow them!

loaded language: language that primarily plays on the emotions. It does not make an argument at all, in truth, but is only a form of manipulation. See Rule 5.

non sequitur: drawing a conclusion that "does not follow," that is, a conclusion that is not a reasonable inference from, or even related to, the evidence. This is a very general term for a bad argument. Try to figure out specifically what is supposed to be wrong with it.

overgeneralizing: generalizing from too few examples. Just because your student friends are all athletes or business majors or vegetarians, it doesn't follow that *all* of your fellow students are the same (remember Rules 7 and 8). You can't generalize even from a large sample unless it is demonstrably representative. Take care!

overlooking alternatives: forgetting that things may happen for a variety of reasons, not just one. For example, Rule 19 pointed out that just because events E_1 and E_2 may correlate, it does not follow that E_1 causes E_2. E_2 could cause E_1; something else could cause *both* E_1 and E_2; E_1 may cause E_2 *and* E_2 may cause E_1; or E_1 and E_2 might not even be related. **False dilemma** is another example: there are usually many more options than two!

persuasive definition: defining a term in a way that may seem to be straightforward but that in fact is **loaded**. For example, someone might define "Evolution" as "the atheistic view that species develop as a result of mere chance events over a supposed period of billions of years." Persuasive definitions may be favorably loaded too: for example, someone might define a "conservative" as "a person with a realistic view of human limits."

petitio principii: Latin for **begging the question**.

poisoning the well: using **loaded language** to disparage an argument before even mentioning it.

> I'm confident you haven't been taken in by those few holdouts who still haven't outgrown the superstition that . . .

More subtly:

> No sensitive person thinks that . . .

post hoc ergo propter hoc (literally, "after this therefore because of this"; sometimes just called the *post hoc* fallacy): assuming causation too readily on the basis of mere succession in time. Again a very general term for what Chapter V tries to make precise. Turn to Chapter V and try to figure out if other causal explanations are more plausible.

red herring: introducing an irrelevant or secondary subject and thereby diverting attention from the main subject. Usually the red herring is an issue about which people get heated quickly, so that no one notices how their attention is being diverted. In a discussion of the relative safety of different makes of cars, for instance, the issue of which cars are made in America is a red herring.

straw man: A caricature of an opposing view, exaggerated from what anyone is really likely to hold, so that it is easy to refute. See Rule 5.

The "Resources" section on this book's companion Web site has links to books and Web sites devoted specifically to fallacies.

CHAPTER EXERCISES

Exercise Set 10.1: Identifying fallacies (part 1)

Objective: To give you practice identifying fallacies.

Instructions: Most of the following arguments commit one of the fallacies from this list:

- *Ad hominem*
- *Ad ignoratiam* (appeal to ignorance)
- *Ad misericordiam* (appeal to pity)
- *Ad populum*
- Begging the question/circular argument/*petitio principii*
- Complex question
- Equivocation
- False cause
- False dilemma

Some of the arguments in this exercise set do not commit any fallacy. For arguments that you think commit one of these fallacies, state the name of the fallacy that the argument commits and explain how the argument commits that fallacy. For arguments that you think do not commit any of these fallacies, write "No fallacy." Note that some fallacies may appear more than once and others may not appear at all.

Tips for success: Some of the fallacies below may be clear to you immediately. For others, you will probably need to look carefully at the descriptions and examples above to see which fallacy the argument commits. In some cases, there may even be more than one way to interpret the argument.

The two fallacies that beginners usually find most confusing are the fallacy of equivocation and begging the question.

To understand the fallacy of equivocation, consider the fact that words sometimes have more than one meaning. For example, consider this (paraphrased) exchange from the Pixar film *Cars*:

> LIGHTNING MCQUEEN: Race cars don't need headlights because the track is always lit.
> RUSTY: Yeah, well, my brother's always lit, but he still needs headlights.

Lightning is using the word *lit* to mean "illuminated." Rusty uses *lit* to mean "drunk." (If you watched *Cars* when you were little, this joke probably went over your head.) At first glance, it sounds like Rusty has offered a rebuttal of Lightning's claim that he doesn't need headlights. But suppose that we changed the dialogue to clarify the different meanings of *lit*:

> LIGHTNING MCQUEEN: Race cars don't need headlights because the track is always lit.
> RUSTY: Yeah, well, my brother's always drunk, but he still needs headlights.

The joke is ruined, the exchange no longer makes sense, and Rusty doesn't even come close to rebutting Lightning's claim.

Arguments that commit the fallacy of equivocation are a lot like this exchange. They look, at first, to be good arguments, but that's only because they're using a single word or expression in more than one way. Once you clarify the different meanings of the words, the arguments no longer look like good arguments. Typically, substituting synonyms will make it clear that one of the premises is either false or irrelevant to the conclusion.

Most examples of the fallacy of equivocation are a bit silly. That's because the "serious" examples are often harder to understand. Consider, for instance, the following argument, adapted from the philosopher John Stuart Mill:

> We ought to pursue whatever is desirable. Since all people desire happiness, happiness is clearly desirable. Therefore, we ought to pursue happiness.

Mill's critics point out that in the first sentence, *desirable* means "worthy of desire." In the second sentence, though, *desirable* means "able to be desired," just as *visible* means "able to be seen." But when we replace *desirable* with those phrases, the last premise is clearly irrelevant to the conclusion that we ought to pursue happiness: Since the first premise only claims we ought to pursue whatever is *worthy* of desire, the fact that happiness is able to be desired tells us nothing about whether we ought to pursue it. As you can see, this equivocation is a bit more subtle than the one from *Cars*. (It's not *all* that subtle, though. Could someone as smart as Mill really have made such an elementary mistake? Or is there a more charitable way of interpreting his argument?)

Moving on to the fallacy of begging the question: People increasingly use the phrase "begs the question" to mean "raises the question," as in "The mayor's speech begs the question of how the city is going to pay for all of those projects." When logicians say that an argument begs the question, however, they mean something quite different. Remember that an argument is supposed to convince you of something that you didn't already believe. When an argument begs the question, it requires you to accept the conclusion *before* you can accept one of the premises. In the example about the Bible, given above, you have to accept that God exists *before* you can accept that God wrote the Bible. Thus, an argument based on the premise that God wrote the Bible can't be a good argument for the claim that God exists.

Another way of begging the question is to include a premise that is nothing more than a restatement of the conclusion in different words. For instance, someone who says, "Justice is necessary for peace because you can't have peace without justice," is begging the question in this way. Their only premise ("You can't have peace without justice") is just another way of stating their conclusion ("Justice is necessary for peace"). Thus, the argument doesn't provide you with a reason for thinking that justice is necessary for peace unless you already believe that justice is necessary for peace. This is why begging the question is also sometimes called circular reasoning. Like a road that takes you in a circle, an argument that begs the question might appear to take you somewhere new, but it doesn't. The destination—that is, the conclusion—is not really different than the starting point—that is, the premises.

Some people have the idea that any argument that makes a questionable assumption is begging the question. This is incorrect. In order to count as begging the question, the argument must assume the very conclusion that it is trying to prove. Otherwise, it's just a regular bad argument.

Most of the other fallacies above are violations of or deviations from rules that you have seen earlier in this book. To figure out which fallacy a passage commits, check first to see if it is one of the types of arguments that we considered in Chapters II through VI. If so, check whether it violates any of the rules in that chapter. That will guide you in thinking about what kind of fallacy the argument commits.

If you can't identify the fallacy by considering the rules from a particular chapter, see if you can explain, in a general way, what is wrong with the argument. Then, look through the list of fallacies above and see which fallacy fits that general description.

Explaining how an argument commits a particular fallacy involves explaining the definition of the fallacy and citing *specific* features of the argument that show that the argument fits that definition. Pay close attention to the sample exercise below to see how that's done.

Sample

What's there to talk about? There are twelve people in this room, and eleven of them think the defendant is guilty. It's plain as day, and nobody but you even had to think twice about it. Come on. Admit it! He's guilty!

Adapted from: 12 Angry Men, *directed by Sidney Lumet (Los Angeles: United Artists, 1957)*

<u>Ad populum.</u> An argument <u>ad populum</u> tries to get someone to "go along with the crowd" in deciding what to believe. The conclusion of this argument is that the defendant is guilty. The only reason offered for that conclusion, however, is that eleven out of twelve people in the room believe that it is true. No reason is given to think that those eleven people are right or know better than the one person who does not believe it. The speaker wants the listener to go along with everybody else in believing that the defendant is guilty.

This response states which fallacy the argument commits, briefly defines that fallacy, and then explains, with reference to specific details of the argument, how the argument commits that fallacy. It does not simply say, "This argument commits the ad populum *fallacy because it tries to convince someone that something is true by pointing out that everyone else believes it." Such a response simply repeats the definition of the fallacy, without giving any indication of how this argument fits that definition.*

---

1. The death penalty is wrong because it's murder.

    Adapted from: "Capital Punishment and Warfare: Murder, or Justice," Beware the Darkness, Aug 20, 2010, http://bewarethedarkness.wordpress.com/2010/08/20/capital-punishment-murder

2. You want people who have entered this country illegally to go back to their home countries. So tell me: Why do you hate immigrants?

    Adapted from: Jorge Ramos, "D. A. King Interview (August, 2013)," The Official Website of Jorge Ramos Álvaros, Aug 19, 2013, http://jorgeramos.com/en/d-a-king-interview-august-2013/

3.   Few pediatricians are trained to diagnose mental illness. Without that training, pediatricians can't prescribe proper treatment for children with mental illness. This poses a huge problem for children with mental illness, because it means they can't get access to vital medical care.

Adapted from: Harold S. Koplewicz, letter to the editor, New York Times, *Sep 12, 2010, http://www.nytimes.com/2010/09/12/opinion/l12drug.html*

4.   The opponents of clean energy laws, such as a carbon tax or a cap-and-trade plan for carbon emissions, are either fools or idiots. Think about it. Either they don't mind our country being addicted to oil and dependent on oil-funded dictators or they think that some kind of global pandemic is going to wipe out at least 2.5 billion people in the next few decades. The first option is foolish. The second is idiotic.

Adapted from: Thomas L. Friedman, "What They Really Believe," New York Times, Nov 17, 2009, http://www.nytimes.com/ 2009/11/18/opinion/18friedman.html

5.   Atheists are hypocrites. Atheism is the view that there are no gods. But everyone, even the atheists themselves, have gods— things in their life that they elevate, worship, praise, and generally pour all of their emotional energy into. How can someone who has gods of his or her own say that there are no gods? You just can't do it.

Adapted from: "Atheists' Stupid Statements #2," YouTube, Jan 26, 2011, http://www.youtube.com/watch?v=Mzxh1YuAVtc

6.   Soviet cosmonaut Gherman Titov orbited Earth seventeen times, but he saw no angels in the heavens. Thus, angels do not exist.

Adapted from: Asif A. Siddiqi, The Red Rockets' Glare: Spaceflight and the Soviet Imagination, 1857–1957 *(Cambridge University Press, 2010), 74*

7.   Everything that any person has ever done is caused by that person's own desires and motivations. In other words, everything that a person does is done to satisfy the person's own desires. Acting to satisfy one's own desires is selfish. And as everybody knows, good

people are not selfish—at least not all the time. Thus, at the end of the day, no one is really a good person.

Adapted from: Joel Feinberg, "Psychological Egoism," in Reason and Responsibility, *13th ed., edited by Joel Feinberg and Russ Shafer-Landau (Belmont, CA: Wadsworth, 2007), 531*

8. If the United States had the same income distribution today as it did in the 1970s, the average American would be earning $120,000. The fact that the average American is now earning just $40,000 is Ronald Reagan's fault. Before Reagan came into office, CEOs made 78 times as much as their minimum-wage workers. Today, they make almost 3,500 times as much!

Adapted from: SemDem, "Obama v. Reagan," Daily Kos, *Feb 7, 2014, http://www.dailykos.com/story/2014/02/07/1275771/- Obama-v-Reagan-Fun-comparison-I-did-to-piss-off-a- wingnut-on-Reagan-s-B-day*

9. Some liberal intellectuals in Saudi Arabia want to relax the strict religious laws that govern that country. They claim that such re- forms are necessary to ensure the ongoing security of the country. But really, they're just perverts who want to flirt with girls and see half-naked women parading around in bathing suits at the beach. The Saudi government doesn't need to listen to them.

Adapted from: Neil MacFarquhar, "In Saudi Arabia, Royal Funds Buy Peace for Now," New York Times, *Jun 8, 2011, http://www.nytimes.com/2011/06/09/world/ middleeast/09saudi.html*

10. There must be some mistake. The people to whom we sold our customers' information aren't identity thieves. We checked their identities, and they all had sparkling clean records.

Adapted from: Scott Adams, Dilbert, *Oct 14, 2010*

Model responses for odd-numbered exercises can be found on page 407.

Need more practice? Go to the companion Web site for this book. Click on the link for "Appendix I." You will find a list of Web sites that discuss fallacies and give examples, often drawn from sources like the ones used in this book. Read the examples given on those sites and write your own explanations for how they fit the definition for a particular fallacy.

Exercise Set 10.2: Reinterpreting and revising fallacious arguments (part 1)

Objective: To give you practice developing productive responses to fallacious arguments.

Instructions: Review each of the arguments in Exercise Set 10.1. If you think that the argument commits a fallacy, then explain how you could reinterpret, revise, or rewrite the argument to avoid that fallacy, keeping as close to the original content and spirit of the argument as you can. If you think that an argument does not commit a fallacy, just write, "No fallacy."

Tips for success: It is tempting to think that once an argument is diagnosed with a fallacy, the argument is hopeless. On this view, identifying a fallacy in someone else's argument means that you don't have to take the argument seriously anymore.

A more constructive response to fallacious arguments is to recognize a fallacy as an opportunity to *improve* the argument. Sometimes this involves adding more premises or making explicit some important assumptions. Sometimes it involves toning down the rhetorical language in the argument to emphasize the legitimate point that the argument is making. Sometimes it means making a different argument that is nonetheless very close to the original argument. Just as the appropriate treatment for a medical condition depends on the diagnosis, so the appropriate treatment for a fallacious argument depends on the specific fallacy that the argument commits.

Ad hominem arguments, for instance, are sometimes misguided ways of criticizing someone else's claims. If you rebut someone's argument by calling him or her a bigot, for instance, you've committed an *ad hominem* fallacy. But if his or her argument uses an unreliable premise that reflects some kind of bigotry, then it would be entirely appropriate to point out that the premise is false, perhaps because it rests on a false stereotype.

Appeals to ignorance can sometimes be repaired by adding an additional premise. After all, the lack of evidence for a particular claim *can* be evidence that the claim is false, if there has been a serious attempt to look for evidence for that claim. Thus, adding a (true!) premise saying that there has been such an attempt can turn a fallacious appeal to ignorance into a reasonable argument. You might need to explain why a lack of evidence *in this case* counts as a good reason to think that the claim is false.

A heartbreaking appeal to pity might just be a loaded way of arguing that a person's hardship really does merit special treatment in this case. After all, hardship is *sometimes* a legitimate reason for special treatment. Focusing on the legitimate reasons that the hardship merits special treatment, rather than on the hardship itself, can therefore be an effective way to remedy a fallacious appeal to pity.

Ad populum arguments invoke "the people" as an authority. In some cases, "the people" might very well be an authority on something. In those cases, the thing to do is to point out *why* it's reasonable to believe what "everyone" is saying.

Question-begging arguments often arise simply because the speaker doesn't recognize that one of his or her premises assumes the truth of the conclusion. See if you can replace that premise with a similar but non-question-begging premise that leads to the same conclusion—perhaps with the addition of another premise or two.

"Complex questions" work by suggesting that a certain assumption is true without offering evidence for it. Although some people may use complex questions as an intentional ruse, many complex questions arise simply because the speaker takes the assumption to be beyond doubt. In either case, the appropriate treatment is to ask for evidence or reasons for that assumption. This gives the speaker the chance to defend the assumption if he or she has good reasons to believe it.

Equivocation is one of the few fallacies that can rarely be salvaged or reinterpreted in a more charitable way. Never say never, though. Consider John Stuart Mill's argument for the desirability of happiness, which we discussed in the "Tips for success" for Exercise Set 10.1. Mill's defenders interpret that argument as implicitly claiming that there is a special connection between the two senses of *desirable*—namely, that something's being desired by everyone is *evidence* that it is worthy of desire. Thus, even though the argument seems to equivocate on *desirable*, perhaps it's not as hopeless as it seems.

When an argument appears to commit the fallacy of false cause, it may simply be that the argument's author has failed to provide enough background information. With additional premises, the claim that one thing causes another might be more plausible. At any rate, the best response to a fallacy of false cause is to work sincerely toward finding the true cause(s) of the effect in question.

This list of proposed "treatments" for various fallacies is not complete, of course. Again, different cases call for different responses.

Admittedly, some arguments really are beyond hope. In such cases, nothing you can do can make a decent argument out of the fallacious one. If you think that one of the arguments in this exercise set is beyond repair in this way, say so and explain why. More generally, if you encounter a fallacy that's truly beyond repair, don't gloat about it. Instead, see if the person has other reasons to accept the conclusion. After all, it would be an appeal to ignorance to say, "Since your argument doesn't work, your conclusion is false!"

Sample

What's there to talk about? There are twelve people in this room, and eleven of them think the defendant is guilty. It's plain as day, and nobody but you even had to think twice about it. Come on. Admit it! He's guilty!

Adapted from: 12 Angry Men, *directed by Sidney Lumet (Los Angeles: United Artist, 1957)*

This argument appears to commit the <u>ad populum</u> fallacy by appealing to the "crowd's" beliefs to justify the conclusion. Given that the context for this argument is a jury's deliberation, we might reinterpret the argument along these lines: "All twelve jurors heard and saw all of the same evidence in the courtroom. Eleven of us found that evidence extremely compelling. You don't know any more than we do about the case, so if you disagree, either you've made some kind of mistake or we have. And it seems more likely to me that one of us has made a mistake than that eleven of us have. So I think it's reasonable to believe that you've made some kind of mistake." The additional premises make it clear why the speaker takes the agreement of the other eleven jurors to be a good reason to believe that the twelfth juror is wrong.

This response highlights the alleged fallacy and then offers a more charitable interpretation of the argument, according to which it does not commit a fallacy. Note that the reinterpreted argument is presented in a much less antagonistic way, which helps promote discussion rather than frustration. More importantly, the response uses specific details of the argument in its explanation, rather than relying on vague generalities about how to reinterpret or revise a specific kind of fallacy. This is important because not all instances of a particular fallacy are amenable to the same kind of reinterpretation. As in this case, reinterpreting an argument can involve stating important assumptions that went unstated in the original version of the argument. In this example, that means pointing out that all of the jurors have seen and heard the same evidence about the case. (For those who have seen 12 Angry Men, *spelling the argument out this way also explains one way in which the argument goes wrong. The twelfth juror* does *have some additional evidence: Because he owns a switchblade just like the defendant's, he knows that the prosecution was wrong in claiming the knife was unusual. And as it turns out, the twelfth juror eventually convinces the others that he's right. The defendant is not guilty!)*

This way of thinking of the argument relates to a topic of discussion among philosophers who study epistemology, or the theory of knowledge: How, if at all, should we change our beliefs when we discover that other thoughtful people who have access to all of the same information disagree with us on a particular topic? So far, at least, philosophers can't agree on the answer to that question.

Model responses for odd-numbered exercises can be found on page 409.

Need more practice? Working with a partner, have each partner write arguments that each commit one of the fallacies listed in this Appendix. Trade arguments and see how many you can reinterpret or revise to avoid committing a fallacy.

Exercise Set 10.3: Identifying fallacies (part 2)

Objective: To give you practice identifying the fallacies listed above.

Instructions: Most of the following arguments commit one of the following fallacies:

- Loaded language
- *Non sequitur*
- Overgeneralizing
- Overlooking alternatives
- Persuasive definition
- Poisoning the well
- *Post hoc ergo propter hoc*
- Red herring
- Straw man

Some of the arguments in this exericse set commit none of these fallacies. For arguments that commit one of these fallacies, state the name of the fallacy that the argument commits and explain how the argument commits that fallacy. For arguments that do not commit any of these fallacies, write "No fallacy." Note that some fallacies may appear more than once and others may not appear at all.

Tips for success: As in Exercise Set 10.1, some of the fallacies in this exercise set may be clear to you immediately. For others, you will probably need to look carefully at the descriptions and examples above to see which fallacy the argument commits.

You may have noticed that several of these fallacies are very closely related. For instance, "poisoning the well" often involves a specific way of using loaded language, and *post hoc ergo propter hoc* is a specific way of overlooking alternatives. It's best to be as specific as possible in identifying fallacies. Thus, when you find an argument that commits the *post hoc* fallacy, say that it's an instance of *post hoc ergo propter hoc*, not just that it overlooks alternatives. This provides a more precise characterization of the argument's flaw.

More generally, many fallacious arguments include loaded language. There are often deeper problems with the argument, though. Thus, for many of these passages, you'll need to think carefully about which of several possible answers best captures the most serious problem with the argument.

Sample

As every Iowan knows, Iowa has seen some major floods in the last few years. Now some ivory tower academics are saying that these floods are because we have changed the landscape so much—draining fields with pipes, straightening streams, filling in wetlands, and whatever else we do. But this is just stupid. The reason for the floods is pretty obvious: it's been raining cats and dogs. Rivers don't flood like this just because someone put in a parking lot.

Adapted from: Joel Achenbach, "Iowa Flooding Could Be Act of Man, Experts Say," Washington Post, Jun 19, 2008, http://www.washingtonpost.com/wp-dyn/content/article/2008/06/18/ AR2008061803371.html

This argument commits the straw man fallacy. The argument is criticizing the view that Iowa's severe flooding has happened because of changes in land use. The argument even explains the view a little bit by giving examples of land-use change (e.g., filling in wetlands). But in rejecting that view, the argument caricatures it as the view that the floods happened "because someone put in a parking lot." It <u>would</u> be absurd to blame the floods on someone's putting in a parking lot, but that wasn't the original view at all.

This response cites specific aspects of the argument to support the claim that the argument commits the straw man fallacy. This is much more effective than simply repeating the definition of the fallacy, since it makes it easy to see how this argument fits that definition.

There are several questionable aspects of this sample argument. For instance, its use of loaded language (e.g., "ivory tower academics" and "just stupid") is problematic. The biggest problem with the argument, though, is that in criticizing another view, the argument caricatures that view in order to make it seem absurd. That's what the straw man fallacy consists in—caricaturing another view in order to make it easier to criticize.

1. I went on a walk with my daughter this afternoon, and three different bicyclists ignored stop signs and almost ran us over. Cyclists really think they're above the law!

    Adapted from: Scott Simon, Twitter post, Jun 26, 2014, 7:31 am,
    https://twitter.com/nprscottsimon

2. First, doctors diagnosed the president of Paraguay with cancer. Then the presidents of Venezuela and Brazil. And not long after that, the previous president of Brazil and the president of Argentina were diagnosed with cancer within a few days of each other. There's only one possible explanation for all of those Latin American leaders getting cancer: The United States government has developed the technology to induce cancer and is using it to try to assassinate leaders it doesn't like.

    Adapted from: Juan Francisco Alonso, "Chávez Suspects That the U.S. May Be Behind His Illness," El Universal (Caracas), Dec 28, 2011, http://www.eluniversal.com/nacional-y-politica/111228/chavez-suspects-that-the-us-may-be-behind-his-illness

3. The Court was asked to decide the simple question of whether, when Congress wrote "established by the State" in the Affordable Care Act, it actually meant "established by the State or the Federal Government." On any rational reading, these plainly

mean different things. But through some absurd interpretive jig-gery-pokery involving other parts of the Affordable Care Act, the Court has caved in to its desperate need to save this wretched law. This is pure applesauce. The Court decided wrongly.

Adapted from: King v. Burwell, 576 U.S. _____ (2015) (Scalia, J., dissenting)

4. Liberals want to take away our right to own guns. Some people complain that this violates our constitutional rights as Americans. And I agree with those people, of course—I mean, it's as clear as can be in the Constitution. But forget about the Constitution for a minute. Suppose I just dropped out of the sky—no political system, no Bill of Rights, no nothing. I would have the right to defend myself and my family, right? And here these liberals want to say that I don't have that right—that I can't defend myself against robbers or murderers or whatever. And that's just crazy, regardless of what you think about the Constitution.

Adapted from: "Ted Nugent on Gun Control," YouTube, Feb 6, 2008, http://www.youtube.com/watch?v=nurM0mY9N10

5. Batman is clearly a criminal. Why else does he wear a mask? Why does he conceal his identity? He hides who he is because he is an outlaw! And think about this: whenever we hear about Batman or see pictures of him, he is with criminals! Only a criminal would spend so much time with other criminals!

Adapted from: "Dizzoner the Penguin," Batman, Twentieth Century Fox Television (Nov 3, 1966)

6. So Monsanto—one of the biggest biotech companies in the world—puts out all these lies about how its genetically modified crops are essential to ending world hunger, how the crops are per-fectly safe, and so on—all kinds of propaganda like this. But did you know that they've actually patented those seeds? And that they ban farmers from saving seeds from *crops those farmers grew themselves* to replant the next year? Monsanto's not interested in helping anybody. They're just looking out for their bottom line. So

don't believe them when they say that genetically modified crops are essential to ending world hunger.

Adapted from: "Real Time with Bill Maher: Episode 294," HBO, Sep 20, 2013

7.   THOMAS HUXLEY: Based on the theory of evolution, I believe that humans are descended from apes.
BISHOP E. R. WILBERFORCE: Do you? Was the ape your grandmother or your grandfather?

Adapted from: Isabella Sidgwick, "A Grandmother's Tales," MacMillan's Magazine, LXXVIII, Oct 1898, 433–34

8.   During the Ebola outbreak in West Africa during 2014, there were ten confirmed cases of Ebola in the United States. Before Obamacare became the law of the land, there had never been a single case of Ebola in the United States. So as you can see, Obamacare has led to Americans getting Ebola.

Adapted from: Peter Sullivan, "Cruz Advisor's 'Bad Joke': No Ebola Before ObamaCare," The Hill, Oct 23, 2014, http://thehill.com/blogs/ blog-briefing-room/221747-cruz-advisors-bad-joke-no-us-ebola-before-obamacare

9.   A politician is someone who tells you what you want to hear and then does whatever he or she wants to do. That's why politicians can't be trusted.

Adapted from: Harry Browne, "The Quintessential Politician," HarryBrowne.org, Jun 22, 2004, http://harrybrowne.org/articles/Reagan'sLegacy.htm

10.   Ladies and gentleman of the jury, I'll admit that the plaintiff's attorneys make a good case. I almost felt pity for the guy. They almost even convinced me that my client is guilty—that my client, a small-town school cafeteria chef in Colorado, really did swindle these record companies out of all of that money. But consider this. Chewbacca, from the *Star Wars* movies, is a Wookie. He comes from the planet Kashyyyk. He's eight feet tall. And yet— and yet, ladies and gentlemen!—he lives on a moon called Endor with a bunch of two-foot-tall Ewoks! Ewoks, ladies and gentlemen! Does that make sense? No! No, it does not. It makes *no* sense.

And so, you see, if Chewbacca lives on Endor, you must acquit! My client is not guilty!

Adapted from: "Chef Aid," South Park, Comedy Central (Oct 7, 1998)

Model responses for odd-numbered exercises can be found on page 411.

Need more practice? Find news sites on the Web that allow users to comment on news stories. Look for stories on controversial topics and read the comments about those stories. Many of the comments will offer arguments about the news stories, about related (or unrelated) topics, or about other comments. See how many fallacies you can identify in those comments.

Exercise Set 10.4: Reinterpreting and revising fallacious arguments (part 2)

Objective: To give you practice developing productive responses to fallacious arguments.

Instructions: Review each of the arguments in Exercise Set 10.3. If you think the argument commits a fallacy, explain how you could reinterpret, revise, or rewrite the argument to avoid that fallacy, keeping as close to the original content and spirit of the argument as you can. If you think an argument does not commit a fallacy, just write, "No fallacy."

Tips for success: As in Exercise Set 10.2, your goal here is to offer something more productive than simply diagnosing fallacies. Your response will need to be tailored to the specific fallacies that you identify.

When a conversational partner overlooks alternatives, the most productive response is to point out other salient alternatives and ask whether those alternatives change your partner's conclusions. Acknowledging those alternatives may force the speaker to give up the argument, since the original argument may not work once he or she takes those alternatives into account. In some cases, however, adding new alternatives doesn't change the ultimate conclusion. So don't jump to any conclusions yourself when you notice that someone has overlooked alternatives.

When someone uses loaded language in presenting an argument, ask yourself what you would think of the argument if all of the loaded language were replaced with neutral language. Just because an argument is couched in loaded language doesn't necessarily mean that it's a bad argument. It just means that you need to beware of getting carried away by emotion when you evaluate the argument. The same goes for poisoning the well. Ask yourself what you would think of the person's claim or argument if he or she had not "poisoned the well" by associating the claim or argument with something unsavory.

What looks like a *non sequitur* to you might look like a strong argument to someone who knows some additional information that links the argument's premises to its conclusion. If you suspect that someone's argument is a *non sequitur*, ask for clarification rather than attacking the argument. If the author isn't available to clarify the argument for you, see if you can fill in any missing premises yourself. What must the author be assuming if he or she takes the premises of the argument to be good reasons for the conclusion? Are those assumptions defensible?

Someone who appears to be generalizing from one or two examples might simply have offered those examples as illustrations, not evidence. Ask yourself or the argument's author whether there are other plausible reasons to think that the generalization is true. Giving other reasons might involve giving additional examples, but it might involve other strategies, such as citing sources.

As with other fallacies that smuggle assumptions into an argument, like circular reasoning and complex questions, the fallacy of persuasive definition is not always committed with malice aforethought. Don't write off an argument just because the definition is loaded. Ask yourself whether the argument works with a more neutral definition or if you can give additional premises that would justify the assumption that's built into a persuasive definition.

An argument that seems to commit *post hoc ergo propter hoc*, like an argument that commits the more general fallacy of false cause, may just be lacking in background information. There may be additional premises that make it more plausible to think that the alleged causal connection is real. Ask yourself or the argument's author what those reasons might be.

Red herrings are most effective when they drag an emotionally charged issue into a debate. Often this happens only because the person committing the fallacy is emotionally invested in the issue, and the fallacy works (when it does) because the hearer is emotionally invested in the issue too. But just because someone brings up an irrelevant point doesn't mean that he or she hasn't also given good reasons to accept some conclusion. Try to ignore the red herring altogether and see if you can find a decent argument in what's left over.

Straw man fallacies sometimes contain a grain of truth. Although they often present overly simple responses to overly simplified arguments, more elaborate versions of those responses might actually be legitimate criticisms of the argument that was being caricatured.

As with the discussion of fallacies in Exercise Set 10.2, this list of "treatments" is far from comprehensive. Different circumstances will call for different responses. Remember that the goal of arguing is not to show *who* is right, but to discover *what* is right. Here the invitation is to focus on what each argument can offer, not on how it falls short.

Sample

As every Iowan knows, Iowa has seen some major floods in the last few years. Now some ivory tower academics are saying that these floods are because we have changed the landscape so much—draining fields with pipes, straightening streams, filling in wetlands, and whatever else we do. But this is just stupid. The reason for the floods is pretty obvious: it's been raining cats and dogs. Rivers don't flood like this just because someone put in a parking lot.

Adapted from: Joel Achenbach, "Iowa Flooding Could Be Act of Man, Experts Say," Washington Post, Jun 19, 2008, http://www.washingtonpost.com/wp-dyn/content/article/2008/06/18/ AR2008061803371.html

In Exercise Set 10.3 we said that this argument commits the straw man fallacy. If we interpret it charitably, though, the claim that "rivers don't flood like this just because someone put in a parking lot" is just a rhetorical flourish. It's a way of saying that the dramatic floods in Iowa are too big to be the result of man-made changes to the environment, including all of the changes that the "ivory tower academics" mention. To improve the argument, we would need additional premises to show that the amount of rain that Iowa has seen in recent years is enough to have caused floods even without those man-made changes.

This response quickly identifies the fallacy that the argument appears to commit and then immediately moves on to explaining how to reinterpret and improve it. Notice that the response suggests an interpretation of the last sentence that yields the strongest argument. Ultimately, the question is not whether that is the interpretation that the author intended, but whether there is a possible interpretation that allows us to learn from the argument.

This response suggests that the argument could be improved by adding premises that show that such heavy rain would have caused floods even without the man-made changes. Before doing some research, most people probably don't know whether such premises can be found. The point of this exercise, though, is to say what would need to be done to improve the argument, even if it turns out that it's difficult to do so.

Need more practice? The "Need more practice?" section after Exercise Set 10.3 suggested that you look for fallacious arguments in the comment sections of online news sites. For each fallacious argument that you find on those sites, ask yourself whether there is a way to reinterpret or revise the argument to avoid the fallacy.

Model responses for odd-numbered exercises can be found on page 414.

Exercise Set 10.5: Two deductive fallacies

Objective: To practice distinguishing *modus ponens* and *modus tollens* from affirming the consequent and denying the antecedent, and to better understand why the last two are fallacies.

Instructions: Each of the arguments below fits the form of either *modus ponens, modus tollens,* affirming the consequent, or denying the antecedent. State which form each argument fits. For arguments that affirm the consequent or deny the antecedent, describe a scenario in which the antecedent of the conditional would be false and the consequent would be true. (Remember that in "if **p**, then **q**," **p** is the antecedent, and **q** is the consequent.)

Tips for success: Affirming the consequent and denying the antecedent look a lot like their non-fallacious relatives, *modus ponens* and *modus tollens.* Each starts with an "if–then" sentence. Each asserts or denies some part of that "if–then" sentence as its second premise, and then infers the truth or denial of the other part as its conclusion. Take a look at all four together:

modus ponens	*modus tollens*
If **p** then **q**.	If **p** then **q**.
p.	Not-**q**.
Therefore, **q**.	Therefore, not-**p**.
affirming the consequent	**denying the antecedent**
If **p** then **q**.	If **p** then **q**.
q.	Not-**p**.
Therefore, **p**.	Therefore, not-**q**.

Despite the superficial similarities, there is a crucial difference between the top two—*modus ponens* and *modus tollens*—and the bottom two—affirming the consequent and denying the antecedent. The top two are valid deductive argument forms. The bottom two are not. They are fallacies. To determine which form an argument fits, symbolize the argument, just as you did for the arguments in Chapter VI. Then carefully compare your symbolization of the argument to the patterns above.

Remember the definition of "validity" from Chapter VI: A deductive argument is valid when the form of the argument is such that it is *impossible* for the premises to be true and the conclusion to be false.

If "if **p** then **q**" is true, and **p** is also true, then it is impossible for **q** to be false. (If **p** were true and **q** were false, then "if **p** then **q**" would be false.) Likewise, if "if **p** then **q**" and not-**q** are both true, then it is impossible for not-**p** to be false.

Even if we assume that "if **p** then **q**" is true, however, we can usually come up with a scenario in which **p** is false while **q** is true. (When we can't, that's because "if **p** then **q**" is also true!) Such a scenario illustrates why affirming the consequent is invalid, because the possibility of such a scenario shows that it's *possible* for the conclusion of the argument to be false even when the premises are true. In that same scenario, not-**p** will be true, and not-**q** will be false. Thus, the scenario also illustrates why denying the consequent is invalid. For example, it's true that if my only pet is a dog, then my only pet is a mammal. But suppose that my only pet is a cat. Then it's true that my only pet is a mammal, but false that my only pet is a dog. So, if you reasoned that because my only pet isn't a dog, it's not a mammal, you'd reach a false conclusion; likewise if you reasoned that because my only pet is a mammal, my only pet is a dog.

Notice that you will not need to say whether any of the premises are actually true or false. Validity does not depend on whether the premises are true. It depends only on the connection between the premises and the conclusion—whether it would be possible for the conclusion to be false *if* the premises *were* true.

Sample

If Rosalyn is babysitting Calvin tonight, then Calvin will have to go to bed early. Calvin's going to bed early. So Rosalyn must be babysitting Calvin tonight.

Adapted from: Bill Watterson, Calvin & Hobbes, *Feb 7, 1989*

Affirming the consequent. The antecedent would be false and the consequent true if Calvin's parents send him to bed early on a night when he doesn't have a babysitter.

This response correctly identifies the form of argument as affirming the consequent. It then briefly describes a scenario in which the antecedent of the conditional (i.e., "Rosalyn is baby-sitting Calvin tonight") is false, but the consequent (i.e., "Calvin will have to go to bed early") is true. Thus, the scenario illustrates why affirming the consequent is an invalid form of argument: If you learned that Calvin was going to bed early—which is true in this scenario—and concluded that Rosalyn is babysitting him—which is false in this scenario—you'd have moved from true premises to a false conclusion. That will never happen when you're using valid arguments.

1. If Bob gave someone a bribe, then Bob should not be punished but the person who accepted the bribe should. Bob gave someone a bribe. Therefore, Bob should not be punished, but the person who accepted the bribe should be punished.

    Adapted from: Subhadip Sircar, "Kaushik Basu Says Make Bribe-Giving Legal," India Real Time, Mar 30, 2011, http://blogs.wsj.com/indiarealtime/ 2011/03/30/kaushik-basu-says-make-bribe-giving-legal/

2. If the government owned your children, then it would be okay for the government to require you to vaccinate your children. But the government doesn't own your children. Therefore, it's not okay for the government to require you to vaccinate your children.

    Adapted from: Philip Rucker and Rosalind S. Helderman, "Vaccination Debate Flares in GOP Presidential Race, Alarming Medical Experts," Washington Post, Feb 2, 2015, http://www.washingtonpost.com/politics/chris-christie-remarks-show-vaccines-potency- in-political-debate/2015/02/02/f1c49a6e-aaff-11e4-abe8-e1ef60ca26de_story.html

3. If Mr. Shue isn't good enough to perform on Broadway, then he'll keep working as a teacher. It turns out that Mr. Shue is good enough to perform on Broadway. Therefore, Mr. Shue isn't going to keep his job as a teacher.

    Adapted from: Glee, Episode 41 ("Rumours"), first broadcast May 3, 2011 by Fox, directed by Tim Hunter and written by Ryan Murphy

4. If time travel is possible, then we can easily learn about the past. We can easily learn about the past. Therefore, time travel is possible.

    Adapted from: H.G. Wells, The Time Machine (1895; repr., Madison, WI: Cricket House Books, 2011), 7

5.   If the Earth circles the Sun, then the planets will sometimes appear to move backward in the sky. The planets sometimes appear to move backward in the sky. Therefore, the Earth circles the Sun.

Adapted from: Nicolas Copernicus, On the Revolutions of Heavenly Spheres *(1543; repr., Philadelphia: Running Press, 2004), 346*

6.   You would follow me if you loved me. But you won't follow me. I guess you don't love me after all.

Adapted from: Georges Bizet, Carmen (Vocal Score), *libretto by Henri Meilhac and Ludovic Halévy, trans. Theodore Baker (Mineola, NY: Dover, 2002), 203*

7.   If the Man in Black's drink was poisoned, then he will die soon. The Man in Black will not die soon. Therefore, the Man in Black's drink was not poisoned.

Adapted from: The Princess Bride, *directed by Rob Reiner (Los Angeles: 20th Century Fox, 1987)*

8.   If you don't play the lottery, then you can't win the lottery. You do play the lottery. Therefore, you can win the lottery.

Adapted from: "Mega Millions Has People Dreaming of Riches," YouTube, Dec 31, 2010, http://www.youtube.com/watch?v=YbMc-N9EGgo

9.   If this girl is possessed by a demon and I sprinkle holy water on her, then she should react violently. I sprinkled ordinary water on her, not holy water. Therefore, she should not react violently.

Adapted from: The Exorcist, *directed by William Friedkin (Burbank: Warner Bros., 1973)*

10.   If the tropical rainforests are not saved, then countless species and many unique cultures will be lost forever. Countless species and many unique cultures will be lost forever. Therefore, the tropical rainforests will not be saved.

Adapted from: "Rainforest Facts," Save the Rainforest, n.d., http://www.savetherainforest.org/savetherainforest_007.htm

Model responses for odd-numbered exercises can be found on page 416.

Need more practice? Working with a classmate, generate a list of ten "if–then" sentences. Write one argument based on each of those ten sentences, with some arguments following the form of modus ponens, some modus tollens, some affirming the consequent, and some denying the antecedent. Swap lists with your partner and see how quickly you can identify which arguments are which..

Critical thinking activity: Relating rules and fallacies

For an activity to help you connect the fallacies in this Appendix to the rules from Chapters I through VI, see the "Relating rules and fallacies" assignment sheet (p. 485) in Part 3.

Exercise Set 10.6: Constructing fallacious arguments

Objective: To improve your understanding of fallacies.

Instructions: Construct an argument that commits each of the fallacies listed below. Then, explain how the argument commits that fallacy.

Tips for success: It's easier to construct some kinds of fallacies than others. For instance, constructing an *ad hominem* fallacy is simple. Pick a person who endorses a particular position and write an argument that tries to prove that position to be false by attacking the person.

Other fallacies can be more difficult to write. One approach is to begin with the most distinctive feature of the relevant fallacy. For instance, the most distinctive feature of the fallacy of equivocation is the use of a single word or expression with multiple meanings. So, to write an argument that commits the fallacy of equivocation, begin by picking a word that has multiple meanings and try to build an argument around those meanings. Similarly, a false dilemma begins with a forced choice between two options, even though there are other options available. So, to write a false dilemma, begin by identifying a situation in which there are at least three options, and then write an argument that involves a forced choice between just two of those options.

Another approach is to think about which rule(s) a fallacy violates. Once you've figured that out, you can write an argument that follows the relevant rules and then tweak it to turn it into a fallacy. For instance, over-generalizing involves a violation of Rules 7 and 8. If you write a good argument for a generalization, you can turn it into a fallacy of overgeneralization by reducing the number of examples used in the argument.

Whatever your approach, it may help to begin by picking a specific conclusion for your fallacious argument. Then, think about good or bad ways of arguing for that conclusion. If you can find a good argument for it, see if you can change it to turn it into a fallacy.

If you want to make this even more challenging for yourself, try to write "realistic" fallacies—that is, fallacies that someone might actually mistake for good arguments.

Sample

Straw man.

"My history professor says that everyone should study world history because that's the only way to understand what's going on in the world today. What a self-absorbed jerk. A lot of people understand the world just fine without getting a PhD in history!"

This argument commits the straw man fallacy because it caricatures the history professor's position in order to show that it's incorrect. The history professor says that everyone should "study world history." The argument misrepresents this position as the claim that everyone should get a PhD in history. You can study world history by taking a class or two—or even by reading books in your free time; you don't need to get a PhD to study world history. Thus, the fact that you can understand the world without getting a PhD in history doesn't undermine the professor's claim that everyone should study world history in order to understand the world.

This response presents an argument that clearly commits the straw man fallacy. It then explains how the argument commits the fallacy, drawing on specific details of the fallacious argument to do so.

---

1.   Complex question

2.   Straw man

3.   Equivocation

4.   Persuasive definition

5.   *Post hoc ergo propter hoc*

6.   Begging the question

7.   *Ad hominem*

8.   False dilemma

9.   *Ad ignorantiam* (Appeal to ignorance)

10. Red herring

Model responses for odd-numbered exercises can be found on page 418.

Need more practice? Working with a friend or classmate, pick five or ten fallacies from this Appendix. Construct arguments that commit each of the fallacies you've chosen. Exchange arguments with your partner and try to identify the fallacies that he or she created. To make it harder, throw in an argument or two that doesn't commit any of these fallacies

Critical thinking activity: Identifying, reinterpreting, and revising fallacies

For a group activity that helps you recognize fallacies, see the "Identifying, reinterpreting, and revising fallacies" assignment sheet (p. 486) in Part 3.

Critical thinking activity: Critical thinking public service announcements

For an out-of-class activity that helps you understand specific fallacies and strategies for avoiding them, see the "Critical-thinking public service announcements" assignment sheet (p. 487) in Part 3.

Appendix II
Definitions

Some arguments require attention to the meaning of words. Sometimes we may not know the established meaning of a word, or the established meaning may be specialized. If the conclusion of your argument is that "Wejacks are herbivorous," your first task is to define your terms, unless you are speaking to an Algonquian ecologist.[1] If you encounter this conclusion elsewhere, the first thing you need is a dictionary.

Other times, a term may be in popular use but still unclear. We debate "assisted suicide," for example, but don't necessarily understand exactly what it means. Before we can argue effectively about it, we need an agreed-upon idea of what we are arguing *about*.

Still another kind of definition is required when the meaning of a term is contested. What is a "drug," for example? Is alcohol a drug? Is tobacco? What if they are? Can we find any logical way to answer these questions?

When terms are unclear, get specific

A neighbor of one of the authors was taken to task by the city's Historic Districts Commission for putting up a four-foot model lighthouse in her front yard. City ordinances prohibit any yard fixtures in historic districts. She was hauled before the commission and told to remove it. A furor erupted and the story got into the newspapers.

Here the dictionary saved the day. According to *Webster's*, a "fixture" is something fixed or attached as to a building, such as a permanent appendage or structural part. The lighthouse, however, was moveable—more like a lawn ornament. Hence, it was not a "fixture"—seeing as the law did not specify any alternative definition. Hence, not prohibited.

When issues get more difficult, dictionaries are less helpful. Dictionary definitions often offer synonyms, for one thing, that may be just as

---

1. "Wejack" is the Algonquian name for a weasel-like animal of eastern North America that in English is called a fisher. "Herbivores" are animals that eat only or mostly plants. Actually, wejacks are not herbivorous.

Rule D1

unclear as the word you're trying to define. Dictionaries also may give multiple definitions, so you have to choose between them. And sometimes dictionaries are just plain wrong. *Webster's* may be the hero of the last story, but it also defines "headache" as "a pain in the head"—far too broad a definition. A bee sting or cut on your forehead or nose would be a pain in the head but not a headache.

For some words, then, you need to make the term more precise yourself. Use concrete, definite terms rather than vague ones (Rule 4). Be specific without narrowing the term too much.

> Organic foods are foods produced without chemical fertilizers or pesticides.

Definitions like this call a clear idea to mind, something you can go on to investigate or evaluate. Be sure, of course, to *stick* to your definition as you go on with your argument (no equivocation).

One virtue of the dictionary is that it is fairly neutral. *Webster's* defines "abortion," for example, as "the forcible expulsion of the mammalian fetus prematurely." This is an appropriately neutral definition. It is not up to the dictionary to decide if abortion is moral or immoral. Compare a common definition from one side of the abortion debate:

> "Abortion" means "murdering babies."

This definition is loaded. Fetuses are not the same as babies, and the term "murder" unfairly imputes evil intentions to well-intentioned people (however wrong the writer may think they are). That ending the life of a fetus is comparable to ending the life of a baby is an arguable proposition, but it is for an argument to *show*—not simply *assume* by definition. (See also Rule 5, and the fallacy of persuasive definition.)

You may need to do a little research. You will find, for example, that "assisted suicide" means allowing doctors to help aware and rational people arrange and carry out their own dying. It does not include allowing doctors to "unplug" patients without their consent (that would be some form of "involuntary euthanasia"—another category). People may have good reasons to object to assisted suicide so defined, but if the definition is made clear at the outset, at least the contending parties will be talking about the same thing.

Sometimes we can define a term by specifying certain tests or procedures that determine whether or not it applies. This is called an *operational* definition. For example, Wisconsin law requires that all legislative meetings be open to the public. But what exactly counts as a "meeting" for purposes of this law? The law offers an elegant criterion:

> A "meeting" is any gathering of enough legislators to block action on the legislative measure that is the subject of the gathering.

This definition is far too narrow to define the ordinary word "meeting." But it does accomplish the purpose of this law: to prevent legislators from making crucial decisions out of the public eye.

Exercise Set 11.1: Making definitions more precise

Objective: To give you practice making definitions more precise.

Instructions: For each of the following definitions, think of an example of something that should be covered by the definition but isn't and/or of something that is covered by the definition but shouldn't be. Then, suggest a better definition that correctly classifies the example(s) you gave.

Tips for success: Definitions provide a way to carve up the world into things that are "covered" by a term and things that aren't—that is, things to which the term applies and things to which it does not. This is often difficult to do.

Even a relatively good definition can run into two kinds of problems: It can include something that it ought not to include, and it can exclude something that it ought not to exclude. (Or both!) For instance, as we noted above, the dictionary's definition of *headache*—"a pain or ache in the head"—incorrectly includes a bee sting on your head as a headache. This is a case of the definition being too broad or covering too much. On the other hand, a definition like "a pain or ache in the head caused by tension or illness" would exclude things that shouldn't be excluded, like headaches caused by dehydration or loud noises. This is a case of a definition being too narrow or not covering enough.

The first step in each exercise in this set is to think of something that exemplifies one of these problems. One good way to begin looking for examples is to ask yourself whether the definition seems too narrow or too broad. If it's too broad, try to think of things that fit the definition, but to which you wouldn't apply the term. If it's too narrow, try to think of things to which you would normally apply the term, but which don't fit the definition..

The second step in each exercise in this set is to suggest a better definition for the term being defined. One criterion for improving your definition is that it should correctly classify the example you gave in the first part of the exercise. Thus, if you gave an example of something that was included when it shouldn't be, you will need to make the definition narrower. If you gave an example of something that was excluded when it shouldn't be, you'll need to make the definition broader. Take care, though, that it does not introduce new problems that didn't exist with the original definition. Especially, make sure that changing the definition doesn't over-compensate in the other direction—make a too-narrow definition too broad, for example. You want to include all and only the things that intuitively "fit" under the term being defined.

Sample

Arguably, even a country that guarantees freedom of speech and freedom of the press may have the right to restrict the sale of pornography. "Pornography" is any material—audio-visual or written—that is sexually explicit.

Adapted from: Caroline West, "Pornography and Censorship," Stanford Encyclopedia of Philosophy, *May 5, 2004, http://plato.stanford.edu/entries/pornography-censorship/*

This definition of "pornography" includes educational materials that are sexually explicit but not pornographic (e.g., medical textbooks or textbooks for sex education classes). A better definition of "pornography" would be "sexually explicit audio-visual or written material that is specifically designed to stimulate sexual arousal."

This response specifies the term being defined and offers an example of something that is included by the original definition, but shouldn't be. It then suggests a better, narrower definition. The definition may not be perfect, but it's a big improvement.

---

1. In many cities, you need a permit to hold a parade. A "parade" is a ceremonial procession that includes people marching.

   Adapted from: "Parade," WordNet, n.d., http://wordnetweb.princeton.edu/perl/webwn?s=parade

2. A person is "presumed dead" if he or she has been missing for at least seven years and there has been no evidence during that time of his or her being alive.

   Adapted from: Eric Zorn, "Declaring Death Doesn't Always Take 7 Years," Chicago Tribune, *Nov 29, 2007, http://blogs.chicagotribune.com/news_columnists_ezorn/2007/11/missingdead.html*

3.   Many school districts would like to ensure that their schools are staffed by highly qualified teachers. A "highly qualified elementary school teacher" is one who holds at least a bachelor's degree and has passed a rigorous state examination to demonstrate subject knowledge and teaching skills in reading, writing, mathematics, and other areas commonly included in elementary school curricula.

Adapted from: 20 United States Code §7801

4.   Some universities prohibit students from throwing parties in the dormitories. A "party" is a gathering of six or more people in a room where alcohol is being served.

Adapted from: "Alcohol and Other Drug Biennial Review—2010," St. Bonaventure University Office of Student Life, 2010, http://www.sbu.edu/campus-life .aspx?id=6098

5.   It is morally wrong for an adult to knowingly give a child poison. A "poison" is any product that can harm a person or animal if it is used incorrectly or in the wrong dosage.

Adapted from: "Poison Law & Legal Definition," U.S. Legal, n.d., http:// definitions.uslegal.com/p/poison/

6.   Achieving "success" in life means holding a stable, respectable job in which you earn a lot of money.

Adapted from: Dennis Nishi, "How to Define Success for Yourself," Wall Street Journal, Oct 25, 2014, http://www.wsj.com/articles/ how-to-define-success-for-yourself-1414284614

7.   In order to protect a valued way of life, people should strive to buy as much of their food as they can from family farms. A "family farm" is a farm that is owned by a single family.

Adapted from: Leslie A. Duram, Encyclopedia of Organic, Sustainable, and Local Foods (Santa Barbara, CA: Greenwood, 2010), 144

8.   I am challenging myself to go without dessert for a month. I consider "dessert" to be any sugary baked good (e.g., pie, cake, or cookies), ice cream, or candy.

Adapted from: Sarah Robles, "January's No Soda Challenege," Pretty Strong, Feb 6, 2013, http://prettystrongblog.blogspot.com/2013/02/januarys-no-soda-challenge.html

9.   Anyone found guilty of terrorism should be imprisoned for life. "Terrorism" is any activity that is a criminal act in the jurisdiction where it is performed and is apparently intended to intimidate a civilian population or influence the policy or action of a government.

Adapted from: 6 United States Code §101

10.   An "unhealthy relationship" is any relationship in which one person inflicts physical, sexual, or emotional violence on the other.

Adapted from: notMYkid, "Unhealthy Relationships," notmykid.org, n.d., http://notmykid.org/unhealthy-relationships/

Model responses for odd-numbered exercises can be found on page 421.

Need more practice? Even dictionary definitions aren't perfect, as the example of "headache" shows. Working with a group of classmates, look for dictionary definitions that are too narrow or too broad. (You might see who can find the greatest number of inappropriate definitions in ten minutes or how many inappropriate definitions the whole group can find in five minutes.) Give an example of something that is inappropriately included or excluded by each definition. Then, as a group, try to work out better definitions for each word.

When terms are contested, work from the clear cases

Sometimes a term is *contested*. That is, people are arguing over the proper application of the term itself. In that case, it's not enough simply to propose a clarification. A more involved kind of argument is needed.

When a term is contested you can distinguish three relevant sets of things. One set includes those things to which the term clearly applies. The second includes those things to which the term clearly does *not* apply. In the middle will be those things whose status is unclear—including the things being argued over. Your job is to formulate a definition that

1. *includes* all the things that the term clearly fits;

2. *excludes* all the things that the term clearly does not fit; and

3. draws the *plainest possible line* somewhere in between, and *explains* why the line belongs there and not somewhere else.

For example, consider what defines a "bird." Exactly what is a bird, anyway? Is a bat a bird?

To meet requirement 1, it is often helpful to begin with the general category (*genus*) to which the things being defined belong. For birds, the natural genus would be animals. To meet requirements 2 and 3, we then need to specify how birds differ from other animals (the *differentia*). Our question therefore is: precisely what differentiates birds—*all* birds and *only* birds—from other animals?

It's trickier than it may seem. We can't draw the line at flight, for example, because ostriches and penguins don't fly (so the proposed definition wouldn't cover all birds, violating the first requirement) and bumblebees and mosquitoes do (so the proposed definition would include some non-birds, violating the second).

What distinguishes all and only birds, it turns out, is having feathers. Penguins and ostriches have feathers even though they don't fly—they're still birds. But insects do not, and neither (in case you were wondering) do bats.

Now consider a harder case: What defines a "drug"?

Start again with the clear cases. Heroin, cocaine, and marijuana clearly are drugs. Air, water, most foods, and shampoos are clearly *not* drugs—though all of these are "substances," like drugs, and are all ingested or applied to our body parts. Unclear cases include tobacco and alcohol.[2]

---

2. Unclear in another way are substances such as aspirin, antibiotics, vitamins, and antidepressants—the kinds of substances we buy in "drugstores" and call "drugs" in a pharmaceutical sense. But these are *medicines*—not "drugs" in the moral sense we are exploring.

Our question, then, is: Does any general description cover *all* of the clear cases of "drugs" and *none* of the substances that clearly aren't drugs, drawing a clear line in between?

A "drug" has been defined—even by a presidential commission—as a substance that affects mind or body in some way. But this definition is far too broad. It includes air, water, food, and so on, too, so it fails on the second requirement.

We also can't define a "drug" as an *illegal* substance that affects mind or body in some way. This definition might cover more or less the right set of substances, but it does not meet requirement 3. It does not explain why the line belongs where it is. After all, part of the point of trying to define "drug" in the first place might well be to decide which substances *should* be legal and which should not! Defining a "drug" as an illegal substance short-circuits this project. (Technically, it commits the fallacy of begging the question or circular argument.)

Try this:

> A drug is a substance used primarily to alter our state of the mind in some specific way.

Heroin, cocaine, and marijuana obviously count. Food, air, and water don't—because even though they have effects on the mind, the effects are not specific, and are not the primary reason why we eat, breathe, and drink. Unclear cases we then approach with the question: Is the *primary* effect *specific* and on the *mind*? Perception-distorting and mood-altering effects do seem to be the chief concern in current moral debates about drugs, so arguably this definition captures the kind of distinction people really want to make.

Should we add that drugs are addictive? Maybe not. Some substances are addictive but not drugs—certain foods, perhaps. And what if a substance that "alter[s] the state of the mind in some specific way" turns out to be *non*-addictive (as some people have claimed about marijuana, for example)? Is it therefore not a drug? Maybe addiction defines "drug *abuse*," but not "drug" as such.

Exercise Set 11.2: Starting from clear cases

Objective: To give you practice developing definitions for unclear and contested concepts.

Instructions: For each of the terms below, give one example of something to which the term clearly applies, one example of something to which it clearly does not apply, and one example of something to which it is unclear if the term applies. Then, in light of those examples, suggest a definition for the term and say briefly why it is a good definition and how it clarifies the unclear case.

Tips for success: Just as Rule D2 suggests, begin by thinking about clear cases—that is, cases where the term clearly applies or clearly does not apply. Ask yourself what separates the cases where the term clearly applies from those where it clearly doesn't apply. What is true of all and only the cases to which the term applies? Let your answer to that question guide you in framing a definition.

Think carefully about what your proposed definition implies for some unclear cases. Which of them end up being covered by the term under your definition? Are you satisfied covering those examples, but not the others? The answer to that question—as with the answer of many definitional questions—depends on your interest in the term.

For instance, consider the term "military vehicle." Tanks and fighter jets are clearly military vehicles. Subcompact sedans made by Toyota or Ford are clearly not military vehicles. Humvees are somewhere in the middle. They are used as military vehicles, but they have also been sold and used as civilian vehicles (Hummers). How you draw the line between military and non-military vehicles will very likely depend on why you are interested in defining "military vehicles" in the first place. If you are trying to define "military vehicle" because you are trying to decide what kind of vehicles should not be available to the public, you might want to focus on how dangerous the vehicle is. If you are interested in figuring out which vehicles to include in a museum of military history, you might want to focus on whether the vehicles were ever actually used by the military. For the purposes of this exercise set, you are not given a particular reason for defining the term, but it may help you to think about the question, "Why might it matter how this term is defined?" If you can think of several different reasons why it might matter, pick one of them, state it explicitly, and use it to guide your thinking.

Sample

Slow

The definition of "slow" will depend on context. Suppose we are defining "slow" in the context of vehicles used for everyday travel, like commuting to work or going to the grocery store. A golf cart, with a top speed of about fifteen miles per hour, is clearly slow. A Tesla Model S, with a top speed of over 130 miles per hour, is clearly not slow. A Vespa LX 50 scooter, with a top speed of thirty-nine miles per hour, is a borderline case. It's fast for a scooter, though relatively slow for riding on highways. One plausible definition of "slow" for a vehicle is "unable to maintain a speed of at least twenty miles per hour." This means that Vespas and similar vehicles don't count as slow, since they can achieve speeds of more than twenty miles per hour,, but golf carts do count as slow. That seems right, since Vespas could keep up with cars and motorcycles on most roads, but golf carts couldn't.

This response begins by pointing out that what we mean by "slow" depends dramatically on context. After all, slow for a street-legal, civilian motor vehicle is very different from slow for a sloth or slow for a rocket. The response then stipulates a context arbitrarily. It could just as well have stipulated "slow for a large African mammal" or "slow [to move] for a chess master"—although it would have to have used different examples, or different kinds of examples, in that case!

After clarifying the context for its definition, this response offers a case that is clearly covered by the term (namely, golf carts) and a case that is clearly not covered (namely, the Tesla Model S electric car). It also explains briefly why those cases are clear cases by citing their top speeds. It then gives a borderline example (namely, Vespas) and justifies its suggestion that this example really is unclear. Finally, the response suggests a definition, explains how the definition resolves the unclear case, and briefly makes an argument for resolving the unclear case in that way.

Just as focusing on "everyday vehicles" is certainly not the only context you might have chosen, "unable to maintain a top speed of more than twenty miles per hour" is not the only plausible definition you might have given. Especially in an area where most travel requires getting on a highway, "unable to maintain a speed of at least forty miles per hour" might be a better definition. Context matters!

1.   Bald

2.   Adult

3.   Fast-food restaurant

4.   Expensive

5.   Brave

6.   Weapon

7.   Made in America

8.   European

9.   Natural

10. Consensual sex

Model responses for odd-numbered exercises can be found on page 427.

Need more practice? Browse the headlines in your favorite newspaper or magazine, looking for unclear terms. Identify cases to which the terms clearly apply, cases to which they clearly do not apply, and borderline cases. Then, check the articles under the headlines to see whether the article is about a clear case or a borderline case.

Definitions don't replace arguments

Definitions help us to organize our thoughts, group like things with like, and pick out key similarities and differences. Sometimes, after words are clearly defined, people may even discover that they do not really disagree about an issue at all.

By themselves, though, definitions seldom settle difficult questions. We seek to define "drug," for example, partly to decide what sort of stance to take toward certain substances. But such a definition cannot answer this question by itself. Under the proposed definition, coffee is a drug. Caffeine certainly alters the state of the mind in specific ways. It is even addictive. But does it follow that coffee should be banned? No, because the effect is mild and socially positive for many people. Some attempt to weigh benefits against harms is necessary before we can draw any conclusions.

Rule D3

Marijuana is a drug under the proposed definition. Should *it* (continue to) be banned? Just as with coffee, more argument is necessary. Some people claim that marijuana has only mild and socially positive effects too. Supposing they're right, you could argue that marijuana shouldn't be banned even though it is a drug (like coffee). Others argue that it has far worse effects and tends to be a "gateway" to harder drugs besides. If they're right, you could argue for banning marijuana whether it is a drug or not.

Or perhaps marijuana is most akin to certain antidepressants and stimulants—medicines that (take note) turn out to be drugs on the proposed definition, but call not for bans but for *control*.

Alcohol, meanwhile, is a drug under the proposed definition. In fact, it is the most widely used drug of all. Its harms are enormous, including kidney disease, birth defects, half of all traffic deaths, and more. Should it be limited or banned? Maybe—though there are counterarguments too. Once again, though, this question is not settled by the determination that alcohol is a drug. Here the *effects* make the difference.

In short, definitions contribute to clarity, but seldom do they make arguments all by themselves. Clarify your terms—know exactly what questions you're asking—but don't expect that clarity alone will answer them.

Critical thinking activity: Defining key terms in an essay

For an out-of-class activity that gives you practice in defining terms in the context of an argumentative essay, see the "Defining key terms in an essay" assignment sheet (p. 488) in Part 3.

Critical thinking activity: Defining difficult terms

For an in-class group activity that gives you practice in defining difficult terms, see the "Defining difficult terms" assignment sheet (p. 489) in Part 3.

Appendix III
Argument Mapping

When you are dealing with complex arguments, drawing a diagram or "map" of the argument can help you understand the argument's structure. This is important because it helps you understand how the different parts of the argument relate to one another, what parts might need more support, and how problems with one part of the argument affect problems with another part of the argument.

An argument map is like a flow chart of an argument. It shows visually how the various premises relate to one another and how they lead to the argument's main conclusion. You can also use them to help you write argumentative essays (remember, for example, Rule 36: Your argument is your outline!) and organize your oral presentations. A variety of argument "mapping" methods are also widely used in formal debating.

Learning to draw argument maps is an extension of learning to analyze arguments. Basic argument analysis involves distinguishing premises from conclusions (Rule 1) and presenting the premises in a natural order (Rule 2). More detailed argument analysis involves understanding exactly what role each premise plays in supporting the argument's main conclusion. Argument mapping is just a way to represent that detailed analysis graphically.

The elements of an argument map are numbers, which represent the premises and conclusion in an argument, and arrows, which connect the premises and conclusions.

Start with the following very simple argument:

> The New York Yankees have won more World Series championships than any other team in baseball history. Therefore, the New York Yankees are the greatest team in baseball history.

The first step in mapping this argument is to identify all of the claims in the argument, just as we did in Exercise Set 1.1. We can do that by bracketing each claim and assigning a number to it, like this:

> [1] [The New York Yankees have won more World Series championships than any other team in baseball history.] Therefore, [2] [the New York Yankees are the greatest team in baseball history.]

The second step is to distinguish the argument's conclusion from its premises (Rule 1). The conclusion indicator "therefore" shows us that claim (2) is the conclusion. This leaves claim (1) as the only premise in the argument. So far, this is nothing new.

The new step comes in representing the relationship between claims (1) and (2) graphically, which we do as follows:

In this diagram, (2) represents the conclusion of the argument ("The New York Yankees are the greatest team in baseball history") and (1) represents the argument's premise ("The New York Yankees have won more World Series championships than any other team in baseball history"). We put the conclusion—(2)—at the bottom of the argument map, and we use a downward arrow to indicate that (1) "leads to" (2)—that is, that (1) is a premise for (2).

Most arguments, of course, aren't that simple. For one thing, most arguments have more than one premise. How about this one?

> Participating in musical ensembles, like orchestras and choruses, is fun. Participating in musical ensembles also teaches valuable lessons about discipline and teamwork. Therefore, children should be encouraged to participate in musical ensembles.

Once again, the first thing to do is to bracket all of the claims in the argument and assign a number to each one:

> ¹[Participating in musical ensembles, like orchestras and choruses, is fun.] ²[Participating in musical ensembles also teaches valuable lessons about discipline and teamwork.] Therefore, ³[children should be encouraged to participate in musical ensembles.]

Next, we want to distinguish the premises from the conclusion. Again, the conclusion indicator "therefore" points the way: (3) is the conclusion, and (1) and (2) are premises.

We can use arrows to represent the relationships among these claims, as follows:

As always, we put the argument's conclusion—in this case, (3)—at the bottom of the argument map. We put the premises above it and draw arrows from the premises to the conclusion. Here, the arrow from (1) to (3) indicates that (1) is a premise for (3), and the arrow from (2) to (3) indicates that (2) is also a premise for (3).

In some arguments, two or more premises work together, as it were, to support a conclusion. Consider, for instance, this argument:

> ¹[Children should be protected from media that might encourage them to do dangerous things.] ²[Violent video games might encourage children to do dangerous things.] Therefore, ³[children should not be allowed to purchase violent video games without parental consent.]

Once again, we need to distinguish premises from conclusion, and once again we see that (3) is the conclusion and (1) and (2) are premises for (3). Notice, however, that premises (1) and (2) are "linked" in a special way: they only support (3) when they are combined, rather than providing independent reasons for (3). In this case, (1) is only a reason for (3) because (2) is true, and (2) is only a reason for (3) because (1) is true. If either of these premises were false, the other premise would cease to be a good reason for (3).

Given that (1) and (2) are related in this special way, we need to draw our argument map differently if it is to represent the relationships among the claims accurately. We can represent the link between (1) and (2) as follows:

$$(1) + (2)$$
$$\downarrow$$
$$(3)$$

We link (1) and (2) by drawing a plus sign between them, and then we draw a single arrow from the linked pair to (3). This shows that (1) and (2) *jointly* support (3).

Contrast this argument with the earlier argument about musical ensembles. In that earlier argument, each premise provided an independent reason to believe the conclusion. The fact that participating in musical ensembles is fun is a reason—all on its own—to encourage children to participate in them. It would count as a reason to encourage participation even if participating didn't teach valuable lessons. Likewise, the fact that participating in musical ensembles is a reason—all on its own—to encourage children to participate in them, and it would count as a reason even if participating weren't fun. Thus, we drew separate arrows from (1) to (3) and from (2) to (3), indicating that each premise leads to the conclusion independently of the other premise.

This highlights one advantage of argument maps over premise-and-conclusion outlines of arguments. Argument maps enable you to show the relationships between premises. Premise-and-conclusion outlines don't.

The other major advantage of argument maps comes when we consider more complex arguments, like this one:

> ¹[There is a finite amount of oil in the world.] Thus, ²[we cannot continue to use oil for fuel forever.] That's why ³[we need to develop alternative sources of energy.]

We've bracketed and numbered the claims in this argument. But when we go to distinguish premises from conclusions, we see a problem. Both (2) *and* (3) are introduced with conclusion indicators ("Thus" and "That's why"). Which is the conclusion?

If we step back and look at the argument as a whole, we can see that the main point of the argument is that we need to develop alternative sources of energy. Thus, the *main* conclusion of the argument is (3). (2) is offered as a reason for (3), which makes (2) a premise of the argument. So why does it also have a conclusion indicator in front of it? Because (2) is supported by (1)—or to put it another way, (1) is offered as a reason for (2). Thus, (2) acts as both a premise *and* a conclusion, like a middle link in a chain. A claim that serves as both a premise and a conclusion is called a *subconclusion*. The argument-within-an-argument that leads to the subconclusion is called a *subargument*.

Argument maps enable us to represent these relationships graphically:

(1)
↓
(2)
↓
(3)

As always, we put the main conclusion—(3)—at the bottom of the argument map. We put (2) just above it, with a downward arrow connecting (2) to (3). We then put (1) above (2), with a downward arrow connecting (1) to (2). This argument map shows at a glance that (1) is offered as a reason for (2), which in turn is offered as a reason for (3).

We can combine the techniques we've used so far to map more complex arguments, as well. In fact, the more complex the argument, the more helpful the map. Consider this argument:

> [1][A standard layout should be required for all Web sites.] [2][A standard layout would save users time] because [3][everyone would know exactly where to go for the information they want.] Also, [4][a standard layout would make it easier for people to put up their own Web sites.] This is because [5][a standard layout could be based on one simple template] and [6][a layout based on one simple template would make "do it yourself" programs easy to create and teach.] [7][Designers wouldn't have to spend as much time coming up with their own layouts, either.]

Some careful analysis of this argument shows that the last three claims are premises for (4), although (5) and (6) are linked to one another and (7) is independent. (3) is a premise for (2). (2) and (4) are independent premises for the main conclusion, (1). Explaining that in words makes it tough to follow; it's *much* easier to see all of this if we draw a picture! We can map this argument as follows:

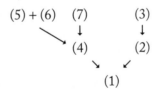

This argument map represents the complexity of this argument much more clearly than any premise-and-conclusion outline could. It shows each sub-argument clearly. It evens reveals the structure of the subarguments: Not only do (5), (6), and (7) all lead to (4), but (5) and (6) are linked, whereas (7) is independent. (2) and (4) are independent premises for the main conclusion, rather than linked premises.

The "Resources" section on this book's companion Web site has links to further reading and resources for argument mapping, including links to argument mapping software.

Exercise Set 12.1: Mapping simple arguments

Objective: To give you practice drawing argument maps.

Instructions: Copy each argument below. Bracket and number the conclusion and all of the premises of each argument. Then, work out an argument map for the argument.

Tips for success: Drawing argument maps will take some time to learn—but it *is* a skill that you can learn with a bit of practice, and it is extremely useful for any kind of argument analysis.

The first step in mapping an argument is identifying and numbering all of the premises and the conclusion of the argument. Remember that, as in Exercise Sets 1.1 and 1.2, not every sentence in a passage is a premise or conclusion of an argument. Bracket the claims that are premises or conclusions and assign a number to each.

All of the arguments in this exercise set are relatively simple in structure. Some exercises will require you to distinguish between linked and independent premises. Others will ask you to identify a series of subarguments that have one premise each—just like the three-step argument above about oil and alternative energy sources.

In distinguishing linked from independent premises, try pretending that one of the two premises is false and then ask yourself whether the other one still provides a reason for the conclusion. If not, then the premises are linked, and you should put a plus sign between them in your argument map. If each premise would be a good reason for the conclusion on its own, then the premises are independent, and you should draw a separate arrow from each premise to the conclusion.

Sample

The meat company Bell & Evans has introduced a more humane method of slaughtering chickens. Bell & Evans is a financially successful company. Therefore, humane handling of animals is compatible with financial success. I wonder if fast-food companies will get the memo?

Adapted from: Tracy Reiman, letter to the editor, New York Times, *Oct 30, 2010, http://www .nytimes.com/2010/10/31/opinion/lweb31chicken.html*

¹[The meat company Bell & Evans has introduced a more humane method of slaughtering chickens.] ²[Bell & Evans is a financially successful company.] Therefore, ³[humane handling of animals is compatible with financial success.] I wonder if fast-food companies will get the memo?

$$(1) + (2)$$
$$\downarrow$$
$$(3)$$

The first part of this response involves bracketing and numbering the claims in the original argument. (Notice that the last sentence of the passage is not bracketed because it is neither a premise nor a conclusion in the argument.) Numbering the claims is necessary so that we know what the numbers in the argument map represent.

The second part of this response involves actually drawing a map of the argument. Once you've identified all of the claims in the argument, all you need to do to map the argument is figure out which claim is the main conclusion and whether the premises are linked or independent.

In this case, the main conclusion is (3), so the response puts (3) at the bottom of the argument map. This argument map shows that the premises—(1) and (2)—are linked. This is because (1) doesn't show that humane practices are compatible with financial success unless (2) is true (and vice versa). (Why not? Suppose that Bell & Evans had switched to a more humane method of slaughtering chickens and gone bankrupt as a result. In that case, Bell & Evans' new practice would not be a reason to think that humane handling of animals is compatible with financial success.)

1. American swimmer Michael Phelps has more Olympic medals than any other athlete. At his peak in the 2008 games in Beijing, Phelps dominated his sport in a way that no one else has. That's why Michael Phelps is the greatest Olympian ever.

Adapted from: Michael Wilbon, "Phelps Greatest Olympian Ever?" ESPN, Aug 2, 2012, http://espn.go.com/olympics/summer/2012/swimming/story/_/ id/8222710/2012-olympics-michael-phelps-greatest-ever-debate

2. Liberals seem to think that government spending is good for the economy. Economic growth, however, comes from private investment. Taxing citizens and spending their money is not a form of private investment. Thus, taxing citizens and spending their money does not promote economic growth.

Adapted from: Rich Case, letter to the editor, Los Angeles Times, *Feb 28, 2011, http://articles.latimes.com/2011/feb/28/opinion/la-le-0228-monday-20110228*

3. Most Americans live too far from their place of work for it to be practical to ride a bicycle to work. This makes bike paths largely a waste of money—as a solution to traffic problems, at least. The government should find other ways to reduce traffic besides building expensive bike paths.

Adapted from: Lily Gray, letter to the editor, Los Angeles Times, *Mar 7, 2011, http://articles.latimes.com/2011/mar/07/opinion/la-le-0307 -monday-20110307/3*

4. The state needs to ensure that DNA tests are available to all defendants in capital murder trials. The state has an obligation to ensure that justice is done in criminal courts—especially when the death penalty is at stake. The only way to do justice is to ensure that all available evidence, including DNA tests, is available in capital murder trials.

Adapted from: Sam Millsap, letter to the editor, New York Times, *Oct 23, 2010, http://www.nytimes.com/2010/10/24/opinion/l24dna.html*

5. By reducing student debt, eliminating tuition at medical schools would enable more new doctors to become primary care physicians. We have a shortage of primary care physicians in this country. Therefore, medical schools ought to be free.

Adapted from: Peter B. Bach and Robert Kocher, "Why Medical School Should Be Free," New York Times, *May 28, 2011, http://www.nytimes.com/2011/05/29/opinion/29bach.html*

6. "Recommerce" companies buy used electronics or other goods and resell them elsewhere. For instance, recommerce companies enable people to sell their old cell phones for cash. Selling old cell phones to recommerce companies also avoids adding more electronics to

landfills. Clearly, selling old cell phones to recommerce companies is the smart thing to do.

Adapted from: Israel Ganot, letter to the editor, New York Times, *Jun 27, 2010,*
http://www.nytimes.com/2010/06/28/opinion/lweb28phone.html

7. Some Western European countries are banning Muslim women from wearing the burqa on the grounds that it is an insult to women's dignity. If Europeans are truly concerned with Muslim women's dignity, then they should be addressing not only the burqa but also highly sexualized images of (non-Muslim) women in the European media. After all, if they're so worried about Muslim women's dignity, they ought to be concerned with *all* women's dignity. And if they are concerned with all women's dignity, then they ought to be just as concerned about highly sexualized portrayals of women in, say, European advertising as they are about the burqa.

Adapted from: Gabriele vom Bruck, letter to the editor, The Economist,
Jun 3, 2010, http://www.economist.com/node/16270944

8. It's ridiculous that people are blaming the celebrities whose nude photos were stolen by hackers and splashed all over the internet. If someone at the Post Office had opened a sealed envelope containing a celebrity's nude Polaroid photos, everyone would blame the Post Office worker, not the celebrity who mailed the photos. But having your photos stolen from a password-protected online system is just like having them stolen from a sealed envelope that you sent through the mail.

Adapted from: Jimmy Kimmel Live, *"Jimmy Kimmel's Leaked iCloud Photo,"* YouTube,
Sep 3, 2014, https://www.youtube.com/watch?v=HU32jCGk8hQ

9. Happiness in life is reserved for those who care more about being happy than about being "successful." The signs of so-called success in modern life—a big house, a fancy car, designer clothes, etc.—are expensive. Having enough money to buy expensive things requires working so hard that you don't have time to enjoy all the expensive things you've bought. Besides, true happiness doesn't

come from owning the kinds of things that are considered signs of success, anyway.

Adapted from: Daniel Dickinson, letter to the editor, New York Times, *Jul 5, 2010,*
http://www.nytimes.com/2010/07/06/opinion/l06sex.html

10. People often think that because of their notorious practice of human sacrifice, the Aztecs were much more barbaric than the Europeans of the time. This isn't true. The Aztecs were sacrificing about 3,500 people a year in the 1500s. If England's population at the time had been as large as that of the Aztec empire, the English would have executed about twice that many people each year. And English executions of the time were every bit as barbaric as Aztec sacrifices.

Adapted from: Charles C. Mann, 1491: New Revelations of the Americas before
Columbus, *2nd ed. (New York: Vintage Books, 2011), 136–37*

> Model responses for odd-numbered exercises can be found on page 430.

Need more practice? Draw argument maps of each of the arguments in Exercise Sets 1.1, 1.2, 6.1, and 6.2. For even more practice, map the arguments in the letters to the editor in your favorite newspaper or magazine.

Exercise Set 12.2: Mapping complex arguments

Objective: To give you practice mapping more complex arguments.

Instructions: Draw an argument map for each of the following arguments.

Tips for success: As with mapping simple arguments, the first step in mapping complex arguments is to identify, bracket, and number each claim in the argument. Remember that you only need to number the premises and the conclusion. Any other sentences, such as those providing background information or expressing thoughts that are only indirectly related to the argument, need not be included.

The second step in mapping an argument is figuring out how the various premises relate to one another and to the main conclusion. There are several ways to go about this, and you should find the strategy that works best for you.

One strategy is to work backward. Start by identifying the main conclusion and put it at the very bottom of the argument. Then, figure out which of the premises lead immediately to the main conclusion. Those go one row up from the main conclusion. (Don't worry yet whether they are linked or independent.) Next, look at each premise in that row and ask yourself what reasons the argument gives for each of *those* premises. Put those reasons one more row up from the main conclusion, being sure to keep track of which premises lead to which subconclusions. Repeat this process until you have placed all of the premises on your map.

Once you have figured out which premises lead to which (sub)conclusions, look at each subargument and ask yourself whether the premises of that subargument are linked or independent. Start by looking at pairs of premises. Suppose that one of those premises is false, and ask yourself whether the other premise still counts as a reason to accept the premises' immediate conclusion. If so, then the premises are independent. If not, then they are linked.

Some people prefer a less systematic approach to mapping arguments. One such approach is to proceed as if you were solving a jigsaw puzzle. See which "pieces" of the argument "fit together" by thinking about which claims lead to which other claims and which claims are linked to which other claims. As you connect premises into subarguments, the overall structure of the argument may become clearer, enabling you to connect all of the pieces into a single argument map. You could even use numbered index cards or sticky notes to represent the claims and try arranging them in different ways on a table or wall.

Whatever approach you take, remember that you will probably need to try out several different possibilities for each argument before you find one that you think is correct.

Sample

Uranium emits rays similar to X-rays. These rays arise either from an interaction between the uranium and its surroundings or from the uranium itself. If the rays arise from an interaction between the uranium and its surroundings, then the amount of radiation should vary with temperature, illumination, or other factors. The radiation, however, is constant: it does not vary with temperature, illumination, or other factors. Thus, the radiation does not arise from an interaction between the uranium and its surroundings. The radiation, therefore, comes from the uranium itself.

Adapted from: Marie Skłodowska Curie, "Radium and Radioactivity," Century Magazine
(Jan 1904), 461–66

uranium emits rays similar to X-rays. ¹[These rays arise either from an interaction between the uranium and its surroundings or from the uranium itself.] ²[If the rays arise from an interaction between the uranium and its surroundings, then the amount of radiation should vary with temperature, illumination, or other factors.] ³[The radiation, however, is constant: it does not vary with temperature, illumination, or other factors.] Thus, ⁴[the radiation does not arise from an interaction between the uranium and its surroundings.] ⁵[The radiation, therefore, comes from the uranium itself.]

$$(2) \ + \ (3)$$
$$\downarrow$$
$$(4) \ + \ (1)$$
$$\downarrow$$
$$(5)$$

This argument is the same as the sample argument for Exercise Set 6.5. (Page 152. Go back and look!) Notice how much more clearly an argument map reveals the structure of the argument, as compared to the premise-and-conclusion outline used in Exercise Set 6.5.

As explained in Exercise Set 6.5, premises (2) and (3) jointly lead, via modus tollens (Rule 23), to (4). Premises (4) and (1) jointly lead, via disjunctive syllogism (Rule 25), to the main conclusion, (5). (Hint: The premises of the deductive argument forms introduced in Chapter 6 are always linked.)

To piece this argument together, it helps to begin by identifying the main conclusion: (5). Once you've found the main conclusion, ask yourself which of the premises lead directly to the main conclusion. Premises (1) and (4) do the trick. What role, then, do (2) and (3) have in the argument? Since (4) is introduced by the conclusion indicator "Thus," we can guess that it's a subconclusion. This means that there must be reasons given for it in the argument. (2) and (3) work as reasons for (4), so we place them above (4) in our argument map as the premises of a subargument.

If you bracketed and labeled the first sentence of the passage—the one that provides the background information that uranium emits rays similar to X-rays—you might have trouble figuring out where it fits into the argument map. If you find a claim that doesn't seem to fit into the argument map anywhere, it might be because it's not really part of the argument at all.

1.   Governments ought not to pay ransoms to terrorists who have kidnapped people. Doing so encourages terrorists to kidnap more people. Paying ransom also provides the terrorists with the resources to kill even more people. Therefore, even though ransoming hostages can save the hostages' lives, paying ransom ultimately leads to more deaths. As hard as it may be to accept, it's more important to minimize the overall harm that terrorists do than it is to save any specific hostage.

Adapted from: Peter Singer, "Refusing to Pay Ransoms Saves Lives in the End," Denver Post, Dec 13, 2014, http://www.denverpost.com/opinion/ci_27126654/ refusing-pay-ransoms-saves-lives-end

2.   Basketball brings in a lot of money for a lot of universities. This money depends on the hard work and dedication of student athletes. Thus, student athletes contribute a great deal to many universities' finances. Yet, these athletes receive little compensation— often no more than the cost of tuition—compared to the amount of money they bring in. Clearly, student athletes deserve more compensation for their work.

Adapted from: Ramogi Huma, "A Fair Day's Pay for a Fair Day's Work," U.S. News & World Report, Apr 1, 2013, http://www.usnews.com/debate-club/ should-ncaa-athletes-be-paid/a-fair-days-pay-for-a-fair-days-work

3.   Drugs ought to be legalized. Attempting to ban drugs is futile. Countries all over the world have tried for decades to ban various drugs. None of the attempts have been successful. Furthermore, making drugs illegal contributes to the development of failed states by empowering criminal drug cartels around the world. The other problems associated with legalizing drugs are more manageable than the problems with criminalizing them too.

Adapted from: "How to Stop the Drug Wars," The Economist, Mar 5, 2009, http://www.economist.com/node/13237193

4.   Archaeologists have found Viking artifacts on Baffin Island in northern Canada. Admittedly, these artifacts could have arrived there by trade. But archaeologists have also found ruins of a large, old stone structure. Since the native people of Baffin Island only built small, cozy structures, the structure must have been built by Vikings. The Vikings wouldn't have built such a large structure

unless they'd actually settled on the island. Thus, the Vikings actually settled on Baffin Island for a time.

Adapted from: Heather Pringle, "Vikings and Native Americans," National Geographic, *Nov 2012, http://ngm.nationalgeographic.com/2012/11/vikings-and-indians/pringle-text*

5.   I see your wife is out of town. How do I know? Since the female detective you're working with is wearing men's deodorant, I take it she borrowed someone else's deodorant this morning. And since it smells the same as your deodorant, it stands to reason that she's wearing your deodorant. Which she would only do if she'd woken up at your place after spending the night there. So she spent the night ar your place—I'm right so far, aren't I? Of course I am. And since you're married, she wouldn't have spent the night with you unless your wife was out of town. *That's* how I know.

Adapted from: Sherlock, "A Study in Pink," BBC, Jul 25, 2010

6.   Contrary to what popular science programs on TV might have you believe, the brain is not elegantly designed. From a design perspective, it's a mess. Consider neurons, the basic cells that make up the brain. Neurons are inefficient means of transmitting signals. They transmit signals slowly. They use an enormous amount of energy in the process too. And they often fail to transmit the signal they are trying to transmit! At a slightly higher level, the brain has parts that are redundant. For instance, we have two completely distinct visual systems—one ancient, one modern. At an even higher level, many brain systems that are only needed some of the time are always "on." This is a waste of energy, and it leads to some unintended and undesirable side effects.

Adapted from: David J. Linden, The Accidental Mind *(Cambridge, MA: The Belknap Press, 2007), 5–14, 47–48*

7.   When one person knowingly causes a fatal injury to another, that is murder. Capitalism deprives many people of the basic necessities of life. It requires them to live in cramped, squalid, toxic conditions. It leaves them without resources for medical care. It leaves them unable to afford the most minimally nutritious food. It leaves them no respite from work, save sex and drink.

Furthermore, because capitalism leaves wealth and power in the hands of the few, it leads to power structures that prevent the oppressed from taking the necessities of life by force. Being deprived of the necessities of life leads to death just as surely as does being actively harmed. Society knows full well that capitalism has this effect. Thus, society is committing murder by allowing capitalism to continue.

Adapted from: Friedrich Engels, The Condition of the Working Class in England *(1845; repr. New York: Oxford University Press, 1999), 106–7*

8. Our galaxy is so big that intelligent life must have developed elsewhere in the galaxy too. And our galaxy is so old that spacefaring civilizations should have visited every corner of it many times. So aliens must know that we're here. And yet, none of those aliens have contacted us. If they know that we're here but we haven't heard from them yet, then they must have made a conscious choice not to contact us. Therefore, aliens must have made a conscious choice not to contact us.

Adapted from: George Dvorsky, "11 of the Weirdest Solutions to the Fermi Paradox," io9, Mar 20, 2013, http://io9.com/11-of-the-weirdest-solutions-to-the-fermi-paradox-456850746

9. Our distant ancestors lived in very small societies. On a normal day, everyone they met would be someone they had known all of their lives. These societies did not interact very much with other societies. Just about everything they ate, everything they wore, and every tool they used was made within that group. Today, of course, we live in vast societies. We can look out at a busy city street and see, all at once, more people than our ancestors saw in their entire lives. We live in a global trading system. Indeed, our world is unimaginably different from the world of our distant ancestors. Our minds, however, are designed for the life of our distant ancestors. Thus, our minds may not be well adapted to the special challenges of the modern world.

Adapted from: Kwame Anthony Appiah, Cosmopolitanism: Ethics in a World of Strangers *(New York: W. W. Norton, 2007), xi–xii*

10. If people see a child about to fall down a well, they will immedi-
     ately want to help the child. This desire will not come from self-
     interested motives. It will not come from the desire to win the
     favor of the child's parents. It will not come from the desire to
     gain a reputation for heroism or to avoid a reputation for callous-
     ness. This shows that people naturally want to help others avoid
     suffering. Since people naturally want to help others avoid suffer-
     ing, and helping others to avoid suffering is part of being a good
     person, all people have it within themselves to be a good person.
     If you have it within yourself to become a good person, then you
     can make yourself a good person by focusing on your own virtue.
     Thus, you can make yourself a good person by focusing on your
     own virtue.

Adapted from: Mengzi, Mengzi, *translated by Bryan W. Van Norden*
(Indianapolis: Hackett Publishing Company, 2008), 46

Model responses for odd-numbered exercises can be found on page 434.

Need more practice? Draw argument maps of the arguments from Exercise Set 1.6, from the exercises in Chapters II through V, from Exercise
Set 6.4, and for the arguments that you created for the exercise sets in
Chapter VII. For even more practice, map the arguments in the editorials
or op-eds in your favorite newspaper. The companion Web site for this
book also has links to classic texts for argument analysis. Find them under
the "Resources" link on the site and map the arguments you find in the texts.

Critical thinking activity: Argument mapping workshop

For an activity that gives you practice mapping arguments, see the "Argument mapping
workshop" assignment sheet (p. 490) in Part 3.

Critical thinking activity: Developing your own arguments using argument maps

For an activity that gives you practice using argument maps to develop your own arguments
in more detail, see the "Developing your own arguments using argument maps" assignment
sheet (p. 492) in Part 3.

Part 2

Model Responses to Selected Exercises with Commentary

Model responses to all odd-numbered exercises in the Exercise Sets of Part 1 appear below. Both strong and weak model responses are given for some exercises. Many responses are followed by commentary that explains the particular strengths and/or weaknesses of the response. For most of the exercises in this book, there will be more than one good response. The responses below are offered only as guides to help you understand what a good response to the exercises looks like.

MODEL RESPONSES FOR CHAPTER I: SHORT ARGUMENTS

Exercise Set 1.1: Distinguishing premises from conclusions

Model Response for Exercise 1

[Racial segregation reduces some persons to the status of things.] Hence, <u>segregation is morally wrong</u>.

The main clue in this argument is the word "Hence," which is a conclusion indicator. Since "Hence" introduces the clause "segregation is morally wrong," that clause is likely to be the conclusion. Furthermore, it makes more sense to see "Racial segregation reduces some persons to the status of things" as a reason for thinking that segregation is morally wrong, rather than the other way around.

Note that the word "Hence" is not underlined in the response. Conclusion indicators point you to the conclusion, but they are not part of the conclusion itself.

Model Response for Exercise 3

Most people experience no side effects from the yellow fever vaccine. <u>People with egg allergies shouldn't get the yellow fever vaccine,</u> though, because [some part of the vaccine is grown inside eggs.]

In this argument, the premise and conclusion are part of a single sentence. The premise indicator because *is your clue that the last clause is the premise and the first clause is your conclusion. Because is a special indicator word in this respect. It usually comes in between the conclusion and a premise. Thus, it helps you identify both the conclusion and a premise. Note that the first sentence is just background information. It is neither a premise nor a conclusion. You don't need to bracket it or underline it.*

Model Response for Exercise 5

Positron-emission tomography, better known as PET, is a method for examining a person's brain. Before undergoing PET, the patient inhales a gas containing radioactive molecules. <u>The molecules are not dangerous for the patient</u> because [they break down within a few minutes, before they can do any damage.]

The argument in this passage comes in the last sentence. Once again, the conclusion and premise are joined together with because. *And again, the first two sentences are just giving you background information; they tell you what positron-emission tomography is and what kind of molecules the argument is about.*

Model Response for Exercise 7

Some people buy college degrees on the Internet because they're trying to pretend that they went to college. <u>That's a waste of money,</u> since [it's easy to make a college degree on your computer,] and [a degree that you make yourself is just as good as a degree that you bought on the Internet.]

The only genuine indicator word in this argument is the premise indicator since. *That's your clue that you're about to see a premise. If you were still having trouble identifying the conclusion after you've found those premises, ask yourself which of the remaining sentences the premises would be good reasons for. In this case, it makes sense to take the premises as reasons to think that buying college degrees online is a waste of money. It doesn't make sense to take the premises as reasons to think that people do buy college degrees online. Thus, we can mark "That's a waste of money" as the conclusion of the argument.*

   Notice that we have marked the last two clauses as separate premises. You could also have marked everything after "since" as one long premise, but in general, it's better to treat each independent clause as its own premise. (Remember: An independent clause is a clause that could be a complete sentence on its own. For instance, "it's easy to make a college degree on your computer" is an independent clause, whereas "a degree that you make yourself" is not.)

The first sentence is background information. It is neither a premise nor the conclusion of the argument. So why does it have a "because" in it? Remember that not every instance of "because," "since," or other common premise indicators is actually an indicator word. In this case, "because" connects a piece of background information to an explanation of that information. An explanation differs from an argument in that an argument gives you a reason to think that something is true, whereas an explanation merely helps you understand why or how something is true.

Model Response for Exercise 9

In the film Interstellar, the main characters travel through a "wormhole," which is a tunnel through space-time that would enable space travelers to zip from one part of the universe to another. In theory, wormholes are possible, but it's probably impossible to use wormholes to travel around the universe. [Keeping wormholes open long enough to travel through them would require enormous amounts of "negative energy,"] and [it's probably impossible to generate that much negative energy.]

Many people who are new to analyzing arguments have trouble with arguments like this. For starters, there are no indicator words. In order to identify the conclusion and the premises, you have to ask yourself what the author's main point is. One way to do this is to ask yourself which clauses(s) or sentence(s) provide a reason to believe which other independent clause(s) or sentence(s). In this case, it makes most sense to interpret the author as using the last sentence to give us reasons to think that it's probably impossible to use wormholes to travel around the universe.

A further question is whether to mark the last sentence as a single premise or as two separate premises joined by and. In most cases, this won't matter too much, but a safe rule of thumb is to divide things into two separate premises when they make two separate claims. The last sentence here makes two separate claims—one about what's required to keep a wormhole open and one about whether it's possible to meet that requirement. That's why we've marked them as two separate premises.

Exercise Set 1.2: Outlining arguments in premise-and-conclusion form

Model Response for Exercise 1

(1) LeBron James will eventually surpass Michael Jordan in MVP awards, All-Star appearances, total points scored, and many other records.

(2) It is quite possible that James will even win as many championships as Jordan did.

(3) So far, Jordan is the greatest basketball player ever.

Therefore, (4) LeBron James will eventually become the greatest player of all time.

The word therefore *is a conclusion indicator. It's one way to see that the conclusion of this argument is that James will eventually become the greatest basketball player of all time. All of the other sentences in this passage make sense as reasons for that conclusion, so you should include each of them as premises in the argument.*

Notice that this premise-and-conclusion outline of the argument does not merely copy the entire sentence verbatim from the passage. It changes the sentences slightly so that each sentence stands on its own: For instance, compare the second sentence of the passage to premise (2) in the response. If you saw only the original sentence, outside of the context of the passage, you might not know that it was about James. The outline overcomes this problem by replacing "He" with "James." In general, it's helpful to replace pronouns with proper names when outlining arguments.

Model Response for Exercise 3

(1) A team of researchers led by Brendan Nyhan of Dartmouth gave some parents information from the Centers for Disease Control and Prevention stating that there is no evidence that vaccines cause autism.

(2) The team gave other parents no information about vaccine safety.

(3) When compared to parents who received no information, parents who received the information were no more likely to vaccinate their children.

Therefore, (4) simply providing information about vaccine safety does not increase the proportion of parents who get their children vaccinated.

This exercise gives a simple example of scientific reasoning. Accounts of scientific reasoning are often presented as stories about what a group of scientists have done, but you can usually reconstruct the scientists' reasoning from the story. In this case, the story starts with an explanation of the scientists' hypothesis—that is, the idea they wanted to test. They wanted to test the idea that giving parents information about vaccine safety would increase the proportion of parents who vaccinate their children. The word concluded *in the last sentence tells you that you're about to read the conclusion of the researchers' reasoning: In this case, the conclusion is that their hypothesis was false—that providing information about vaccine safety does not make parents more likely to vaccinate their children.*

Notice that the reasons given for this conclusion don't just consist of observations the researchers collected. The researchers did an experiment: They gave information only to some parents, and then they compared the behavior of those parents to the behavior of parents who did not receive that information. Scientific reasoning often works this way. You start with a hypothesis, and then you do an experiment to generate exactly the kinds of observations you need to test your hypothesis, and then you reason from your observations to a conclusion.

Model Response for Exercise 5

(1) In 1908, something flattened eight hundred square miles of forest in a part of Siberia called Tunguska.

(2) Scientists discovered that a lake in the area has the shape of an impact crater that would have been created by an asteroid or comet.

Therefore, (3) the Tunguska event was caused by an asteroid or comet.

The fact that there are other popular theories about what caused the "Tunguska event" might make us more skeptical about the conclusion of this argument. Since they are not reasons for that conclusion, though, we do not include them when outlining this argument in premise-and-conclusion form.

Note that, like the previous exercise, this argument illustrates the scientific method in action. Since there are numerous competing hypotheses about the cause of the Tunguska event, scientists try to find ways to test those different hypotheses. Developing and testing multiple hypotheses is an important part of doing good science. Drawing conclusions from those tests requires careful reasoning.

Model Response for Exercise 7

(1) People behave much more cautiously when they know that their life is on the line.

Therefore, (2) People would drive much more cautiously if there were a spear mounted on the steering wheel of every car.

(3) We should do everything we can to encourage cautious driving.

Therefore, (4) all cars should have a spear mounted on the steering wheel, aimed directly at the driver's chest.

This argument contains a subargument—that is, an argument within an argument. Premise (1) is a reason for (2), and (2) is a reason for the main conclusion. Thus, we call (2) a subconclusion. We indicate that (2) follows from (1) by writing "Therefore" before (2). (For more on subarguments and subconclusions, see page 271 in Appendix III.)

Just because this argument seems ridiculous (but is it really?) doesn't mean that we can't put it in premise-and-conclusion form. Putting an argument in premise-and-conclusion form is a very different task from figuring out whether it is a good argument.

Model Response for Exercise 9

(1) It is possible for someone to wonder whether her life is meaningful even if she knows that she has enjoyed her life.

Therefore, (2) a meaningful life is not the same as an enjoyable life.

(3) Someone who is alienated from her life or feels like her life is pointless, even if she is doing things that might seem worthwhile from an objective perspective, is not leading a meaningful life.

Therefore, (4) a meaningful life is not the same as a life spent on objectively worthwhile projects.

Therefore, (5) neither enjoyment nor objectively worthwhile projects, each considered separately from the other, are sufficient for a meaningful life.

Like the argument in exercise 7 of this set, this argument contains subarguments. Premise (1) is a reason for premise (2) and premise (3) is a reason for premise (4). Premises (2) and (4), taken together, are reasons for the main conclusion, (5).

A more precise and visually appealing way to represent the structure of arguments is to literally draw a picture of them, creating what is

*sometimes called an argument map. In this case, we can represent the rela-
tion between these various premises and their subconclusions and final conclusion like this:*

$$(1) \qquad (3)$$
$$\downarrow \qquad\quad \downarrow$$
$$(2) \quad + \quad (4)$$
$$\downarrow$$
$$(5)$$

*We introduce argument maps in Appendix III (p. 268). You won't need
them to do the other exercises in this book, but studying argument mapping
may help you understand and construct more complex arguments.*

Exercise Set 1.3: Analyzing visual arguments

See the companion Web site for this book for model responses to Exercise
Set 1.3.

Exercise Set 1.4: Identifying reliable and unreliable premises

Model Response for Exercise 1

(1) Anybody could become a zombie.

(2) Zombies are constantly looking to eat the brains of the living.

Therefore, (3) you should always be prepared to escape from or fight
back against a zombie attack.

The premises of this argument are unreliable because it is a widely
known fact that zombies don't exist. Thus, it's false that anybody
could become a zombie (premise 1), and it's false that zombies are
constantly looking to eat the brains of the living (premise 2).

*This response explicitly addresses each premise in the argument. It explains
that the premises are unreliable because they rest on an assumption that is
widely known to be false.*

*Some people do believe in zombies, of course, and so they would not accept
this response's justification for rejecting the premises. However, we do not
need complete agreement on the truth or falsity of a premise to decide whether
it's reliable or unreliable. Use your judgment to decide whether there is
enough agreement or controversy about a particular premise to make it a*

good starting point for an argument. If in doubt, specify what you think the argument's target audience is, and state whether members of that audience would accept the premise.

Model Response for Exercise 3

(1) A true education involves accumulating knowledge and educating one's emotions.

(2) A liberal arts education exposes students to history, science, math, literature, and the arts.

(3) Exposure to literature and the arts speaks directly to our emotions.

Therefore, (4) a liberal arts education is an essential part of any "real" education.

Premises (2) and (3) are reliable because they are widely accepted facts. Premise (1) is unreliable because the use of the vague expression "true education" makes it too hard to tell whether it's true. What counts as a "true education?" At the very least, we would need to see an argument for the claim that a "true education" involves accumulating knowledge and "educating the emotions."

Sometimes it's hard to know whether a premise is reliable because it's hard to know exactly what the premise means. That is arguably the case with the first premise in this argument. The best way to try to make such premises reliable is to make the claim as precise as possible (see Rule 4 and Appendix II) and offer reasons for it.

Model Response for Exercise 5

(1) By looking at the ratios of radioactive materials to products of radioactive decay in a piece of rock, we can estimate the age of the rock fairly well.

(2) Radiometric dating reveals that some large rock formations in the Earth's crust are up to four billion years old.

Therefore, (3) the Earth itself is at least four billion years old.

Premise (1) is reliable because it is a widely known fact that you can estimate the age of a rock by looking at radioactive materials in the rock. However, depending on the audience, some readers might not know that, and so it would be even better if the argument cited a source to support this claim. Premise (2) is unreliable because it is neither widely known nor supported by a source or an argument in this passage. Thus, we can't be sure whether it's true.

This response omits several sentences from the passage. These sentences are explaining terminology (e.g., "radioactive" and "radiometric dating") or giving examples, not providing reasons to accept the conclusion of the argument. That's why we don't include them in our premise-and-conclusion outline of the argument.

The response claims that premise (1) is reliable because it's a widely known fact. The response also admits that some people might deny or be unaware that premise (1) is true. Remember that what counts as a "widely known fact" will vary with the intended audience of the argument. This is why the difference between a premise's being reliable *and its being true is so important: A fact is a fact whether anyone knows it or not. Just because a premise is true, though, doesn't mean that it's a reliable starting point for an argument. Since arguments are supposed to take us from things that we justifiably believe to be true to things that we* didn't *previously know, we have to start with premises that are reliable—that is, premises that we justifiably believe.*

Finally, the response points out that premise (2) is unreliable in the context of this argument. Remember that this is not *saying that premise (2) is false. It's just saying that we don't have a good reason to accept it in the context of this argument. If the premise is true and there are good sources that show that it's true, the author of the argument could have avoided this problem by citing those sources.*

This argument illustrates yet another important aspect of scientific reasoning: Science builds on itself. That is, scientific arguments rest on premises that were themselves shown to be true through previous scientific investigation, and we can't expect every argument to restate the entire chain of reasoning supporting every single premise. (Instead, we often expect arguments to cite their sources, so that readers can follow up if they're unsure of the truth of a particular claim.) This argument, for instance, rests on an established body of knowledge about how different kinds of carbon atoms decay over time. Understanding scientific arguments, therefore, often requires knowing a bit about lots of different things. That's one reason to get a broad scientific education.

Model Response for Exercise 7

(1) As of 1988, polio remained endemic in only six countries: Niger, Egypt, India, Pakistan, Afghanistan, and Nigeria.

(2) By 2006, Niger and Egypt were polio free.

Therefore, (3) we are getting closer to the elimination of polio.

Premise (1) is unreliable because it is not widely known, and the argument offers no source or subargument to back it up. It may well be true, but an argument such as this, for a general audience at least, cannot just assert it without offering some sort of support. Premise (2) is reliable because it's supported by a good source—the World Health Organization.

The difference between premise (1) and premise (2) in this argument is that premise (2) is supported by a source, whereas premise (1) is not. The source cited to supported premise (2) is a good one, although as you'll see in Chapter IV, the argument would be better if it told you when and where the World Health Organization said that Niger and Egypt were polio free.

Model Response for Exercise 9

(1) Every time you eat meat, your meal is the result of the suffering and death of an animal.

(2) It's disgusting to put a piece of a dead animal's carcass into your mouth and chew it.

(3) There is plenty of great vegetarian food.

(4) Vegetarianism is healthier than eating meat.

(5) By becoming a vegetarian, you'd be joining the company of great people like Leonardo da Vinci, Isaac Newton, Thomas Edison, Paul McCartney, Shania Twain, and Tobey Maguire.

Therefore, (6) you should be a vegetarian.

Premise (1) is mostly reliable. It's obvious that when you eat meat, your meal is the result of an animal's death. Most meat, but not all, comes from animals who suffered (e.g., in factory farms or slaughter-houses) in order to produce that meat. Premise (2) is unreliable. It's too subjective and controversial a statement to count as a good starting point. Since many people do not find it disgusting to eat meat, and eating meat involves putting a piece of an animal's carcass in your mouth, apparently they don't agree that that's disgusting! Premise (3) is fairly reliable. Most people by now know that there is a lot of great vegetarian food, especially when you look at cuisines other than American cuisine.

Premise (4) is unreliable because it's too vague a statement. Some vegetarian diets are healthier than some omnivorous diets, but other vegetarian diets are unhealthy. In order to be reliable, the premise would have to be more precise about the kinds of diets it has in mind—and probably about the ways in which vegetarian diets are healthier. Finally, premise (5) is partly reliable, since it's widely known that some of those people (like Paul McCartney) are vegetarians, but not well known that some of the others are or were vegetarians.

This response proceeds systematically through each premise, offering nuanced evaluations of each of them. Some of the premises are only partly reliable, and the response explains which parts are reliable and which parts are not.

Notice that premises (2) and (3) are both "subjective" statements, but the response claims that one premise is reliable while the other is not. Many people are tempted to dismiss all subjective statements as "mere opinion," but even some subjective statements are sometimes accepted widely enough to provide good starting points for a debate. For instance, "A cool swim on a hot summer day is wonderful" is a subjective statement, but most people would probably accept it as a reliable premise in an argument. The same goes for ethical statements. "Abortion is always immoral" is too controversial to count as a reliable premise, but "It's wrong to torture people for fun and profit" is so widely accepted that most people would think it odd to say that it's an unreliable premise.

Exercise Set 1.5: Decomplexifying artificially abstruse quotations

Model Response for Exercise 1

I have a feeling we're not in Kansas anymore.

You may not come up with the exact wording of the original quotation. If you don't, that's fine; just aim for clarity and directness. Responses like "I don't think we're in Kansas anymore" or "I don't feel like we're in Kansas anymore" would be perfectly good.

Model Response for Exercise 3

Brevity is the soul of wit.

Notice that in the "complexified" version of this quotation, the clause between the dashes simply repeats the first part of the sentence without adding any new content. Thus, it can be cut entirely from the simplified version; there is no need to say, "Brevity, or conciseness, is the soul of wit." Just figure out the basic meaning of the entire quotation and restate it as plainly as possible.

Model Response for Exercise 5

We must be the change that we wish to see in the world.

Notice that parts of the "complexified" version of the quotation are simply redundant. For instance, the complexified version ends with "the world that we inhabit." Since it's clear from the context that "the world" means "the world that we inhabit," rather than some other world (Jupiter?), you can delete the words "that we inhabit" without changing the meaning of the sentence.

Model Response for Exercise 7

Early to bed, early to rise, makes a man healthy, wealthy, and wise.

This response substitutes single words (e.g., "healthy") for longer phrases (e.g., "[having a] good physical constitution"). Having a large vocabulary should help you say the same thing in fewer *and better-focused words, not more.*

Model Response for Exercise 9

A woman without a man is like a fish without a bicycle.

Among many other changes, this response substitutes the more common phrase "is like" for the less common "is akin to." Take care when using unusual phrases in place of more common words. Sometimes it is very effective, but sometimes it just makes you sound like you're trying to "sound smart."

Exercise Set 1.6: Diagnosing loaded language

Model Responses for Exercise 1

Example of a strong response to this exercise

This argument contains at least five instances of loaded language. The first sentence presumably refers to supporters of the U.S. military's "Don't Ask, Don't Tell" policy that allowed homosexuals to serve in the military if and only if they hid their sexual orientation. Calling supporters of the policy "religious fanatics" casts them in a negative light, and calling the policy "anti-gay discrimination" casts the policy in a negative light. The sentence could just say, "Supporters of 'Don't Ask, Don't Tell' lost the political battle over homosexuals in the military." The rest of the argument uses the phrases "dangerous," "hatemongering," and "fearmongering" to describe those same people; all of these carry strong negative connotations. The word "dangerous" could be deleted without affecting the argument. "Hatemongering against homosexuals" could be replaced with "opposition to homosexuality" and "fearmongering against other groups" with "emphasis on other groups of people."

This response does three things: It identifies specific words or phrases that are "loaded" with emotional overtones, it explains why they are loaded, and it suggests neutral alternatives for each of them.

Example of a weak response to this exercise

The argument contains loaded language: "religious fanatics," "hatemongering," and "fearmongering."

While this response does identify several instances of loaded language, it neither explains what makes them loaded nor suggests more neutral alternatives. It also overlooks some more subtle instances of loaded language.

Model Response for Exercise 3

This argument uses several loaded expressions: "dirty little secret," "monstrously cruel mistreatment," and "senseless animal cruelty" all have strong negative overtones. The first two could be avoided by describing the factory farm's practices in neutral terms (e.g., by describing the size of the crates in which factory-farmed chickens are kept), leaving it to the reader to decide whether those practices are "monstrously cruel." The expression "senseless cruelty to animals" could be replaced with "treating animals in this way." Finally, by saying that "morally decent people abhor" such practices, the argument suggests that anyone who is not outraged by factory farms is morally indecent; this might be expressed more modestly by asserting that "Many people believe it is wrong to treat animals in this way."

Sometimes there is no neutral substitute for a particular expression because of the way a sentence is written. Avoiding loaded language sometimes requires rewriting entire sentences, as this response recommends.

Model Response for Exercise 5

This argument relies on a more subtle use of loaded language: the phrase "imaginative little fable" suggests—without argument—that the boy's claim about losing the knife is false. Likewise, the question, "You don't really believe that, do you?" suggests that anyone who believes the "fable" is gullible or stupid, but it doesn't actually give any reasons for thinking that the boy's claim is false.

Note that the words "murder weapon" and "murderer," which might count as loaded language in other contexts, are not loaded in this context. The argument is about someone who is on trial for murder. The knife in question was used to kill someone; it really is a murder weapon. If the boy did commit the crime, as the argument tries to show, then he is, literally, a murderer.

Model Response for Exercise 7

This argument uses positive loaded language. Words and phrases like "new and innovative," "accomplishments," "achieve," and "make this school a better place for you, for me, and for all of our other wonderful classmates" evoke warm, fuzzy feelings without giving any substantive information about what Tracy Flick intends to do to improve the school.

Not all loaded language is negative: some can be loaded in the other direction. Such language aims to get listeners to like the speaker or the argument without providing good reasons to do so. Often, positive loaded language aims to make the listeners feel good about themselves, which is a powerful way to get them to feel good about whatever it is they're listening to.

Exercise Set 1.7: Evaluating letters to the editor

Model Responses for Exercise 1

Example of a strong response to this exercise

This letter does a decent job distinguishing its conclusion from its premises (Rule 1). Although it doesn't use any indicator words, the structure of the letter makes it clear that the first sentence is the main conclusion. The letter presents its premises in a natural order (Rule 2). The premises are reasonably reliable (Rule 3), since they're pretty much common sense, although some people might deny that all responsible gun owners have to keep their guns in a gun safe. (Maybe a trigger lock is enough in a household without children, for instance.) The argument could probably be made more concise (Rule 4), since the first sentence and the last clause basically say the same thing. While none of the language is particularly loaded (Rule 5), comparing marijuana edibles to guns is a bit inflammatory. Comparing them to prescription drugs might prevent some readers from getting riled up. The letter does a fairly good job using consistent terms (Rule 6), although the first and last sentences have slightly different terms for explaining where marijuana edibles should be stored.

This response proceeds methodically through each of the six rules from Chapter I. It explains in some detail how the letter follows (or fails to follow) each rule. It also offers nuanced evaluations in cases where the argument mostly obeys a rule but could do better.

Example of a weak response to this exercise

This letter follows most of these rules: Rules 1, 2, 4, and 6. One rule it maybe does not follow is Rule 3, "Start from reliable premises." And it totally violates Rule 5! Comparing marijuana to guns is totally ridiculous and really loaded language.

Although this response mostly agrees with the strong response above, this one is far too quick and too vague. It does not address each rule individually—it just lists them without explaining how the letter follows them. When it addresses Rule 3, it simply says that the argument might not follow the rule. It does not explain how the argument runs afoul of Rule 3, nor does it indicate how badly it violates Rule 3. Are all of the premises unreliable—or just one? Are the premises clearly false—or just, maybe, questionable? Why? Finally, in claiming that the argument violates Rule 5, the response offers a very quick assertion that it's "ridiculous" and "really loaded" to compare marijuana to guns, but it doesn't say why. (For more on when and how it's reasonable to compare seemingly different things, see Chapter III!)

Model Responses for Exercise 3

Example of a strong response to this exercise

This letter to the editor does a poor job with Rules 1 and 2. The conclusion is presumably that we "ought to be ashamed of the level of discourse in our politics," but this is buried in the middle of the letter. The argument would be much clearer if the author switched the third and fourth sentences. That way, the sentence about "innuendo and idiocy" would be next to the sentence about "honest discussion," where it belongs, and the conclusion would come at the end of the letter. The letter does a decent, but not great, job with Rule 3. All three premises probably resonate with most people's experience, but they're stated as vague, sweeping generalizations. The letter does a good job following Rule 4. A few words, like "thoughtful," could be deleted without changing the meaning, but the letter is straightforward and concise. The letter does a poor job following Rule 5. The expressions "run screaming" and "idiocy" all cast politicians in a strongly negative light. "Idiocy" could be deleted and "avoid" could be substituted for "run screaming." As for Rule 6, the letter does reasonably well, though it uses "discussion," "discourse," and "debate" as synonyms instead of picking one and sticking with it.

This response offers concrete, constructive suggestions for making the letter follow each rule.

Example of a weak response to this exercise

This argument is great, and it makes a really important point. The conclusion (Rule 1) is about how politicians avoid intelligent debate, which is so true (Rule 3). The argument makes perfect sense to me (Rule 2), and it's not overly abstract (Rule 4) or loaded (Rule 5).

This response praises the argument largely because the author agrees with the argument's conclusion. The response tries to connect its praise of the letter with various rules, but it does so briefly and incorrectly. Following Rule 1 is not a matter of the reader identifying or accepting the conclusion; it's a matter of the argument making it easy for the reader to recognize premises and conclusions. Rule 2 is about the arrangement of the premises being sensible and easy to follow: commentary on it should focus on the order and "flow" of the premises. Rule 3 is not about the truth of the conclusion, *but about the reliability of the* premises.

This response does offer brief assessments of Rules 4 and 5, though it doesn't support its claims. The response makes no mention of Rule 6. In general, evaluating an argument is not about whether you accept the argument's conclusion. It involves asking targeted questions about how well the author presents the argument and how well the premises support the conclusion.

Model Responses for Exercise 5

Example of a strong response to this exercise

The use of "Thus" as a conclusion indicator and the presentation of the ideas in a natural order (Rule 2) make it easy to distinguish the conclusion of this argument from its premises (Rule 1). As for premise reliability (Rule 3), the main issue is whether the second premise is reliable. It might be true that these discoveries took a long time to impact health care, but it's not common knowledge and the argument doesn't give us good reason to believe it, so the premise is unreliable. The language is all straightforward (Rule 4) and the argument doesn't use much loaded language (Rule 5), except perhaps the phrase "overly enthusiastic scientists." The argument does not violate Rule 6 by using different words for the same idea.

This response highlights the connection between Rule 1 and Rule 2. When someone presents ideas in a natural order, it is easier to identify the conclusion of the person's argument.

Example of a weak response to this exercise

This argument follows Rule 1 and 2. It does not follow Rule 3 because the second premise is unreliable. It follows Rules 4, 5, and 6.

This response is better than the weak responses to the earlier exercises in that it addresses each rule individually and even gives a brief explanation of how the argument violates Rule 3. However, it does not *justify its claims that the argument follows Rules 1, 2, 4, 5, and 6. Nor does it justify its claim that the second premise is unreliable.*

Model Responses for Exercise 7

Example of a strong response to this exercise

This letter makes it clear what the general conclusion of the argument is, and it's clear that the rest of the letter consists of reasons for the conclusion (Rule 1). With respect to Rule 2, the letter presents its ideas in a natural order, except for the last sentence. That sentence should probably come before the third sentence. All of the premises are reliable (Rule 3) because they're common knowledge, and the letter avoids overly abstract writing (Rule 4). The premises avoid loaded language (Rule 5), but the conclusion is fairly inflammatory, and it doesn't say exactly what the author wants us to believe or do. Should people be writing letters to their local governments? Holding used book sales or buying bumper stickers that say "Support Your Local Library"? Forming angry mobs and picketing the homes of politicians who want to cut library funding? We can't tell which of these the author means from the command "Fight for your library!" The letter does not use different words to express the same idea (Rule 6).

This response explains the ways in which the argument follows or violates each rule. It explains in detail why the conclusion contains more emotional power than substance by illustrating the various things that the conclusion could be taken to mean.

Example of a weak response to this exercise

The argument doesn't use any conclusion indicators, so it fails Rule 1. It presents its ideas in a natural order (Rule 2), except that the last sentence seems out of place. When it comes to Rule 3, the argument needs a lot more work. How does the author know that my local library has books on the topics that she mentions? She hasn't been to every library in the country. She hasn't justified the claim that libraries encourage people to read for pleasure, either. She needs to give statistics to support that claim. As for the claim that there are limits to what you can find on the Internet, I'll bet the author just hasn't looked hard enough. The conclusion builds more on overtone than substance (Rule 5), but the rest of the language in the letter is fine (Rules 4 and 6).

This response is detailed, but it applies two of the rules incorrectly. An argument does not necessarily need to use conclusion or premise indicators in order to follow Rule 1. As long as the argument makes clear what the conclusion is and what the premises are, which this argument does, it follows Rule 1. With respect to Rule 3, this response is far too demanding. It's reasonable to assume that most libraries have books on the topics mentioned in the letter, even if the letter's author hasn't been to every library. It's also reasonable to assume that libraries promote reading for pleasure, even without detailed statistics. Finally, since many people have had the experience of looking for information on the Internet and not being able to find it, it's more reasonable to think that there are limits to what you can find on the Internet than to think that the author simply hasn't looked hard enough. Remember that premises do not need to be beyond doubt in order to be reliable. Following Rule 3 only means providing premises that the argument's audience can accept as reasonable starting points.

Model Responses for Exercise 9

Example of a strong response to this exercise

This letter is definitely clear about the main message, but it's actually somewhat unclear about which claim is supposed to be supported by the other claims (Rule 1). Is the fact that Fred Snowden would be appalled a reason to think that the University of North Carolina's behavior constitutes a blight on all American universities? Or is it the other way around? It's hard to tell. There's no particular flow or order to the ideas presented, either, in violation of Rule 2. Furthermore, most of the premises are rather vague, sweeping statements, so the argument doesn't do very well on Rule 3. The only premise that's not vague is about Fred Snowden's emphasis on academics, but that's neither common knowledge nor backed up by a source, further weakening the argument's performance on Rule 3. The argument could be much more concrete and concise (Rule 4). For instance, the author could replace the vague phrase "scandalous decision to defraud the NCAA" with a more concrete description of what the university did. Relatedly, the author frequently uses loaded language (Rule 5), like "scandalous decision to defraud." At least the argument does not violate Rule 6 by using terms inconsistently.

Again, this response addresses each rule individually and explains how the argument follows the rule (or doesn't), offering specific examples to support its claims.

Example of a weak response to this exercise

This letter fails Rule 3 miserably. I have no idea who Fred Snowden is, other than some coach for University of Arizona. And I have no idea why I should care what Fred Snowden thinks. Why is this letter writer wasting our time talking about him, rather than about the issues in North Carolina?

This response focuses too narrowly on one particular problem with the argument. The entire response is a criticism of the letter's claims about Fred Snowden. The response is correct that the letter's author gives us no particular reason to believe his claims about Snowden, and that this is a problem with respect to Rule 3. But the response says nothing about how any of the other claims fare with respect to Rule 3. Nor does it address how well the argument follows any of the other rules from this chapter.

Furthermore, the response misunderstands a key point about premise reliability. The response complains that Fred Snowden's beliefs have nothing to do with the scandal in North Carolina. This is true. But the question of whether a premise is reliable is just a question about the premise itself, not about the relationship between the premise and the conclusion. We'll look at how well particular premises support their conclusions in future chapters.

MODEL RESPONSES FOR CHAPTER II: GENERALIZATIONS

Exercise Set 2.1: Finding relevant examples

Model Response for Exercise 1

Pigeons, parakeets, and swans

Appropriate examples for this generalization must be birds and they must be able to fly. Pigeons, parakeets, and swans all fit the bill.

Notice that there are some borderline examples, too. Chickens, for example, can't fly very far or very well, but they can fly. Do they count? Sticking with clear-cut examples provides better support for the generalization, so stay away from those debatable cases.

The generalization in this exercise is false, of course. Some birds, such as ostriches and penguins, can't fly. Thus, even though it's easy to produce lots of examples of birds that can fly, that doesn't entitle us to conclude that all birds can fly. It's often possible to find examples to support any generalization, true or false. Thus, being able to trot out a few good examples isn't enough to show that a generalization is true.

Model Response for Exercise 3

Neil Armstrong, Buzz Aldrin, and Ken Mattingly

This generalization is about people who walked on the moon in the twentieth century. It says that they were all Americans. So, appropriate examples for this case would be people who both walked on the moon in the twentieth century and are American. Neil Armstrong, Buzz Aldrin, and Ken Mattingly were all American astronauts who walked on the moon in the 1960s or 1970s.

Notice that these criteria are slightly more complicated than in the earlier generalizations. An American who walks on the moon in the twenty-first century wouldn't count, despite being a person who walked on the moon and was an American.

Model Response for Exercise 5

Pineapple, orange, and guava

Appropriate examples for this generalization must meet two criteria: they must be fruits and they must be sweet (when ripe). Notice that some people might dispute certain examples: If you gave butternut squash as an example, some people might object that it's not a fruit—even though it technically is. Some people might object that it's not sweet enough to count as "sweet."

The same kinds of problems crop up in collecting data for scientific studies. Scientists often deal with these problems by defining their terms in much more detail. For instance, instead of using vague terms like sweet, *they might specify that most fruits contain at least a certain amount of sugars per gram. (But what about* fruit *and* ripe, *which are also vague?) For more on definitions, see Appendix II.*

For the purpose of this exercise, sticking with clear-cut examples allows you to avoid those difficulties.

Model Response for Exercise 7

Australia, Italy, and Canada

Appropriate examples for this generalization must be developed, democratic countries that do not practice capital punishment. Australia, Italy and Canada are all developed, democratic countries, and none of them practice capital punishment.

As with the generalization in exercise 5, this generalization is actually false. The United States and Japan are developed, democratic countries, and both use capital punishment.

Notice also that this generalization leaves some crucial details open to interpretation. How developed must a country be to count as "developed"? How democratic must it be to count as "democratic"? And for that matter, what counts as "practicing capital punishment"? For instance, Russia hasn't abolished capital punishment, but it has had a moratorium on executions since 1996. Does it "practice capital punishment"? (For that matter, is it democratic?)

In most cases, there may not be a single best interpretation of the generalization. What matters most is that you pick one definition and stick to it.

Model Response for Exercise 9

John Lennon, Elton John, and Adele

Appropriate examples for this question must be musicians, they must be famous, and they must be from England.

Once again, you may need to think carefully about what this generalization means before you choose examples. Who counts as a musician? Do songwriters or orchestral conductors count? Who counts as famous? Everyone has heard of John Lennon, so that's easy. Elton John is clearly famous too. But what about Adele? She's famous among younger music fans, but your parents and grandparents probably don't know who she is. (Neither does one of the co-authors of this book.) What about someone like the English cellist Jacqueline du Pré? Classical music aficionados consider her one of the greatest cellists of all time, but most people have probably never heard of her. Is she famous? As with exercise 7, what matters is that you pick one interpretation of the generalization and stick with it.

Exercise Set 2.2: Improving biased samples

Model Response for Exercise 1

This argument could be improved by sampling all likely Republican voters throughout the United States, rather than looking just at people who attended the Republican National Conference. The "political junkies" who attended that conference are probably more politically involved than the average voter, since most voters wouldn't bother to go. And there are probably more people at that particular conference who support the libertarian candidate who won, since the conference is close to his home state and drew "busloads" of libertarian supporters.

This response explains what group you would need to sample to improve the argument, and it explains clearly why the existing sample—namely, people attending this conference—is not representative of the group discussed in the conclusion—namely, Republican voters in general. If you're having trouble figuring out whether a sample is biased, ask yourself how the people or things in the sample are likely to differ from other people or things in the group discussed in the argument's conclusion.

Notice that the response cites details from the argument—e.g., the fact that conference attendees are "political junkies"—to support its reasoning.

Model Response for Exercise 3

The conclusion of this argument is that foreign universities are enrolling more and more American students. This is a generalization about foreign universities as a whole. However, all of the examples are from Scotland and Ireland. To support the claim that students are flocking to "foreign universities," as opposed to universities in the UK, Ireland, and Canada, for instance, we would need to look at universities elsewhere in the world, especially in non–English-speaking countries. After all, American students are much more likely to go an English-speaking university than a non–English-speaking university.

As this response points out, the conclusion is about a very large group: all universities outside the United States. The examples, though, are all drawn from a very specific subgroup. To improve the argument, we need to look at a wider set of examples.

The response not only identifies the way in which the examples are unrepresentative, but explains why that sample bias undermines the argument.

Model Response for Exercise 5

This argument looks only at drivers who chose to switch from their old insurance provider to Allstate. This results in a biased sample because it excludes everyone who decided not to switch. The argument would be stronger if it looked at a random sample of all drivers (e.g., by calling people who were randomly selected from a list of everyone with a driver's license) rather than just those who decided for themselves to switch to Allstate. That would give us a more accurate estimate of how much the average driver could expect to save (or lose) by switching to Allstate.

This is a subtle example of allowing people to decide for themselves whether to be included in the sample. Social scientists run into this sort of problem all the time when they're trying to figure out the impact of some program, policy, or action. For instance, consider the fact that Americans who marry at a young age are more likely to divorce than people who wait to marry later in life. Does this mean that the average person would be less likely to get divorced if he or she waited another five years to get married? Or is it that the kind of people who marry young are also the kind of people who are likely to get divorced, so that they would still be more likely to get divorced, even if they waited another five years to marry? You can't tell just by comparing the average divorce rates for people who married young to those who married later. You need more sophisticated techniques, such as comparing people who are similar except in that they married at different ages. Those techniques are well beyond the scope of this book, but you can learn about them by taking a statistics course. The need for such statistical sophistication is one reason that social science is so challenging.

Model Response for Exercise 7

This argument ignores all of the organisms throughout history who have had offspring but not managed to raise them to adulthood. Thus, to construct an unbiased sample, it would have to look at organisms whose children did not survive to have offspring of their own—which might well include most offspring.

As the author of this facetious argument points out, each of us comes from a long, unbroken line of organisms that succeeded in raising their offspring to an age where those offspring could have offspring of their own. But this, as the author says, is "the mother of all sampling bias," for it excludes precisely those organisms whose offspring did not survive. Just as the sample exercise for this exercise set looks only at college graduates who work at Schnucks, this argument looks only at organisms who succeeded (however minimally) as parents. To avoid this kind of error, be sure that your sample doesn't automatically exclude anything that wouldn't support the conclusion.

It's also worth noting that many of the examples might not really be examples of organisms that were good parents in any reasonable sense of the term: An organism that creates thousands of offspring and leaves them all to fend for themselves hardly qualifies as a good parent, but as long as just one of those offspring survives, it could have lots of descendants today through that one survivor.

Model Response for Exercise 9

Since the conclusion of this argument is about Americans convicted of serious crimes, the examples need to be drawn randomly from all prison inmates convicted of serious crimes. Although the argument doesn't specify this, the Innocence Project presumably looks for inmates for whom there is evidence of (or at least a high likelihood of) a wrongful conviction, since those are the kinds of cases with which they're concerned, and cases where they're likely to have the greatest chance of reversal. To improve the argument, we would need to pick long-term inmates at random and have the Innocence Project defend them.

This response identifies another subtle source of sample bias: The examples are selected by someone whose primary goal is not to do an objective study of the criminal justice system. The Innocence Project is trying to free people who have been wrongly imprisoned, and so they quite understandably look for people who are likely to be innocent. If they are doing their job well, we should expect many of their clients to be exonerated.

The unrepresentative nature of this sample is not a problem for the Innocence Project. It is a problem for any attempt to conclude, on the basis of the Innocence Project's cases, that many Americans are wrongfully imprisoned.

Exercise Set 2.3: Identifying relevant background rates

Model Response for Exercise 1

First, we need to know how many cars there are on campus: that is, we need to know (or readily be able to calculate) the theft <u>rate</u> on campus. Second, we would need to know what the rate of car thefts is in the surrounding area. If there are few cars on campus or a very low theft rate in the surrounding area, then it's not as big an accomplishment if there have been no car thefts on campus.

We could get even more precise here by figuring out how we're going to count the number of cars on campus. Are we looking at the number of cars on campus on, say, an average weekday morning at 10 a.m.? The average number of cars parked on campus overnight? The total number of cars parked on campus at any point during the month? All of these suggestions are ways of refining the basic idea that we need to know how many cars there are on campus.

Model Response for Exercise 3

We need to know the rate of people in non-high-paying jobs who also say they love their jobs. Only then can we tell whether having a high-paying job is really connected to loving your job.

Even though this argument presents rates (two out of three, or 66 percent; and 75 percent), its conclusion implicitly compares these rates to another rate—namely, the rate at which people who do not have high-paying jobs say that they love their jobs. (Compare this to a claim like, "Nine out of ten mothers in Texas love their children." Before we can draw any special conclusions about mothers in Texas, we would need to know how many mothers in other places love their children.)

Model Response for Exercise 5

We would need to know several things to justify this conclusion. First, we would need to know how many <u>other</u> financially troubled people who turned to hoodoo saw an improvement in their financial situation. That is, we need a <u>rate</u>, and not merely a few, probably unrepresentative examples (without even last names!). Second, we would need to know the rate at which people who did <u>not</u> turn to hoodoo also saw an improvement in their financial situation. Only by comparing the two rates can we decide whether people who turn to hoodoo are <u>more</u> likely to recover from financial troubles.

We're implicitly comparing people who turned to hoodoo to people who did not turn to hoodoo. Thus, if we're going to say that hoodoo is connected to financial recovery, we need to know the rate of financial improvements for both groups.

Scientists have a technique for comparing background rates to determine if two events really are connected. They use something called a "control group." The basic idea is to get two groups of people (or animals, trees, etc.) that resemble each other very closely, and then expose one of those groups to the "treatment" in question (e.g., hoodoo). That group is called the "experimental group." The other group, which does not get the "treatment," is the control group. This allows scientists to calculate the rate at which members of each group experience the expected effect (e.g., recovery from financial troubles). They can then compare the rates for the experimental group and the control group to see if people in the experimental group really do have a significantly greater (or lesser) chance of experiencing the effect in question.

Model Response for Exercise 7

We need to know how many Take 5 tickets the New York lottery sells every day. This would enable you to figure out the <u>percentage</u> of tickets that win, which is what you would need to know to decide whether buying one ticket gives you a good shot at winning.

The relevant background rate here is the percentage of winning tickets. The information we need to calculate that rate is the number of winning and non-winning tickets sold.

Notice that the number of tickets sold is probably much higher than the number of people who play the lottery in a given day, since some people buy multiple tickets. Thus, you need to focus on the number of winning tickets and not just the number of people who won the lottery.

Another way in which the argument might be deceptive is that it doesn't distinguish between different types of "winners." Lotteries sometimes pay a large number of very small prizes so they can claim that an impressive number of tickets were "winning tickets." This is almost surely the case in New York, since there's no way the lottery could support one hundred thousand big prizes every day. Of those one hundred thousand tickets that the ad touts as having won money, then, only a very few—maybe only one or two, if any—actually won big money, which is what we usually mean by "winning the lottery." In general, like all forms of institutionalized gambling, lotteries are a profit-making enterprise, so you know before you even start that in the long run the state will come out ahead.

Suppose that only one ticket in one hundred thousand wins big. One person goes home with (say) five hundred grand, but the holders of the other 99,999 (more or less) go home with little or nothing. At a one-in-a-hundred-thousand rate (.001 percent), you are more likely to get a huge payback by just randomly giving your money away to strangers.

Model Response for Exercise 9

To determine which is more dangerous—measles or the measles vaccine—we'd need to know what fraction of people who get measles died (i.e., the death rate from measles) and what fraction of people who get a measles vaccine died (i.e., the death rate from the vaccine). Far more people get the measles vaccine than get measles. So, even if the death rate from the measles vaccine were much lower than the death rate from measles, the total number of deaths from the vaccine would probably be higher.

Being able to think critically about numbers is crucial to think clearly about vaccines. Measles kills only about 0.2% of people who contract it. That's two in every thousand people. Serious reactions to the measles vaccine occur in about one in every three thousand people who get the shot. Thus, even if all of the deaths reported in this argument really were caused by the measles vaccine (rather than simply happening after an adverse reaction to the vaccine), careful consideration of the background rates suggest that getting the vaccine really is safer than getting the measles. One of the ironies of this debate is that there were so few measles cases in the United States because so many people had been vaccinated against it.

The current controversy about vaccines depends in part on the difficulty of thinking clearly about statistics. (It also depends in part on common mistakes in reasoning about causes. See Chapter V to learn more about arguments about causes.) It's easy for people on both sides of the debate to produce statistics that seem convincing, and debunking the bad arguments often depends on a subtle understanding of things like the importance of background rates. So, next time you get involved in a debate about vaccines, remember to think very carefully about the reasoning you encounter, and do your best to (politely) encourage others to do the same.

Exercise Set 2.4: Evaluating simple arguments that use numbers

Model Response for Exercise 1

This argument tries to convince you to buy a security door brace by claiming that "up to 80 percent of forced entries" occur through a front door or a window. This is misleading for many reasons. First, why does it say "up to 80 percent"? Does this mean that, as a national average, nearly 80 percent of forced entries occur through a front door or window, or does it mean something less impressive? Also, the statistic mentions only forced entries. How many burglaries result from forced entries, as opposed to other methods of entry? And notice that the statistic is for entries through a front door or window. What share of those forced entries occur through a window, for which a door security brace wouldn't help?

This response explains what the argument tries to do with statistics and then explains, in a methodical way, why that statistic may be misleading. To do this, it suggests various interpretations of the statistics and explains why some plausible interpretations do not support the argument's conclusion.

This argument is adapted from a YouTube video that functions as an advertisement, even though it's disguised as an informational video.

Unfortunately, advertisers frequently do try to mislead with statistics. This response does better than simply stating that the argument's authors have an ulterior motive. It identifies specific aspects of the statistic that raise doubts about its reliability.

Model Response for Exercise 3

This argument chooses comparisons that are somewhat biased in favor of beef: it compares the lowest cholesterol (lean) beef with high-cholesterol forms of other foods, such as cheese. A fairer comparison would be to low-fat cheese, for example. But the fundamental problem with the argument is that it doesn't compare beef to any foods other than quite fatty ones. It is entirely possible that <u>all</u> of these foods are high in cholesterol! Nothing in this argument even begins to show what a low or moderate or healthy (not-high) level of cholesterol would be, or that beef is anywhere near that level.

Notice that according to these very data, lean beef has the same level of cholesterol as fried chicken, which is not exactly reassuring. Meanwhile, though you'd never guess it from this argument, fruits and vegetables have no cholesterol whatsoever.

Yet another thing to note is that three ounces is a fairly small helping of beef (or any main dish). But the 73 milligrams of cholesterol in that three ounces of beef is already more than a third of the total *recommended maximum daily intake of cholesterol according to some studies (around 200 mg). A little common sense should already make you suspicious of this argument, but you may have to do a little research to realize just how bad it really is.*

Model Response for Exercise 5

This argument compares humans' cumulative carbon dioxide emissions to the cumulative emissions from volcanoes over all of geological history. It notes that our emissions are tiny in comparison to those volcanic emissions—less than one-thousandth of a percent. This is misleading because it's comparing human emissions over, say, ten thousand years to natural emissions over four and a half <u>billion</u> years. Furthermore, the argument gives no reason to think that this comparison is relevant. Why would it even matter how humans' emissions stack up against all the volcanic emissions in geological history?

Throwing around very small (or very big) numbers can make an argument sound very impressive. After all, "less than one-thousandth of a percent" doesn't sound like very much. But it's easy to make anything sound very small (or very big) by picking the right units. For instance, Bill Gates (the world's richest person) owns just 0.0003 percent of all the world's wealth. That doesn't sound like much, does it? And if you save for college by putting a quarter in a piggy bank every week, it would take you over nine thousand years to save enough to pay the average cost of tuition at a private college—even if costs didn't rise. Sounds like a lot, doesn't it?

The lesson here is to pay close attention to the units in an argument, not just to the numbers themselves. Are the numbers expressing distance in feet or miles? Are they expressing costs in pennies or dollars—or maybe in millions of dollars? Sometimes, as in this case, you'll need to think carefully about what those units are. Be especially wary if the units seem unusual—like "fractions of the cumulative volcanic emissions over the past four and a half billion years."

There's another lesson, too. Just because something sounds like a little (or a lot) doesn't mean that it has a minor (or major) impact. A lethal dose of arsenic, for instance, is just three millionths of an adult's body weight. So just because a number is very small doesn't mean you can assume that it doesn't matter.

Model Response for Exercise 7

The conclusion of this argument is that we can't believe much of what anyone says. In other words, it's about the <u>percentage of statements</u> that are true. The premise, though, is about the <u>percentage of people</u> to whom the average person lies. Since the conclusion and the allegedly relevant statistic are about different things, the statistic doesn't support the conclusion. To see why, suppose that I say 100 things to each of 100 people during the week, for a total of 10,000 statements. If I tell one lie to a third of those people, I've lied to nearly 34 percent of the people, but only 33 out of 10,000 statements—a third of one percent—were lies.

This response explains how the statistic in the argument isn't talking about exactly the same thing as the conclusion. This is a good example of the importance of asking what exactly the statistic is saying and whether it really shows what the argument needs it to show. Since the point is put rather abstractly in the first part of the response, the response gives an example to clarify the idea.

There is at least one other issue with this argument, which is the definition of "lie." Suppose that you are feeling ill. You pass a coworker in the hall, and she asks, "Hi, how are you?" If you say, "Fine, thanks," is that counted as a lie in the study? That could make a big difference in what you think of the claim that people lie to 34 percent of people during a typical week. To find out for sure, you would need to read the original study, which you can probably find through your school's library. (Ask a librarian!)

Model Response for Exercise 9

This argument uses extremely precise numbers to convey an air of authority, but it doesn't provide the background information we need to make sense of the relevant statistics. In general, the argument gives rates of increase without giving underlying numbers. But what should we make of a 171 percent increase in gun homicides, for instance, if we don't know how many gun homicides there were the previous year? Furthermore, the argument isn't clear about whether the increases are increases in crimes <u>per person</u> ("per capita", as it's usually put) or just in the <u>total number</u> of these crimes. Since the population of Australia is increasing, the total number of crimes could go up even when the number of crimes per capita stays the same or goes down.

This response notes the purpose of the extremely precise statistics in the argument before zeroing in on the argument's main flaws. First, it gives only rates of change, *without giving actual numbers. In this case, this is a serious flaw. According to Snopes.com, there were nine gun homicides in Victoria in 1996 and nineteen in 1997. That turns out not to be a statistically significant increase. (That is, even though homicides more than doubled, both numbers are so tiny compared to the total population as to be basically the same from a statistical perspective.)*

Second, the argument focuses on the rate of change in the total number *of crimes, not on the rate of change in* crime rates. *This matters because changes in the total number of crimes do not always coincide with significant changes in an area's crime rate—that is, in the percentage of people who are victims of a crime. For instance, the total number of crimes in an area will change as the area's population grows, even if the crime* rate *stays the same. To say that crime is getting better or worse in an area, we need to focus on changes in the crime rate, not just in the raw numbers.*

It's worth noting, of course, that even if violent crimes did go up after the gun ban, that doesn't prove that the gun ban caused *crime to go up. To learn how to construct and evaluate arguments about what caused what, see Chapter V.*

Exercise Set 2.5: Finding counterexamples

Model Response for Exercise 1

Javier Bardem is a Hollywood movie star, but his native language is Spanish.

The generalization in this exercise is about Hollywood movie stars. It says that all Hollywood movie stars are native English speakers. Thus, to find a counterexample to the generalization, we need to find someone who is a Hollywood movie star but is not *a native English speaker. Javier Bardem grew up in Spain, and his native language is Spanish, so he is a counterexample to the generalization.*

Model Response for Exercise 3

Platypuses

The generalization in this exercise is a negative generalization about mammals. It says that they do not lay eggs. Thus, a counterexample to this generalization would be a mammal that does lay eggs. Platypuses, which live in Australia, are mammals, but they lay eggs. (There are only four other species of mammals that do so.)

Model Response for Exercise 5

The Holy See (Vatican City)

This exercise is more difficult than it might appear because the generalization is open to interpretation. The Holy See is the only fully recognized, independent country that is not a full-fledged member of the United Nations, making it the only clear counterexample to this generalization. (The Holy See is a "permanent observer" at the UN, but since "membership" in the UN is clearly defined, that part of the generalization is less open to interpretation.)

Areas that consider themselves to be independent countries, but are not generally recognized as such, pose a special problem for this generalization. Take Taiwan (the Republic of China), for instance. Taiwan is not a member of the United Nations, although it used to be. Taiwan regards itself as an independent, sovereign country, but China and most other countries do not. Thus, its status as a counterexample to this generalization is disputed. In general, it's best to avoid disputed counterexamples if you can find undisputed counterexamples.

Model Response for Exercise 7

Egg salad

This generalization is about salads. It says that all salads are made from vegetables. This leaves a lot of room for interpretation. What, exactly, counts as a salad? And does the generalization mean that the salad is made en-tirely from vegetables, mostly from vegetables, or at least partly from veg-etables? For that matter, what counts as a vegetable?

Egg salad is presumably a salad, and its main ingredient, obviously, is eggs, which are not vegetables. Thus, it is a counterexample to the generalization.

What about Greek salad, which typically includes tomato (technically a fruit), cucumber and bell peppers (both of which are also technically fruits), olives (fruit), cheese, and onion? Strictly speaking, it is mainly fruits and cheese, though it includes at least one vegetable (onion). Whether Greek salad counts as a clear counterexample depends on your interpretation of the generalization. (Also, many people think that tomatoes, cucumbers, bell pep-pers, and olives are vegetables, despite their actually being, technically, fruits. See Appendix II for more on definitions.)

If you find yourself unable to decide whether something is a counter-example, try refining the generalization to resolve the interpretive prob-lems. For instance, if you can't decide whether Greek salad is a counterexample to the generalization "Salads are made of vegetables," try making the gen-eralization more precise: Greek salad is a clear counterexample to "Salads are made entirely of vegetables," but it is clearly not a counterexample to "Salads contain at least some vegetables."

Model Response for Exercise 9

There are no counterexamples to this generalization

This is another tricky case. The generalization is about mammals, and it says that all mammals have hair. The generalization might mean that all types of mammals typically have hair (at least at some stage of their lives). If that's what it means, then the generalization is clearly true; it's part of the definition of a mammal that it has hair. (Even whales and dolphins have a few hairs when they are very young.) On the other hand, it might mean that every individual mammal has hair. In that case, it might be false. In-dividuals may sometimes lose all of their hair due to an autoimmune disease. Are they counterexamples to this generalization?

Exercise Set 2.6: Evaluating arguments for generalizations

Model Responses for Exercise 1

Example of a strong response to this exercise

This argument is very weak. It violates Rule 7 by giving only one example. It presumably does not follow Rule 8, either, since voters are very diverse, making it impossible for one person to be a representative example of all voters. The argument would be stronger if the author stated how many voters she watched, since that would give us the background rate (Rule 9). There are no statistics in the argument, so Rule 10 doesn't apply here. If the author had considered counterexamples (Rule 11), I'm guessing she would have noticed that most people do not take very long to vote.

This response addresses each rule and offers fairly detailed explanations for its claims about how well the argument follows each rule. It even mentions Rule 10, if only to say that it's not relevant. In the case of Rule 11, the response offers a reasonable guess about what would have happened had the argument considered counterexamples.

Example of a weak response to this exercise

This argument is bad. It only gives one example—a single voter who took too long in the voting booth. This violates Rule 7. That's a problem because you can't generalize about all voters just by looking at a single example. Maybe that voter had trouble reading and so it took him or her a really long time to read the ballot.

While this response does get to the heart of the matter, it would be better if it considered all of the rules from this chapter. It's true that the argument is weak because it doesn't follow Rule 7, but it's worth pointing out the argument's other flaws too. A good response addresses every rule.

Model Responses for Exercise 3

Example of a strong response to this exercise

This argument is not very strong. It does give several examples (Rule 7), but they are not representative (Rule 8). The argument is about all empires, but the examples are all from the twentieth century. While the author might expect us to know how many empires there have been in the last century, she would do well to think about how many empires there have been throughout history (Rule 9). There are no statistics in this argument, so Rule 10 doesn't apply. There are lots of counterexamples, which the author ignores (Rule 11). Think of the Roman Empire, the Ottoman Empire, the Holy Roman Empire, and the Spanish Empire, not to mention China.

In addition to touching on each rule from this chapter, this response explains in detail how the argument fails on Rules 8 and 11. In discussing Rule 11, the response gives specific counterexamples (though it could elaborate).

Example of a weak response to this exercise

This argument follows Rule 7, but not Rules 8, 9, or 11. The argument doesn't use any statistics.

For the most part, this response just states which rules the argument does and does not follow. It does not explain how the argument follows or fails to follow each rule.

Model Responses for Exercise 5

Example of a strong response to this exercise

This is a weak argument, but for subtle reasons. On the one hand, it gives lots of examples—314 of them, to be exact (Rule 7). And because it's looking at all 3,141 counties in the United States, it's not "cherry picking" just the counties that support its conclusion (Rule 8) or ignoring counterexamples (Rule 11). The problem here has to do with background rates (Rule 9) and the use of statistics (Rule 10). Because of the very low background rate of people developing kidney cancer, the statistics given in the argument don't support the conclusion that people in rural counties have a lower risk of developing kidney cancer. In densely populated counties, even a low background rate will lead to lots of cases of kidney cancer. But in sparsely populated counties, that same rate would often mean that no one in the county develops kidney cancer in a given year. So, it's no surprise that those counties have the lowest rates of kidney cancer. But that's different than saying that people in those counties have a lower risk of kidney cancer.

This response acknowledges what the argument does well and then explains, in detail, why the argument's use of statistics fails to support its conclusion.
    The flaw in this argument illustrates a common mistake based on "small sample sizes"—that is, statistics generated by looking at small groups. When you have a random process at work in a small group, you're far more likely to get "extreme" results than when you have that same process at work in a

large group. For instance, suppose that you toss four quarters in the air, and your professor tosses a hundred quarters in the air. When the coins land, it would be much more likely that all of your coins landed heads than that all of your professor's coins did. But this doesn't mean that your quarters have a greater chance (or a greater "risk") of landing heads.

To avoid this sort of problem, scientists prefer to look at large samples, where statistical flukes are much rarer. The size of the group that you need depends on a lot of factors, including the rarity of the events you're trying to study. For instance, if you're trying to study the common cold, which occurs quite frequently, you won't need nearly as large a group as if you're trying to study kidney cancer, which is rare.

Example of a weak response to this exercise

This is a strong argument. It gives over three hundred examples (Rule 7), drawn from a complete survey of all American counties (Rule 8). Because it gives us the total number of counties, we can calculate the percentage of counties that have low rates of kidney cancer (Rule 9). The argument could be a bit more detailed about its statistics (Rule 10) by, for example, telling us the average rate of kidney cancer in those safest 341 counties. The argument does not ignore counterexamples (Rule 11).

This response does address each rule from this chapter. However, it doesn't apply them very well. For one thing, notice how much clearer the discussion of Rules 8 and 11 was in the strong model response, which explains in detail how the argument follows those rules. But more importantly, this response displays a mechanical, unthinking application of Rules 9 and 10. In the case of Rule 9, this response calculates a percentage based on the two numbers that we're given. That's sometimes helpful, but not in this case. As shown in the strong model response, there are deeper, more subtle issues at work here related to statistics and background rates. In general, remember that the rules give you a checklist of things to think about, but you'll need to apply them carefully and thoughtfully, not mechanically.

Model Response for Exercise 7

This argument is weak. It uses only one example (Rule 7), and that example is not particularly representative of power companies in Georgia (Rule 8). Business operates very differently in China than in the United States, so we may not be able to draw good inferences about an American reactor from the experience of a Chinese construction project. The argument does not tell us how many power companies are building AP1000 reactors, so we don't know the background rate (Rule 9). The argument doesn't run afoul of Rule 10, but only because there are no other statistics involved. The argument does not consider counterexamples (Rule 11). Are there other companies that have built or are building AP1000 reactors? What have their experiences been?

This response proceeds methodically through each rule, pointing out the ways in which the argument falls short of each one. In some cases, the response even explains why violating the rule creates a problem. For instance, it points out that the unrepresentativeness of the example in the argument makes it difficult to draw inferences about a power plant in Georgia.

Model Response for Exercise 9

This argument is fairly weak. The argument gives ten examples. This is a fairly small sample, so the argument doesn't do a great job with Rule 7. We don't know whether the examples are representative, so we don't know how well the argument does with Rule 8. Where did the unnamed "fight promoter" get his list of twenty-three boxers? Were those boxers more likely than average to have brain damage? Furthermore, what distinguishes the ten boxers that Dr. Matland found from the thirteen that he didn't? Maybe brain-damaged boxers were easier to find because they had been in more fights and were therefore better known. The argument does not allow us to determine the background rate of any of the ailments that Dr. Matland identified (Rule 9), especially because we don't know how old the boxers were when Dr. Matland found them. After all, the background rate of dementia in thirty-year-olds is much lower than in seventy-year-olds. There are no statistics involved in the argument, so we don't need to worry about Rule 10. Dr. Matland did look at every boxer he could find, and he presumably looked just as hard for non-damaged boxers and for damaged boxers, so he is not ignoring counterexamples (Rule 11).

Like the model response to exercise 7 in this exercise set, this response proceeds methodically through each rule from this chapter and explains how the argument violates each one.

Exercise Set 2.7: Arguing for and against generalizations

Model Responses for Exercise 1

Example of a strong response to this exercise

This generalization is false. A surprising number of U.S. presidents <u>were</u> born in Ohio or Virginia—namely, Grant, Hayes, Garfield, Benjamin Harrison, McKinley, Taft, and Harding in Ohio and Washington, Jefferson, Madison, Monroe, William Henry Harrison, Tyler, Taylor, and Wilson in Virginia. That's just over a third of all U.S. Presidents. The majority, however, were born elsewhere. Four each were born in Massachusetts and New York; two each in North Carolina, Texas, and Vermont; and the birthplaces of the rest are in over a dozen other states.

This response begins by recognizing all of the presidents born in Ohio and Virginia—a nice move—but also makes it clear that there are not enough of them to show that the generalization is true. It then identifies the specific states in which fourteen other presidents were born, although it doesn't name the presidents, and asserts that the rest were not born in Ohio or Virginia either. This covers all the presidents, and thus provides a sufficient number of examples (Rule 7). The author of the argument summarizes the relevant background rate (Rule 9) by pointing out that the sixteen presidents born in Ohio and Virginia make up only about a third of all presidents. In this case, the author probably can count on the audience knowing roughly how many U.S. Presidents there have been—forty-four as of 2015 (Rule 9). There are no other relevant statistics involved in this argument, so the argument doesn't run afoul of Rule 10, either.

Example of a weak response to this exercise

This generalization is false. Neither Barack Obama, George W. Bush, Bill Clinton, George H. W. Bush, nor Ronald Reagan were born in Ohio or Virginia.

This response is weak because it looks only at a few U.S. presidents, and only at the most recent ones. It misses all of the supporting examples and also most of the counterexamples. Look farther!

Model Responses for Exercise 3

Example of a strong response to this exercise

This generalization is false. A lot of classical music is exciting. Think of the opening of Beethoven's Fifth Symphony or the "Ode to Joy" at the end of his Ninth Symphony. Think of the "Gloria" from Bach's Mass in B Minor, the "Hallelujah Chorus" from Handel's <u>Messiah</u>, Mozart's <u>Don Giovanni</u>, Tchaikovsky's "1812 Overture," Wagner's "Ride of the Valkyries," Mahler's Symphony No. 2, the finale to Stravinsky's <u>Firebird</u>, or Copland's "Fanfare for the Common Man." That doesn't even get into composers like Brahms, Strauss, Mussorgsky, Verdi, Mahler, Ravel, Bartók, Prokofiev, or Shostakovich. These are all exciting pieces, even to people who don't listen to a lot of classical music.

This response begins by asserting that the generalization is false. It then offers an alternative generalization, meant to show that the original generalization is false: A lot of classical music is exciting. (Note that this isn't the only way to argue against the claim that classical music is boring. You might argue that classical music is interesting, rather than exciting.)

The response then gives many examples to support the claim that a lot of classical music is exciting (Rule 7). It gives ten specific examples of exciting pieces of classical music and then mentions nine additional composers who wrote exciting music. The composers and pieces come from a wide range of time periods and countries, providing a nicely representative sample of classical music (Rule 8). We know, of course, that there are many more classical composers and classical pieces than those mentioned here, so the argument doesn't need to tell us that these examples cover just a small fraction of all classical music (Rule 9). Since the conclusion here is just that "a lot" of classical music is exciting, though, that's okay.

Of course, it would be easier to decide whether the examples given in this argument are good examples if we had a good definition of "exciting music."

Example of a weak response to this exercise

This generalization is false. A lot of classical music is very interesting once you understand it, and some of it is downright exciting. The problem is that people don't really know how to appreciate it. If you don't know what you're listening for, Bach's fugues, for instance, are kind of boring. But if you know what's going on, a fugue can be as exciting and interesting as any murder mystery.

Like the previous response, this response begins by claiming that the generalization is false and offering an alternative. However, the argument for that alternative cites only one example of exciting classical music—Bach's fugues—and even then it admits that Bach's fugues are only exciting and interesting to those who really understand them. The response spends more time explaining why people think that classical music is boring than actually arguing that it's not. Throughout this exercise, concentrate on giving examples and using statistics to support your claims about each generalization, rather than supporting your claims in other ways.

Model Responses for Exercise 5

Example of a strong response to this exercise

This generalization is false. The U.S. Parachute Association reported 2.2 million skydiving jumps in 2007. From those 2.2 million jumps, there were only 821 injuries and eighteen deaths. That's a death rate of less than one in ten thousand and an injury rate of four in one thousand. According to <u>Bandolier</u>, a journal written by Oxford scientists, that's only a slightly higher death rate than tennis.

This response begins by stating that the generalization in question is false. It then uses statistics to support that generalization, including a comparison to tennis—an activity that most people would never consider dangerous.

Notice that it takes a little bit of interpretation to see that the claim "Skydiving is dangerous" is making a generalization. The claim says that many or all people who go skydiving face significant risks. A good way to show that something is not risky is to show that few people get hurt or die while doing it. That's what this argument sets out to do.

Notice that after finding the death rate, the argument puts that rate in context by comparing it to something else that people don't consider dangerous. This is often helpful in dealing with vague terms like dangerous.

Example of a weak response to this exercise

This generalization is true. Think about it. Throwing yourself out an airplane thousands of feet in the air is obviously dangerous. There are so many things that could go wrong, from a parachute that doesn't deploy correctly to landing in the water and getting tangled in your ropes. Why do you think they require people to take special classes and make their first jumps tied to a professional instructor?

This argument demonstrates a common mistake people make when arguing for (or against) a generalization. Rather than looking at particular examples—that is, working out the statistics to tell you how likely you are to get injured—this argument gives other kinds of reasons for thinking that skydiving is dangerous. But the proof is in the number of people who do (and don't!) get injured while skydiving. After all, maybe the kinds of problems that the argument mentions are exceedingly rare. In that case, even though

they would obviously be very bad for you if they happened, they're so un-
likely to happen as to pose only a minor risk.

Model Responses for Exercise 7

This generalization is false. There are generalizations that have no
exceptions. For instance, the generalizations "All triangles have three
sides" and "All mountains over 8,000 meters above sea level are in
Asia" have no exceptions.

Proving that a universal generalization is false is easy. All you need to do is
produce a counterexample. This response gives two counterexamples to the
claim that "All generalizations have exceptions"—which means, of course,
that this generalization applies to itself because it, too, has exceptions!

MODEL RESPONSES FOR CHAPTER III: ARGUMENTS BY ANALOGY

Exercise Set 3.1: Identifying important similarities

Model Response for Exercise 1

Being a student and having a job both involve specific tasks that
you're expected to do at specific times. Both give you the chance to
develop new skills. You can get kicked out of school/lose your job if
you don't perform well.

This response gives three similarities between being a student and having a
job. But how can you tell whether those similarities are "important?" The
first step is to avoid obviously silly or trivial similarities. Beyond that, ask
yourself what conclusions someone might draw based on the similarities you
mention. Taking this response as an example, someone might give the fol-
lowing argument by analogy: "You should take advantage of being a stu-
dent by learning as much as you can from your studies. Having a job is like
being a student in that both give you the chance to develop new skills. Thus,
you should take advantage of having a job by learning as much as you can
from your work."

You don't need to include an argument as part of your response, but if you can think of one—especially one that has an important, interesting, or un-expected conclusion—then you can be confident that your similarity is an important one.

Model Response for Exercise 3

First-degree murder and euthanasia both involve intentionally causing someone's death. Both are illegal (in most places, at least).

While there are obvious differences between first-degree murder and eutha-nasia, your task here is to focus on the similarities. Even if you don't like the idea of comparing two things, you can almost always find some important ways in which they are similar. Remember: saying that two things are similar in certain respects is not saying that they're the same or even that they are similar in most respects.

Analogies can be helpful tools in thinking about difficult ethical issues. One important skill in thinking about ethical issues is learning to recognize relevant similarities and differences between two actions or two situations.

Model Response for Exercise 5

The shape of the continents drawn on the globe is the same as the shape of the continents on Earth. Two cities that are on opposite sides of the globe are on opposite sides of the Earth. If one river is to the north of another river on the globe, it's also north of that other river on Earth.

This response points out various similarities between a globe and the Earth that make the globe a good model of the Earth. To say that one thing is a good model of the other is just to say that the two are similar in ways that enable us to learn about the second thing by studying the first. Think of a model train. Studying a model train enables us to learn what the different parts of a real train are, how they're connected, etc. A globe is just a model of the Earth, much like a model train is a model of a real train. A globe shows where different geographical features (e.g., continents, rivers, and moun-tains) are in relation to one another or where different cities or countries are in relation to one another. You can learn a lot about the Earth by looking at a globe—for instance, which countries share borders with one another, where various rivers go, which cities are close to the ocean, and so on. When we draw these conclusions about the Earth, based on what we see on the globe, we're using an argument by analogy, along these lines: "The Amazon River flows into the Atlantic Ocean on the globe. The position of a river on the globe is similar to the position of that river on Earth. Therefore, the Amazon River flows into the Atlantic Ocean on Earth."

Models are important in scientific reasoning. They enable us to draw conclusions about one thing (e.g., the weather, proteins, or human immune systems) by looking at something else (e.g., computer models of the weather, physical models of a protein, or other animals' immune systems) that's easier to study. Drawing these conclusions involves using arguments by analogy.

The similarities in your response don't have to relate to the use of globes as models. We've picked these similarities as a way of illustrating how models work.

Model Response for Exercise 7

Earth and a watch both consist of many parts that fit together in intricate ways that enable them to achieve some apparent purpose.

This response gives only one similarity. That's fine; it's all that's strictly required of you in the instructions. To find important similarities between the Earth and a watch, you need to think quite abstractly. The eighteenth-century philosopher William Paley famously used an analogy between the universe and a watch to argue that the universe had been designed by an intelligent creator. In his Natural Theology, *Paley notes that the watch seems to serve a purpose and that if the parts were made or assembled in a different way, the watch would not serve that purpose. Many parts of nature, such as an eye, are the same way: they serve a purpose, and if the parts were "made" or "assembled" differently, they would not serve that purpose. Since we take the apparent design of the watch as proof that it had a designer, we should take the apparent design of nature as proof that it had a designer—or so Paley argued.*

We examined a very similar argument in the discussion of Rule 12. Do you think that Hume's criticism of the analogy between the universe and a house extends to Paley's analogy between the universe and a watch?

Model Response for Exercise 9

Mice and humans are both mammals. Both can get cancer. Many things that are toxic to mice are also toxic to humans.

The similarities mentioned in this response partly explain why biologists and biomedical researchers often use mice as models for humans. (If you missed it, go back right now and check out our discussion after the model response to exercise 5, where we said that models are important in scientific reasoning.) When scientists say that they're using mice as models to study, say, cancer in humans, they mean that they're studying cancer or cancer treatments in mice and then drawing conclusions—using arguments by analogy!—about how cancer or cancer treatments work in humans.

A professional biologist, of course, could cite much more specific similarities between mice and humans. Those more specific similarities are important for thinking that mice really are good models for studying specific biological processes in humans. Even if you're a budding biologist yourself, though, you shouldn't expect to be able to come up with those sophisticated similarities just yet.

Exercise Set 3.2: Identifying important differences

Model Response for Exercise 1

One (usually) pays to be a student, but one gets paid to do a job.

The differences that you cite in this exercise set need not have anything to do with the similarities that you noted in Exercise Set 3.1. You can use the same standard, though, for deciding whether your differences are important: Ask yourself whether you could imagine this difference affecting the strength of an argument by analogy.

Model Response for Exercise 3

First-degree murder involves killing someone against their will, whereas euthanasia involves helping someone die with their consent or upon their request. Euthanasia is, according to the definition used here, necessarily performed by a doctor, whereas murder can be committed by anybody.

Euthanasia involves helping a terminally ill patient die. In some cases, called "passive euthanasia," this involves nothing more than stopping or withholding lifesaving treatment at the patient's request. In other cases, called "active euthanasia," it involves prescribing or even administering a lethal dose of medication. One big difference between murder and any form of voluntary euthanasia is that euthanasia requires the patient's consent. Bioethicists—philosophers who study ethical questions in biology and medicine—disagree about whether euthanasia—especially active euthanasia—is morally acceptable.

The second difference—that, by definition, only doctors can perform euthanasia—highlights an important point about analogies. Sometimes differences can actually strengthen an argument by analogy. Suppose you wanted to argue that euthanasia is morally wrong because it is relevantly similar to murder. Many opponents of euthanasia think that the fact that euthanasia is performed by a doctor, despite being a difference between euthanasia and murder, actually makes it more likely that euthanasia is wrong. After all, doctors are supposed to help people, not harm them, and killing people certainly sounds like a way of harming them. (But is it always?)

Model Response for Exercise 5

The Earth has an atmosphere, whereas the globe does not. The globe is hollow, whereas the Earth has various layers beneath the surface, such as the mantle and the core. Globes often have dark lines to represent the borders between countries, but there are no such lines on the Earth itself (in most places).

In discussing the model response to exercise 5 in the previous exercise set, we explained that the globe is a good model of the Earth in that it enables us to draw certain conclusions about the Earth by studying the globe. The first two differences cited in this model response show that any scientific model has its limits. A globe is useful for learning about geography, but it's not useful for learning about weather or about geological processes going on under the Earth's surface. The third difference—that borders show up as dark lines on the globe, but not on the Earth—shows that even in areas for which our model is good, such as geography, we have to think carefully before drawing inferences. The model won't resemble the thing being modeled in every way, and we can end up drawing false conclusions if we don't think about the differences between them.

Model Response for Exercise 7

There are scientific explanations for how the Earth and its intricacies could have developed without being intentionally designed, but there is no such explanation for how watches could have come into existence. The Earth has a far greater ability to "repair" itself than a watch does.

Both of these differences are important, but they are important for different reasons. The first difference is important if you are considering William Paley's argument for the existence of a creator. (See Model Response 7 in Exercise Set 3.1 for a discussion of Paley's argument.) The second difference is probably not important for Paley's argument, but it might be important for arguments about how we treat the Earth or how we respond to ecological problems.

Model Response for Exercise 9

Mice are far less intelligent than humans. Compared to human embryos, mouse embryos have higher levels of an antioxidant called glutathione.

This response mentions one obvious difference and one difference that requires scientific training to discover—or even understand. Both differences show the limits of using mice as models for understanding humans. The importance of the first difference is clear. The second difference seems minor, but it turns out to be tragically important: Because of this specific difference in antioxidant levels between mouse and human embryos, which was documented by a scientist named Jürgen Knobloch and his colleagues in 2008, mice are immune to certain damaging effects of a drug called thalidomide. Thalidomide caused devastating birth defects in humans in the 1960s, but studying thalidomide in mice wouldn't have revealed the dangers to humans because of this subtle difference in their biology. On the other hand, the artificial sweetener saccharin was long thought to cause bladder cancer in humans because it does so in mice. After further study, however, it was shown that the biological differences between mice and humans mean that in the specific case of saccharin, the fact that it causes bladder cancer in mice does not show that it causes bladder cancer in humans. The United States government removed saccharin from the list of possible carcinogens in 2000. The general lesson here is that using mouse models can tell us a lot about humans, but in any given case, there's a chance that mice and humans differ in subtle ways that undermine the analogy. (Incidentally, one reason to think that mice are generally good models for humans is based on the sort of argument we explored in Chapter II: There are lots and lots of examples in which lessons learned from studying mice turned out to apply to humans, too.)

Exercise Set 3.3: Evaluating arguments by analogy

Model Responses for Exercise 1

Example of a strong response to this exercise

This is a reasonable start to an argument for the possibility of life on Europa, but there are still serious problems with it. It's a good start because the argument identifies a very important similarity between Earth and Europa—namely, having large oceans of (liquid) water. Water is essential for life as we know it, and so Europa's oceans provide a strong reason to think that life is <u>possible</u> on Europa. However, life requires other things, too, like a source of energy. The argument doesn't say whether Europa is like Earth in other ways that would be important for sustaining life. Another big problem with this argument is that there are important differences between Earth and Europa. The biggest difference is that Europa's oceans are much colder and darker than Earth's, and so they may not be able to generate or sustain life. There may be further differences too, which are not addressed by the argument. Perhaps the oceans on Europa are so acidic, for instance, that it would be hard for life to survive there. The last big problem with the argument is that the conclusion is too strong. The argument gives a decent reason to think that there <u>might</u> be life on Europa, but not a decent reason to think that there <u>is</u> life on Europa.

This response does several things. First, it gives a nuanced overall assessment of how well the argument follows Rule 12. Second, it discusses why the similarity mentioned in the argument is relevant to the conclusion. Third, it touches on a very important difference between Earth and Europa, explains why it's relevant to the conclusion, and mentions another possible difference. Finally, the response recognizes that the argument would be better if it had a more cautious conclusion. That's more constructive than just saying that the argument fails.

Still, the response could be even better. It would be stronger if it included more information about the similarities and differences between Earth and Europa, rather than just speculating about what those similarities and differences would be. That would require more research.

Example of a weak response to this exercise

This is a bad argument by analogy. It mentions one important similarity—that both Earth and Europa have oceans of water—but it doesn't mention any of the differences. Besides, water may be necessary for life on Earth, but that doesn't mean it's necessary for life on other planets. Maybe scientists just need to have more imagination about what kinds of life forms could exist.

While this response makes some good points, there are three major problems with it. First, it doesn't explain in detail why the similarity is relevant to the conclusion. Second, it neither identifies any differences between Earth and Europa nor explains why any particular difference is relevant. Third, the response goes off on a tangent about whether water is necessary for life on other planets. This is a very interesting point, but it is not relevant to assessing this argument, since the fact that Europa could harbor other kinds of life doesn't undermine the point that it could harbor Earth-like life. Many students are tempted by the open-ended nature of analogies to include irrelevant material in their evaluations of arguments by analogy. Stay focused on why the similarities and differences are relevant to the conclusion.

Model Response for Exercise 3

This is a good argument by analogy. Although it only identifies one similarity between texting while driving and driving drunk, that similarity provides a very strong reason to accept the conclusion. Since one big reason not to drive drunk is because it decreases your ability to avoid road hazards, showing that texting while driving also decreases your ability to avoid road hazards provides a very strong reason to think that people shouldn't text while driving. There are important differences, of course. The most important, perhaps, is that a driver can put down the phone if traffic becomes heavier or conditions more dangerous. A drunk driver can't suddenly become sober when necessary. Thus, it's easier to be responsible about texting while driving than about driving while drunk. Still, given that we can't always predict when hazards are going to appear, the similarity outweighs the difference just mentioned.

This response explains clearly why the similarity is relevant to the conclusion. It also identifies an important difference between the two things being compared, and it explains why that difference is important.

Most importantly, the response explicitly states that the similarity between texting while driving and driving while drunk outweighs the difference. It even explains why the similarity outweighs the difference. This is why the response claims that the argument is a good one. You might disagree about the relative weight of the similarity and differences; you might think that the drunk's inability to sober up on command makes the differences more important than the similarity. In that case, you are less likely to find this argument compelling. Since it can be very hard to reach agreement on the proper weighting of different reasons, such a disagreement can be very difficult to resolve. In those cases, the best thing to do is to look for other arguments for or against the same conclusion. But what matters most for the purposes of this exercise, again, is your assessment of the relevant similarities and differences between drunk driving and driving while texting.

Model Response for Exercise 5

This is not a very strong argument by analogy. The relevant similarity is that the mice avoid strangers and novelty, as autistic people do. This similarity is important because it suggests that whatever is going on in the brains of the affected mice might be the same as what's going on in the brains of autistic people. And if that's true, then whatever is causing that condition in the mouse brains might also be causing autism in humans. Displaying some behaviors that are typical of autistic humans, however, is not necessarily the same as being autistic. Furthermore, it seems like a stretch to use mice as a model for something as complicated as autism. While Naviaux's research raises interesting possibilities for understanding autism, the argument presented here doesn't provide a very strong reason to think that autism in humans is caused by the kind of "hyperactive response" found in Naviaux's mice.

As with exercise 9 in each of the previous two exercise sets, this exercise deals with the use of mice as models for humans. This response does a good job of explaining why the similarity is supposed to be relevant to the conclusion. It goes on to say that the similarity, while relevant, is not strong enough to support the conclusion. The response would be better if it offered more evidence to think that autism is too complicated to be studied by using mice as models. (What kind of evidence might you give? See Chapter IV!)

Notice that the response doesn't say that the conclusion of the argument is false. In fact, it even admits that the argument offers a good reason to investigate the conclusion further. But the response denies that this argument, by itself, gives us enough reason to accept the conclusion. Lots of good science is like this: It doesn't establish that a particular claim is correct, but it provides enough evidence to continue taking that claim seriously and to investigate it further.

Model Responses for Exercise 7

Example of a strong response to this exercise

This is a reasonably strong argument by analogy. The similarity between the two arguments, which is implied but never stated, is that both argue that a person should learn to do something by hand even if they always, in fact, use machines to do it for them. That is, both arguments have the same underlying logic. This is relevant to the conclusion because if two arguments have the same underlying logic and one of them is a bad argument, then the other is also a bad argument. There is one important difference between the argument about students and calculators and the one about farmers and equipment. Students often use calculators to do things that they <u>could</u> do by hand if they knew how. For instance, a student who knows how to take the derivative of an equation <u>could</u> do it without a calculator. Farmers use equipment like farm equipment to do things that they could not plausibly do by hand, like single-handedly tilling many acres of fields. Still, since very few students ever need to take derivatives or do other advanced math by hand, the similarity outweighs the difference.

The argument by analogy in exercise 7 is unusual in that its purpose is to prove something about another argument. Specifically, its purpose is to prove that the "math argument"—the one about students and calculators—is a bad argument. To do this, the analogy compares the "math argument" to a similar argument that is obviously bad. In effect, it says, "Argument A is like Argument B. Argument B is obviously bad. Thus, Argument A must be a bad argument too." This is sometimes a very effective tactic in refuting someone else's arguments.

This model response to the analogy does a good job explaining how the "math argument" and the "farmer argument" are alike. It also does a good job identifying an important difference between the two arguments and explaining why the similarity outweighs the difference.

In general, comparing one argument to another argument can be an effective way to show that the first argument is flawed. If you can establish that the two arguments share the same underlying logic and that the second argument is flawed, you can often show that the first argument shares the same flaw.

Example of a weak response to this exercise

This is a weak argument by analogy. It identifies only one similarity between being a student and being a farmer, which is that both students and farmers use equipment. The argument ignores the fact that they use very different kinds of equipment.

There are several problems with this response. Most importantly, it misses the fact that the exercise is comparing two arguments, *and only indirectly comparing students and farmers. Second, it does not explain the importance of the similarity or difference that it mentions.*

Model Response for Exercise 9

This is a somewhat decent argument by analogy. It's difficult to decide whether the similarities between Zhang and Stuart are more important than the differences or vice versa. The similarity is that they both gave money to a university in a country that was not their own. This is important because, other things being equal, if it's okay for one person to do something, it's okay for another person to do the same thing. However, other things are not equal here: the difference between Zhang and Stuart is that Stuart came from a wealthier country and raised money for a university in a poorer country. Zhang is giving money to a university that is already among the wealthiest in the world, even though his country is much poorer than the United States. Thus, you might think that Chinese universities deserved Zhang's help more than Yale did. Someone who thinks that it is very important to donate money where it is most needed will probably think that this difference is more important than the similarity. On the other hand, someone else might think that Zhang's personal reasons for donating to Yale are more important than questions about whether the money could do more good elsewhere.

This is a nicely nuanced response. If you find yourself unsure about whether an argument by analogy works, you might adopt the strategy used in this response: identify the important similarities and differences, and then explain why some people would weight them in one way while others would weight them in a different way. You might find yourself drawn to one way of weighting them rather than another. (But be careful! It's tempting to weight them in whatever way supports the conclusion you want to believe.)

This argument illustrates another common use of arguments by analogy: trying to show that an action is (or would be) right or wrong by comparing it to another action that is right or wrong. A similar form of argument is common in some legal systems: for instance, defense attorneys might argue that their client's actions were legal because they were just like someone else's actions, which were found to be legal in an earlier case.

Exercise Set 3.4: Constructing arguments by analogy

Model Response for Exercise 1

Stealing a DVD from a store is wrong. Downloading a movie without paying for it is like stealing a DVD from a store. Both involve acquiring something that somebody created without paying the creators for it (and without the creators' permission). Thus, downloading movies without paying for them is wrong.

The key to exercise 1 is to find an activity that is similar to downloading movies but that is clearly wrong (or clearly not wrong, if you are arguing that downloading movies is not wrong).

Model Response for Exercise 3

It is not illegal to smoke cigarettes. Smoking cigarettes is like riding a motorcycle without a helmet in that both significantly increase your chances of dying in particular ways. Thus, riding a motorcycle without a helmet should not be illegal.

This argument does what it is asked to do, but it still may be rather weak. The relevant consideration is not actually that cigarette smoking is legal. It's that cigarette smoking should *be legal. If you just point out that smoking is legal, as in this argument, the analogy could just as well work the other way—to show that since it's illegal to ride a motorcycle without a helmet (in some places), it should be illegal to smoke cigarettes! When constructing arguments by analogy, be sure that you're emphasizing the right thing.*

Model Response for Exercise 5

When the United States overthrew Saddam Hussein during its 2003 invasion of Iraq, a large statue of Hussein was pulled off its pedestal in Baghdad's Firdos Square. The destruction of the statue symbolized the overthrow of the old Iraqi government. The mutilation and burial of the Olmec heads is like the destruction of the statue in Firdos Square in that both involve getting rid of a symbol of a particular ruler (or set of rulers). Thus, the burial of the heads may have been part of a revolution or invasion that toppled the government of San Lorenzo.

This response compares the Olmec heads to a specific example of the destruction of a large political monument. (There are plenty of similar examples you might have picked to make the same argument.) That's more helpful than just comparing it to "the destruction of political monuments during revolutions or invasions," since it makes it easier to identify specific similarities and differences.

This exercise illustrates the use of analogies in the scientific process of "hypothesis formation." That's a fancy way of saying that scientists sometimes come up with a hypotheses by reasoning by analogy. If an archaeologist used this argument to come up with the hypothesis that the heads were destroyed as part of a revolution of invasion, the next step would be to look for evidence that supports or contradicts that hypothesis. For instance, if there is some other Olmec city that suddenly becomes more prominent around the same time that the heads were buried in San Lorenzo, that would support the hypothesis that the heads were destroyed as part of an invasion.

Model Response for Exercise 7

It is silly to argue that humans shouldn't use radiation therapy to cure cancer on the grounds that humans do not naturally use radiation therapy. Arguing that humans shouldn't be vegetarians because we are not naturally vegetarians is just like arguing that humans shouldn't use radiation therapy on the grounds that it's unnatural. Both arguments infer that we shouldn't do something from the fact that we don't naturally do it. Thus, it's silly to argue that humans shouldn't be vegetarians on the grounds that we are not naturally vegetarians.

This response illustrates an important strategy in reasoning. One way to refute an argument is to give another argument that is similar to the first but very clearly flawed. The power of this strategy, which logicians call "refutation by logical analogy," is that you can use it even if you're not sure how to explain what's wrong with the original argument. In this example, we don't need to say exactly why it's silly to argue from a premise about what's natural to a conclusion about what we ought to do. We only need to show an example of that reasoning that is clearly flawed. (See the model response to exercise 7 in Exercise Set 3.3 for another example of a refutation by logical analogy.)

MODEL RESPONSES FOR CHAPTER IV: SOURCES

Exercise Set 4.1: Identifying biased sources

Model Responses for Exercise 1

Example of a strong response to this exercise

The employees at a major electronics store chain may be biased sources. They may tell you to buy the warranty, even if it is mostly unnecessary, if they get bonuses or other perks for selling warranties and other add-ons.

At least, you'd want to ask the salesperson some pointed and specific questions, like how frequently appliances like the one you are buying actually break.

Example of a weak response to this exercise

A good friend who bought the extended warranty on a new television is a biased source. He or she is just going to tell you to buy the warranty to avoid looking stupid by admitting that the warranty is not worth buying.

This response exaggerates an otherwise legitimate concern about bias. Most people don't like to admit to making a mistake. If your friend now thinks that buying the warranty was a mistake, he or she may not like to admit it. This minor bias, though, is probably overcome by the fact that this person is your good friend. A good friend presumably cares more about helping you than about admitting a mistake.

This holds a larger lesson. Lots of people have minor biases on any given issue. This doesn't necessarily disqualify them as impartial sources. The question is whether their interest in telling you the truth outweighs whatever minor biases they may have.

Model Response for Exercise 3

The president of one of the top-ranked universities in the United States is a biased source. Part of a university president's job is to promote that university, and so no matter what he or she really thought, the president of a top-ranked university is going to insist that his or her university is the best.

Model Responses for Exercise 5

One biased source would be a celebrity who gets a lot of money and publicity by writing books about how vaccines weaken children's immune systems. Such a celebrity would have a lot to lose by acknowledging that vaccines don't weaken children's immune systems.

The kind of celebrity described in this response is a classic case of someone with a strong financial incentive to push for a particular answer to the question. Vaccine manufacturers would be too.

Some people are tempted to say that pediatricians are a biased source on this topic. After all, pediatricians make money by providing medical services, and vaccines are one kind of medical service. Furthermore, if vaccines really did weaken children's immune systems, that would provide pediatricians with more business in the future, since their patients would be more likely to get sick in the future. People sometimes make similar kinds of arguments about public health researchers who study vaccines—or about scientists who study other controversial topics, such as climate change. The thinking is that those scientists want to reach a particular conclusion (e.g., that vaccines are safe or that climate change is dangerous) in order to keep the grant money flowing.

But money is not the only thing that motivates people. Professional and social norms matter, too. In medicine, those norms require doctors to promote their patients' health—and even more importantly, not to harm their patients. The overwhelming majority of pediatricians recommend or even insist that parents vaccinate their children. If vaccines were actually dangerous, this would mean that most of the medical profession had turned its back on one its core values. Likewise, the norms in science require researchers to pursue the truth rather than a politically predetermined answer. These sorts of norms are crucial to protecting the integrity of medicine and science, and so even though there are surely some bad eggs who violate those norms, most doctors and scientists take them very seriously.

In short, when you're thinking about whether a source counts as biased, you'll need to balance these sorts of motivations against other kinds of incentives.

Model Response for Exercise 7

A politician who is running for office on a strong anti-abortion platform is a biased source. Such a politician may exaggerate the likelihood of complications for two reasons. First, if the politician can convince you that abortion is dangerous, you may be more likely to support his or her campaign. Second, anti-abortion candidates may be reluctant to say anything that sounds like a concession to supporters of abortion rights, since highly ideological voters might interpret that as being "soft on abortion." Single-issue politicians have a special incentive to exaggerate, even more so in the heat of a campaign.

Notice that this response does not say that all politicians are biased sources on this question or they are insincere in their beliefs. Instead of condemning an entire group, the response specifies that politicians running on a "strong anti-abortion platform" would not count as impartial sources on this subject. The same goes, of course, for politicians running on a strong pro-choice platform.

Model Responses for Exercise 9

Example of a strong response to this exercise

The principal of a struggling private school is a biased source. Since the school would benefit from school vouchers, and this particular principal's school is in need of financial help, the principal has a clear incentive to get you to believe that vouchers would improve education.

Example of a weak response to this exercise

A biased source would be a university researcher who published a research paper showing that school vouchers would improve education. He or she wouldn't want to be proven wrong.

The second response makes another common mistake. Some people think that anyone who has taken a position in a debate is automatically a biased source. Unless you have some specific reason to think otherwise, however, it's reasonable to assume that the researcher has reached his or her conclusion based on a careful assessment of the evidence, not on the basis of personal bias. Being biased is not the same as having a view on an issue; being biased is having a view that is determined by something other than good reasons.

Exercise Set 4.2: Identifying independent sources

Model Response to Exercise 1

A travel guidebook for Canada and someone who lives in Vancouver and goes to Whistler frequently.

Model Response to Exercise 3

Your philosophy professor or the Web site of Jim Pryor, a philosophy professor at New York University, whose site contains useful tips on writing good papers.

This assumes, of course, that Jim Pryor isn't your professor! If he is, you could turn to any of several helpful books instead, such as Lewis Vaughn's Writing Philosophy.

Model Response to Exercise 5

The U.S. Centers for Disease Control and Prevention (CDC) and a scientific paper published in a reputable academic journal, though you'd have to make sure that neither one cites the other.

On a question this technical, any source aimed at a mass audience, such as a newspaper, will have to get its information from a more technical source, such as a scientific paper. So if you cited a newspaper, you'd really be relying indirectly on the scientific study that the newspaper's journalists had read. Citing that study yourself wouldn't then count as citing another independent source.

This model response explicitly points out that you'd have to check whether either of your sources cites the other. Just about every scientific study relies heavily on previously published work by other scientists. That's how science works: One group of scientists builds on the research done by earlier scientists. To find out whether a particular study is getting its information from somewhere else, you'll have to track down the original paper. (Ask your librarian for help!) Then find the sentence or paragraph where the researchers make the claim you're interested in and see if there's a citation to another source. If so, that other source is the one you want. (Unless, of course, that source just got the information from some other source....)

Model Response to Exercise 7

Your grandmother or grandfather and birth records from the area where your great-grandmother was born.

Finding independent, well-informed sources on this topic may be harder than it appears. If your grandparents are no longer living, you can't ask them. (Your grandparents might also be unsure or misinformed about exactly where your great-grandmother was born—especially if she was born in a different country.) If you have no idea where your great-grandmother was born, you can't very well track down birth records from that area, such as birth certificates or a record of births in a local parish. Even if you do know where she was born, it might be difficult or impossible for you to go there and find birth records. In many areas, birth records may not even exist for your great-grandmother's generation.

You might need to enlist an expert's help just to find the right documents here. Genealogists might be able to help you track down the right area—though you should beware the biases created by genealogists' financial incentive to find you a convincing lead—and local librarians or archivists at local historical societies might be able to point you to the right documents. In general, librarians are extremely helpful in locating appropriate sources.

Model Response to Exercise 9

A respected social scientist who studies the criminal justice system and a genuinely non-partisan think tank.

Note that genuinely unbiased researchers on such a controversial topic may not be easy to find! The best thing to do on such a topic might be to get input from as many experts as you can.

Exercise Set 4.3: Evaluating arguments that use sources

Model Response to Exercise 1

This argument does a fairly poor job following Rule 13. The argument relies on a study by a Dr. Vasile, but it provides nothing more than the author's name and his professional affiliation. We don't know when or where Dr. Vasile published his study, which makes the source hard to find. As an aerospace engineer, Dr. Vasile is presumably an informed source (Rule 14). We have no particular reason to think that he is biased, so the argument does a decent job with Rule 15. The argument does not follow Rule 16; it does not attempt to cross-check Dr. Vasile's study. Rule 17 does not apply here.

This response systematically addresses each of the rules from this chapter. It gives a nuanced analysis of Rule 13 rather than simply saying that the argument does or doesn't follow the rule. This response explains why Dr. Vasile is an informed source.

Although it might not affect whether you think Vasile is a good source, you could strengthen this argument by explaining Vasile's reasons for thinking that it's unwise to blow up an asteroid. Some of these, at least, are not highly technical (like: then you get a thousand small pieces which could be a lot harder to deal with than one big one). A weakness of the argument as it stands is that it requires us to simply take one expert's word for something that we could readily be invited to think through for ourselves.

Model Response to Exercise 3

This argument is terrible. The argument cites its sources (Rule 13) only in the vaguest way. There is no way to determine what infomercial it is talking about or who the spokesman is. The spokesman may or may not be informed (Rule 14), but he is clearly not impartial (Rule 15). After all, he's being paid to say great things about "the product." The argument makes no effort to cross-check sources (Rule 16). The argument does not use any Web sources (Rule 17).

If you're paying attention to the sources of these arguments, you might have noticed that the argument in exercise 3 comes from the satirical newspaper The Onion. *The point of* The Onion *article from which the argument is adapted is precisely that infomercials are highly suspect sources of information.*

Onion *articles occasionally circulate on social media sites as true stories. One of the co-authors of this book even had a student cite the online version of* The Onion *in a research paper—a vivid illustration of the importance of Rule 17!*

Model Response to Exercise 5

This argument does a decent job following Rule 13. It gives the date and venue for Stephen Hawking's speech, which would make it fairly easy to learn more about his remarks. It's hard to find a more informed source (Rule 14) on black holes than Hawking, and Hawking doesn't stand to gain anything by admitting that he's been wrong for decades (Rule 15). The biggest problem with this argument is that it doesn't cross-check Hawking's claim (Rule 16). Do other experts agree with him, or is Hawking's new view of black holes controversial? Mightn't he (and we) be wiser to avoid, for now, taking _any_ definitive view of such an obscure matter?

Like the model responses to exercises 1 and 3, this response proceeds systematically through the rules from this chapter. It does not mention Rule 17, since the argument does not rely on any sources from the Web. It also gives reasons for each of its claims.

The last line of the response highlights the fact that even the experts might not know very much about some topics. And even when the experts do know a lot about a topic, sometimes they're wrong about a particular aspect of it. Science is never fully settled; even things that seem beyond doubt are occasionally discovered to be false. That's why many scientists say that science is not a set of facts; it's a method for discovering facts.

The example in this exercise also highlights that science is not just based on authority. Stephen Hawking, whose life was dramatized in the 2014 film A Theory of Everything, *is one of the best-known astrophysicists alive. But that doesn't mean that he has a monopoly on the truth in astrophysics.*

Model Response to Exercise 7

This argument uses sources well. It clearly cites its main source, including the specific issue of the journal where the researchers published their study (Rule 13). It cross-checks that source against an independent source (Rule 16). Both sources are informed (Rule 14), since one was published in a prestigious medical journal and the other is a professor at a well-known university, and there's no reason to suspect that they are biased (Rule 15). This argument does not rely on Web sources, so Rule 17 is not relevant.

Model Response to Exercise 9

This argument uses sources reasonably well, but it could be better. The argument identifies its source as NHANES (Rule 13), and it explains what NHANES is, in a way that shows that we can treat it as an informed (Rule 14) and impartial (Rule 15) source. However, the argument could do a better job with Rule 13 by explaining how someone could access the NHANES data that it cites. The argument doesn't cross-check its sources (Rule 16), but this may be because there are no good independent sources. It's expensive to collect detailed data on such a large population, so there may not be any sources that are anywhere near as reliable as NHANES on this issue. It's not clear whether the NHANES data is from the Web, but if it is, the CDC is clearly a reliable Web source (Rule 17). Despite these problems, the argument uses sources well enough that we can trust its conclusion.

This response acknowledges that the argument could be better in some specific ways, but it also recognizes that the argument is good enough to establish its conclusion. Arguments can be convincing even if they aren't perfect. The response also recognizes that the topic of this argument might make it difficult or impossible to cross-check sources. Again, when it is very difficult or expensive to gather a particular kind of information, there may not be more than one independent source.

Exercise Set 4.4: Using sources in arguments

Model Response to Exercise 1

This claim is false. According to the Food and Agriculture Organization of the United Nations, Italy, France, and Spain each produces more wine than does the United States. The data available from their FAOSTAT Web site show that France produced over five million tons of wine in 2012, Italy produced roughly 4 million tons, and Spain produced over three million tons, whereas the United States produced just under three million tons. The Wine Institute, an advocacy group for California wine producers, also reports that France, Italy, and Spain produce more wine than does the United States. Their report is available from the "Statistics" section of their Web site.

This response cites two independent sources to confirm that the United States produces less wine than some other countries. Both sources are well informed about wine production, and neither is likely to be biased. (Since the Wine Institute advocates for California wine producers, we might be suspicious of their impartiality if the question were about, say, the quality of California wines, but it's harder to distort the truth about quantities produced—and besides, they wouldn't lie about the United States producing less wine than other countries.) The response cites its sources in a rather informal way, but it provides enough information that we could find the relevant sources easily.

Model Response to Exercise 3

This claim is false. According to the World Health Organization's Fact Sheet #330, on "diarrhoeal disease," diarrhea kills about 760,000 children under five each year. The fact sheet is dated April 2013, and it is available on the WHO Web site.

This response clearly cites its source, which was published by a well-informed and impartial organization. The response also notes the date of the fact sheet, which is important for a topic like this, since statistics about global public health generally change over time. If you are using old sources, you should think about whether things might have changed since those sources were published.

Model Response to Exercise 5

This claim is true. David G. Anderson, a professor of anthropology at the University of Tennessee, specializes in the early settlement of what is now the southeastern United States. In a paper presented at the Paleoamerican Odyssey Conference in 2013, Anderson and his colleagues summarize evidence from a range of scholarly papers on evidence about the early settlement of the Americas. This evidence shows that humans lived in the Americas <u>at least</u> 13,000 years ago, but probably arrived a few hundred or even a few thousand years before that. Furthermore, a survey of experts by Amber Wheat, published in the Society for American Archaeology's <u>SAA Archaeological Record</u> in 2012, found that 58 percent of respondents thought humans had arrived in the Americas at least 15,000 years ago.

You could, of course, write an entire paper—or an entire book!—on this topic. But this response does several important things to try to establish that the experts agree that humans arrived in the Americas at least 13,000 years ago. It identifies informed, unbiased sources (Rules 14 and 15), which it cites relatively clearly (Rule 13). The response emphasizes that each of the two sources rely on a range of other experts to establish their conclusion; the people that this response cites are not maverick researchers bucking the scientific consensus. And that's what Rule 16 is really about: showing that the experts generally agree on your conclusion. Of course, the majority of scientists sometimes gets it wrong, but those of us who are not experts need very strong reasons to think that the majority of experts are wrong about something. So, establishing that most experts agree on something does give us non-experts a good reason to accept the experts' claim.

Model Response to Exercise 7

This claim is true. According to the Web site for the Insurance Institute for Highway Safety (http://www.iihs.org), the only minivans to receive a "Top Safety Pick" award for 2015 were the Honda Odyssey, the Toyota Sienna, and the Kia Sedona. Honda and Toyota are Japanese companies, and Kia is Korean.

This argument points readers to the IIHS's Web site and highlights exactly what the IIHS said that allows the argument's author to conclude that the safest minivans in the United States are made by Asian car companies.

MODEL RESPONSES FOR CHAPTER V: ARGUMENTS ABOUT CAUSES

Exercise Set 5.1: Brainstorming explanations for correlations

Model Response to Exercise 1

Maybe studying philosophy trains one to think in the ways that are required to do well on the GRE. (That is, maybe studying philosophy causes one to be able to do well on the GRE.) On the other hand, maybe students who are already likely to do well on the GRE (e.g., because they are already good at the kinds of tasks the GRE tests) are more likely to choose to study philosophy, because the skills that are useful on the GRE are also useful in philosophy. Of course, it's possible that both of these causes are at work: Maybe people with the skills to excel on the GRE are more likely to study philosophy <u>and</u> studying philosophy further improves those skills.

This response suggests three different explanations of the observed correlation. The first is that studying philosophy causes high GRE scores. The second is that there is some common cause of both high GRE scores and studying philosophy. The final suggestion is more nuanced: maybe both of the first two suggestions are partly correct.

Notice that this response says a little bit about why the different explanations might be plausible. Specifically, it notes that studying philosophy might improve the skills needed for the GRE and that having those skills might increase the chances that one will choose to study philosophy.

For this exercise, you do not need to attempt to figure out which explanation is the most likely. You're just brainstorming plausible explanations.

Model Response to Exercise 3

Maybe the shorter days of autumn cause the leaves to turn colors and the geese to fly south. Or, it could be a coincidence: Maybe the geese head south because of something further south, like the reappearance of a new food source, that just happens to occur when the leaves are changing color in the north. I suppose it's also possible that the geese are responding to the color of the leaves, flying south to escape colors that they don't like.

This response does more than just say that the correlation could be a coincidence. It offers a suggestion for how that coincidence could come about.

Model Response to Exercise 5

It could be that graduating from college causes you to earn more over the course of your life, perhaps because college improves people's skills, access to professional networks, and so on. Alternatively, it could be that people who have the capacity, support, etc. to finish college are more likely to earn a lot of money, regardless of whether they went to college. Or it could be a combination of both of those things.

The "Tips for success" for this exercise set mention several possible explanations for a correlation. Not all of them make sense in every case. For instance, it's clear that earning more money later in life doesn't cause you to have graduated from college earlier in life. (Of course, not everyone goes to college earlier in life, but the number of older students is small compared to the number of younger students.) So, while you can use the possibilities from the "Tips for success" to generate ideas, think carefully about whether each possible explanation makes sense.

    On the other hand, don't give up on alternatives just because you think you have a good explanation for a correlation. It's important to have multiple "working hypotheses" in science—that is, multiple ideas about what's causing the thing you're interested in.

Model Response to Exercise 7

Perhaps turmeric contains some compound that protects people against Alzheimer's. Alternatively, there may be a genetic trait that is common among Indians, but not Americans, that predisposes people to like the taste of turmeric and to have lower incidence of Alzheimer's. This would be a common factor that causes both turmeric consumption and low incidence of Alzheimer's. Or it could just be a coincidence: one difference between Indians and Americans (maybe just accidents of culture) causes the disparity in turmeric consumption and another, unrelated difference causes the disparity in Alzheimer's incidence.

Model Response to Exercise 9

Either it's just a coincidence or Tecumseh's brother's curse has caused these presidents to die in office.

While this correlation is real, it's worth noting that the argument in exercise 9 doesn't tell you how many U.S. presidents died in office after being elected in a year that didn't *end in zero. (See Rule 9.) If lots of presidents had died in office, there might be no correlation here to explain. Whenever someone claims that there is some especially astonishing correlation, take a good critical look at the evidence!*

Exercise Set 5.2: Identifying the most likely explanation

Model Responses to Exercise 1

Example of a strong response to this exercise

The most likely explanation is the combined one: students who already have the skills to excel on the GRE are more likely to study philosophy, and studying philosophy further improves those skills. In order for either part of this explanation to be plausible, it must be the case that the skills needed for the GRE, such as critical thinking and careful reading, are also used in philosophy. But if the same skills are needed in both contexts, then those who already have them are more likely to study philosophy, since they're likely to enjoy philosophy and be good at it from the start, and those who study philosophy are likely to improve those skills even more. Thus, the combined explanation is more plausible than either explanation alone.

This response gives a detailed justification for the claim that the third, combined explanation (from the model response to exercise 1 in Exercise Set 5.1) is more plausible than the other explanations. Notice that this response touches on all of the possible explanations given in exercise 1 from Exercise Set 5.1.

Example of a weak response to this exercise

Obviously, the most likely explanation is the combined one. It's more likely than the simple explanation that studying philosophy causes one to do better on the GRE. It's also more likely than the simple explanation that having the skills to do well on the GRE causes one to study philosophy.

This response does not give any specific reasons for thinking that the "combined" explanation is the most plausible. It simply asserts (and then re-asserts twice more) that the combined explanation is more likely than each of the other explanations. Someone who didn't understand why the combined explanation is more likely than the others would not learn anything from this response.

Model Response to Exercise 3

The best explanation is that the autumn weather causes the leaves to turn colors and the geese to fly south. Because of the shorter days, leaves do not generate enough energy from sunlight; as a result, they turn colors and fall off. The shorter days also prompt migratory behavior in birds. Since the seasonal migration of many bird species is a well-known fact, and changes in leaf color are also well known to relate to seasonal changes, this is unlikely to be a coincidence. It is also unlikely that the geese are fleeing from the leaves, since cage-raised birds, who are not exposed to leaves that change color, also display some of the same behaviors as migrating birds during the fall.

Chances are that you didn't know that caged birds exhibit some of the same behaviors as migrating birds during the fall. Yet, this fact can help support the claim that geese are not responding to visual cues, such as leaf color. This is a nice example of how knowing more about a topic can help you make better judgments about what causes what.

Model Response to Exercise 5

The best explanation is a complex one: college causes higher earnings and having the right kind of abilities, support, etc. causes both higher graduate rates and higher earnings. This is because both explanations clearly have a grain of truth to them: College does teach you new, valuable skills that can lead to higher paying jobs. It also connects you to other people who are more likely to have higher paying jobs, and that network can help you get a higher paying job yourself. On the other hand, people who have the abilities you need to graduate from college (e.g., discipline and perseverance) and good financial and social support from friends and family are likely to get better paying jobs, get promoted, etc. than those who lack those skills. Finally, people who face obstacles to graduating from college, such as chronic illness or especially demanding family situations, might also have trouble finding or keeping high-paying jobs.

When it comes to causal relationships, sometimes the best answer really is the complicated one. In situations like these, however, the more interesting question is often how much each factor contributes to the final outcome. For instance, how much of a college graduate's extra earnings are caused by graduating from college, as opposed to that person's personal abilities and social situation?

In some cases, it's possible to answer these sorts of questions by using a "randomized control trial," in which some people (or animals or whatever) are randomly assigned to a different group (e.g., to the group that gets a particular medicine or the one that gets a plain sugar pill). This enables scientists to measure how big of an effect a particular cause has. Those kinds of trials are much easier to do in some sciences, such as medicine or cognitive psychology, than in others, such as sociology or economics. In general, they're easier to do in the natural sciences than in the social sciences. In the social sciences, researchers often have to rely on sophisticated statistical techniques to measure the effect of something like a college education.

Model Response to Exercise 7

There are so many differences between Indian and American diets, environments, and cultures that it seems hasty to conclude that higher turmeric consumption leads to lower Alzheimer's incidence. Furthermore, it seems unlikely that a single genetic mutation would both predispose someone to like turmeric and make them less likely to develop Alzheimer's. Thus, the best explanation at present seems to be that the correlation is coincidental. If, however, someone discovered a mechanism by which turmeric could reduce the incidence of Alzheimer's, then we would have good reason to believe that there is a causal relationships at work here.

Notice that this response does not rule out the possibility that there is a causal connection. Nor does it leap to conclusions based on a correlation that could conceivably have a causal explanation. Instead, it notes that the best explanation at present—that is, given what we currently know—is that the correlation is coincidental, and it specifies what we would need to discover in order to think that the relationship is causal.

It turns out that some researchers believe that they have found a mechanism by which turmeric reduces the risk of Alzheimer's: a compound called curcumin that is found in turmeric. This is another case in which knowing lots of background information improves your critical thinking abilities—and thus another reason to get a broad education!

Model Response to Exercise 9

The only plausible explanation for this correlation is coincidence. Of the eight presidents who died in office, seven were elected in years ending in zero (though not always for the first time). Of those, four were assassinated and three died of different kinds of natural causes. (Harrison himself died because he caught pneumonia giving an overly long inaugural address in the rain.) In order for the so-called Curse of Tippecanoe to have **caused** these deaths, it would somehow have had to cause both Harrison's bombast and the two other natural deaths as well as motivate all four assassins, none of whom had any obvious interest in Native American issues, to kill their respective victims. Since there is no plausible explanation for how this could happen, it is implausible that the curse caused the deaths.

This response highlights the lack of a plausible explanation for how one thing could have caused another. The lack of any such explanation is often a good reason to think that a correlation is just coincidental. Notice the difference between this exercise and exercise 7. The model response for that exercise reached the more modest conclusion that unless someone can discover a mechanism by which turmeric causes reduced rates of Alzheimer's disease, the correlation is probably a coincidence, whereas this model response argues straight out that the correlation is a coincidence. The reason for this difference is that we know that foods can affect people's health. We just don't know whether turmeric affects people's health in this particular way. By contrast, we have no evidence whatsoever that curses kill people.

Exercise Set 5.3: Evaluating arguments about causes

Model Responses to Exercise 1

Example of a strong response to this exercise

In addition to violating the rule from Chapter I about avoiding loaded language, this argument does only a mediocre job following the rules from Chapter V. It follows Rule 18 by citing the study of 11,000 Australians to establish the inverse correlation between television watching and longevity. It seems like the authors probably thought about alternative explanations (Rule 19), since they list several, but they could do a better job spelling out the different options. The argument suggests some reasons to think that the most plausible explanation for the correlation is that watching television (indirectly) causes poor health (Rule 20), and it does a good job recognizing the complexity of the causal connections here (Rule 21), but it doesn't offer any evidence to show that those suggestions are correct. For instance, it doesn't actually show that people who watch more television eat more junk food or exercise less than other people, and it doesn't show that being isolated or lonely leads to worse health outcomes.

This response begins by explaining how the argument establishes that a correlation really exists. It then works systematically through Rules 19, 20, and 21. Even better, it offers more than a superficial evaluation of the argument with respect to those rules: For instance, the response recognizes that by suggesting various causal mechanisms, the authors show that they've thought about alternative explanations, even if they don't explicitly say so. Furthermore, the response doesn't blindly accept the argument's explanation for the correlation, noting that the argument doesn't offer any evidence to support the assumptions behind their explanations.

Example of a weak response to this exercise

This argument follows Rule 18. There is a correlation between increased television watching and dying younger. The argument also follows Rules 19 and 20. The correlation is best explained by saying that watching television causes you to die younger.

This response offers no argument or analysis but only assertion. It doesn't explain how the argument establishes the existence of a correlation. Nor does it offer any critical analysis of the argument's reasons for thinking that there's a causal connection between watching television and dying younger. Someone who was unsure how good this argument is wouldn't be any better off after reading this response.

Model Response to Exercise 3

Example of a strong response to this exercise

This is a silly causal argument. At the time the argument was made, there was technically a correlation between legalizing marijuana and sending a team to the Super Bowl (Rule 18). But not only does the author fail to mention alternative explanations (Rule 19), she proposes an explanation that is almost certainly not the most likely one (Rule 20). The fact that cities in Colorado and Washington sent their teams to the Super Bowl shortly after those states legalized marijuana is just a coincidence: There's no plausible explanation for how legalizing marijuana could have improved their teams' performance.

Coincidental correlations are most likely to occur when you're looking at a very small number of events. For example, imagine that you and a friend each drew two cards at random from a normal deck of playing cards, and you both got one ace and one jack. That would be a surprising coincidence, but you wouldn't think there's anything unusual going on. But suppose that you each drew twenty cards in a row and you got the same card every time. That would make you think that there was something funny going on. The same trickery leads to other kinds of spurious correlations, such as the correlation that Tyler Vigen reports between the number of people who drown in a swimming pool in any given year and that number of films featuring Nicolas Cage in that year.

Example of a weak response to this argument

What a dumb argument. There's obviously no causal connection between legalizing marijuana and going to the Super Bowl. It's just a coincidence.

The problem here isn't that this response is incorrect. After all, the argument was just a joke. But it's still worthwhile taking the time to practice explaining why *the argument is so bad. That is, it's worthwhile explaining how you know that the correlation is just a coincidence.*

Model Response to Exercise 5

Example of a strong response to this exercise

This is a fairly weak causal argument. It begins by asserting an inverse correlation between military service in Vietnam and income a decade later (Rule 18). The author mentions some other possible explanations (Rule 19), but argues that those can't be right because the draft was random (Rule 20). The argument overlooks two sources of complexity, however (Rule 21). First, it ignores the fact that some people were able to avoid the draft (e.g., by staying in school), and that wealthier, better-connected people might have been more likely to do that <u>and</u> more likely to earn higher incomes later. Second, the argument generalizes too quickly from the example of American men serving in the Vietnam War to <u>all</u> people serving in the military anywhere at any time. Maybe there was something special about Vietnam, or about the American economy in the 1970s and '80s.

In addition to all the usual hallmarks of a good response, such as proceeding methodically through each rule, this response does three especially noteworthy things. First, it uses concrete details from the argument to support its evaluation: In discussing Rule 20, it cites the argument's point about the draft being random to explain how the argument works toward the best explanation. Second, it exhibits careful thought about why military service in Vietnam and income in the 1980s might be inversely correlated. Third, it doesn't get carried away with the alternative explanations. It describes them as additional sources of complexity, rather than as completely undermining the argument.

Keeping in mind the caveats expressed in this model response, the military draft served as what social scientists call a "natural experiment." In commenting on the model response to exercise 5 in Exercise Set 5.2, we noted that social scientists usually have to use statistical methods to measure the effect of something, since they can't randomly assign people to serve in the military, graduate from college, etc. But sometimes there's a way to get pretty close to a randomized experiment: finding situations in the world where people have already been (more or less) randomly chosen for something, and then they see what happened to those people as opposed to people who were not chosen.

Example of a weak response to this exercise

This is a great argument! It really goes to show that veterans are treated unfairly by establishing that serving in the military causes people to have worse job prospects! More people need to be aware of this issue!

In addition to all the usual hallmarks of a weak response, such as failing to connect the response to any of the relevant rules, this response does two especially regrettable things. First, it leaps from the claim that veterans earn less than non-veterans to the claim that veterans are being treated unfairly. Maybe they are, but this argument hasn't shown that. For all that's been said in this argument, maybe serving in Vietnam helped veterans see what's important in life and that led many of them to choose jobs that were more personally rewarding than financially rewarding. Second, the response shows a lack of critical thinking about other possible explanations of the observed correlation. Thus, it concludes that the argument is stronger than it is. When you're passionate about an important issue, such as the fair treatment of veterans, it's tempting to accept weaker arguments just because you want to be able to use them to support your favorite position. But in the end, you don't do yourself any favors by leaning on weak evidence.

Model Response to Exercise 7

This argument follows Rule 18. It cites "a recent study by researchers at the Hebrew University of Jerusalem" to show that there is a correlation. (This would be better if it gave names or a more detailed citation.)

It doesn't do a great job with Rules 19 and 20, though. Assuming that the study was published in a reputable journal, it's unlikely that the correlation is just a coincidence, since it came from a controlled scientific experiment. However, given the information that we have here, it's too soon to rule out the possibility that the drug caused depression-like behavior and bone loss independently. All drugs have side effects, and bone loss could be a side effect of the drug. Perhaps the argument would be stronger in this respect if it acknowledged more complexity (Rule 21) about the various ways in which the drug may have led to bone-density loss.

Controlled scientific experiments like this one are powerful tools for exploring causal relationships, but even here it can be difficult to figure out what causes what. If you buy the researchers' story about "depressed" mice losing bone density because they become less active, then you'll probably think that the most plausible connection is that depression-like behavior causes bone loss. If you think that story is too speculative, then you might think that the best explanation of the correlation is that the drug caused both depression-like behavior and bone-density loss.

Model Response to Exercise 9

This is a fairly strong causal argument. It begins by asserting a correlation (Rule 18), although it doesn't say anything about how we know that this correlation exists. It considers several different possible explanations of the correlation (Rule 19), ranging from vegetarianism causing a higher IQ to various ways that higher IQs might cause vegetarianism. It then gives reasons to prefer some of those explanations over others (Rule 20). Finally, it admits that the true explanation of the correlation is probably some complex combination of the proposed mechanisms by which higher IQs cause vegetarianism (Rule 21).

This response notes that, as stated, the argument does not justify its claim that there is a correlation between childhood IQ and vegetarianism in adulthood. This is one reason that the argument is only "fairly" strong. The response also cites specific aspects of the argument, such as the proposed explanations of the correlation, to support its own claims about how well the argument follows various rules.

Exercise Set 5.4: Constructing arguments about causes

Model Responses to Exercise 1

Example of a strong response to this exercise

Smoking cigarettes does cause lung cancer. According to the "Fact Sheet on the Health Effects of Cigarette Smoking" on the CDC's Web site, men who smoke are twenty-three times more likely to develop lung cancer than men who don't, and female smokers are thirteen times more likely to develop lung cancer than female non-smokers. Thus, there is a strong correlation between smoking and lung cancer. It's also implausible that getting lung cancer makes people smoke, since most people start smoking long before they get lung cancer. Furthermore, there is a clear mechanism by which smoking causes cancer. Cigarette smoke contains toxic chemicals. When smokers inhale these chemicals into the lungs, the chemicals damage cells in their lungs, eventually leading to lung cancer. The existence of this mechanism, along with the strength of the correlation between smoking and cancer, makes it very unlikely that the correlation is simply a coincidence.

This response does four things particularly well. First, it states its claim clearly at the beginning. Then, it cites a reliable source to establish a correlation between smoking and lung cancer. (It could have done even better by giving a Web address for the fact sheet.) Then, it considers and rejects another explanation for the correlation. Finally, it briefly explains how smoking causes lung cancer.

Example of a weak response to this exercise

Smoking cigarettes causes lung cancer. Everyone knows that smokers get lung cancer more often than non-smokers. That's because cigarette smoke has tar and chemicals in it, like arsenic.

This response does provide the major elements of a causal argument: It makes a clear causal claim. It asserts that there is a correlation between the cause and the effect. It explains vaguely how cigarette smoke causes cancer. However, it appeals to common knowledge to establish a correlation. This is better than nothing, but not much. Sometimes things that "everyone knows" turn out to be false. Furthermore, it does not address any alternative explanations for the correlation.

Model Response to Exercise 3

Earthquakes do cause volcanic eruptions. A study by scientists at the University of Oxford, reported on January 12, 2009 on the Web site ScienceDaily, shows that large earthquakes are followed by up to four times as many volcanic eruptions as usual. The scientists suggest that the earthquakes disturb the magma underneath nearby volcanoes. This leads to a buildup of pressure under the volcanoes, issuing in eruptions. The study's careful statistical analysis shows that this is unlikely to be a coincidence. There is no obvious third factor causing both earthquakes and eruptions. Volcanic eruptions do cause earthquakes, which makes the causal connection between earthquakes and eruptions complicated. However, since the eruptions in the study happened _after_ the large earthquakes—sometimes several months afterward—the eruptions didn't cause these earthquakes. Thus, at least some large earthquakes cause volcanic eruptions.

This response appeals to a careful statistical analysis to support the claim that the correlation is not merely coincidental. Statisticians can often estimate how likely a correlation is to result from pure chance. When scientists report that an effect is "statistically significant," they usually mean that there's only a 1-in-20 (or sometimes a 1-in-100) probability that the effect resulted from pure chance. Note, however, that even a very small effect can still be statistically significant; statistical significance only has to do with the probability that an observed effect is just a coincidence.

Model Response to Exercise 5

Sleeping with lights on as an infant does not cause nearsightedness. Although an article in the prestigious scientific journal <u>Nature</u>, published in <u>1999</u>, found a correlation between sleeping with lights on and becoming nearsighted later in life, the best explanation is not that one causes the other. Subsequent studies in <u>Nature</u> showed that nearsighted parents were more likely to leave the lights on in a baby's room. Children of nearsighted parents are more likely to become nearsighted themselves. These subsequent studies showed that, once we control for parents' nearsightedness, there is no correlation between sleeping with the lights on and nearsightedness. Thus, there is a factor that causes both nearsightedness and sleeping with the light on as an infant—namely, having nearsighted parents, who presumably don't want to wander into a darkened room at night when they wouldn't be wearing their glasses.

This response illustrates an important point about the scientific process. When one group of scientists discover a correlation between two things, they often suggest that there might be a causal connection between them. This spurs other scientists to investigate the connection between these two things; they may find a better explanation for the correlation. Of course, the media often exaggerates the initial suggestion of a causal link, leading to news stories about "the myth that X causes Y" being disproven by new studies. When you read about a study showing a correlation between two things, look for follow-up studies that try to explain or debunk that correlation. One good way to find follow-up studies is with scholarly search engines like Google Scholar (which is free) or Web of Science (which is probably accessible through your library's Web site).

Model Response to Exercise 7

Attending religious services regularly probably does make people happier. "Are We Happy Yet?," a 2006 report by the Pew Research Center, finds that people who attend religious services at least once a week are much more likely to say that they are "very happy" than those who seldom or never attend religious services. The relationship between religious attendance and happiness is certainly very complicated. There are probably other factors that cause both happiness and religious attendance. For instance, maybe people from religious families tend to be closer to their family, which can make people happier and encourage them to go to religious services. However, going to religious services provides a great deal of social interaction, which makes people happier, and may contribute to a sense of purpose in life, which also makes people happier.

This response illustrates the difficulty of determining causal relationships in the social sciences. There are so many factors involved in creating happiness that it is extremely difficult to disentangle them. It is best to be modest about such claims, as this response is: it concludes only that religious attendance "probably" makes people happier. Notice that nothing in this response implies that the only way to become happy is through religious attendance. Other activities provide social interaction and a sense of purpose, as well. Remember to expect complexity in causal relationships!

As suggested in the commentary of the previous model response, the 2006 study spurred follow-up studies probing the connection between religious attendance and happiness. One such study, published in December 2010 in the American Sociological Review, *concludes that the gains in happiness come from the strengthened social networks that people build by attending religious services. Remember to look for follow-up studies whenever you're evaluating a scientific finding.*

MODEL RESPONSES FOR CHAPTER VI: DEDUCTIVE ARGUMENTS

Exercise Set 6.1: Identifying deductive argument forms

Model Response to Exercise 1

<u>Modus ponens</u>: p stands for "I am thinking," and q for "I exist."

*To get started symbolizing the argument in exercise 1, notice that the first sentence is an "if–then" sentence. Those are often good places to start. Let **p** stand for the part of that sentence between "if" and "then." Let **q** stand for the part after "then." Notice that the second sentence is the same as **p** and the last sentence is the same as **q**. Once we label them accordingly, we see that the argument matches the form of modus ponens.*

Model Response to Exercise 3

<u>Modus tollens</u>: p stands for "The Great Spirit desired me to be a white man," and q for "The Great Spirit made me a white man."

When people express deductive arguments in plain English, they'll often use slightly different grammatical tenses to say more or less the same thing (e.g., "the Great Spirit had desired me to be a white man" versus "the Great Spirit desired me to be a white man"). Most of the time, you can just ignore those grammatical differences.

Model Response to Exercise 5

<u>Modus tollens</u>: p stands for "scraping stingers out worked better than pulling stingers out," and q stands for "scraping the stingers out should leave smaller welts than pulling the stingers out."

This argument illustrates one connection between deductive logic and scientific reasoning. A key part of scientific reasoning is "hypothesis testing," in which scientists first figure out what they should expect to observe in a particular situation if a hypothesis were correct; then put themselves in that situation; and finally, check whether they observe what they expected. If they didn't, that's a reason to conclude that the hypothesis is false, just as the researchers described in this argument did.

*   At least, that's the cartoon version of how science works. In real life, things are more complex. Maybe the scientists were wrong about what the*

hypothesis means for the situation in question. Maybe they didn't create quite the right situation. Maybe their measurements were off. It takes rigorous experimentation and careful thought to show that the hypothesis has really been "falsified"—that is, shown to be false. In terms of deductive logic, what's going on is often that the if–then sentence in the argument isn't strictly true: It's possible that the hypothesis could be correct, and yet the scientists should not expect to observe what they think they should. In short, modus tollens *is a helpful way to think about what's going on in hypothesis testing, but only if you remember that the if–then sentences in science aren't always 100% accurate.*

Model Response to Exercise 7

<u>Modus tollens</u>: p stands for "Rodale Press's self-help books really work," and q for "After reading a Rodale Press self-help book, most Rodale Press customers would not need more of their self-help books on the same topic."

The idea that is symbolized by **q** *is stated in two different ways in the argument for exercise 1: Steve Salerno says that "one would not expect people to need further help from us." The next sentence says that "most of his company customer's did need further help from them—on the same topic—after reading their self-help books." It doesn't matter what exact terms you use to explain what* **q** *stands for, as long as you recognize that both of those clauses express the same idea and can be labeled with the same letter.*

To be fair, Rodale Press does publish books other than self-help books, and we doubt that Salerno means to say that Rodale's self-help books are less effective than other publishers' self-help books.

Model Response to Exercise 9

Dilemma: p stands for "I'm just a poor old country boy," q stands for "I'm a demon," and r and s both stand for "you'd better be nice to me."

An equally good way to answer this questions would be to say that **p** *stands for "I'm just a poor old country boy,"* **q** *stands for "I'm a demon,"* **r** *stands for "you'd better be nice to me," and the argument takes the following form: Either* **p** *or* **q***. If* **p***, then* **r***. If* **q***, then* **r***. Therefore,* **r***. That might not look quite like a dilemma at first. After all, aren't dilemmas supposed to yield conclusions of the form "* **r** *or* **s***"? But since* **p** *and* **q** *each entail* **r***, the conclusion here would be "* **r** *or* **r***," which is the same as* **r***. As we hinted in discussing the*

*"Hedgehog's dilemma," this is actually a common use of dilemma: By show-
ing that there are only two possibilities, and that either one leads to the
same conclusion, you can show that the conclusion must be true.*

Exercise Set 6.2: Identifying deductive argument in more complex passages

Model Response to Exercise 1

<u>Modus tollens</u>: p stands for "The points of light are stars," and q for
"The points of light will be arranged randomly like the other stars."

*Don't be thrown off by the background information in this passage. Look for
the logical connectives (in this case, "if") and then look for restatements of
the ideas linked by the connectives. Notice that this is another example of
hypothesis testing, as we discussed in connection with the model response to
exercise 5 in Exercise Set 6.1.*

Model Response to Exercise 3

<u>Modus ponens</u>: p stands for "People living without a government are
prone to steal from and kill one another," and q for "The thing to do is
to set up a government to force everyone to behave."

Model Response to Exercise 5

<u>Modus tollens</u>: p stands for "Burning was the release of phlogiston"
and q stands for "Burning metals would cause them to lose weight."

*One thing that makes this example somewhat difficult is that p and q are
expressed in slightly different ways at different times. For instance, q is first
expressed as "Burning metals causes them to gain weight," but not-q is expressed as "Burning metals would cause them to lose weight." And although
p is initially expressed as "Burning was the release of phlogiston," the conclusion (not-p) is stated in a more general way: "The phlogiston theory was
incorrect." You'd only recognize that "the phlogiston theory was incorrect"
counts as not-p if you realize that the phlogiston theory says that "burning
is the release of phlogiston." (Strictly speaking, "burning is not the release of
phlogiston" and "the phlogiston theory is incorrect" say slightly different*

things. But for purposes of understanding the reasoning in this argument, we can treat them as equivalent.)

This exercise illustrates another important feature of hypothesis testing in scientific reasoning. You might think that scientists immediately gave up the phlogiston theory when they learned that metals gained weight when burned. But many didn't. Instead, they amended the phlogiston theory. For instance, some scientists proposed that phlogiston had "negative weight," so that losing phlogiston involved gaining weight, in something like the way that releasing helium from a balloon causes it to fall. The point is that testing a hypothesis requires holding constant a wide range of background assumptions. So, when the test of a hypothesis appears to undermine that hypothesis, it might be because one of those background assumptions is false.

Model Response to Exercise 7

<u>Modus tollens:</u> p stands for "Celebrity endorsements do not signal a better product or a more trustworthy company," and q for "Consumers do not respond to celebrity endorsements."

This argument can be confusing because p and q are expressed in a negative way—that is, in terms of what celebrity endorsements do not do and what consumers do not respond to. Many people are tempted to use p to stand for "Celebrity endorsements signal a better product or a more trustworthy company" and q to stand for "Consumers respond to celebrity endorsements." That's fine as long as you recognize that the first premise of the argument is then "if not-p then not-q." The second premise would be not-not-q (or, equivalently, q), leading to the conclusion p. As you can see, though, it's simpler to use p and q as in the model response above.

Model Response to Exercise 9

<u>Modus ponens:</u> p stands for "Bertrand Russell did not believe in God or immortality," and q for "Bertrand Russell was not a Christian."

There are a few tricky things about this argument. First, the second premise and the conclusion are stated in a negative way, as they were in exercise 7 of this exercise set.

Another tricky thing about this argument is that it shifts between talking about "someone" and talking about Bertrand Russell. The first premise just says that if "someone" does not believe in God and immortality, then that person is not a Christian. The second premise says that Bertrand Russell did not believe in God or immortality. We haven't developed the technical tools to formalize this argument completely, but it should be clear that Russell would have allowed us to rephrase his argument as: "If Bertrand Russell did not believe in God or immortality, then he could not truly have been a Christian. Russell did not believe in God or immortality. Thus, Russell was not a Christian."

Exercise Set 6.3: Drawing conclusions with deductive arguments

Model Response to Exercise 1

Using <u>modus tollens</u>, we can conclude that the SAT is not a useful test.

Let p stand for "The SAT is a useful test" and q stand for "The SAT tests skills like research and critical analysis." The premises would then be "if p then q" and not-q. Modus tollens lets us infer not-p from those premises. In this case, not-p stands for "The SAT is not a useful test."

Model Response to Exercise 3

Using disjunctive syllogism, we can conclude that if the "continental drift" hypothesis is correct, then there will be fossils in eastern South America that can be found nowhere else but in western Africa.

Let p stand for "the 'continental drift' hypothesis is correct," q stand for "there would have been animals that lived nowhere but near the place where the old supercontinent split apart," and r stand for "there will be fossils in eastern South America that can be found nowhere else but in western Africa." The premises are then "if p then q" and "if q then r." The conclusion of a hypothetical syllogism is an if–then sentence that begins like the first premise and ends like the second premise—in this case, "if p then r."

Whenever you have two "if–then sentences" in an argument, you should check to see if they fit together in the right way to form a hypothetical syllogism. If they don't, check to see if the argument is a dilemma.

This argument illustrates another role that deductive reasoning plays in scientific reasoning. Wegener first proposed his idea of continental drift in 1915, claiming that continents could combine and separate over periods of millions of years. On an oversimplified view of science, this might seem like an unscientific hypothesis, since no one can directly observe anything that happens over millions of years. How, then, can you test such a hypothesis? To overcome this problem, scientists use deductive and other kinds of reasoning to figure out what observations they could make to test the hypothesis. In this case, Wegener reasons that if his hypothesis is true, then we should be able to find some fossils that appear only in South America and Brazil. In fact, there are such fossils—most famously, those of a freshwater reptile called a Mesosaurus. *Note, however, that this merely provides evidence for Wegener's hypothesis, rather than a deductively valid proof of it. (Can you see why?)*

Model Response to Exercise 5

Using disjunctive syllogism, we can conclude that light consists of waves.

*Let **p** stand for "light consists of tiny particles" and **q** stand for "light consists of waves." We would then symbolize the two premises as "**p** or **q**" and "not-**p**." Disjunctive syllogism allows us to infer **q**: "Light consists of waves."*

*The physicist Thomas Young offered an argument like this one after conducting his famous "double-slit" experiment in 1801. In a mind-bending turn of events, modern physics has shown that Young's conclusion was right but that one of his premises was wrong: light is a wave, and so **q** is true, but light is also a particle, making the premise not-**p** false! (Remember, using a valid deductive argument form like disjunctive syllogism doesn't always means that your conclusions will be true. It only guarantees that your conclusion will be true* if *all of your premises are true.)*

As with exercise 5 in the previous exercise set, this example illustrates the importance of background assumptions in hypothesis testing. Young assumed that light had to be either a particle or wave—not both. That seems like a very reasonable assumption, but it turns out to be false.

Model Response to Exercise 7

Using dilemma we can conclude that either people's colleagues will resent their time offline or their colleagues will appreciate their time offline.

*Let **p** stand for "individuals could try to cut back their smartphone use on their own," **q** for "individuals could try to cut back their smartphone use in cooperation with their colleagues," **r** for "people's colleagues will resent their*

*offline time," and **s** for "people's colleagues will appreciate their offline time."
The third sentence is **p** or **q**. The fourth is if **p** then **r**, and the last sentence is
if **q** then **s**.*

Model Response to Exercise 9

Using <u>modus ponens</u>, we can conclude that the computer files couldn't
have been created in 2003.

*Let **p** stand for "The computer files were created with Microsoft Office 2007"
and **q** stand for "The computer files couldn't have been created in 2003." We
can then symbolize the last two sentences in the exercise as **p** and if **p** then
q. (Remember from the previous exercise set that "**q** if **p**" means if **p** then **q**!)*

    *Note that you won't always find premises in the order you expect. The typi-
cal form for modus ponens is: "If **p** then **q**. **p**. Therefore, **q**." Here, the order
of the premises is reversed. Feel free to rearrange the premises to make them
fit the rules—just be very careful not to change the premises in the process!*

    *You might have been tempted to conclude that the computer files weren't
created in 2003. That would be a reasonable thing to say, although it's is a
different (and weaker) claim than saying that they couldn't have been created in 2003. The logical relationships between the way things are, the way
things might be, and the way they have to be are studied in a branch of
deductive logic called modal logic.*

Exercise Set 6.4: Working with *reductio ad absurdum*

Model Response to Exercise 1

<u>To prove:</u> No man has had sex in space.

<u>Assume the opposite:</u> A man has had sex in space.

<u>Argue that from the assumption we'd have to conclude:</u> Some guy has
had sex in space and didn't tell anyone about it.

<u>But:</u> It's really hard to believe that a guy could have had sex in space
and not tell anyone about it.

<u>Conclude:</u> No man has had sex in space.

*The first step in fitting this argument to the form of reductio ad absurdum
is to recognize that the conclusion of the argument is that no man has had
sex in space.*

Like all reductio *arguments, this argument asks us to assume—for the sake of argument—that the intended conclusion is false. That is, it asks to assume that some man has had sex in space. There are two clues that this is the claim to put in the "assume the opposite" line of the* reductio *form: First, the author of the argument says, "Suppose, just for the sake of argument." Second and more importantly, the claim "A man has had sex in space" is the opposite of the conclusion. (If we were to symbolize the conclusion as* **p***, this claim would be not-***p***.) You won't see the first clue in every* reductio *argument, so it's important to learn to recognize the second clue, too.*

When you put the assumption that some man has had sex in space together with the premise that no one has admitted to having sex in space, you're forced to conclude that some man has had sex in space and kept quiet about it. Notice that for the purposes of this exercise, we don't need to identify exactly how the assumption leads to that conclusion; we just need to identify the ridiculous conclusion itself.

That conclusion is ridiculous (according to the author of this argument) because no man could keep such information to himself. Since assuming that some man has had sex in space leads to a ridiculous conclusion, we can conclude that no man has (yet!) had sex in space. Again, notice that the conclusion (on the last line of your reductio *form) is the same as the claim that the argument is trying to prove (on the first line of your* reductio *form). This should be the case for all of your answers in this exercise set.*

Like many reductio *arguments, the assumption in this argument leads to a conclusion that is very hard to believe but is not literally impossible. Some people might not find it hard to believe that a man could keep quiet about having had sex in space; such people would not find this argument very persuasive.*

Model Response to Exercise 3

<u>To prove:</u> My roommate is not real.

<u>Assume the opposite:</u> My roommate is real.

<u>Argue that from this assumption we'd have to conclude:</u> My roommate doesn't age.

<u>But:</u> All real people age.

<u>Conclude:</u> My roommate is not real.

Once again, we begin by identifying the main conclusion of the argument and then assuming the opposite. Through some chain of reasoning, which you don't need to include in your reductio *form, this assumption leads to the claim that the author's roommate doesn't age.*

Notice that the claim that "all real people age," which is listed here on the "But" line of the reductio *form, is not actually stated in the argument. This is common in* reductio *arguments, because the claim that goes on that line is often so obvious that it doesn't need to be stated. It's part of your task in explaining the* reductio *to figure out what goes in that space in the formalized version of the argument.*

Model Response to Exercise 5

<u>To prove:</u> It is impossible to accelerate something to the speed of light.

<u>Assume the opposite:</u> It is possible to accelerate something to the speed of light.

<u>Argue that from the assumption we'd have to conclude:</u> The thing you accelerated to the speed of light would have a length of zero.

<u>But:</u> Nothing can have a length of zero.

<u>Conclude:</u> It is impossible to accelerate something to the speed of light.

Notice that the argument that leads from the assumption to the claim that the thing you've accelerated would have a length of zero depends on Einstein's theory of relativity. Thus, instead of rejecting the assumption that it is possible to accelerate something to the speed of light, we could reject the theory of relativity. This is usually the case in reductio *arguments: You could avoid rejecting your assumption by rejecting another premise of the argument instead.*

Even if you are unsure about which premise you want to reject, you can use reductio *arguments to draw inferences about the implications of a theory. For instance, Einstein used this argument to show that his theory of relativity implied that you can't accelerate anything to the speed of light. That's one reason that he insisted on keeping the premise that his theory of relativity was correct, rather than the assumption that one can accelerate something to the speed of light; he was trying to see what else would be true if we assumed that this theory were true.*

A common variation on this argument points out that, according to the theory of relativity, it would take an infinite amount of energy to accelerate something to the speed of light—but it's impossible to apply an infinite amount of energy to anything.

Model Response to Exercise 7

<u>To prove:</u> There must be life on other planets in the Milky Way.

<u>Assume the opposite:</u> There is no life on any other planet in the Milky Way.

<u>Argue that from the assumption we'd have to conclude:</u> The probability of life arising on Earth is basically zero.

<u>But:</u> Life did arise on Earth.

<u>Conclude:</u> There must be life on other planets in the Milky Way.

This argument is a fancy way of expressing the idea that it's really hard to believe that Earth is the only habitable planet on which life developed. But don't be fooled: the fact that something has a probability of almost zero doesn't mean it's impossible. Consider, for instance, that the probability of any given ticket winning the Powerball lottery jackpot is one in 175,223,510 or 0.000000005707. Yet, people do sometimes win that jackpot. By analogy, even if the probability of life arising on Earth is basically zero, that doesn't strictly contradict the claim that life did arise on Earth. But then again, remember that some reductio *arguments don't rely on strict contradictions. (And furthermore, if you've read Chapter III and thought about using analogies to refute arguments, you'll know to look for important differences between the lottery and the development of life. Can you think of any?)*

Model Response to Exercise 9

<u>To prove:</u> There is no largest prime number.

<u>Assume the opposite:</u> There is a largest prime number, N.

<u>Argue that from the assumption we'd have to conclude:</u> There is a prime number that is larger than N.

<u>But:</u> N can't be the largest prime number if there is a prime number that is larger than it is.

<u>Conclude:</u> There is no largest prime number.

Mathematicians frequently use reductio ad absurdum *to prove mathematical theorems. They often call these arguments "proofs by contradiction." They use this name because mathematical* reductio *arguments lead to contradictions—such as the claim that N both is and is not the largest prime number. Since contradictions can't be true, they make for very strong* reductio *arguments. You don't run into the problem of someone thinking that your "absurd" result is actually true.*

This argument can be a bit difficult to follow, especially if you're unfamiliar with prime numbers. For the purposes of this exercise, the key is to focus on identifying the various parts of the reductio, *rather than worrying about exactly how we get from the assumption that N is the largest prime number to the claim that there is a prime number that is larger than N. Understanding the gist of the argument requires understanding a common technique in mathematical* reductio *arguments: When you assume the existence of some number, you get to give that number a name. In this case, the author assumes the existence of a largest prime number, which he names N. The goal of this argument is to show that even when we assume that N is the largest prime number, we can in fact identify an even larger prime number. That leads to the contradiction that N is and is not the largest prime number.*

To see how this works, consider a similar but simpler argument: "There is no largest number. To see why, assume that there is a largest number. Call it X. Now, consider the number that you get by adding one to X. Call that number Y. (That is, Y = X + 1.) Y is larger than X. Therefore, X is not actually the largest number. Therefore, there is no largest number." Like the argument about the largest prime, this argument works by showing that even if you pick a number such that all you know about it *is that it's supposed to be the largest number there is, you can always find a number that is larger than it is.*

When you encounter proofs by contradiction in your math classes, try fitting them into the form of reductio ad absurdum.

Exercise Set 6.5: Identifying deductive arguments in several steps

Model Response to Exercise 1

Dilemma and disjunctive syllogism: p stands for "God is able to prevent evil," q stands for "God is unable to prevent evil," r stands for "God is not all powerful," and s stands for "God is not perfectly good."

The premises in the argument in this exercise are given in the order one would expect for dilemma and disjunctive syllogism. The only thing that makes this tricky, other than the large number of statements involved, is that the passage includes some explanatory sentences that are not part of the argument itself.

Incidentally, the problem raised by the argument in this exercise is known in the philosophy of religion as "the problem of evil." Philosophers and religious people have responded to it in many different ways. Some accept that if God is all powerful and perfectly good, then there is no evil in the world and then use modus ponens *to conclude that there is no* genuine *evil in the world—only things that seem "evil" to us because we do not understand God's plan. Others take the approach used in this argument, inferring that God is not perfect and all powerful. (In fact, some take the existence of evil as evidence that God does not exist at all.) Still others deny the alleged connection between God's power and goodness and the existence of evil. Perhaps God allows evil because he wants us to have free will. Perhaps, in his perfect wisdom, he sees evil as a means to achieving some higher purpose.*

Model Response to Exercise 3

Hypothetical syllogism (twice) and <u>modus ponens</u>: p stands for "Miss Windham has had thirty perms in her life," q for "Miss Windham knows not to wet her hair after getting a perm," and r for "Miss Windham would not have gotten in the shower after getting a perm." These three claims make up the first hypothetical syllogism, leading to the conclusion if p then r. These claims are followed by s, "Miss Windham is lying about not hearing the gunshot." Putting if p then r together with if r then s leads to the conclusion if p then s. Since it is implied that p is true, we can use <u>modus ponens</u> to infer s, which is the main conclusion of the argument.

The pieces of this argument are presented in order in exercise 3, but not all of the intermediate steps are laid out explicitly there. For instance, nowhere does it actually say, "If Miss Windham has had thirty perms in her life, then she would not have gotten into the shower after getting a perm." This intermediate conclusion is implied by the argument. This is quite common, since it would be pedantic to reiterate each intermediate conclusion throughout the argument.

As with many arguments that combine hypothetical syllogisms and modus ponens, *it is possible to interpret this argument as a series of* modus ponens *arguments instead. On this interpretation, we would formalize the argument as follows: p. If p, then q. Therefore, q. If q, then r. Therefore, r. If r, then s. Therefore, s. Both of these are fine, although the use of hypothetical syllogism is closer to the original text of the argument.*

Model Response to Exercise 5

Hypothetical syllogism and <u>modus ponens</u>. Let p stand for "the speed of north-south seismic waves indicates that most crystals in the inner core are aligned north-south" and q stand for "the speed of seismic waves traveling through the center of the inner core indicates that most crystals in the center inner core are aligned east-west." Let r stand for "the inner core has its own 'inner inner core.'" The two if-then sentences toward the end of the paragraph are if p then q and if q then r, respectively. By hypothetical syllogism, these entail if p then r. Earlier in the paragraph, the sentence "This shows that the crystals in the inner core are aligned in a north-south direction" means that same thing as p. <u>Modus ponens</u> gets us the main conclusion, r.

As with exercise 3, some steps of this argument aren't made explicit, such as the inference from if p then q and if q then r to if p then r. And as with exercise 3, you could interpret this as a series of modus ponens *arguments rather than a hypothetical syllogism. What makes this argument harder to follow than the one in exercise 3 is the technical nature of the content. But you don't actually need to understand exactly what the argument is saying in order to understand its logical structure.*

This argument highlights an often overlooked feature of science: While schoolteachers usually emphasize that science involves making lots of observations, science also requires a lot of careful reasoning—including deductive reasoning. The seismologists discussed in this exercise certainly looked at many observations of the seismic waves generated by earthquakes. To get from those observations to an interesting conclusion, however, they had to construct a long chain of careful reasoning. (In fact, if you read the original scientific paper from which this argument is adapted, the reasoning is even more complicated than it appears in this exercise.) Science is not really a matter of "look and see." It's more a matter of "look and see and think."

Model Response to Exercise 7

Hypothetical syllogism, <u>modus tollens</u>, and disjunctive syllogism. Let p stand for "I am awake" and q stand for "I am still dreaming." Let r stand for "everything in my apartment looks and feels like it does in real life," and s for "this carpet will feel like wool." The first two sentences can be interpreted as "p or q." The third sentence is "if p then r," and the fourth is "if r then s." Putting these together with hypothetical syllogism entails "if p then s." The fifth sentence, which says that the carpet feels like polyester, can be interpreted as "not-s," since the carpet doesn't feel like wool if it feels like polyester. Putting not-s together with "if p then s" yields the sixth sentence, not-p, by <u>modus tollens</u>. Putting not-p together with "p or q" (from the first sentence) leads to the final conclusion, q, by disjunctive syllogism.

*As with the argument in exercise 5, this argument skips over some of the intermediate steps, such as the conclusion of the hypothetical syllogism ("if **p** then **s**"). It also states some of the premises in rather indirect ways. For instance, the first two sentences don't use the word "or," but together they express the same idea as the sentence, "Either I am awake or I am still dreaming." That's why we can interpret them as "**p** or **q**." Furthermore, the claim that the carpet feels like polyester is not literally the same as the sentence, "The carpet does not feel like wool." In the context of this argument, however, the claim about the carpet feeling like polyester is to say that the carpet does not feel like wool. (If you wanted to be more rigorous about this, you could add an extra deductive argument here: "The carpet feels like polyester. If the carpet feels like polyester, then it does not feel like wool. Therefore, the carpet does not feel like wool." This would give you not-**s**.) As a general rule, when faced with complex deductive arguments, you may need to add a few steps yourself to make the argument fit the rules precisely. Alternatively, you may need to reinterpret some of the claims in the arguments to make them fit together with the other claims more precisely. Just be careful not to change the meaning of the claims when you reinterpret them!*

Model Response to Exercise 9

Disjunctive syllogism and <u>modus ponens</u>. To see clearly how this works, it helps to rewrite the argument a little bit. Let p stand for "Segregation laws fit with the moral law," q for "Segregation laws are unjust," and r for "One has a moral obligation to disobey segregation laws." We can then read the argument as follows: "p or q. Not-p. Therefore, q. If q then r. Therefore, r."

As with exercise 9 in Exercise Set 6.2, we haven't covered enough formal logic to handle all of the complexities of this argument. To understand the basic form of the argument, we need to simplify it a bit. While the original argument is more complex than the one presented in this model response, King would presumably recognize the argument in this response as a version of the argument he presented—at least as applied to the specific case of segregation laws.

MODEL RESPONSES FOR CHAPTER VII: EXTENDED ARGUMENTS

Exercise Set 7.1: Identifying possible positions

Model Response to Exercise 1

(1) Yes

(2) No

(3) Yes, but only for people over 18

(4) Yes, but only for medical uses

(5) No, but possession of marijuana should carry only a small fine

As this response illustrates, identifying good answers may require thinking carefully about what the question means. What counts as "legalizing" marijuana? Does it mean that anyone may grow, sell, buy, and use marijuana? Or does it mean that people are allowed to grow and use marijuana on their own, but are not allowed to sell it? Or grow and sell it only for certain purposes? Thinking about the different interpretations of the question will help you identify more nuanced answers.

Model Response to Exercise 3

(1) Yes

(2) No

(3) Only if the developers help to expand the species' habitat elsewhere

There are many different conditions under which you might think it is appropriate for a developer to destroy the habitats of endangered species. Endorsing some of these conditions is so close to a simple "Yes" or "No" answer that they're not worth considering. For instance, "Yes, as long as the developer could not make as much money building elsewhere" is pretty much like just saying Yes. (If the developer could make more money elsewhere, why would he or she build in the endangered species' habitat anyway?) Similarly, "No, unless the alternative is that some people become homeless," is usually tantamount to just saying No.

You might not know which conditions you want to attach to your answers now. That's okay. When you are working on an extended argument, you can always revisit and reconsider your answers later.

Model Response to Exercise 5

(1) By looking at their students' standardized test scores at the end of the year

(2) By comparing their students' standardized test scores at the beginning of the year to their scores at the end of the year

(3) Based on student evaluations

(4) By having principals from other schools observe their teaching

(5) Some combination of the above

You don't need to invent all of your answers from scratch. Almost any topic you consider has already been considered by someone else. It's usually worth your time to find out what answers other people have proposed. They may have come up with ideas that wouldn't have occurred to you.

Notice that it may be possible to combine potential solutions to a problem. For instance, if test scores and student evaluations both have shortcomings as measures of teacher performance, schools might measure teacher performance more accurately by looking at both *test scores and student evaluations.*

Model Response to Exercise 7

(1) By relying on national pension schemes, such as Social Security

(2) By putting a set fraction of their paychecks into a savings account each month

(3) By buying stocks

(4) By buying bonds

(5) By buying a mix of stocks and bonds

(6) People in their twenties should not be saving for their retirement.

Some questions are "loaded," meaning that they frame an issue in such a way that they seem to preclude certain answers. (See also the fallacy of "Complex Question" in Appendix I.) Asking how twenty-somethings ought to save for retirement seems to assume that they should be saving for their retirement. It's important to recognize when a question has such built-in assumptions and to consider answers that reject those assumptions, as the last answer in this response does. (Technically, those won't be answers to the question, but they might still be appropriate responses to someone who asks the question.)

Exercise Set 7.3: Sketching arguments for and against positions

Model Response to Exercise 1

An argument for the position:

(1) Requiring national service of all eighteen-year-olds would force teenagers to interact with fellow citizens from very different walks of life.

(2) Interacting with fellow citizens from very different walks of life instills a deeper understanding of and appreciation for the diversity of the United States.

(3) It would be a good thing for all American citizens to acquire a deeper understanding of and appreciation for the diversity of the United States.

Therefore, (4) national service should be required of all American eighteen-year-olds.

An argument against this position:

(1) The United States prides itself on being a free country.

(2) In a free country, the government does not tell adults what to do with their lives.

Therefore, (3) national service should not be required of all American eighteen-year-olds.

This response offers two basic arguments: one for the stated position and one against it. Both arguments have only a few premises. (Depending on your argument, you might need four or five premises—or you might only need one.)

Many of these premises are in need of further defense or clarification. For instance, someone might justifiably want to know why it would be a good thing for all American citizens to acquire a deeper understanding of their country's diversity. Don't worry about providing that justification here. You can fill in the details later.

Model Response to Exercise 3

An argument for this position:

(1) Once a species goes extinct, it is gone forever.

(2) Losing something forever is a serious problem.

Therefore, (3) the extinction of an endangered species is a serious problem.

An argument against this position:

(1) Species have gone extinct throughout the planet's history.

(2) When species have gone extinct in the past, new species appear or move in to take the place of the species that have gone extinct.

Therefore, (3) the extinction of an endangered species is not a serious problem.

The first of the two arguments in this response is more of a philosophical argument. It addresses the significance of a permanent loss. You may be able to come up with arguments like this just by thinking through the issue, although you can always do some research to see what others have said about it too. The second argument depends on certain facts about the history of life on Earth. You may need to do some research to come up with this argument—or at least, you may need to do some research when it comes time to support the premises. (See Rule 31.)

You should consider both kinds of arguments. Many debates can't be settled with just one type of argument or the other. You'll need to dig up some facts, and you'll need to think carefully about the issues involved in your argument.

Model Response to Exercise 5

An argument for the position:

(1) According to WebMD, only about one in every 2,000 children in the United States had autism in the 1980s.

(2) According to WebMD, about one in every 150 eight-year-olds in the United States is now on the autism spectrum.

Therefore (3) autism is becoming more common (at least in the United States).

An argument against the position:

(1) Statistics about children "with autism" now include children with a wide range of developmental disorders on the autism spectrum, rather than just those with autism.

(2) Children on the autism spectrum were much less likely to be diagnosed as having a developmental disorder in the past than they are now.

Therefore (3), the increasing prevalence of autism spectrum diagnoses does not reflect an increase in the prevalence of autism.

Each of these arguments raises an important point in the debate over the rise of autism spectrum disorders. Each argument is also seriously incomplete: The first argument doesn't address the points raised in the second argument, and the second argument doesn't show that changing definitions and increased awareness account for all of the increase in diagnoses. But at this point in the process, you're not trying to come up with the most complete arguments you can; you're just trying to sketch the basic ideas behind each position. That's what these arguments do.

Model Response to Exercise 7

An argument for the position:

(1) It is possible to die from an overdose of alcohol.

(2) It is not possible to die from an overdose of marijuana.

Therefore, (3) alcohol is more dangerous than marijuana.

An argument against the position:

(1) People who use marijuana sometimes move on to other, more dangerous drugs, like cocaine or heroin.

(2) It is much less common for alcohol use to lead to doing harder drugs.

Therefore, (3) marijuana is more dangerous than alcohol.

The second argument in this response relies on the idea that marijuana is a "gateway" drug. Defenders of marijuana use might complain that this argument is misleading. They might claim that on closer inspection, the premises do not really support the conclusion. It is often worth considering popular arguments for or against a position, even if you think those arguments are ultimately misguided. Doing so can help you understand why people disagree with you on a topic and what you might say to change their mind. (Of course, you might also discover that their arguments are more powerful than you think. That might change your mind!)

Model Response to Exercise 9

An argument for this position:

(1) People can't properly understand debates about many important topics, including political topics, if they don't understand statistics.

(2) It's important for people to understand debates about important topics, including political topics.

Therefore, (3) everyone should be required to take at least one course in statistics.

An argument against this position:

(1) People learn enough about statistics in regular math classes in high school.

Therefore, (2) it's false that everyone should be required to take at least one course in statistics.

This exercise asks you to customize the position being debated by filling in the blank with an academic subject of your choosing. This response filled in the blank with "statistics." You, of course, are free to choose something different—including a subject that you really don't *think everyone should be required to take.*

Exercise Set 7.5: Developing arguments in more detail

Model Response to Exercise 1

(1) For a study published in December 2012, researchers from the Boston University School of Medicine examined the brains of eighty-five deceased patients, in which they found evidence that repeated concussions had caused a kind of brain damage called "chronic traumatic encephalopathy," which has symptoms similar to Alzheimer's disease.

(2) In 2014, the Committee on Sports-Related Concussions in Youth found that most studies of repeated concussions show "unfavorable changes" in patients' cognitive abilities, such as memory and processing speed.

Therefore, (3) concussions—especially repeated concussions—are very dangerous.

When confronted with claims from certain specialized disciplines, such as medicine, it's often best to look for recent authoritative sources to support the claim. Remember, though, to cross-check your sources: When you set out to find a source to support a particular claim, you're likely to overlook or ignore sources that contradict that claim. Making a conscious effort to check for sources that contradict the claim can help you catch unreliable premises or studies that have later been disproven.

Model Response to Exercise 3

(1) Pigs that live on factory farms live in small, crowded pens.

(2) Pregnant pigs are confined to even smaller, individual stalls, which are frequently too small to allow the pig to turn around.

(3) Factory-farmed pigs do not get to participate in the social behaviors that are an important part of a normal pig's life.

(4) Confining intelligent, social creatures, like pigs, to small pens and depriving them of an important part of a normal life is cruel.

Thus, (5) it is cruel to force pigs to live on factory farms.

This response suggests several features of factory farms that make it cruel to force pigs to live there. Notice that this argument could be developed further. For instance, how do we know that factory-farmed pigs live in small, crowded pens, etc.? An even more developed form of this response might offer sources to back up the claims about life on a factory farm. As a first pass, though, this response does a good job of spelling out the reasons for thinking that it is cruel to force pigs to live on factory farms.

Model Response to Exercise 5

(1) If people are constantly afraid of everyone else, then they will be afraid to invest their time and effort in producing things that others can take from them.

(2) If people are afraid to invest their time and effort in producing things that others can take from them, then there will be no business or industry.

Thus, (3) if people are constantly afraid of everyone else, then there will be no business or industry.

This response uses a hypothetical syllogism (Rule 24) to spell out the connection between fear of others and a lack of business and industry. Hypothetical syllogism is often useful for spelling out causal connections.

Model Response to Exercise 7

(1) Barbara Thompson, Pat Levitt, and Gregg Starwood—all from the Department of Pharmacology at Vanderbilt University—published a paper in <u>Nature Reviews Neuroscience</u> in 2009, in which they review several studies showing that using cocaine during pregnancy leads to long-lasting, negative effects on cognitive ability and attention.

(2) A parent who intentionally does something that will cause his or her child to have cognitive deficits is seriously harming that child.

Therefore, (3) a pregnant woman who uses cocaine is seriously harming her child.

This response provides an argument for the claim that a pregnant woman who uses cocaine is seriously harming her child. Instead of looking for a source that says exactly that, however, the response uses a source to support the more specific claim that cocaine negatively impacts cognitive development. This provides deeper insight into how cocaine use during pregnancy can result in harm to a child.

Model Response to Exercise 9

(1) If you were a brain-in-a-vat, then your experiences might be identical to the experiences you would have if you were a normal person.

(2) If your experiences as a brain-in-a-vat might be identical to the experiences you would have if you were a normal person, then you might not be able to tell whether you are a brain-in-a-vat or a normal person, since you can't distinguish between two things that are identical.

Therefore, (3) if you were a brain-in-a-vat, then you might not be able to tell that you were a brain-in-a-vat.

This response uses hypothetical syllogism (Rule 24) to argue for the claim that if you were a brain-in-a-vat, then you might not be able to tell that you were a brain-in-a-vat. This is often a promising strategy when you are trying to provide an argument for a conditional (i.e., "if–then") sentence.

Exercise Set 7.7: Working out objections

Model Response to Exercise 1

The argument claims that "parents ought not to put their kids at serious risk." But parents can't—and shouldn't—try to protect their kids from all risks. For instance, allowing teenagers to date puts them at risk of having their hearts broken, but prohibiting them from dating limits an important part of their personal development. So, the argument doesn't work.

This objection argues that a particular premise in the argument is false. It does that by arguing that the premise is "too strong"—i.e., that it claims too much. In response to this objection, we might want to modify the premise in question. We could change it to something like, "Parents ought not to put their kids at serious risk unless doing so is necessary for achieving an important goal." Of course, then you'd have to show that encouraging kids to play high-impact sports is necessary for achieving an important goal. (What goal? Why is it important? Are there other ways of achieving it?)

Model Response to Exercise 3

The second premise of this argument is, strictly speaking, false. It is not wrong to be cruel in general; it is wrong to be cruel <u>to persons</u>. This is because only persons count when it comes to morality. Pigs are not persons. Therefore, it is not wrong to be cruel to pigs.

Even if you think that an objection is misguided, thinking about objections can help you improve your arguments. Perhaps you think that it is wrong to be cruel to non-human animals, even if they are not persons. Or perhaps that in the relevant sense, pigs are persons—quite a different claim. Thinking about why someone might reject one of your premises might help you see ways in which you need to develop your argument further.

Model Response to Exercise 5

The first premise of this argument is false. If there were no government, people might be afraid of strangers, but they would still have friends and relatives whom they trust.

The objection we considered in the model response to exercise 1 showed that the conclusion of the argument needed to be revised. This objection in this response shows that one of its premises needs to be revised. Perhaps we don't want to say that without a government, everyone would fear every-one. Maybe we want to say something less sweeping—something like, "If there is no government, then people will be afraid to interact with strang-ers." This might still be enough to make a powerful argument.

Model Response to Exercise 7

The first premise of this argument is too strong. If a pregnant woman is not eating the foods needed to ensure a healthy pregnancy, a doctor isn't obligated to report her to the authorities. The doctor ought to help the woman improve her diet.

In response to this objection, we might want to look for a different principle that could explain why doctors ought to report cocaine-using pregnant women to the authorities. Maybe doctors ought to report child abuse, and using cocaine during pregnancy counts as child abuse.

Model Response to Exercise 9

The argument in this response depends on the claim that there is no way, other than on the basis of one's experience, to know that one isn't a brain-in-a-vat. This claim needs to be defended. Maybe there are sophisticated philosophical arguments—or unsophisticated ones!—that show that we're not brains-in-vats. Unless that claim is supported, the argument doesn't work.

Remember that not all objections involve claiming that one of the premises in an argument is false. There are other kinds of flaws that can weaken an argu-ment. In this case, the flaw is that the argument involves an unsupported—and therefore unreliable—premise (Rule 3).

Exercise Set 7.9: Brainstorming alternatives

Model Response to Exercise 1

Alternative 1: Governments should start a media campaign, including public service announcements, to make texting while driving as socially unacceptable as drinking and driving.

Alternative 2: Governments should require car manufacturers to install devices that block cell phone reception inside moving cars.

Alternative 1 is the best option. The original proposal will be no more effective than existing laws against texting while driving—maybe even less so, since drivers might see texting while driving and using their phone's GPS navigation as equivalent, since they would both be breaking the same law. Besides, it's impractical to ban the use of GPS navigation. Alternative 2 would not only make it harder to use GPS navigation, but it would prohibit passengers in the car from sending texts, making calls, looking up nearby gas stations or restaurants, and so on. This major inconvenience would probably drive people to find ways to disable the blocking device.

Sometimes coaxing people into doing something is more effective than forcing them to do it. After all, people are much more willing to cooperate with you when you convince them that you're asking them to do the right thing.

Note that the solutions to most problems tend to create problems of their own—or, at the very least, to require paying some cost in terms of time, money, or energy. Therefore, it's important to consider the balance of benefits to costs in evaluating a proposal, rather than just choosing the proposal that would most effectively accomplish your chosen goal. Alternative 2, for instance, would be very effective at discouraging texting while driving, but it would create all sorts of new problems. When you're thinking about ways to solve a problem, be sure to think about what other problems you might be creating in the process.

Model Response to Exercise 3

Alternative 1: Governments should increase funding for their space agencies.

Alternative 2: Governments should establish prizes for companies that achieve specific space-related goals.

In the short run, Alternative 2 is the best option. It gives some direction and public support to space exploration, but it allows a wide range of actors to pursue their own approaches to the task. It is better than Alternative 1 because government space agencies have a hard time pursuing multiple approaches simultaneously and taking risks. Alternative 2 is better than the original proposal because there is not enough money to be made in space exploration in the short run.

Remember that no proposal exists in a vacuum. You need to take the circumstances into account when choosing a proposal. You might think that privatizing space exploration is the best option in the long run, but that doesn't necessarily mean that it's the best option right now.

Model Response to Exercise 5

Alternative 1: Newspapers should become not-for-profit organizations that get funding through grants and donations.

Alternative 2: Newspapers should collect demographic information about their sites' users and provide targeted advertisements to each user, which will enable the newspapers to charge advertisers a higher fee.

Alternative 1 is the best option. A news service funded through grants and donations would not have to worry as much about catering to the tastes of advertisers or delivering sensationalist stories that attract lots of viewers for advertising purposes. The original proposal would simply drive users to other news sites. Alternative 2 might boost revenues somewhat, but it is unlikely to generate enough money to pay for quality reporting on important issues.

Model Response to Exercise 7

Alternative 1: Governments should run advertising campaigns to encourage healthier habits.

Alternative 2: Governments should subsidize healthier foods so that they are cheaper than fast foods and sugary soft drinks.

Alternative 1 is the best option. It is probably the least effective in terms of encouraging healthier habits, but it is the only one that is acceptable. The government should not impose taxes just to get people to stop doing things that the government doesn't like. Nor should it spend taxpayers' money to subsidize products that the government wants people to buy. Such subsidies would be unfair and open to corruption (i.e., to lobbyists spending lots of money to get politicians to subsidize their products). Thus, neither the original proposal nor Alternative 2 is acceptable.

Sometimes the option that achieves the stated goal most efficiently is not the best alternative, since that option might be morally or politically unacceptable, have serious negative side effects, etc.

Model Response to Exercise 9

Alternative 1: Schools should impose harsh penalties, such as suspension or expulsion, on unruly students.

Alternative 2: School districts should provide parenting lessons to parents of young children and counseling to older children as a means of preventing or reducing behavioral problems.

The original proposal is the best alternative. Schools that have intro-duced uniforms report that discipline, academic performance, and students' self-image all improve as a result of the uniforms. Thus, introducing uniforms achieves several important goals. Alternative 1 may improve discipline within the school, but it means that unruly students won't get as good an education, which might lead to even bigger problems for those students later in life. Alternative 2 might help, but it would be more expensive and difficult to implement than Alternative 1.

Note that this response's argument for the original proposal includes at least two claims that are controversial: First, what reason do we have to believe that schools that have introduced uniforms see the results that this response claims? (Are there reliable studies of the effects of school uniforms?) Second, would Alternative 2 really be more expensive and difficult to implement than Alternative 1? Thus, the argument in this response is ripe for further research and development. (See Exercise Set 7.3.)

MODEL RESPONSES FOR CHAPTER VIII: ARGUMENTATIVE ESSAYS

Exercise Set 8.1: Writing good leads

Model Response to Exercise 1

As surprising as it may seem, a diet that includes beef from range-fed cattle causes less animal suffering than an entirely vegetarian diet.

This hard lead clearly lays out the main conclusion of the argument. This is an especially effective way to start off when your conclusion is surprising or otherwise likely to grab the reader's attention all on its own.

Model Response to Exercise 3

Imagine that your child has been kidnapped. The police have caught the kidnapper, but he refuses to say where he's keeping your child. The kidnapper's iPhone might contain clues about where he's been—and where your child might be. Wouldn't you want the police to be able to access the data on that iPhone? So why has Apple made it impossible for them to do that?

This soft lead begins with an imaginary scenario that vividly illustrates the main reason for thinking that Apple (and Google) ought to reverse the change to their encryption software. Another approach here would be to track down an actual case in which police used a suspect's cell phone to solve a crime.

You could just as easily have gone with a hard lead for this exercise, although it might take two sentences to do it: "Apple and Google have made law enforcement's job harder by encrypting the data on everyone's phones. This was a mistake." Nothing says a hard lead has to be a single sentence.

Model Response to Exercise 5

College students ought to think twice before writing off the humanities.

This response does two things. First, it identifies the main point of the essay: Students should seriously consider studying the humanities. Second, it hints at the fact that there is something to be said against studying the humanities. (After all, if there is nothing to be said for "writing off the humanities," why do college students need to "think twice" before doing it?)

Model Response to Exercise 7

No high school newspaper would run a story that used the "n-word" to refer to an African-American. Mark Twain's Huckleberry Finn, however, uses the word over two hundred times, and it is a staple of the high school English curriculum. The difference is that Huck Finn is a classic of American literature.

This is a "softer" lead than the model responses to most earlier exercises in this set. It uses a (very brief!) imaginary scenario to lead the reader into the issue of Twain's use of the "n-word."

Notice that these introductory sentences set up the main argument, which centers on Huckleberry Finn's *status as a literary masterpiece, but they don't actually say what the main point of the essay is. They don't mention the new edition of the novel, from which the offending word has been removed, and they don't state the author's main position, which is that the book should be left unedited. In fact, this lead is compatible with an argument that the book* ought *to be censored but is not, because people are squeamish about editing a "classic of American literature."*

It's okay if you don't state the main conclusion of the essay in the first few sentences, but be sure to state it somewhere in the introductory paragraph(s).

Model Response to Exercise 9

Of the top ten family films on the Internet Movie Database (IMDB), exactly one has a female protagonist. This is not an anomaly. In general, family films portray women as highly sexualized, ditzy characters who rarely do anything as heroic or significant as their male co-stars.

This lead mixes a hard and a soft approach. The first sentence uses an interesting fact to illustrate the main point of the essay. The third sentence states that main point explicitly. The second sentence ties the other two sentences together.

Exercise Set 8.2: Making definite claims and proposals

Model Response to Exercise 1

Version 1: Schools should look at the change in students' test scores between one year and the next to measure teacher's effectiveness.

Version 2: Schools should hire recently retired teachers to observe other teachers in the classroom in order to evaluate how well each teacher is doing.

The original proposal in this question is so vague as to be almost meaningless. How else would you evaluate a teacher except by looking at how well they're teaching? The question is what, precisely, schools should do to figure out how well teachers are teaching.

This response suggests two very different approaches to measuring teacher effectiveness. Both responses could be made even more precise. For the first version, we might specify what kinds of tests we should use. For the second version, we might specify how often the teachers should be observed, how many different observers should evaluate them, what rubric should be used in evaluating them, etc.

It's often a judgment call about whether to include those extra details in your first statement of your claim or proposal. If you can include the details without making the claim too long or hard to understand, it's often worth doing. If including the details muddies your message, then leave them for later.

Model Response to Exercise 3

Version 1: It ought to be illegal to harm any endangered bird or mammal.

Version 2: There ought to be a law that prohibits the killing of any member of an endangered species or the destruction of the habitat of any endangered species.

There are three sources of vagueness in the original proposal: Which endangered species are "important"? Which species count as "endangered"? And what does it mean to say that such species should be "protected"?

Both of the proposals in this response address the first and third sources of vagueness, but they do so in different ways. Version 1 implies that only endangered birds and mammals count as "important" endangered species. (This isn't particularly plausible, but at least it's clear!) Version 1 also implies that "protecting" those species means making it illegal to harm any member of that species. (But what counts as harming them?) Version 2 gets rid of the word "important" and asserts that all *endangered species should be protected. It also spells out what it means to "protect" those species: Make it illegal to kill members of the species or to destroy their habitat.*

What about the word "endangered"? It is vague, but it's not going to be easy to clarify it in a single sentence. Alternatively, you could adopt one of the technical definitions used by government agencies that deal with endangered animals. Or you could just say something like, "An 'endangered species' is any species that appears on the U.S. Fish & Wildlife Service's Endangered Species List." (See Appendix II: "Definitions," p. 256.)

Model Response to Exercise 5

Version 1: People in the richest 10 percent of the population are more likely to have used marijuana, cocaine, or heroin than are people in the poorest 10 percent of the population.

Version 2: People in the richest 1 percent of the population are more likely to use illegal narcotics than are people living below the federal poverty line.

There are three sources of vagueness in the original claim: the terms rich *and* poor, *the word* use, *and the word* drug. *Each of these could be made more specific in various ways, and Version 1 and Version 2 take different approaches to each of them.*

Let's start with the different ways this response deals with the vagueness of rich *and* poor. *Version 1 treats* rich *and* poor *similarly, asking us to look at the top and bottom 10 percent of the wealth distribution. Version 2 uses criteria that have more cultural salience: the "top 1 percent" is often taken to have special significance for thinking about economic inequality, and the federal poverty line provides an official dividing line between the poor and the non-poor.*

It would be possible to adopt a more scientifically sophisticated approach here by looking at correlations between wealth and the probability of drug use, rather than just comparing people at the very top and bottom of the wealth distribution. Such an approach would require a more technical approach to statistics than we've introduced in this book.

Model Response to Exercise 7

Version 1: The majority of Americans are Christian.

Version 2: America's laws and public institutions should honor and be guided by Christian beliefs and values.

The oft-repeated claim that "America is a Christian nation" could mean many different things, and at least some of the disagreement about it might stem from failing to get clear about what it means. If it just means that the majority of Americans are Christian, then it's easy enough to figure out whether it's true, but it's harder to say just what follows in terms of how Christianity should influence American laws and institutions. If the claim is supposed to mean something closer to Version 2, then you're going to need a very different kind of argument to show that it's true.

As with the first exercise in this exercise set, both Version 1 and Version 2 in this model response could be made more precise. Is Version 1 talking about American citizens? And is it talking about people who answer "Yes" when asked if they're a Christian? People who attend a Christian church regularly? Or what? In Version 2, what exactly does it mean to say that American laws should "honor and be guided by Christian beliefs and values?" Despite this vagueness, both versions are much clearer than the original claim that "America is a Christian nation."

Model Response to Exercise 9

Version 1: There are technologically sophisticated civilizations on other planets, with technology at least as advanced as our own.

Version 2: There are life forms on other planets, but they may be no more sophisticated than bacteria and other single-celled organisms here on Earth.

This response highlights the fact that a proposal that looks quite definite might actually be quite vague. The response offers two wildly different versions of the basic claim that there is life on other planets. According to Version 1, that "life" includes intelligent life forms capable of advanced technology. According to Version 2, that "life" might be no more complex than some of the simplest organisms on Earth.

Exercise Set 8.4: Detailing and meeting objections

Model Response to Exercise 1

Monkeys, however, are relatively intelligent, social animals. They can feel fear, loneliness, and pain. Sending a monkey to Mars, it might be objected, would be like locking a monkey in a metal shipping container with several years' worth of food and letting it starve to death when the food runs out. A person who did that to a monkey on Earth would be locked up for animal cruelty. Thus, we can see why someone might conclude that sending a monkey to Mars is also animal cruelty, and therefore that the Russians shouldn't do it.

While it's true that a Mars-bound monkey would suffer fear and loneliness, the difference between sending a monkey to Mars and locking one in a shipping container is that the Mars mission has a greater purpose: the advancement of an important scientific goal—namely, landing humans on Mars. This greater purpose, in my view, justifies imposing a significant degree of suffering on an animal. Thus, it's okay for the Russians to send a monkey to Mars.

This response dives right into the objection, developing it into a complete argument. Specifically, it uses an argument by analogy to support the claim that the Russians shouldn't send a monkey to Mars.

After developing the objection, the response meets the objection by explaining why that argument by analogy fails. Sending a monkey to Mars is not relevantly similar to locking a monkey in a shipping container because the former serves a greater purpose whereas the latter does not. Thus, the response tries to show that while the objection makes a valid point about the effects of the mission on the monkey, this point doesn't undermine the original argument. Whether you think the response is successful will depend in part on whether you think that the "greater purpose" of a mission to Mars really justifies imposing that kind of suffering on a monkey.

Model Response to Exercise 3

Critics of euthanasia object that legalizing euthanasia will actually make people more likely to abuse it. As long as euthanasia is illegal, it is easy to tell when doctors have done something wrong: If they prescribe a lethal medication for a patient, they have violated the law. Thus, doctors will be cautious about helping patients commit suicide because they do not want to serve jail time. If euthanasia were legal, according to these critics, it would be harder to tell when doctors have broken the law, and so more people would take the risk of abusing euthanasia.

This objection assumes that we cannot build safeguards into laws about euthanasia. As long as we require careful documentation that doctors have followed the necessary steps before assisting patients with euthanasia, it should be easy to tell when they abuse the right to help patients commit suicide. Thus, legalizing euthanasia would not increase doctors' ability or tendency to abuse it.

This response restates the main idea of the objection and then develops an entire argument to support that main idea. It then offers a rebuttal that is designed to show why the objection fails.

Notice the use of the phrase "according to these critics" in the last sentence of the first paragraph. That phrase helps remind the reader that we're still talking about an objection, not about the author's own views.

Model Response to Exercise 5

Some people will object that women's rights are irrelevant here. The far more important issue, they will say, is the welfare of the children who are born to unwed mothers. Many people believe that children need to grow up in a home with a stable, traditional, husband-and-wife family. Only this kind of environment, it is thought, provides children with the stability and the proper role models that they need to become successful, well-adjusted adults.

This view ignores the wide variety of families in modern society. Many people live together and have children without getting married. Many people divorce after having children, and their children split their time between their parents' homes. Others raise children by themselves, or with the help of friends and extended family. Children from homes like these turn out just fine—just as many children from "traditional" households develop behavioral or emotional problems.

This response repeatedly distances the author from the views of the objectors. This can be appropriate when you want to emphasize your disagreement with the objection's premises in addition to its conclusions. (Compare this with the model response to exercise 3, in which the author and the imaginary objector could probably agree on some of the premises of the objection.)

Notice that the response does nothing to back up the claim that children from non-traditional households "turn out just fine." In order to convince skeptics, this response would need to cite good sources to support that premise.

Model Response to Exercise 7

Some might object that what really matters in college is not where you go, but what you do while you're there. There are plenty of very successful people who did not go to elite colleges. What makes them successful is that they work hard, make smart choices about the kinds of classes they take and the extracurricular activities that they are involved in, and pursue opportunities, such as internships, that advance their careers.

This does not undermine the basic point, however, that elite colleges provide their students with important benefits compared with other schools. Hard work and smart choices are important, but they will bring greater rewards if they are combined with the greater support, better resources, and better opportunities offered by elite colleges. Thus, the objection simply misses the point of the argument.

In detailing the objection, this response begins by rephrasing the main point of the objection—namely, that "what you do" matters more than "where you go." It then offers some reasons to think that what you do matters more than where you go. For instance, it notes that there are many successful people who did not go to elite colleges. That is, it provides premises to support the conclusion that where you go to college is not as important as what you do while you're there.

In responding to that objection, the response explains why the objection does not undermine the main argument. The conclusion of the main argument is that going to an elite college brings substantial benefits over going elsewhere. The objection, therefore, is somewhat beside the point. The main argument isn't claiming that you can't be successful elsewhere; it's only claiming that, other things being equal, going to an elite school brings greater benefits than going elsewhere.

Model Response to Exercise 9

Many parents will object that they are merely "protecting their investment." Many parents pay enormous sums of money to send their children to college. They do this because they expect that attending college will benefit their children. Some students might not reap those benefits on their own, though, because they have a hard time adjusting to college. In the worst case scenario, difficulties adjusting to college could lead to bad outcomes, such as failing out of school. Parents who stay in constant contact with their children are just trying to avoid such outcomes. This is a reasonable strategy for many parents, even if it limits their children's chances to become more independent. It is like choosing to put money in a savings account rather than investing in risky stocks: the returns might be lower, but so is the risk of a very bad outcome.

For parents who have good reason to think that their child will have serious difficulty adjusting to college, this is a reasonable concern. However, most freshmen do adjust to college life without constant parental supervision. Furthermore, there is surely a middle ground between the kind of constant supervision that inhibits independence and the totally "hands-off" approach that leaves students at risk of failure. Thus, the need to protect one's investment does not justify constant supervision of most freshmen.

In detailing the objection, the response begins by restating the main point of the objection—namely, that parents are protecting their investment. It then explains what the objection means and then gives strong reasons to think that this is a reasonable thing to do. (Notice the investment-related argument by analogy that's used to support the objection.)

In responding to the objection, the response takes a nuanced approach. It acknowledges the legitimate points made in the objection, but it notes that these points only apply to some freshmen and that they do not entirely justify the need for constant parental supervision even of those freshmen. The main conclusion of the original remains plausible: Parents need to let college freshmen manage their own lives.

Especially when presented with a powerful objection, this kind of nuanced response is often appropriate. Do not pretend that there are no good reasons on the other side of a debate. You can acknowledge those reasons while still defending your own position.

MODEL RESPONSES FOR CHAPTER IX: ORAL ARGUMENTS

Exercise Set 9.1: Reaching out to your audience

Model Response to Exercise 1

We all know that we have a lot of choices in how we eat. Do we pick up burgers at the drive-thru or cook our own food at home? Should we eat beef? What about chicken? Fish? Farmed fish or wild fish? The list goes on. Let's suppose for the moment that I'm trying to decide whether to eat beef or go completely vegetarian, and I want to make whatever decision will cause the least animal suffering. How many of you think that, if I want to minimize animal suffering, I should eat beef? How many think I should go completely vegetarian? Well, it turns out the answer is: eat beef. Here's why.

This response starts by eliciting an experience that everyone in the audience has: deciding what to eat. And then it invites the audience members to engage with the presentation by asking them to answer a question, presumably using a show of hands. Finally, it grabs their attention by revealing that the correct answer to that question is not the one that most of them probably expected.

Model Response to Exercise 3

Think about all of the photos, texts, and other stuff on your cell phone right now. Is there anything on there that you wouldn't want most people to see? If so, you're probably glad that Apple and Google have made it harder for hackers to break into your cell phone. But here's something you might not have thought about: Apple and Google have now made it so hard to break into a phone that even the police can't do it—not even if they need the information on that phone to prosecute dangerous criminals. That's a problem, and Apple and Google should fix it.

Like the response to exercise 9.1, this response opens with a question for the audience. Unlike exercise 9.1, however, it's probably best to let the audience members keep their answers to themselves in this case. This response also contains a little "plot twist." The first few sentences make it seem like the speaker supports stronger encryption, but then pivots to introduce an argument against stronger encryption. As long as you're crystal clear about what position you're actually taking, this can be an effective device for grabbing listeners' attention and winning some sympathy from people who might otherwise resist your final conclusion.

Model Response to Exercise 5

Imagine two boxes: Box A and Box B. I offer to sell you one of these boxes—your choice. I won't tell you what's in them, but I will tell you this: Both boxes cost $200,000. Box A contains something that you can resell for a million dollars. Box B contains something that you probably can't resell at all. Which one do you want to buy? Of course, you're going to buy Box A, right? Why wouldn't you?

Well, what if I then told you that Box B contained the love of your life? Wouldn't you remember that maybe money is not the measure of all worth?

Now imagine that the boxes represent different college educations. Box A is a degree in accounting. Box B is a degree in the humanities. Sure, Box A is a more lucrative investment, but I'm going to try to convince you that Box B might actually be more worth buying. The question really is: Is a degree in the humanities more like a bad investment or the love of your life?

This response aims to engage the audience by asking them to make a decision about an imaginary situation. Specifically, it creates an abstract situation that parallels the topic of the presentation without revealing exactly what that topic is.

Once the topic is revealed, this opening sets a challenge for the presenter—to convince the audience that the presenter's main point is correct, despite an obvious reason to think it's not. This is often an effective strategy when you think your audience will initially be skeptical about your main point.

Of course, the people in your audience may have different views about your topic. Maybe some people in your audience currently think that a degree in the humanities is a waste of time, but others already agree that such a degree is worthwhile. An opening like this connects to both groups of people by challenging the first group of people and getting the second group of people on your side.

Model Response to Exercise 7

Think of all the words that would have gotten you in trouble if you had said them in your high school English class. Now, think about how many books you read in your high school English class that used one or more of those words over and over again. What are they? Maybe The Catcher in the Rye comes to mind, but that's pretty mild, really. The one that stands out most in my high school experience, at least, is Huckleberry Finn. Huck Finn is full of the "n-word"—over two hundred instances of it. At least, it was full of it until recently: A new edition has just come out that replaces the "n-word" with the word "slave." I'm going to argue today that this is a mistake. Teachers should stick to the original text, "n-word" and all.

Like the response to exercise 3 in this set, this response asks the audience to recall something from their own experience. It also asks audience members to report about their experience by asking them which books contain "inappropriate language." (Depending on the sensitivities of your classroom, you might even ask students to call out some of the words that would have gotten them in trouble in high school. This kind of "ice breaker" activity can be helpful when your audience is bored, tired, or otherwise apathetic.) After asking audience members to report on their experiences, the response establishes a connection between the presenter and the audience by having the presenter share his or her personal experience about reading The Catcher in the Rye *and* Huckleberry Finn *in high school. Finally, it transitions to the main topic of the presentation and states the main conclusion of the presentation quite bluntly. (See Rule 42: It helps to give your audience clear signposts telling them where you're going.)*

Model Response to Exercise 9

I don't know about you, but I'm pretty sure that if you put on the soundtrack to the Disney movie <u>The Little Mermaid</u>, I could sing along to the whole thing. That's because my sister loved <u>The Little Mermaid</u>. She watched it over and over again. And what did she see when she, as a little girl, watched <u>The Little Mermaid</u>? She saw a sexy cartoon mermaid who wore nothing but a seashell bra, who made ditzy mistakes like combing her hair with a fork, who needed to be rescued by brave Prince Eric (a male) and watched over by Sebastian the Crab (also male) and her father (also male). The only powerful female character in the movie is Ursula the Sea Witch, the hideous, evil villain. And if you think about <u>your</u> favorite childhood movies, I'll bet you'll find something similar: the female characters—especially the "good" ones—tend to be sexy, ditzy, and in need of male help. These movies, I submit, send bad messages about gender roles to our nation's children.

This response begins with a quirky fact about the presenter—one that, depending on the speaker's personality, might elicit a laugh from the audience. Revealing unusual or even slightly embarrassing things about oneself is an effective way to engage the audience's interest and get them to lower their guard.

The response continues with a brief story about the experiences of the presenter and someone he or she knows. This is followed by an invitation to compare the presenter's experience to one's own experience. Having engaged the audience's interest and made them think about some of their own experiences on the topic, the response reveals the main point of the presentation.

Exercise Set 9.3: Reframing arguments in a positive way

Model Responses to Exercise 1

Example of a strong response to this exercise

If you're trying to lose weight, I've got good news for you! Researchers have discovered a way to help your body metabolize sugars more effectively, which can help prevent obesity and diabetes. And it's simple: Stay away from diet soda. It turns out that the artificial sweeteners in those diet sodas change the kinds of bacteria that live in your intestine, which in turn makes it harder to metabolize sugars. Of course, eating a well-balanced diet and getting regular exercise are also essential, but for those of us who are trying to lose weight, it's always helpful to find one more trick for trimming fat.

Notice that this response contains almost exactly the same information, but with a completely different "spin." Instead of putting a negative spin on the fact that diet sodas make it harder to lose weight, this response emphasizes the positive side of that fact: Staying away from diet sodas might make it easier to lose weight. (Be careful here! It's tempting to say that giving up diet soda will help you lose weight, but strictly speaking, the information you're given in this exercise doesn't actually say that your gut bacteria go back to "normal" when you give up diet soda. You'd need to do more research before coming to that conclusion.)

Example of a weak response to this exercise

If you're overweight and drinking diet sodas to try to lose a few pounds, I've got bad news for you. It turns out that the artificial sweeteners in those sodas make it harder for your body to metabolize real sugars, which in turn makes it harder to lose weight. Ultimately, though, I think that's a good thing. Once people know that you can't shed extra weight by switching to diet soda, they'll probably try harder to avoid gaining weight in the first place! So sorry if you're already overweight, but at least this research might help other people.

In some sense, the main message of this response isn't that different from the message of the strong response, but it's framed in a way that will be discouraging—and maybe even insulting—to audience members who are overweight. When thinking about whether your message is "positive," think about how different kinds of audience members are likely to feel when they hear it.

Model Responses to Exercise 3

Example of a strong response to this exercise

It used to be that museums were willing to accept archaeological artifacts that had been stolen from ancient sites or smuggled out of their home countries. Most museums have since thought better of these illicit methods of acquiring artifacts. Since no one else is funding new excavations, however, it is difficult for museums to acquire new artifacts. By funding excavations themselves, archaeological museums can not only acquire new artifacts but also further their missions of increasing the world's knowledge about ancient sites.

Whereas the original passage focused on a problem, this response focuses on the solution to the problem. It also focuses on the positive changes that have led to the problem—namely, the fact that museums are no longer willing to accept stolen or smuggled artifacts.

Example of a weak response to this exercise

Museums that display archaeological artifacts have gotten over their nasty habit of buying stolen artifacts. It's important that museums continue to expand their collections. In order to make this a reality, though, everyone needs to pitch in to finance excavations. We can do it!

This response differs from the strong response mainly in that it ignores the concrete proposals given in the strong response and focuses only on the vague, feel-good idea that if everyone "pitches in," museums can expand their collections through legitimate means. Offering something positive requires more than being optimistic. It requires offering a realistic plan or proposal for solving a problem.

Model Responses to Exercise 5

Example of a strong response to this exercise

Everyone wants good posture. The good news is that there are a few simple things that people can do to get good posture. For instance, sleeping in a proper position, such as on your back; adjusting the lighting and seating at your desk; getting eyeglasses, if you need them, so that you still see the computer screen while sitting properly; and paying attention to good posture at the gym can all lead to improvements in your posture. In fact, you can improve your posture right now by sitting up straight through the next presentation!

The original passage focused on the things that people were doing wrong. This response turns those things around and uses them as examples of simple changes that people can make to improve their posture.

As a general rule, if you want to get people to do something, it's more effective to tell them about other people who are *doing it than to complain about the other people who* aren't *doing it.*

Example of a weak response to this exercise

Having good posture is easy! A few simple changes to your sleeping position and your working or studying setup should have you standing up straight in no time. There's no excuse for your slouching now!

Besides lacking the detail of the stronger response, this response goes overboard with the positivity. Nothing in the original passage suggests that developing good posture happens overnight. When you promise that something is easy when it isn't, you're setting people up for disappointment. Don't be afraid to tell your audience that their goals are hard to achieve. Just be sure to offer them a path that will lead them toward those goals, rather than dwelling solely on the obstacles in their way.

Model Responses to Exercise 7

Example of a strong response to this exercise

Hispanic students are now enrolling in college at a higher rate than blacks or non-Hispanic whites. Many are still struggling to graduate, however, because only half are prepared for college-level English courses and only one in three for college-level math. We can hope that new programs aimed at improving Hispanic students' academic performance can boost those numbers, ensuring that the college graduation rate catches up with the enrollment rate.

The statistics presented in the original passage are discouraging. Putting a bright face on them is challenging. One way to do this is focus on the bright spots, such as the high college enrollment rate and the introduction of new programs to boost academic performance. Another, more subtle way is to reframe the statistics in terms of students who are prepared for college-level work, rather than those who aren't. Since these changes only go so far in putting a positive spin on things, this response avoids unwarranted optimism by concluding only that "we can hope" that the new programs will improve graduation rates.

Example of a weak response to this exercise

Some people think that Hispanic high school graduates aren't prepared for college. Sure, maybe many such students don't graduate, but at least they're enrolling in college at a higher rate than other groups. And half of them show up ready to excel in college-level English courses. That sounds pretty good to me—especially when you compare it to where we used to be.

Like the stronger response, this response focuses on the students who are doing well by noting that about half of Hispanic students are prepared for college-level English courses. (Be careful not to exaggerate the good news, though! Being told that half of Hispanic students are unprepared isn't enough to infer that the other half are prepared to "excel" in college-level English courses!) Stating that high enrollment numbers "sound pretty good" shows a positive attitude, but it also shows a certain refusal to face the facts, like an ostrich sticking its head in the sand to avoid bad news. If half or more students are unprepared for college-level work, that is a bad thing. Instead of putting on a happy face and pretending that this is an acceptable situation, it's better to admit that there is a problem and explain why you think it's solvable. Some actual data about "where we used to be" would also be helpful.

Model Responses to Exercise 9

Example of a strong response to this exercise

You have the power to save lives. Through donations to effective charities like the Against Malaria Foundation, you can provide anti-mosquito bed nets to families who otherwise couldn't afford them. These nets literally save the lives of children who would otherwise die of malaria. For every $7,500 in donations, the Against Malaria Foundation can provide enough bed nets to save at least two or three children. That's the same amount that it takes to fund the average "wish" granted by the Make-a-Wish Foundation, but instead of just brightening someone's day, you're saving someone's life. That's not to say that the heartwarming work of the Make-a-Wish Foundation isn't valuable. Rather, it's to say that you have the opportunity and the power to do even more good if you donate to organizations that put your money to the best use possible—and that's something you should really feel good about.

In some ways, the original passage already offers something positive— namely, a way to save kids' lives. But it does so in a fairly antagonistic way. The original passage focuses on the badness of "wasting" money making sick kids feel good. Telling your audience that they're bad people for wanting to support Batkid is not a very effective way of winning their support. This response focuses instead on the goodness of saving lives by donating to the Against Malaria Foundation. It's far less disparaging of the Make-a-Wish Foundation, focusing not on the alleged wastefulness of donating money to them, but on the additional good to be done by donating elsewhere.

Example of a weak response to this exercise

Donating $7,500 to the Make-a-Wish Foundation can help make a sick child's dream come true. Seeing those dreams come true can be a truly heartwarming experience, as when 11,000 people turned out to help a sick five-year-old play "Batkid" for a day. But you can do even more good by donating that same money to other charities—charities that save lives, rather than just brightening someone's day. Sure, brightening a kid's day makes you feel good, but shouldn't saving a kid's life make you feel even better?

While it offers more or less the same message as the strong response, this response weakens its case in three ways. First, it dwells too much on the Batkid example, which tugs at listeners' heartstrings and makes them less willing to see the alternative proposal in a positive light. Second, it fails to provide specifics about the proposed positive alternative. Which charities will save children's lives? How will they do it? Finally, in saying that saving lives should make you feel better about yourself than brightening someone's day, the response risks alienating listeners who, like most people, get more joy out of the Batkid story than out of impersonal statistics about the number of anonymous children who didn't die of malaria.

Exercise Set 9.4: Ending in style

Model Response to Exercise 1

Here's the bottom line: If you care about animal suffering, the question about what to eat isn't as simple as it seems. There's no way to feed ourselves without causing some amount of animal suffering. But as surprising as it may be, certain kinds of animal husbandry, such as range-fed cattle, cause less animal suffering than growing crops. So if you really want to save animals' lives, put down that tofu and pick up a hamburger!

This response reiterates the central argument and ends with a quip that will help the audience remember the main "take-away" from the presentation.

Model Response to Exercise 3

Now that you've heard my argument, think again about that stuff on your cell phone that you don't want other people to see. Maybe it's embarrassing. Maybe it would get you in a bit of trouble with your parents or the dean. But what's more important? Protecting your embarrassing photos? Or protecting people from dangerous criminals? Because as I've argued, the new, stronger encryption reduces law enforcement's ability to fight crime. Apple and Google ought to undo what they've done.

By using the phrase "Now that you've heard my argument," this response explicitly signals that the presentation is coming to an end. It then harkens back to the opening paragraph of the presentation. (Go back to the model responses to exercise 9.1 and see!) This is often an elegant way to wrap things up, especially if you can use your opening example or anecdote to re-capitulate your main argument, as this response does. And as with the model response to exercise 1 in this exercise set, this response closes with an explicit statement of what the speaker wants the audience members to take away from the presentation.

Model Response to Exercise 5

Many of you probably appreciate other, more varied reasons for taking humanities classes, but the three reasons that I've presented today should provide a compelling case even if you don't yet value the humanities for their own sake. Thus, even if you did come to college looking for a major that will "pay off" in some literal, financial sense, it would be a mistake to write off the humanities. They play a vital role in a well-rounded education—as illustrated, for instance, by this very course and, I hope, by this very presentation!

This response articulates the purpose of giving this presentation and reminds the audience why the presentation's topic is relevant to their lives.

Model Response to Exercise 7

I'm sure that the editor of this latest edition of Huckleberry Finn has good intentions. But, as I've argued, his alteration of the text removes an integral part of Twain's text and deprives instructors of a valuable educational opportunity. The text deserves to stay as it is, "n-word" and all.

This response uses the phrase "as I've argued" to signal that the presentation is coming to a close. It concludes with a pithy restatement of the main point of the argument.

Model Response to Exercise 9

In summary, then, the study that I've been discussing today finds three main complaints about films aimed at families with young children: first, there aren't enough female characters; second, the female characters that do appear in the films are scantily clad and sexy; and third, the female characters rarely do anything heroic or especially respectable. So the next time you're wondering where kids get their ideas of gender roles, look no further than the latest "kid-friendly" blockbuster.

This response uses very explicit signposting—"In summary," "first," "second," "third," etc.—to show that the speaker is summarizing the argument. It then relates the argument back to the audience's personal experiences by reminding them of the real-world implications of the argument's topic.

Exercise Set 9.5: Evaluating oral presentations

See the companion Web site for this book for model responses to Exercise Set 9.5.

MODEL RESPONSES FOR APPENDIX I: SOME COMMON FALLACIES

Exercise Set 10.1: Identifying fallacies (part 1)

Model Response to Exercise 1

Begging the question. The conclusion is that the death penalty is wrong. One of the key premises is that the death penalty is murder. But murder is just wrongful killing. (For instance, killing in self-defense isn't murder because it's not morally wrong.) So, saying that the death penalty is murder is just saying that the death penalty is wrongful killing—that is, the death penalty is morally wrong.

Since begging the question (also known as circular reasoning) involves assuming the conclusion in order to justify one of the premises, this response begins by identifying the conclusion. It then explains how the one premise in this argument assumes the truth of that conclusion. In this case, you wouldn't accept the premise of this argument—namely, that capital punishment is murder—unless you already accepted the conclusion that capital punishment is wrong.

Notice that this response does not simply restate the definition of the fallacy. That is, it does not just say that this argument commits the fallacy of begging the question because the premise assumes the truth of the conclusion (which would be more or less begging the question itself). Instead, this response cites specific details to show that the argument meets the definition of the fallacy.

Model Response to Exercise 3

No fallacy.

Medical students, it is said, develop a kind of hypochondria: they constantly suspect themselves and others of having the diseases that they are studying in medical school. When studying fallacies, it is easy to develop a similar enthusiasm for spotting fallacies. Don't be too quick to attribute a fallacy to an argument. Forcing yourself to explain in detail *how the argument fits the definition of a particular fallacy is a good way to avoid the critical thinking student's equivalent of "medical student syndrome."*

Model Response to Exercise 5

Equivocation. The argument uses the word "gods" in two different ways, and the argument doesn't work if we substitute appropriate synonyms for each use of "gods." In defining atheism, the argument uses the word "gods" to mean "deities" in the strict religious sense. In claiming that atheists have gods, however, the arguments uses "gods" to mean something like "things that are esteemed very highly." If we replace "gods" with these synonyms, the argument goes like this: "Atheists don't believe in deities. But they do value certain things very highly. Therefore, atheists do believe in deities, which makes atheists hypocrites." The second premise in that argument is irrelevant to the conclusion. Thus, the argument fails.

In order for an argument to commit the fallacy of equivocation, two things must be true. First, the argument must use a word or expression in more than one way. Second, it must be the case that substituting appropriate synonyms for each use of the word ruins the argument—either by making some of the premises false or by making them irrelevant to each other or the conclusion.

This response not only identifies the word that is used in more than one way (namely, "gods"), but it explains each meaning in detail and why the argument would be faulty if we substituted appropriate synonyms for each use of "gods."

Model Response to Exercise 7

Equivocation. The argument uses the word "selfish" in two different ways. The third sentence effectively defines "selfish" as "acting to satisfy one's own desires." The next sentence claims that "good people are not selfish," where "selfish" probably means something like "concerned only with one's own interests." Since acting to satisfy one's own desires is not necessarily being concerned only with one's own interest—some people desire to help others, including family members, friends, and strangers—this amounts to using "selfish" in two different ways. The claim that people always act on their own desires is significantly different from the claim that good people are concerned with more than their own interests.

The argument in exercise 7 addresses a view that philosophers call "psychological egoism," which is the view that everyone always acts selfishly. As philosophers from Bishop Butler to Joel Feinberg have long argued, however, this view is either plainly false, trivial, or just confused.

This instance of equivocation is far more subtle than the one in exercise 5. You may have to think about it for a while to see that the two uses of "selfish" really are different. (It might help to think about some specific cases in which one person's acting on his or her own desires doesn't count as being concerned only with his or her own interests.) Most of the instances of equivocation that you encounter in "real life" will probably be more like this instance than the more obvious one in exercise 5.

Model Response to Exercise 9

<u>Ad hominem</u>. This argument criticizes the liberal intellectuals' argument by attacking them personally—calling them "perverts" who are only interested in "flirt[ing] with girls" and ogling half-naked women. The argument says nothing about the merits of the claim that relaxing Saudi Arabia's strict religious laws would improve the country's national security, and thus it doesn't provide us any reason to doubt that claim.

This argument identifies the specific attacks made on the Saudi liberal intellectuals and explains why those personal attacks do not discredit the position that they are advocating.

Notice that what counts as a personal attack varies from context to context. Some audiences would see nothing perverted or objectionable in a desire to flirt with girls or to see them in bathing suits. Others, ranging from conservative Saudis to liberal Americans, would disapprove of the liberal intellectuals' alleged sexual objectification of women. The relevant question here is whether the author of the argument is trying to get the argument's audience to reject a position on the basis of someone's (allegedly negative) personal qualities.

Remember that there is one kind of case where someone's personal qualities might be relevant to the strength of their argument. When an argument rests on the speaker's authority, it is relevant to bring up personal flaws that undermine that authority (e.g., by exposing the speaker as biased or uninformed with respect to the topic of the argument).

Exercise Set 10.2: Reinterpreting and revising fallacious arguments (part 1)

Model Response to Exercise 1

This argument begs the question, since the premise is just another way of restating the conclusion. Improving the argument would require replacing the premise with a neutral definition of the death penalty, such as "the execution of a person convicted of a capital crime," and then showing that the death penalty is unjustified killing—i.e., murder.

Someone making an argument like this most likely does not see the premise as another way of stating the conclusion. If pressed to explain the difference between the two, the author of the argument might be able to come up with reasons that the execution of a person convicted of a capital crime amounts to unjustified killing. If he or she can produce such reasons, then this fallacious argument will be transformed into a non-fallacious argument.

This response doesn't specify exactly what premises we would use to show that the death penalty is unjustified killing. Instead, it simply explains what we would have to do to "fix" the fallacy.

Model Response to Exercise 3

No fallacy.

Since the argument in exercise 3 contains no fallacy, there is no need to reinterpret or change it in order to avoid a fallacy.

Model Response to Exercise 5

This argument commits the fallacy of equivocation. Taken as an argument about the falsity of atheism, there is no clear way to avoid this fallacy without writing a completely different argument.

This response ultimately concludes that the argument is beyond saving— that is, that no argument similar to this one could support a conclusion similar to the conclusion of this argument. Instead of rejecting the argument simply because it commits a fallacy, however, this response arrives at this pessimistic conclusion only after considering what it would take to make this argument respectable.

    In general, it is very difficult to reinterpret or revise a fallacy of equivocation. Often, the best thing to do, as suggested in this response, is simply to look for a different argument for the same conclusion.

Model Response to Exercise 7

This argument commits the fallacy of equivocation. By changing some of the argument slightly, we might be able to salvage it. In particular, we could add the premise that many people's desires are primarily concerned with their own interests, change the second-to-last sentence to say, "Good people are not primarily selfish," and change the conclusion to say, "Many people are not good people." This argument may or may not work, but at least it avoids an outright fallacy.

Here is a rare case in which you might be able to save an argument that commits the fallacy of equivocation—but notice that "saving" the argument, in this case, means tweaking the conclusion. Like many fallacious arguments, this argument takes a reasonable claim—that many people act selfishly—and blows it out of proportion. In order to avoid fallacies, we may need to tone down the conclusion and rework the argument a bit.

Notice that the reinterpreted argument is no longer an argument for psychological egoism (i.e., the view that everyone always acts selfishly). It's an argument for the much weaker—and arguably false!—claim that most people are usually selfish. This is an importantly different claim.

Model Response to Exercise 9

This argument is expressed as an <u>ad hominem</u> attack on the liberal intellectuals who are criticizing Saudi Arabia's strict religious laws. It is unlikely that we could reconstrue the accusations against them as a legitimate reason for doubting their claims that relaxing those laws is necessary for Saudi Arabia's national security. But by emphasizing that the liberal intellectuals want Saudi Arabia to be a very different place than it is now, the <u>ad hominem</u> attack at least suggests one important reason that more conservative Saudis might be skeptical of their argument: Perhaps the liberal intellectuals have a very different view of what is genuinely in the country's national interests.

This response briefly restates which fallacy the argument commits and then admits that the argument is probably beyond repair. It also explains why the argument is beyond repair. Still, it tries hard to find something in the fallacious argument that might suggest a more reasonable line of argument.

Exercise Set 10.3: Identifying fallacies (part 2)

Model Response to Exercise 1

Overgeneralizing. An argument commits the fallacy of overgeneralization when it makes a sweeping generalization about a large group based on one or a few examples. This argument takes a few examples of cyclists ignoring a particular law (namely, that they have to stop at stop signs) and generalizes that all cyclists think they are above all traffic laws. It doesn't even say how many cyclists did stop at stop signs. Nor does it take account of the fact that one person taking one walk through part of a city is very unlikely to see a representative sample of all cyclists or intersections.

This response does three things. First, it correctly identifies the most important problem as one of overgeneralization. Second, it restates the definition of overgeneralization. Third, it explains clearly how this particular argument fits that definition, using references to very specific aspects of the argument.

Model Response to Exercise 3

Loaded language. An argument uses loaded language when it relies on emotionally charged language to get the reader to accept its conclusion. This argument uses phrases like "absurd," "jiggery-pokery," and "applesauce," which cast doubt on the Court's decision without actually offering reasons for thinking that Court decided wrongly.

The loaded language in this argument is not exactly inflammatory. (It's hard to get worked up about someone your argument "applesauce" or "jiggery-pokery.") But the language is designed to make the court's decision seem silly and foolish, without giving reasons for thinking so.

For the record, the dissenting opinion from which this argument comes really does contain the phrases "jiggery-pokery" and "pure applesauce," though it never calls the law "wretched" or accuses the court of "caving in."

Model Response to Exercise 5

Overlooking alternatives. This argument overlooks alternative explanations of Batman's mask and the fact that he is only seen with criminals. The most plausible explanation is that he wears a mask so that criminals can't target him in his daily life as Bruce Wayne, and that he's only seen with criminals because he only goes out as Batman when he's going to fight crime.

This response gives a quick explanation of how the argument commits the relevant fallacy and then explains it in more detail. Simply giving the "quick" explanation, though—that the argument overlooks alternative explanations of Batman's mask and his frequent appearance with criminals—would not be enough; such a response is the kind of answer that one could give just by knowing the definition of "overlooking alternatives." So, rather than stopping at that superficial answer, this response uses specific details of the argument to support the claim that the argument overlooks alternatives.

Model Response to Exercise 7

Straw man. A straw man fallacy involves misrepresenting someone's position or argument in order to make it look ridiculous or easy to refute. In this exchange, Bishop Wilberforce commits a straw man fallacy because Huxley is not claiming that his (Huxley's) grandparents were apes. Huxley is claiming only that the extremely distant ancestors of humans were apes.

This exchange allegedly comes from a famous debate in 1860 between Thomas Huxley, an important early proponent of Darwin's ideas about evolution, and Bishop Wilberforce, a critic of evolution.

Model Response to Exercise 9

Persuasive definition. First the argument in exercise 9 defines a politician as someone who says one thing and then does something else; then, based solely on that definition, it concludes that politicians can't be trusted.

Even if it were the case that most politicians said one thing and did another, that would not make it part of the definition of "politician." After all, if we replaced all public office holders with certifiably honest people, we would not be making a linguistic mistake when we referred to them as politicians. This argument tries to smuggle in the premise that politicians say one thing and do another by presenting it as a definition.

As with exercise 3, you might be tempted to say that this argument overgeneralizes. But notice that the argument doesn't even cite a single example of a politician who says one thing and does another. So technically it's not generalizing from any examples.

Exercise Set 10.4: Reinterpreting and revising fallacious arguments (part 2)

Model Response to Exercise 1

This argument overgeneralizes from three examples that the author encountered while on a walk. The first step in improving the argument would be to say whether the author encountered any counterexamples on that walk (i.e., cyclists who did stop at stop signs). If not, the argument would be a little stronger. The next step would be to try to show that the cyclists and intersections that the author saw were really representative, rather than, say, particularly reckless teenagers or notoriously confusing intersections. But to really improve the argument, we'd have to consider more examples of cyclists breaking the law. Depending on how many examples and counterexamples we can find, we might want to revise the conclusion to say only that <u>some</u> cyclists think they are above <u>some</u> traffic laws.

This response cites the specific feature of the argument that makes it tempting to dismiss it as overgeneralizing. It then suggests steps that the argument's author could take to strengthen the argument, noting that the author might need to revise the argument's conclusion.

Model Response to Exercise 3

It would be relatively easy to eliminate the loaded language in this argument, but that would leave it as the bare assertion that the court made a simple mistake in interpretation. Since it's not all that plausible that five Supreme Court justices made such a simple mistake, the argument should go into more detail about why the majority's interpretive approach was wrong.

Sometimes it's hard to tell exactly what an author is getting at when they resort to loaded language. They might have good reasons to feel strongly about something, but until they tell you those reasons, there's not much you can say about how to improve their argument.

Model Response to Exercise 5

This argument overlooks the most likely explanation of Batman's behavior, which is that he is a vigilante who needs to protect his identity from criminals. It is unlikely that this argument could be saved, since we know that Batman is not a criminal.

This response acknowledges that the argument's conclusion is almost surely false and that it is therefore very difficult to "fix" the argument.

Model Response to Exercise 7

This argument seems to commit a straw man fallacy, since Huxley is clearly not claiming that his grandparents were apes. While Wilberforce's argument is unlikely to undermine the theory of evolution, it at least raises a legitimate and interesting question: When a new species evolves from an existing species, at what point in the family tree do we say, "This individual is a member of a new species"? Wilberforce could therefore improve his argument by changing its (implied) conclusion. Instead of implying that the theory of evolution is false, he could claim that this is an interesting challenge for the theory.

Some apparent straw man fallacies, like the one in the sample exercise for this exercise set, are poorly expressed versions of plausible arguments. Others, like the one in this exercise, conceal rather weak arguments. One way to improve a weak argument is to change its conclusion to something less ambitious. This response, for instance, suggests that Wilberforce should not argue that the theory of evolution is false, but only that it faces a specific challenge. This is a less ambitious claim in the sense that it is easier to establish that a theory faces a particular challenge than it is to establish that the theory is false.

Model Response to Exercise 9

This argument uses a persuasive definition. We could reinterpret the definition as a rhetorically edgy way to claim that, as a matter of fact, most politicians do not keep their word. To really make the argument work, then, we would need to add further premises establishing the truth of that generalization.

This response suggests a way to reinterpret the argument to avoid the fallacy. Since the resulting argument would still not be very strong, the response also suggests steps that could be taken to strengthen the argument.

Exercise Set 10.5: Two deductive fallacies

Model Response to Exercise 1

<u>Modus ponens.</u>

Remember not to be thrown off by complicated antecedents or consequents—especially when they contain the word not. *The consequent of the if–then sentence in this exercise is "Bob should not be punished, but the person who accepted the bribe should be punished." You can symbolize that whole sentence as* **q**, *so that the argument symbolizes straightforwardly as If* **p**, *then* **q**. **p**. *Therefore,* **q**. *(See the "Tips for success" section of Exercise Set 6.2 for more advice on symbolizing arguments that contain the word "not" inside an "if–then" sentence.)*

Model Response to Exercise 3

Denying the antecedent. Suppose that, despite being good enough to perform on Broadway, Mr. Shue loves teaching but hates late nights and big cities. In that case, he may well keep his job as a teacher, despite being good enough for Broadway.

Don't be thrown off by the fact that the antecedent of the if–then sentence in this argument is expressed in a negative way—that is, that it says that Mr. Shue is not good enough to perform on Broadway. If we symbolize that statement as **p**, *then the second sentence of this exercise, which says that Mr. Shue is good enough to perform on Broadway, would be not-***p***.*

Note that this model response doesn't simply say, "Suppose that Mr. Shue is good enough to perform on Broadway but will keep his job as a teacher." That is, it doesn't simply ask us to suppose that the antecedent is false but the consequent true. It describes a specific scenario that enables us to understand how that could be the case.

Model Response to Exercise 5

Affirming the consequent. Imagine that the Earth is the center of the universe, with the sun, moon, planets, and stars revolving around it. But suppose that the planets also move in "epicycles," as ancient and medieval European astronomers believed. That means that while they're orbiting the Earth, they're also following smaller circular paths centered on their orbits around Earth. (Picture people in the Mad Tea Party ride at Disney World, each spinning around the center of their own tea cup while the tea cup spins around the center of the ride.) In that case, each planet will sometimes appear to move backward in the sky, but the sun will circle the Earth.

The scenario described in this response, where the Earth is at the center of the universe and the planets moving in epicycles is essentially the old, Ptolemaic theory of the universe (credited to the ancient Roman/Egyptian astronomer Ptolemy). That theory used the idea of epicycles to explain the fact that the planets do sometimes appear to move backward in the sky. You could also have dreamed up even more creative scenarios to show how the planets seem to move backward even if the Earth did not orbit the sun.

This question illustrates an interesting feature of the scientific method. Scientists—like Copernicus, on whose work this exercise is based—regularly think about the implications of their ideas. We can think about these implications in terms of "if–then" relationships, such as the claim that if the Earth circles the sun, then the planets will sometimes appear to move backward in the sky. Scientists then compare those implications with what they observe about the world. When they observe what their hypothesis predicted—e.g., the planets sometimes appearing to move backward—they consider the hypothesis "confirmed." But as you can see from this example, confirmation doesn't provide a deductively valid proof of the hypothesis. To think that it did would be to commit the fallacy of affirming the consequent. All that confirmation can do is provide evidence for that hypothesis. Perhaps the more interesting case is when observations don't match what the scientists expected. Then they have to determine whether the "if–then" sentence in their argument was false or if they should use modus tollens *to conclude that their hypothesis is incorrect.*

Model Response to Exercise 7

Modus tollens.

If you have seen The Princess Bride, *you'll know that the Man in Black is immune to the poison that he drinks during his battle of wits with Vizzini. So, even though he does not die, his drink was poisoned. Thus, the argument in this exercise leads us to a false conclusion. So how can it be valid? It's valid because the validity of an argument does not depend on whether the premises or conclusions* are *actually true. To say that an argument is valid is just to say that its conclusion would be true if the premises were all true.*

But in this case, the first premise—the "if–then" sentence—is false: The Man in Black will not die, even if his cup is poisoned. So the valid argument form modus tollens *is taking us from a false premise to a false conclusion.*

Model Response to Exercise 9

Denying the antecedent. Suppose that the girl is possessed but reacted violently to the ordinary water in order to make the speaker doubt that she is possessed.

It might have taken you a while to realize that in saying that he did not sprinkle holy water on the girl, the speaker was saying that the antecedent of his "if–then" sentence was false. After all, the antecedent is that the girl is possessed by a demon *and the speaker* sprinkled holy water on her. *But notice that if* **p** *is false, then so is* **p and q**.

    In the film The Exorcist, *Father Karras sprinkles ordinary tap water on the girl who is allegedly possessed. The girl reacts violently, which Father Karras thinks is evidence that she's not really possessed. But as you can see from this exercise, Father Karras has overlooked an important possibility.*

Exercise Set 10.6: Constructing fallacious arguments

Model Response to Exercise 1

"Mr. Ashworth, you have steadfastly maintained your innocence throughout this trial. And you've put on a good show. After all, your spending habits haven't changed since the bank robbery, which makes it easy for you to claim you weren't the robber. But what I want to know, Mr. Ashworth, is this: Since you haven't been spending it, did you stash the money in a safe place nearby, or is it already squirreled away in some offshore bank account?"

    This commits the "complex question" fallacy. The question assumes that Mr. Ashworth <u>did</u> steal six million dollars from the bank. Mr. Ashworth can't accept either answer without admitting to stealing the money.

This response uses some additional text to set up the context for the fallacious argument. Many fallacies depend on context in this way, so you should feel free to explain the context in your response—either indirectly, as this response does, or directly, by saying something like, "At a trial for a bank robbery, the prosecution asks the defendant, 'What did you do with the six million dollars that you stole from the bank?'"

This response also explains briefly how the argument commits the fallacy in question.

Model Response to Exercise 3

"The dean says that Chris should be expelled for selling drugs on campus. But other people sell drugs on campus all the time—sometimes even to the dean!—without getting in trouble. After all, caffeine is a drug, and we have a coffee shop on campus. Therefore, it's unfair for the dean to expel Chris."

This argument commits the fallacy of equivocation. It uses the word drug in two different ways. In the first premise, it means "illegal drugs," such as cocaine. In the rest of the argument, it means something like "substances that alter the user's state of mind when ingested." If we substitute these synonyms in for the word drugs, the premises about the dean allowing the coffee shop to sell caffeine become irrelevant and so the argument fails

This response explains why the argument falls apart when we distinguish the two different senses of drug. That's an important step in demonstrating that an argument's use of an ambiguous term really does amount to equivocation.

It's hard to come up with fallacies of equivocation that aren't glaringly obvious or even silly. You might need to resort to something silly for this exercise. That may not be ideal, but it at least shows that you understand what the fallacy is.

Model Response to Exercise 5

"I felt like I was getting a cold last week, so I drank lots of orange juice. This week I feel better. I guess the orange juice did the trick."

This fallacy commits the fallacy of post hoc ergo propter hoc. It assumes that the orange juice caused the speaker to feel better, without considering alternative explanations for the correlation. For instance, maybe the speaker had a very mild cold last week and was going to feel better this week regardless of what he or she did.

This response offers a very common instance of post hoc *reasoning: reasoning about what makes you sicker or healthier. Pay attention to your friends' and families' discussions of their health, and you'll probably spot*

some instances of post hoc *reasoning. But remember: there's no need to act superior when you think someone else has committed a fallacy. Instead, try asking them gently why they think there's a real causal connection between their health and whatever they ate, drank, or did.*

Model Response to Exercise 7

"My dad caught me smoking, and he said that I should quit because smoking is bad for you. What a hypocrite! That guy smokes two packs a day!"

This argument commits the <u>ad hominem</u> fallacy. Instead of responding directly to the dad's argument that the speaker should stop smoking because smoking is unhealthy, it attacks the speaker's dad for being a hypocrite. The speaker's dad's hypocrisy doesn't undermine the strength of his argument. Smoking <u>is</u> bad for you, and that <u>is</u> a good reason to quit, regardless of whether the speaker's dad smokes. Maybe the speaker's dad is desperately trying to stop himself and hopes at least to keep the speaker from getting hooked.

This response highlights another common kind of fallacious argument. Many people are tempted to accept or to use ad hominem *arguments that accuse someone of being a hypocrite. (In fact, it's so common that logicians have a special name for this version of the* ad hominem *fallacy:* tu quoque, *which is Latin for "You too.") As this response explains, however, the other person's hypocrisy doesn't undermine the strength of the argument.*

Remember, the problem with ad hominem *arguments isn't that the personal attack is false or unwarranted. The problem is that personal attacks don't undermine a good argument unless the argument relies on the expertise of the arguer. Being a hypocrite isn't a good thing—but just because someone is a hypocrite (if they really are) doesn't mean his or her arguments aren't good arguments.*

Model Response to Exercise 9

"Our product is perfectly safe. There is absolutely no good scientific evidence to show otherwise."

This argument commits the <u>ad ignorantiam</u> fallacy (appeal to ignorance). It argues that a product is "perfectly safe" by pointing out that there is no "good scientific evidence" to prove that it's not safe. That is, it claims that the conclusion is true just because no one has proven otherwise.

This response highlights the fact that the argument's only reason for believing the product to be safe is because it hasn't yet been conclusively proven harmful (to the arguer's satisfaction, anyway). Without some further premises, that's just an appeal to ignorance. (Of course, it would normally be just as fallacious to say, "That product is dangerous. There's been no research to prove otherwise!") If the argument had included a premise such as, "There have been many rigorous scientific tests of our product's safety," things would be different. After all, if there had been many rigorous tests of the product, and the tests all showed no evidence of harms, you could rewrite the argument as follows: "Our product is perfectly safe. It has been subjected to rigorous testing, and all of the tests have found the product to be safe." This is not appealing to ignorance; it is appealing to positive reasons to think that the product is safe. Similarly, you could establish a presumption that the product is dangerous by pointing out that the product is similar to others that were proven to be dangerous or otherwise providing a reason to demand research proving the product's safety.

MODEL RESPONSES FOR APPENDIX II: DEFINITIONS

Exercise Set 11.1: Making definitions more precise

Model Responses to Exercise 1

Example of a strong response to this exercise

This definition of "parade" would exclude a procession consisting entirely of floats, cars, tanks, etc., without any people marching. A better definition would be "a ceremonial procession through a public area consisting of people marching and/or vehicles."

This response points out a type of parade that is incorrectly excluded by the original definition. It then offers a revised definition that simply adds the excluded category. This is the simplest way to improve a definition: add a word or clause that includes or excludes the examples that were incorrectly excluded or included by the original definition.

Notice that the proposed definition is not as precise as it could be. For instance, it is unclear whether "vehicles" includes only motorized vehicles, like cars and trucks, or if it also includes things like bicycles. What about riding lawn mowers? Are they vehicles? It is also unclear exactly what counts as a "public area" and what counts as the relevant kind of procession. In some sense, Westminster Abbey in London is a public area, and Kate, Duchess of Cambridge, processed down the aisle with several other people when she married Prince William. Was her bridal procession a parade? As these examples illustrate, you may not always be able to make your definitions perfectly *clear, but that doesn't mean that you can't get close or that there's no point in trying.*

Here's another way in which the revised definition is imperfect: Unless you're willing to count horses as vehicles (which seems like a stretch), the revised definition would exclude a procession of people on horseback. That might not be a big problem for modern parades in major cities, but it would exclude many parades in other times and places. This goes to show that when you're coming up with a definition, you might need to think about how it would apply in other places or other periods of history.

Example of a weak response to this exercise

This definition of "parade" would exclude a parade consisting entirely of floats, cars, tanks, etc., without any people marching. A better definition would be "any group of vehicles or people moving in unison down a designated route."

This response correctly identifies a problem with the original definition: it excludes things that it shouldn't exclude. The definition proposed in this response, however, goes too far in the other direction. It includes things that it shouldn't include, such as students walking down a hallway to get to a classroom, people driving down the highway to get to work, contra dancers, and a football team running down the field after a kickoff.

Model Responses to Exercise 3

Example of a strong response to this exercise

This definition of "highly qualified elementary school teacher" would exclude a teacher who has been teaching for thirty years and is widely recognized by her principal, her colleagues, and her students and their parents as a good teacher but has not passed a state exam because she has never taken one. For the purposes of ensuring that teachers are good at their jobs, a better definition would be "someone who either has at least ten years' experience as an elementary school teacher or someone who has at least a bachelor's degree and has passed a rigorous state examination to demonstrate subject knowledge and teaching skills in reading, writing, mathematics, and other areas commonly included in elementary school curricula."

The original definition in exercise 3 is presumably an operational definition. It substitutes a precise but bureaucratic definition of "highly qualified elementary school teacher" for a more natural but less readily quantified definition like "an elementary school teacher who has a strong grasp of the subjects that he or she teaches, the methods for teaching them, and techniques of classroom management in an elementary school setting."

This response recognizes that the original, operational definition overlooks the possibility that people with adequate experience could be highly qualified teachers even if they have never taken a state examination. To remedy this, the response suggests a definition that offers two distinct ways of counting as "highly qualified"—having ten years' experience or getting a bachelor's degree and passing a state examination—and requires only that someone meet one of those criteria to count as "highly qualified."

An alternative response could have focused on examples that are incorrectly included by the definition, such as people who have a bachelor's degree and have passed the exam but who cannot even begin to manage a classroom full of kids.

Example of a weak response to this exercise

This definition wrongly includes someone who secretly hates children. You wouldn't want that person teaching in elementary school, even if he or she had a college degree and had passed the state exam. A better definition would be "someone with a college degree who has passed the state exam and enjoys working with children."

This response runs together two distinct issues. We are trying to define a specific term here—namely, "highly qualified elementary school teacher." This is not quite the same thing as trying to determine which people would be the best choice to teach elementary school. This response is getting at the fact that someone could be a highly qualified elementary school teacher and still not be a good choice to teach elementary school. Since being qualified for a job and being well suited for a job are not quite the same thing, however, we shouldn't try to define them in the same way.

Model Responses to Exercise 5

Example of a strong response to this exercise

This definition of "poison" incorrectly includes guns, which can kill people if used incorrectly, and medicines, which can kill people when used in the wrong dosage. A better definition would be "a non-medicinal chemical substance that can harm a person or animal if ingested."

This response emphasizes things that are incorrectly included by the definition—that is, something that does not obviously count as a poison but nonetheless fits the definition. The response offers two examples instead of one to highlight two distinct problems with the definition. The first problem is that the definition includes things like firearms, which can kill people but are not poisons. To fix this problem, the response changes the definition to include only chemical substances. The second problem is that lots of things that don't count as poisons, such as medicines, will kill a person if used in the wrong dosage. To fix this problem, the response changes the definition to include only non-medicinal substances. (But then, can't overdoses of medicines count as poisoning too? You might well call Poison Control to deal with such an event. How might you amend the definition to fix that problem?)

You might think that the revised definition in this response is too narrow. For instance, it excludes substances, such as alcohol, that could kill someone but are very rarely, if ever, used for that purpose. One way to defend the proposed definition is to argue that such substances might be poisonous if ingested in large quantities, but they are not poisons.

Example of a weak response to this exercise

This definition of "poison" incorrectly includes cars, which can kill people if used incorrectly, and water, which can kill people if they are exposed to too much of it (i.e., if they drown). A better definition would be "a substance that is toxic." Neither cars nor water are toxic, even if they can sometimes kill people.

Like the strong response to this exercise, this response identifies items that are incorrectly covered by the original definition. It then suggests a definition that correctly excludes those items, but only by introducing another equally problematic term: toxic. Since toxic is closely related in meaning to the word poison and is just about as hard to define, defining a poison as "a substance that is toxic" does not bring us much closer to understanding what poison is.

Model Responses to Exercise 7

Example of a strong response to this exercise

This definition of "a family farm" incorrectly includes farms that are owned by a family but managed by a giant corporation and worked exclusively by migrant laborers who have no connection to the family. A better definition would be "a farm that is owned and mostly worked by a single family."

This response emphasizes the owners of a farm are not always the ones who manage or work the farm. The proposed definition is closer to the legal definition of "a family farm" in the United States, which requires that the family that owns a farm manage and work on the farm.

Recognizing defects in a definition may require questioning some assumptions of the terms in the definition. While some people may have assumed that ownership of a farm and management of a farm went together, the flaw in this definition is that this is not always the case.

If you don't know a lot about the term being defined, it can be hard to come up with examples that reveal the flaws in the definition. One approach for identifying such examples is to consult a broad range of definitions—not just in dictionaries, but also in legislation, government documents (e.g., the tax code), newspaper articles, and so on—to see how those definitions differ. Ask yourself what examples would be covered by one definition but not another. That can get you started thinking about ways in which "family farms" might differ from one another.

Example of a weak response to this exercise

This definition of "a family farm" incorrectly includes farms that are owned by giant corporations that are owned by a single family. A better definition would be "a farm that is owned by a family that lives on the farm and does not own a giant corporation."

It is debatable whether the original definition of "a family farm" in this question really includes farms owned by giant, family-owned corporations. There are also far fewer farms owned by giant, family-owned corporations than there are farms that are owned by a family but operated by someone else. (Of course, in terms of physical size, corporation-owned farms might be huge.) Thus, the exceptions identified in the strong response are more important than the exceptions identified in this weak response.

Furthermore, the definition proposed in this response is not much better than the original definition. It includes two extra conditions: the family must live on the farm and they must not own a giant corporation. The first condition is not strong enough. A farm that is operated entirely with hired labor is not a family farm, even if the family lives on the farm. The second condition is too narrow because it focuses only on a very special problem with the original definition, leaving aside the more general problem about who actually operates the farm. You are better off looking for general criteria, rather than addressing problems one by one.

Model Responses to Exercise 9

Example of a strong response to this exercise

This definition of "terrorism" incorrectly includes civil disobedience that includes criminal actions. For instance, if a country made it a criminal act to participate in peaceful protests against the government, then this definition would count such protestors as terrorists. A better definition would be "violent or destructive acts, or threats to perform such acts, that are apparently intended to intimidate a civilian population or influence the policy or action of a government."

This response offers a concrete example to illustrate the more abstract problem that it identifies with the original definition. The response then revises the original definition to exclude the thing that it incorrectly included. Notice that the revised definition also anticipates and fixes an additional problem—namely, the inappropriate exclusion of threats of violence or destruction from the definition of terrorism. Someone who threatens to detonate a bomb in a busy area is arguably as much of a terrorist as someone who actually does so. If you see multiple problems with the original definition, you can use your revised definition to address more than one of them.

Example of a weak response to this exercise

This definition of "terrorism" incorrectly excludes terrorist actions that happen to be legal in the jurisdiction where they are performed. For instance, giant banks caused the 2008 financial crisis by ruthlessly exploiting consumers. They ruined people's lives in the process. But everything the bankers did was allegedly legal, so it doesn't count as terrorism. A better definition would be "an action that causes serious physical, material, or psychological harm to people and that is done in order to get what the actor wants without regard for the people that are harmed in the process."

There are two main problems with this response. First, this response is not trying to find a definition that fits our current notion of terrorism. It is essentially proposing a new, expanded, and rather loaded definition. It's one thing to argue that irresponsible financiers are as bad as terrorists. It's another to try to support that claim by appealing to an unorthodox definition of terrorism. (See Rule D3 in Appendix II, p. 266.)

Second, the definition that this response proposes is far too broad. While it's true that terrorism involves causing serious harm in order to get what one wants, this definition erases the distinctions between terrorism and many other kinds of wrongs. On this definition, a person who cheats on his or her spouse or spray-paints slogans on boxcars might count as a terrorist. Such a broad definition of terrorism is not nearly as useful as one that identifies a particular kind of wrong.

Exercise Set 11.2: Starting from clear cases

Model Response to Exercise 1

Patrick Stewart, who played Captain Picard on <u>Star Trek: The Next Generation</u>, is clearly bald. Brad Pitt is clearly not bald. The actor Kevin Spacey is borderline bald. A good definition of "bald" would be "so little hair growing between the forehead and the crown of the head that the scalp is clearly visible across that entire area when the head is not covered." This definition gives a reasonably simple test for baldness. It excludes people with receding hairlines and shaved heads but includes people, like Homer Simpson, who have just a little bit of hair on the top of their heads. It also includes people who cover their heads with a "comb-over."

This response mentions three examples that many people can likely picture in their heads, making it easy for someone to see—in their mind's eye, at least—what counts as "bald." The definition is quite precise, and the justification for the definition cites the ease with which it is applied and mentions the kinds of borderline cases that are included and excluded. (Consider an alternative definition that focused on, say, hairs per square inch of scalp. This might be a lot more exact, but it would be very difficult to use, since we rarely have a chance to count someone's hairs!)

Model Response to Exercise 3

McDonald's is clearly a fast-food restaurant. The French Laundry, a high-end restaurant in Napa Valley that only serves nine-course meals and is consistently rated as one of the best restaurants in the world, is clearly not a fast-food restaurant. Chipotle Mexican Grill, the chain of "fast casual" restaurants that serve made-to-order burritos and similar food, is a borderline case. A good definition of "fast-food restaurant" is "any restaurant in which there are no table servers, requiring customers to order their food at a counter or cash register." This includes restaurants like Chipotle, since Chipotle does not have table servers. This is better than definitions that focus on, e.g., the price of the food or the speed of service, since it makes sense to say that a restaurant is "expensive for a fast-food place" or "slow for a fast-food place."

This response justifies its proposed definition by contrasting it with other salient approaches to drawing a bright line between fast-food restaurants and other kinds of restaurants.

As usual, where you want to draw the line will probably depend on your interests. If you're a business analyst writing about the rise of chains like Chipotle, you might want a definition that cuts up the restaurant market more finely, so that Chipotle doesn't get lumped into the same category as Taco Bell. In that case, you might focus on other factors, such as how much of the food is delivered to the restaurant frozen or consists of highly processed ingredients.

Model Response to Exercise 5

Suppose we are classifying actions (rather than people) as brave. A middle school student who publicly sticks up for an unpopular student who is being picked on is acting bravely, since it requires standing up to a lot of peer pressure. A teacher who fails to stick up for that student because he is afraid that the students will make fun of him is not acting bravely. A student who secretly encourages his or her friends to stop picking on the unpopular student is a borderline case. A good definition of "brave" would be "willing to face physical or emotional dangers in order to achieve something important." That would probably exclude the student who only sticks up for the unpopular kid in secret, since he or she is not really facing any physical or emotional danger.

You might well have given examples in which people faced physical danger, such as firefighters running into a burning building. If you'd focused only on those examples, you might have defined bravery in terms of willingness to face physical danger. But as this response highlights, willingness to face physical danger is not the only kind of bravery. Coming up with a range of examples that clearly fit and do not fit the term can help you devise a better definition.

Model Response to Exercise 7

A piece of wooden furniture that is crafted by an American woodworker using wood grown in the United States is clearly "made in America." A t-shirt that was manufactured in Bangladesh using cotton that was grown in India and milled in China was clearly not made in America. A Toyota truck that is designed in Japan and assembled in the United States, with some parts made in Mexico, is a borderline case. A good definition of "made in America" is "manufactured or at least assembled in the United States from parts or materials most of which are themselves made in America." That would exclude things that are barely American-made, like a car assembled in the United States but made entirely from parts that were manufactured abroad; but it would include things that include some imported components, like a phone that is manufactured in the United States but contains some copper that was imported from China.

In an age of global industry, it turns out to be harder than you might expect to say where something was made. Since some Americans prefer to buy things that are "made in America," it's important that someone establish a standard definition for that term. It would be easy enough to adopt a very strict definition in which something is "made in America" if and only if it is manufactured entirely in the United States containing materials and parts that were themselves grown, mined, or created in the United States. But that's probably too narrow to reflect the real interests of people who prefer to buy things that are made in America. As it happens, the United States government has settled on a definition much like the one offered in this model response, although the government's definition is more precise.

Model Response to Exercise 9

Earthquakes are clearly natural. Computers are clearly unnatural. Dairy cattle are borderline cases, since they are animals that exist in their present form only because people have domesticated them. A good definition of "natural" would be "came into being and/or came to have its present form without significant human intervention." This definition captures the essential element of human intervention, but it excludes seemingly natural things that have been shaped by humans, like dairy cattle or lakes created as a result of a dam built by people.

This definition proposes a fairly broad definition of "natural." It allows as "natural" those unclear cases where something has been only slightly altered by humans. It excludes those things that have been significantly altered. For instance, a mountainside would still count as natural even if a few people had blazed trails along it. It would not count as natural if the slope were cleared and converted to farmland, or rearranged by bulldozers for a road or subdivision. In some cases, you might need to do some research to figure out whether something meets the definition. You might be surprised, for instance, to learn that modern dairy cattle are significantly different from their undomesticated cousins.

Notice that this definition of "natural" is entirely neutral. Some things that count as "natural" on this definition are bad (e.g., earthquakes) and some things that count as unnatural are good (e.g., computers). "Natural" is one of many terms that are often defined in a loaded way, which makes critical thinking more difficult.

MODEL RESPONSES FOR APPENDIX III: ARGUMENT MAPPING

Exercise Set 12.1: Mapping simple arguments

Model Responses to Exercise 1

[1][American swimmer Michael Phelps has more Olympic medals than any other athlete.] [2][At his peak in the 2008 games in Beijing, Phelps dominated his sport in a way that no one else has.] That's why [3][Michael Phelps is the greatest Olympian ever.]

The argument map in this response shows that the first two sentences of the argument—labeled (1) and (2)—are independent premises for the main conclusion, (3), which appears (as always) at the bottom of the argument map. (The main conclusion is indicated in the original argument by the conclusion indicator "That's why.")

The two premises are independent, rather than linked, because each one provides a good reason—all by itself, without help from the other—for believing the conclusion.

Model Response to Exercise 3

[1][Most Americans live too far from their place of work for it to be practical to ride a bicycle to work.] [2][This makes bike paths largely a waste of money—as a solution to traffic problems, at least.] [3][The government should find other ways to reduce traffic besides building expensive bike paths.]

The argument map in this response shows that each sentence in the argument is given as a reason for the next sentence. Claim (1) is a premise for (2), which is, in turn, a premise for the main conclusion, (3).

There are no conclusion indicators in the argument to give this away. You need to figure it out by thinking about what the main point of the argument is and how the various claims relate to one another.

One way to approach this problem is to think about which arrangements make the most sense. Claim (1) is a good reason to believe (2). Claim (2) is not as convincing as a reason for (1). Thus, it makes more sense to read (1) as a premise for (2) than vice versa. Claim (2), in turn, seems like a good reason for (3). Thus, the arrangement shown in this response's argument map seems like a reasonable interpretation of the argument.

Notice that (1) might seem like a good reason for (3) all by itself. Why not just draw an arrow from (1) to (3)? No doubt you would, if all you were offered were (1) and (3). Remember, though, that your goal here is to diagram the argument as it is written. Since (2) is included as well, we need to try to find a place for it. Claim (2) doesn't make sense as the main conclusion of the argument. It's neither linked with (1) nor independent of (1). Instead, it seems to fit most naturally as a subconclusion in between (1) and (3).

As this example illustrates, mapping arguments takes a fair amount of playing around with different options. (In the authors' view, this is one of the most enjoyable aspects of argument analysis!) Sometimes, the choice between one argument map and another will be a matter of interpretation.

Model Response to Exercise 5

[1][By reducing student debt, eliminating tuition at medical schools would enable more new doctors to become primary care physicians.] [2][We have a shortage of primary care physicians in this country.] Therefore, [3][medical schools ought to be free.]

$$(1) + (2)$$
$$\downarrow$$
$$(3)$$

The first two sentences of the argument are both premises. They jointly lead to the conclusion, which is the third sentence. This is shown in the argument map by linking (1) and (2) with a plus sign and drawing a single arrow to the main conclusion at the bottom of the map.

To see that the premises are linked, rather than independent, consider this: We would have no reason to take steps to increase the number of primary care physicians if we weren't facing a shortage of them, so (1) would not be a reason for (3) if (2) weren't true. And the need for more primary care physicians wouldn't give us a reason to eliminate tuition at medical schools if doing so wouldn't increase the number of primary care physicians, so (2) would not be a reason for (3) if (1) weren't true.

Model Response to Exercise 7

Some Western European countries are banning Muslim women from wearing the burqa on the grounds that it is an insult to women's dignity. ¹[If Europeans are truly concerned with Muslim women's dignity, then they should be addressing not only the burqa but also highly sexualized images of (non-Muslim) women in the European media.] After all, ²[if they're so worried about Muslim women's dignity, they ought to be concerned with all women's dignity.] And ³[if they are concerned with all women's dignity, then they ought to be just as concerned about highly sexualized portrayals of women in, say, European advertising as they are about the burqa.]

$$(2) + (3)$$
$$\downarrow$$
$$(1)$$

Since the main conclusion of this argument appears first in the argument itself—and is labeled (1) in the response—this response puts (1) at the bottom of the argument map. It shows that the premises—labeled (2) and (3) in the argument—are linked, jointly supporting (1). The first sentence in the passage provides background information. It does not constitute a premise in the argument.

If you've read Chapter VI, you'll recognize this argument as an instance of hypothetical syllogism (Rule 24). As a general rule, deductive arguments involve linked premises. (You need "if p then q" and "if q then r" as premises in a hypothetical syllogism. Without one, the other does nothing to support the conclusion "if p then r.")

One common mistake when mapping arguments that use "if–then" sentences is to treat each part of the sentence as a separate claim. It may be tempting, for instance, to separately map the statement "Europeans are truly concerned with Muslim women's dignity" and the statement "they should be addressing not only the burqa but also highly sexualized images of women in the European media", as you would do in Chapter VI to analyze deductive validity. Here this would be a mistake. When you map an argument's structure, map whole premises, like "if p then q," not their constituent statements.

Notice, for example, that this argument is not claiming that Europeans are truly concerned with women's dignity (which is the statement that is symbolized by p in this case). In fact, the argument suggests, but does not say, that Europeans are mainly concerned about something other than women's dignity. The argument is only saying that if Europeans care about Muslim women's dignity, then they ought to address both the burqa and highly sexualized images of women. That entire "if–then" sentence is a single claim, and it needs to be mapped as such.

Model Response to Exercise 9

[1][Happiness in life is reserved for those who care more about being happy than about being "successful."] [2][The signs of so-called success in modern life—a big house, a fancy car, designer clothes, etc.—are expensive.] [3][Having enough money to buy expensive things requires working so hard that you don't have time to enjoy all the expensive things you've bought.] Besides, [4][true happiness doesn't come from owning the kinds of things that are considered signs of success, anyway.]

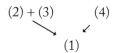

$$(2) + (3) \qquad (4)$$
$$(1)$$

As in Question 7, the main conclusion of this argument appears first in the written version, so it is labeled (1) in the response. Claims (2), (3), and (4) are all premises.

As the argument map in this response shows, an argument can mix linked and independent premises. Premises (2) and (3) in this argument are linked. The fact that signs of success are expensive does not by itself imply that happiness is reserved for those who care more about being happy than about being successful. Neither does the fact that making a lot of money takes a lot of time. It's only when you put those two things together that either counts as a good reason for (1). Premise (4), on the other hand, is a reason for (1) regardless of how expensive the "signs of success" are. Thus, it is an independent reason for (1).

Exercise Set 12.2: Mapping complex arguments

Model Response to Exercise 1

[1][Governments ought not to pay ransoms to terrorists who have kidnapped people.] [2][Doing so encourages terrorists to kidnap more people.] [3][Paying ransom also provides the terrorists with the resources to kill even more people.] Therefore, [4][even though ransoming hostages saves the hostages' lives, paying ransom ultimately leads to more deaths.] As hard as it may be to accept, [5][it's more important to minimize the overall harm that terrorists do than it is to save any specific hostage.]

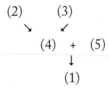

The "jigsaw puzzle" approach works well for this argument. The conclusion indicator therefore signals that claim (4) is either the conclusion or a sub-conclusion. When we think about its relationship to the other claims, we can see that (2) and (3) both work as reasons for (4), but that (4) seems to be a reason for (1) rather than the other way around. So that gives us one sub-argument: (2) and (3) somehow lead to (4). And how do we get from (4) to (1)? By joining (4) to (5). So that gives us the rest of the diagram.

All we need to do now is figure out which premises are linked and which are independent. Since either (2) or (3) would provide a reason for (4) on its own, those premises are independent. What about (4) and (5)? Claims (4), (5), and (1) fit a general pattern that should tip you off: Claim (4) states that an action would have a particular effect. Claim (5) states that we ought not to take actions that have that effect. The main conclusion is that we ought not to take the action described in (4). Whenever you see this pattern—doing x would lead to y, and we ought to avoid y, so we ought not to do x—you should expect the premises to be linked rather than independent. (Can you explain why?)

Model Response to Exercise 3

[1][Drugs ought to be legalized.] [2][Attempting to ban drugs is futile.] [3][Countries all over the world have tried for decades to ban various drugs.] [4][None of the attempts have been successful.] Furthermore, [5][making drugs illegal contributes to the development of failed states

by empowering criminal drug cartels around the world.] ⁶[The other problems associated with legalizing drugs are more manageable than the problems with criminalizing them too.]

This response shows that the main conclusion—(1)—is supported by three independent premises—(2), (5), and (6)—and that (2) is supported in turn by two linked premises—(3) and (4).

To arrive at this argument map, you might begin by identifying (1) as the main conclusion of the argument. Then notice that claims (2), (5), and (6) have nothing to do with one another, except that they are all reasons for (1). This makes them independent premises for (1). Claims (3) and (4), on the other hand, relate more immediately to (2) than to (1). Indeed, they seem to be given in this argument as reasons for (2). So, they go on the line above (2) in the argument map. They are linked, rather than independent, because (3) makes (4) a more powerful reason for (2), and (3) is not a reason for (2) at all unless (4) is true.

Why is that? The fact that every attempt to ban drugs has failed is a good reason to believe that banning drugs is futile if and only if there have been many attempts to ban drugs. Remember Rule 7! Thus, (3) makes (4) a more powerful reason for (2). The fact that many countries have attempted to ban drugs does nothing to show that banning drugs is futile unless those attempts have been unsuccessful. Thus, (3) needs (4) in order to count as a reason for (2).

Model Response to Exercise 5

¹[I see your wife is out of town.] How do I know? Since ²[the female detective you're working with is wearing men's deodorant,] I take it ³[she borrowed someone else's deodorant this morning.] And since ⁴[it smells the same as your deodorant], it stands to reason that ⁵[she's wearing your deodorant.] ⁶[Which she would only do if she'd woken up at your place after spending the night there.] So ⁷[she spent the night at your place]—I'm right so far, aren't I? Of course I am. And since ⁸[you're married], ⁹[she wouldn't have spent the night with you unless your wife was out of town.] <u>That's</u> how I know.

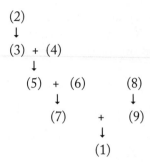

Working backward and paying close attention to premise and conclusion indicators can help you map this complex argument from the BBC's Sherlock Holmes reboot.

The main conclusion is clearly (1). So let's put that at the bottom of the argument map. Claim (9) states that the detective would not have spent the night unless the listener's wife was out of town, where (7) states that the detective did spend the night. Those two claims jointly entail the conclusion, so let's add them as the next layer up.

The premise indicator "since" reveals that (8) is a premise for what comes next, which in this case is claim (9). So let's add (8) as a premise for (9) in our diagram.

Now, how does Sherlock know that the detective spent the night with his listener? After figuring out that she's wearing the listener's deodorant— which is claim (5)—Sherlock reasons that she would only do that if she'd spent the night there—which is claim (6). So let's add those to the diagram above claim (7).

But how did he know that she was wearing his deodorant? Again, follow the indicator words. The word "since" before claim (4) tells us that it's a premise for (5). And since it's claim (3) that makes (4) into a strong reason for (5), we'll put those two together as the premises for (5).

Finally, claim (2) is offered as a reason for claim (3), so that goes on yet another line, completing Sherlock's chain of reasoning.

As this example illustrates, arguments that seem very complicated on the surface often turn out to be nothing more than a chain of relatively easy-to-understand arguments. By focusing on one step at a time, you can often make great progress in understanding what otherwise seems impenetrable.

Model Response to Exercise 7

[1][When one person knowingly causes a fatal injury to another, that is murder.] [2][Capitalism deprives many people of the basic necessities of life.] [3][It requires them to live in cramped, squalid, toxic conditions.] [4][It leaves them without resources for medical care.] [5][It leaves them

unable to afford the most minimally nutritious food.] ⁶[It leaves them no respite from work, save sex and drink.] Furthermore, because ⁷[capitalism leaves wealth and power in the hands of the few], ⁸[it leads to power structures that prevent the oppressed from taking the necessities of life by force.] ⁹[Being deprived of the necessities of life leads to death just as surely as does being actively harmed.] ¹⁰[Society knows full well that capitalism has this effect.] Thus, ¹¹[society is committing murder by allowing capitalism to continue.]

$$ \begin{array}{ccccc} (3) & (4) & (5) & (6) & (7) \\ & \searrow & \searrow & \swarrow & \swarrow \end{array} $$

$$ (1) \quad + \quad (2) \quad + \quad (8) \quad + \quad (9) \quad + \quad (10) $$
$$ \downarrow $$
$$ (11) $$

The key to mapping this argument is to pull the two subarguments out of the main argument. Focus for a moment just on (1), (2), (8), (9), and (10). Together they jointly provide an argument for believing that society is committing murder. But why should we believe that capitalism deprives people of the basic necessities of life? To support this claim, the argument offers (3), (4), (5), and (6) as independent reasons for accepting (2). The argument offers (7) as a reason for accepting (8).

You might also interpret (2), (8), (9), and (10) as jointly leading to an unstated subconclusion—call it (12*)—that society knows that capitalism causes fatal harm to some people. You could then interpret (1) and (12*) as jointly leading to (11). Sometimes, adding unstated subconclusions to an extremely complex argument can help you organize that argument more effectively.

This argument comes from Friedrich Engels' famous account of the conditions of the working class in England in 1844. His book is widely considered a classic study of the social effects of the Industrial Revolution. Engels went on to co-author The Communist Manifesto *with Karl Marx.*

Model Response to Exercise 9

¹[Our distant ancestors lived in very small societies.] ²[On a normal day, everyone they met would be someone they had known all of their lives.] ³[These societies did not interact very much with other societies.] ⁴[Just about everything they ate, everything they wore, and every tool they used was made within that group.] ⁵[Today, of course, we live in vast societies.] ⁶[We can look out at a busy city street and see, all at once, more people than our ancestors saw in their entire lives.] ⁷[We live in a global trading system.] Indeed, ⁸[our world is unimaginably different from the world of our distant ancestors.] ⁹[Our minds,

however, are designed for the life of our distant ancestors.] Thus, [10][our minds may not be well adapted to the special challenges of the modern world.]

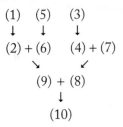

$$
\begin{array}{ccc}
(1) & (5) & (3) \\
\downarrow & \downarrow & \downarrow \\
(2) + (6) & & (4) + (7) \\
\searrow & & \swarrow \\
& (9) + (8) & \\
& \downarrow & \\
& (10) &
\end{array}
$$

Working backward is a useful approach to mapping this argument. The main conclusion is (10)—that our minds may not be well adapted to the challenges of the modern world. The argument condenses the basic reasons for this into two premises: the modern world is radically different from that of our distant ancestors, but our minds are designed for their world, not ours.

The rest of the premises constitute subarguments that are designed to show that our world is unimaginably different from theirs. One strand of this argument focuses on the number and variety of people that we encounter: they encountered very few strangers (because they lived in small societies) whereas we encounter many strangers (because we live in a vast society). The other strand of the argument contrasts the self-sufficiency of ancient societies with our global trading network.

Many arguments, especially those with this level of complexity, can be mapped in multiple ways. For instance, you might group (2) and (4) together as linked premises for (8), in which case you would want to group (6) and (7) together too. Thus, there may be more than one good response to this exercise.

Part 3

Critical Thinking Activities

The following activities provide you with longer, more in-depth, and more collaborative ways to develop your critical thinking skills. Some of these activities can be done in the classroom, some will need to be outside of class, some could be done inside the classroom or at home, and a few combine work done outside with work done inside the classroom.

Many of the activities—such as the "Found arguments" and "Writing a letter to the editor" activities—can be repeated profitably, with or without the listed variations. Others you will want to do only once.

Some of the activities list variations at the end. Of course, your instructor might have other variations in mind—or entirely different activities, perhaps inspired by the activities below. Always find out whether your instructor has alternative or additional instructions for you before beginning one of these activities.

Found arguments

Objective: To give you practice finding and analyzing arguments.

Instructions: Read the discussion of Rules 1 and 2 and complete Exercise Sets 1.1 and 1.2 before beginning this activity. When you are ready, complete each of the following steps in order.

1. *Find a brief argument outside of this class.* Find an argument that is no longer than one or two paragraphs' worth of text. Good places to look for arguments include books, newspapers, and magazines; online sources like blogs and Web forums; audiovisual materials including radio or television broadcasts, movies, or online videos; advertisements and sales pitches; lectures or textbooks from other courses; and conversations that you've had or overheard—really just about anywhere!

2. *Print out, photocopy, or write down the original argument.* If your argument is already in printed form, print it out, cut it out, or photocopy it from the original source. If it's in a video,

conversation, or other non-printed format, write it down,
sticking as closely to the original language as you can.

3. *Rewrite the argument in premise-and-conclusion form.* Begin by
   identifying the conclusion and premises of the argument, just
   as you did in Exercise Set 1.1. Then, organize the premises into
   a numbered list with the conclusion at the end, as in Exercise
   Set 1.2.

Final product: The final product of this activity should consist of a printed
or written version of the original argument and a premise-and-conclusion
outline of the argument.

Variation: Complete the activity as above using a "visual argument"—that
is, an image or video that tries to convince the viewer to do or believe
something without explicitly stating an argument in words. See Exercise
Set 1.3 for advice on creating a premise-and-conclusion outline of an argument based on an image or video.

Variation: Chapters II through VI describe specific kinds of arguments.
After reading one of those chapters, complete the activity as above, but
find an argument of the kind discussed in the chapter you read (e.g., an
argument about generalizations, as discussed in Chapter II).

Variation: After studying Appendix III, complete the activity as above, but
create an argument map of your "found argument," rather than a premise-
and-conclusion outline.

Creating a visual argument

Objective: To help you understand arguments presented in images.

Instructions: Read the commentary for Rules 1 and 2 and complete Exercise Set 1.3 before beginning this activity. When you are ready, complete
each of the following steps in order.

1. *Create a visual argument on any topic you want.* A visual argument
   is an image or video that tries to persuade the viewer to do or
   believe something without necessarily stating an argument in
   words. Your visual argument can be as simple or elaborate as you
   wish—from a hand-drawn stick figure cartoon to a collage of

magazine cutouts to a video that you create. (Before you create a video, be sure that you have the means to display it in class, and your instructor's permission to do so.)

2. *Create a premise-and-conclusion outline of your visual argument.* Write your interpretation of your own visual argument in premise-and-conclusion form, just as you did in Exercise Set 1.3.

3. (Optional) *Analyze the visual arguments created by your classmates.* Bring your visual argument to class. Form a group of three or four people. Share your visual argument with your group and write a premise-and-conclusion outline of the arguments presented by your group members. Compare each person's premise-and-conclusion outline of each argument and pick the two that best capture the message of the image or video.

Final product: The final product of this activity should consist of a visual argument and a premise-and-conclusion outline of that argument. If you completed the optional Step 3, your final product will also include a set of premise-and-conclusion outlines of two or three of your classmates' visual arguments.

Writing a letter to the editor

Objective: To give you practice constructing arguments and expressing them in plain English.

Instructions: Read Chapter I and complete Exercise Sets 1.1, 1.2, and 1.6 before beginning this activity. When you are ready, complete each of the following steps in order.

1. *Find a recent newspaper or magazine article on which you would like to comment.* Many newspapers and magazines publish letters about recent articles. The first step in writing a letter to the editor is to find a recent article about which you have something to say.

2. *Construct an argument that makes a point about your chosen article.* First, figure out what the main point of your letter is; that will be the conclusion of your argument. Then, write a

premise-and-conclusion outline of your argument, similar to those you created for Exercise Set 1.2.

3. *Rewrite your argument as a letter to the editor.* In Exercise Set 1.2, you went from a prose version of an argument to a premise-and-conclusion outline. In this step, take the premise-and-conclusion outline you created in Step 3 and rewrite it in normal prose. Be sure to follow any guidelines, such as word limits, set by your chosen publication.

4. *Send your letter to the editor of your chosen newspaper or magazine.* Most publications accept letters to the editor via email or a form on their Web site. Find out how to submit a letter to your chosen publication and send your letter to the editor. Watch upcoming issues to see if your letter gets published. Good luck!

Final product: The final product of this activity should be an electronic or paper copy of an original letter to the editor. The letter should contain an argument related to a recent newspaper or magazine article. Your instructor may want proof that you have submitted your letter to the editor, such as a copy of your email or a printout of the Web form.

Analyzing unadapted arguments

Objective: To give you practice analyzing arguments in their original contexts.

Instructions: Read the discussion of Rules 1 and 2 and complete Exercise Sets 1.1 and 1.2 before beginning this activity. When you are ready, complete each of the following steps in order:

1. *Identify the conclusion and premises for each of the arguments in the box below.* Unlike the arguments in the exercise sets throughout this book, the arguments below have not been simplified; they have been reprinted here (almost) word for word, in all their original messiness and complexity. This means you'll need to think more carefully about what the main conclusion is and take more care in separating the premises from background information. It may help you to underline the conclusion and bracket the premises, as you did in Exercise Set 1.1.

2. *Write a premise-and-conclusion outline of each argument in the box below.* For each argument, write a premise-and-conclusion outline, as you did in Exercise Set 1.2. Since these arguments were reprinted word for word from their original sources, you may need to rephrase more of the premises than you did in Exercise Set 1.2. When rephrasing premises, be sure not to change their meaning.

Final product: The final product of this activity should consist of a set of ten premise-and-conclusion outlines—one for each argument in the box below.

Variation: After reading Appendix III and completing Exercise Sets 12.1 and 12.2, create argument maps for each of the arguments in the box below.

SOME ARGUMENTS FOR ANALYSIS

1. "Most coca farmers live in remote regions in southern and eastern Colombia. Many farmers need to grow coca in order to earn a living, because decades of government neglect have failed to provide the necessary infrastructure to make it possible to transport perishable food crops from these remote regions to distant markets."

    Gary Leech, Beyond Bogotá: Diary of a Drug War Journalist in Colombia
    (Boston: Beacon Press, 2009), 45

2. "Science has indisputably established the fact that, as Dr. Keith Moore writes in *The Developing Human: Clinically Oriented Embryology,* 7th edition, 'Human development begins at fertilization. This highly specialized, totipotent cell marked the beginning of each of us as a unique individual.' A preborn child is not a potential person, but a person with potential—a whole, distinct, living human being. The difference between you as an embryo or fetus and you today as a college student is only a function of time and nutrition. Since it is a scientific fact that abortion kills a unique and genetically unrepeatable human being, the question [about the morality of abortion] cannot be 'about a woman's control over her own body.'"

    Andrew Guernsey and Jessica Janneck, "A Fetus Is a Human with a Right to Live,"
    The Johns Hopkins News-Letter, *Oct 30, 2014, http://www.jhunewsletter.*
    com/2014/10/30/a-fetus-is-a-human-with-a-right-to-live-26841

3.   "Properly speaking, there are in the world no such men in the world as self-made men. [That term] implies an individual independence which does not exist.
      "Our best and most valued acquisitions have been obtained either from those who stand about us or from those who have gone before us in the field of thought and discovery. We have all either begged, borrowed or stolen—reaped where others sowed, gathered where others strewed."

Frederick Douglass, Self-Made Men, *Address before Students of the Indian Industrial School at Carlisle, Pa.,*
1874, From Library of Congress, Frederick Douglass Papers, http://www.loc.gov/item/mfd.29014/

4.   "We sometimes mistakenly see our careers as the 'selfish' part of our lives because we earn money or make profit, while our altruistic acts—giving to charity, say, or volunteering at the soup kitchen or giving blood—that's the work we do for others. We think *that's* what we do that makes the world a better place. We forget that being good at our job helps others and makes the world a better place, too.
      "Being an extraordinary teacher changes the lives of your students. Being a great boss means creating ways for employees to flourish and use their skills. Running a great restaurant gives people a chance to meet their friends for something more than food—for conversation, for friendship and creating memories. And giving people a chance to pay less for shirts or apples or tires because you've figured out a way to reduce inventory costs and sell those items more cheaply lets people satisfy their desires at a lower cost than they otherwise would have to pay."

Russ Roberts, How Adam Smith Can Change Your Life
(New York: Portfolio/Penguin, 2014), 169–70

5.   "Though from a Western point of view, women's identification [in Chinese culture] with the family or the inner quarters…may seem unduly restrictive, the social significance of these three roles [of daughter, wife, and mother] should not be underestimated. In Chinese tradition, the family is the model for the Empire, and the most necessary part of the social structure. Women's role in the family, therefore, is essential to their role in public life. It also serves as a model for the king, whose success depends on responding to the needs of the people in much the same way that a woman must respond to the needs of her family. Chinese culture envisions the wise and virtuous woman empowering her husband and her children for social leadership, from which the whole family and state will benefit."

Robin Wang, Images of Women in Chinese Thought and Culture
(Indianapolis: Hackett Publishing, 2003), xiii

6. "Obscenity is not within the area of constitutionally protected freedom of speech or press…under the First Amendment. . . . In the light of history, it is apparent that the unconditional phrasing of the First Amendment was not intended to protect every utterance. . . . The protection given speech and press was fashioned to assure unfettered interchange of ideas for the bringing about of political and social changes desired by the people. . . . All ideas having even the slightest redeeming social importance—unorthodox ideas, controversial ideas, even ideas hateful to the prevailing climate of opinion—have the full protection of the [First Amendment] guaranties, unless excludable because they encroach upon the limited area of more important interests; but implicit in the history of the First Amendment is the rejection of obscenity as utterly without redeeming social importance."

    Roth v. United States, 354 U.S. 476 (1957)

7. "Reams of pages of figures have been collected to show the value in dollars of a college education, and stacks of pamphlets have been published to bring these figures—and conclusions more or less based on them—to the attention of potential students. . . . The only thing wrong is that along with the figures and facts goes a totally unwarranted conclusion. . . . It says that these figures show that if you (your son, your daughter) attend college you will probably earn more money than if you decide to spend the next four years in some other manner. This unwarranted conclusion has for its basis the equally unwarranted assumption that since college-trained folks make more money, they make it because they went to college. Actually we don't know but that these are the people who would have made more money even if they had not gone to college. There are a couple of things that indicate rather strongly that this is so. Colleges get a disproportionate number of two groups of kids: the bright and the rich. The bright might show good earning power without college knowledge. And as for the rich ones…well, money breeds money in several obvious ways. Few sons of rich men are found in low-income brackets whether they go to college or not."

    Darrell Huff, How to Lie with Statistics
    (New York: W. W. Norton, 1954), 93–94

8. "If you have to take out student loans, you essentially have two choices: federal student loans and private loans.
    "For most borrowers, federal student loans are the best option. When you start to pay back your federal loans, the interest rate will be fixed, which will help you predict your payments after graduation. And in some cases, the federal

government will pay the interest on your loans while you are in school—these loans are called subsidized loans.

"Other student loans are generally private student loans. The most common private student loans are offered by banks. Their interest rates are often variable, which means your interest rates and payments could go up over time. Private loans can also be more expensive—rates have been as high as 16% over the past couple of years. And when it is time to repay, private loans don't offer as many options to reduce or postpone payments.

"For most people, federal student loans are a better deal than private student loans, so you'll want to take advantage of federal options first."

U.S. Consumer Financial Protection Bureau, "Choose a Student Loan," consumerfinance.gov, n.d., http://www.consumerfinance.gov/paying-for-college/choose-a-student-loan/

9. "After I took office, my administration began briefing all strikes outside of Iraq and Afghanistan to the appropriate committees of Congress. Let me repeat that: Not only did Congress authorize the use of force, it is briefed on every strike that America takes. Every strike. That includes the one instance when we targeted an American citizen—Anwar Awlaki, the chief of external operations for [Al Qaeda in the Arabian Peninsula]. . . .

"[W]hen a U.S. citizen goes abroad to wage war against America and is actively plotting to kill U.S. citizens, and when neither the United States, nor our partners are in a position to capture him before he carries out a plot, his citizenship should no more serve as a shield than a sniper shooting down on an innocent crowd should be protected from a SWAT team.

"That's who Anwar Awlaki was—he was continuously trying to kill people. He helped oversee the 2010 plot to detonate explosive devices on two U.S.-bound cargo planes. He was involved in planning to blow up an airliner in 2009. When Farouk Abdulmutallab—the Christmas Day bomber—went to Yemen in 2009, Awlaki hosted him, approved his suicide operation, helped him tape a martyrdom video to be shown after the attack, and his last instructions were to blow up the airplane when it was over American soil. I would have detained and prosecuted Awlaki if we captured him before he carried out a plot, but we couldn't. And as President, I would have been derelict in my duty had I not authorized the strike that took him out."

Barack Obama, "Remarks at National Defense University," May 23, 2013, http://www.gpo.gov/fdsys/pkg/DCPD-201300361/html/DCPD-201300361.htm

10.   "Friends and fellow citizens: I stand before you tonight under indictment for the alleged crime of having voted at the last presidential election, without having a lawful right to vote. It shall be my work this evening to prove to you that in thus voting, I not only committed no crime, but, instead, simply exercised my citizen's rights, guaranteed to me and all United States citizens by the national Constitution, beyond the power of any state to deny....

"The preamble of the federal Constitution says:

"'We, the people of the United States, in order to form a more perfect union, establish justice, insure domestic tranquility, provide for the common defense, promote the general welfare, and secure the blessings of liberty to ourselves and our posterity, do ordain and establish this Constitution for the United States of America.'

"It was we, the people; not we, the white male citizens; nor yet we, the male citizens; but we, the whole people, who formed the Union. And we formed it, not to give the blessings of liberty, but to secure them; not to the half of ourselves and the half of our posterity, but to the whole people—women as well as men. And it is a downright mockery to talk to women of their enjoyment of the blessings of liberty while they are denied the use of the only means of securing them provided by this democratic-republican government—the ballot."

Susan B. Anthony, An Account of the Proceedings of the Trial of Susan B. Anthony on the Charge of Illegal Voting at the Presidential Election in Nov., 1872 *(Rochester, NY: Daily Democrat and Chronicle Book Print, 1874), 151–53*

Finding misleading statistics

Objective: To give you practice finding and explaining misleading uses of statistics.

Instructions: Read the section on Rule 10 and complete Exercise Set 2.4 before beginning this activity. Then, complete each of the following steps in order.

1.   *Find an argument that uses statistics in a misleading way.* You can find arguments in newspapers, magazines, online, on television shows or videos, advertisements, in conversations with friends or family, etc.

2. *Print out or write down the argument.* If the argument is in a video or other non-written format, write out the argument, sticking as closely as you can to the original language. If the argument is more than one or two paragraphs long, you may choose to summarize the argument.

3. *Explain how the use of statistics in the argument is misleading.* In one or two paragraphs, explain why you think the use of statistics in the argument is misleading. If you can, suggest a way to improve the argument so that it is less misleading.

4. (Optional) *Find the most misleading use of statistics in a small group of your classmates.* Form a group with three or four of your classmates. Have each member of your group share the argument that he or she found and explain why the use of statistics in the argument is misleading. As a group, decide which of the arguments makes the most misleading use of statistics. Choose someone to share that argument with your class.

Final product: The final product of this assignment should be a written document of no more than a few pages. It should contain both the original argument (or your summary of it) and your explanation of how the argument's use of statistics is misleading.

Generalizations about your classroom

Objective: To give you practice constructing arguments for generalizations based on examples that you find yourself.

Instructions: Read Chapter II and complete Exercise Sets 2.6 and 2.7 before beginning this activity. Then, complete each of the following steps in order.

1. *In a small group, write a generalization about your classroom or campus that could be verified in fifteen to thirty minutes.* Examples of generalizations about your classroom include "Most of the students in this room have been to a concert in the last two weeks" or "Nothing in this room is made in the United States." Examples of generalizations about your campus include "Most of the buildings on campus are accessible for people in

wheelchairs" or "There's no space left in the bike racks around campus." Remember, these should be generalizations for which a small group of students could collect an adequate number of examples in about fifteen to thirty minutes (or whatever time limit is set by your instructor). Deciding which generalizations qualify is part of the challenge!

2. *Trade generalizations with another group in your class.* Each group in the class should give its generalization to another group. Each group should receive exactly one generalization from some other group.

3. *As a group, find examples to construct a good argument for or against the generalization that you have been given.* A good argument, in this case, is one that follows the rules from Chapter II. You will need to find and keep track of examples. For instance, if another group gave you the generalization "None of the classrooms in this building are currently set up for small group discussions," you will need to find and make a list of classrooms in your building, noting which ones are set up for small groups. If your generalization includes things around campus, you may need to be creative in getting information about examples. Are you trying to find out what's scheduled in classrooms in many different buildings? Consider looking online rather than trekking all over campus. Be sure to find out from your instructor if there is a time limit on your search.

4. *As a group, write out your argument, based on the examples that you found.* Write out your argument for or against the generalization you were given, much as you did for Exercise Set 2.7. Be sure to state whether the generalization is true or false. Choose someone in your group to share your argument with the class.

Final product: The final products of this assignment should be a list of examples and a written version of your argument. The list should clearly indicate which examples support the generalization and which are counter-examples.

Using analogies to understand unusual objects

Objective: To give you practice constructing arguments by analogy.

Instructions: Read Chapter III before beginning this activity. Then, complete each of the following steps in order.

1. *Find an unusual object.* Find an unusual object—something that will not be familiar to most of your classmates. Check out your local flea markets, antique shops, or specialty stores; think also about specific types of objects that are familiar to you from some prior experience or skill that is not likely to be shared by many others. For example, you can usually find something unfamiliar to most people at a hardware store or craft store.

2. *Write a brief description of the object's purpose or use.* Write down a two- or three-sentence description of the main use or purpose of the object.

3. *Share your object with a small group of classmates.* Form a group of four or five people. Share your object with the other members of your group, but do not share the description of the object's purpose or use.

4. *As a group, use analogical reasoning to try to figure out the use or purpose of your group's objects.* For each of the objects in your group, come up with analogies that suggest possible uses for the object. That is, find similarities between the objects from Step 1 and more familiar objects. Use these similarities as the basis for an argument by analogy to make an educated guess about the object's purpose. Have one group member record these arguments by analogy.

5. *Reveal the true purpose or use of your object to your group.* Share your description of your object's use or purpose with the rest of your group. See how close your group was to figuring out the real purpose of each object.

6. *Choose one object from your group to share with the class.* Choose one of your group's objects to share with your class. Show the

object to the class. Have the rest of the class use analogical reasoning to infer the purpose or use of the object. Then, explain the analogical reasoning that your group used to draw a conclusion about the object's purpose or use. Finally, reveal its actual purpose.

Final product: The final products of this assignment should be a set of unusual objects, a description of the purpose or use of each object, and a written argument by analogy about each object.

Using analogies in ethical reasoning

Objective: To give you practice applying arguments by analogy to ethical dilemmas.

Instructions: Read Chapter III and complete exercise 3.4 before beginning this activity. Then, complete each of the following steps in order.

1. *Write a short paragraph about an ethical problem.* You could write about an ethical problem that you have faced recently, one that you've read about in a book or seen in a movie, etc. The problem should involve a difficult moral or ethical decision.

2. *Construct an argument by analogy to argue for a specific solution to your ethical problem.* Think of a situation that is similar to the one you described in Step 1 except that it is much less ethically puzzling. That is, it should be a situation where most people would agree about the right thing to do. Using an argument by analogy, compare the problem from Step 1 to this other situation in order to argue that the solution to the ethical problem is like the proper response to the other situation. Write this argument out in a paragraph or two.

3. (Optional) *Share your work with a classmate and see if he or she agrees with your solution.* Have a classmate read your work from Steps 1 and 2. Discuss your argument with your classmate to find out whether he or she agrees with your proposed solution to the ethical problem. If he or she does not agree, find out why not.

Final product: The final product of this assignment should be a written document of roughly two or three paragraphs. The first paragraph should describe an ethical problem. The remaining paragraphs should use an argument by analogy to argue for a specific solution to that problem.

Recognizing reliable Web sources

Objective: To help you distinguish between reliable and unreliable sources on the Web.

Instructions: Read Rule 17 before beginning this activity. Then, complete each of the following steps in order.

1. *Find the Web page for this activity on the companion Web site for this book.* Go to the companion Web site for this book. Click on the link for "Part 3." Then, click on the link for "Recognizing Reliable Web Sources."

2. *Examine each of the Web sites linked from the Web page for this activity.* The Web page from Step 1 will contain links to various Web sites. Some of these sites are legitimate sites on which well-informed, relatively impartial experts present information. Others are not (in one interesting way or another). Examine each of the sites carefully, trying to distinguish the sites that make reliable sources from those that do not. For those that do not, try to tell, if you can, what the intention of the site actually is and who its creators might be.

3. *Make a list of sites that would be reliable sources of information and a list of sites that would not be reliable sources of information.* Next to each entry on your list, make a few notes about how you came to the conclusion about the site's reliability as a source.

4. *In a small group, compare lists to devise a list of reliable sources, a list of unreliable sources, and a list of sources about which you are unsure.* If everyone agrees that a particular site is reliable, put it on your group's list of reliable sources. If everyone agrees that a site is unreliable, put it on your group's list of unreliable sources. If your group disagrees on a site, see if you can resolve that disagreement

through discussion or further research. If you can't, put it on your group's list of sources about which you are unsure.

5. *As a class, compile a single list of reliable sources and a single list of unreliable sources.* As a class, compare the lists that each group produced. Try to resolve any disagreements and uncertainties through discussion so that everyone agrees on which sites belong on which list.

Final product: The final product of this activity should be three sets of lists: your own lists of reliable and unreliable sites; your group's lists of sites that are reliable, sites that are unreliable, and sites about which your group is unsure; and your class's lists of reliable and unreliable sites.

Finding good sources

Objective: To give you practice finding good sources to support claims.

Instructions: Read Chapter IV before beginning this activity. Then, complete each of the following steps in order.

1. *Choose a paper of yours from a previous class.* The paper can be on any topic, and it need not be an argumentative essay.

2. *Choose three claims from your paper that could be supported with sources.* In choosing claims, consider both whether the claim is the kind that can be supported by sources and whether you think you can find good sources to support those claims. Pick claims for which you did not already provide sources in the original paper. Write each claim on a separate piece of paper.

3. *Find two good sources to support each claim.* Identify two independent, well-informed, impartial sources that support each of the three claims you identified in Step 2. Write out a complete citation for each source, using Chicago citation style or any style that your instructor requires. For more information about citation styles, see the "Resources" section of the companion Web site for this book.

4. *Write a brief paragraph explaining why the source is a good source to support your claim.* Your paragraph should quote or paraphrase the part of the source that supports the claim. The paragraph should also explain why you think each source is well informed and impartial.

Final product: The final product of this assignment should be a written document of three pages. Each page should have a single claim at the top, all three claims taken from the same paper. Each page should then have citations for two sources and brief paragraphs explaining why those are good sources for supporting the claim at the top of that page.

Bluffing about causal explanations

Objective: To give you practice brainstorming alternative explanations of correlations and working toward the most likely explanation.

Instructions: Read Chapter V before beginning this activity. Then, complete each of the following steps in order.

1. *Working in a small group, identify an interesting or surprising correlation.* Try to find a correlation for which you can think of several plausible explanations.

2. *As a group, decide on the best explanation of the correlation.* If you can find good sources that establish the genuine explanation for the correlation, use that explanation. If you cannot find good sources, follow the rules from Chapter V to decide what you think is the best explanation of the correlation. The best explanation may or may not involve a causal connection between the things or events that are correlated. Write a brief paragraph that presents this explanation of the correlation.

3. *As a group, create two alternative explanations.* Write two separate paragraphs detailing two alternative explanations for the correlation (besides the one you identified in Step 2). Try to make them as convincing as possible.

4. *Read all three explanations to your class.* Do not tell the rest of the class which explanation is the correct one.

5. *Have your classmates vote on which explanation they think is correct.* After the class has voted, reveal which explanation you believe is correct and explain why you think so.

Final product: The final product of this assignment should be three separate explanations for a particular correlation—one correct explanation and two fake explanations.

Reconstructing scientific reasoning

Objective: To give you practice understanding the reasoning behind scientific experiments.

Instructions: Read Chapter I and Chapter V before beginning this activity. When you are ready, complete the following steps in order:

1. *Find a description of a famous experiment in the history of science.* Using your library or the Internet, find a description of a famous experiment in the history of science, such as Galileo's experiment on the speed of falling objects, Thomas Young's experimental test of whether light is a wave or a particle, or Ernest Rutherford's experiment that revealed the basic structure of the atom. After identifying an experiment that you'd like to study, you may need to do a little research to find an adequately detailed description of it. Photocopy or print out this description to turn in later.

2. *Reconstruct the reasoning by which the experimenter reached his or her conclusion.* In your own words, summarize the reasoning behind the experiment. What did the experiment prove? Use that as the conclusion of the argument. What did the experimenter do to prove that conclusion? What assumptions did he or she make in the process? Those are the premises of the argument.

3. *Write out a premise-and-conclusion outline of the experimenter's reasoning.* Rewrite your summary from Step 2 in a premise-and-conclusion outline, just as you did in Exercise Set 1.2.

Final Product: The final product of this activity should consist of a photocopied or printed description of a famous scientific experiment and a premise-and-conclusion outline of the reasoning behind the experiment.

Analyzing arguments in scientific reasoning

Objective: To give you practice recognizing and understanding arguments in scientific sources, including science textbooks.

Instructions: Read Chapter I and Chapter V before beginning this activity. When you are ready, complete the following steps in order:

1. *Identify the conclusion and premises for each of the arguments in the box below.* Unlike the arguments in the exercise sets throughout this book, the arguments below have not been simplified; they have been reprinted here almost word for word, in all their original messiness and complexity. This means you'll need to think more carefully about what the main conclusion is and take more care in separating the premises from background information. It may help you to underline the conclusion and bracket the premises, as you did in Exercise Set 1.1.

2. *Write a premise-and-conclusion outline of each argument in the box below.* For each argument, write a premise-and-conclusion outline, as you did in Exercise Set 1.2. Since these arguments were reprinted word for word from their original sources, you may need to rephrase more of the premises than you did in Exercise Set 1.2. When rephrasing premises, be sure not to change their meaning.

Final product: The final product of this activity should consist of a set of ten premise-and-conclusion outlines—one for each argument in the box below.

Variation: After reading Appendix III and completing Exercise Sets 12.1 and 12.2, create argument maps for each of the arguments in the box below.

Variation: After reading Chapters II through VI, identify the type(s) of argument(s) used in each argument in the box below. (Do the arguments involve arguments from examples? Arguments by analogy? Arguments by authority? Deductive reasoning—which forms?) Optionally, evaluate each argument using the rules from the corresponding chapter(s).

SOME EXAMPLES OF SCIENTIFIC REASONING

1.   "Adolescence is a difficult and frustrating time for some chimpanzees just as it is for some humans. Possibly it is worse for males, in both species. The male chimpanzee attains puberty when he is about eight years old, but he is still nowhere near being full-grown—he weights about 40 pounds as compared to the 90 to 110 pounds of the fully mature male. He will not become sexually mature—capable of siring an infant—for another four or five years. The eight-year-old, although increasingly able to dominate, even terrorize females, must become ever more cautious in his interactions with the big males in order to avoid arousing their aggression. He will not be ranked as socially mature until he is thirteen to fifteen years old—or even older. . . .

    "Usually he does not join in the long sessions of social grooming so beloved by his elders: he sits a few yards away from the mature males grooming himself. When the group climbs into a tree to feed, the adolescent male often sits at a discreet distance from his superiors—at times he even feeds in a neighboring tree. When the mature males start their displays on arrival at some food source, the adolescent male sometimes keeps well out of the way until things have calmed down."

Jane Goodall, In the Shadow of Man, Revised Edition
(Boston: Mariner Books, 2000), 173–77

2.   "*Funisia* is one such example of an early sex-fossil. It is an upright-standing worm-like animal that looks a little like a section of rope. It is revered because it is one of the first animals of which we can say with a degree of certainty that, yes, it was having sex. How can we be so sure? You might imagine digging up hundreds of the things, fossilized mid-coitus, but no—nothing like that has ever been found. Instead, we know of their sex lives because of the 'sprats'. Sprats are young *Funisia*, and in fossils they generally appear in little clusters, each containing individuals all within the same size and age band, which on the face of it doesn't sound very sexy. Except that we see exactly the same thing in modern-day animals like corals and sea-worms, which broadcast sperm and eggs out into the water, often on highly specific nights of the year. Fertilised eggs descend in the water column, hit the floor, grow, and hey presto—sprats. The products of sex. They are a little like sex's trace fossils, like a footprint or fossilised faeces. And it is one of the earliest pieces of evidence that sex was taking place in those early seas."

Jules Howard, Sex on Earth *(London: Bloomsbury Sigma, 2014), 24*

3.   "[T]he first proven major extension of human geographic range since our ances-tors' colonization of Eurasia . . . consisted of the occupation of Australia and New Guinea, joined at that time into a single continent. Many radiocarbon-dated sites attest to human presence in Australia/New Guinea between 40,000 and 30,000 years ago. . . . Within a short time of that initial peopling, humans had expanded over the whole continent and adapted to its diverse habitats. . . .

      "During the Ice Ages, so much of the oceans' water was locked up in glaciers that worldwide sea levels dropped hundreds of feet below their present stand. As a result, what are now the shallow seas between Asia and the Indonesian islands of Sumatra, Borneo, Java, and Bali became dry land. . . . The edge of the Southeast Asian mainland then lay 700 miles easy of its present location. Nevertheless, central Indonesian islands between Bali and Australia remained surrounded and separated by deep-water channels. To reach Australia/New Guinea from the Asian mainland at that time still required crossing a minimum of eight channels, the broadest of which was at least 50 miles wide. Most of those channels divided islands visible from each other, but Australia itself was always invisible from even the nearest Indonesian islands, Timor and Tanimbar. Thus, the occupation of Australia/New Guinea is momentous in that it demanded watercraft and pro-vides by far the earliest evidence of their use in history. . . .

      "Initially, archaeologists considered the possibility that the colonization of Australia/New Guinea was achieved accidentally by just a few people swept to sea while fishing on a raft near an Indonesian island. . . . But believers in the fluke-colonization theory have been surprised by recent discoveries that still other islands, lying to the east of New Guinea, were colonized soon after New Guinea itself, by around 35,000 years ago. Those islands were New Britain and New Ireland, in the Bismarck Archipelago, and Buka, in the Solomon Archi-pelago. Buka lies out of sight of the closest island to the west and could have been reached only by crossing a water gap of about 100 miles. Thus, early Aus-tralians and New Guineans were probably capable of intentionally traveling over water to visible islands, and were using watercraft sufficiently often that the colonization of even invisible distant islands was repeatedly achieved unintentionally."

Jared Diamond, Guns, Germs, and Steel *(New York: W. W. Norton, 1999), 41–42*

4.   It happens that certain material appears in the dream-content which cannot be subsequently recognized, in the waking state, as being part of one's knowledge and experience. . . . The dreamer is therefore in the dark as to the source which the dream has tapped, and is even tempted to believe in an independent produc-tive activity on the part of the dream, until, often long afterwards, a fresh episode restores the memory of that former experience, which had been given up for lost,

and so reveals the source of the dream. One is therefore forced to admit that in the dream something was known and remembered that cannot be remembered in the waking state.

[Joseph] Delboeuf relates from his own experience an especially impressive example of this kind. He saw in his dream the courtyard of his house covered with snow, and found there two little lizards, half-frozen and buried in the snow. Being a lover of animals he picked them up, warmed them, and put them back into the hole in the wall which was reserved especially for them. He also gave them a few fronds of a little fern which was growing on the wall, and of which he knew they were very fond. In the dream he knew the name of the plant, *Asplenium ruta muralis*. . . . [But in] his waking state Delboeuf knew only a few Latin names of plants, and nothing of any *Asplenium*. To his great surprise he discovered that a fern of this name did actually exist, and that the correct name was *Asplenium ruta muraria*, which the dream had slightly distorted. An accidental coincidence was of course inconceivable; yet where he got his knowledge of the name Asplenium in the dream remained a mystery to him.

The dream occurred in 1862. Sixteen years later, while at the house of one of his friends, the philosopher noticed a small album containing dried plants, such as are sold as souvenirs to visitors in many parts of Switzerland. A sudden recollection came to him: he opened the herbarium, discovered therein the *Asplenium* of his dream, and recognized his own handwriting in the accompanying Latin name. The connection could now be traced. In 1860, two years before the date of the lizard dream, one of his friend's sisters, while on her wedding-journey, had paid a visit to Delboeuf. She had with her at the time this very album, which was intended for her brother, and Delboeuf had taken the trouble to write, at the dictation of a botanist, the Latin name under each of the dried plants.

That dreams have at their disposal recollections which are inaccessible to the waking state is a remarkable and theoretically important fact. . . .

Sigmund Freud, The Interpretation of Dreams *(1900).*
Chapter 1, section B. Translated by A. A. Brill, 1913

5.   "For more than a century, 'culture' has been invoked to explain different levels of violence within the United States and between the United States and other nations. . . .

"In the present context the term 'culture' is akin to widely shared belief systems. . . .

"Culture-based theories have great intuitive appeal, but they are tricky to prove empirically. One problem is that belief systems are hard to quantify and often seem to go hand in hand with other factors that facilitate violence, such as disadvantage and the breakdown of order. . . .

"Muddling things further, violence rates can be very different across regions that look pretty similar. Take the filmmaker Michael Moore's examination of the United States and Canada, neighboring nations that share a British heritage and frontier traditions, high levels of economic development, open democratic governance, even popular culture—but have very different levels of gun violence. In *Bowling for Columbine*, Moore suggests that Canadians have less gun violence because they are less volatile and more deferential to collective, consensus approaches to problem solving, a common characterization. But it's also true that Canada has much stricter gun laws than does the United States and much lower rates of handgun ownership. So is Canadian cultural 'niceness' keeping the gun homicide rate low? Or are Canada's gun laws keeping matters in check? Or is it both—the culture gave rise to the laws, which reinforce the culture?

"No one can say for sure, at least for now. But circumstantial evidence leads us to question 'culture' as the overriding explanation for violence (though we believe it may matter in certain circumstances). Our general skepticism stems from the fact that, although the United States has a *gun* homicide rate roughly seven times that of Canada, the two countries actually have comparable rates of *nongun* homicides. Likewise, within the United States, the exceptional rate of southern violence is really a problem of gun violence, not violence by other means. If cultural predispositions were to blame for violence, we would expect to see disparities between the United States and peer nations, and between the American South and other regions, in *nongun* assaults and homicides. But where these differences exist, they tend to be small."

Philip J. Cook and Kristina A. Goss, The Gun Debate: What
Everyone Needs to Know *(Oxford University Press, 2014), 62–64*

6.   "[T]he strongest evidence that a recreational drug can cause brain damage comes from the study of amphetamine, methamphetamine, and the synthetic amphetamine-like drug MDMA (Ecstasy [or Molly]). The results of animal studies show that doses of MDMA approximating those taken by human users result in the degeneration of very fine serotonergic neuron terminals. In rodents, these terminals regrow within a few months after drug use is stopped; but, in monkeys, the terminal loss may be permanent. . . ."

Bryan Kolb and Ian Q. Winshaw, Fundamentals of Human Neuropsychology,
Sixth Edition (New York: Worth Publishers, 2009), 189

7.   "Very clear experimental evidence for the particle-like behavior of photons was uncovered by Arthur Holly Compton in 1922. Compton had been investigating the scattering, or the deflection, of X rays by a target of graphite. . . . According to [classical, non-quantum] theory, X rays are merely light waves of extremely

high frequency. But according to quantum theory, they ought to consist of photons; and since their frequency is much higher than that of ordinary light, the energy of the X-ray photons ought to be much larger than that of photons of ordinary light. . . .

"When Compton bombarded the graphite with X rays of one selected wavelength, he found that the scattered X rays had wavelengths somewhat larger than that of the incident [that is, original] X rays. Classical theory cannot explain such a change of wavelength. . . .

"Compton soon recognized that the change of wavelength could be understood in terms of collisions of photons with electrons, collisions in which the photons behave like particles. . . . When the photon bounces off the electron, the electron recoils and thereby picks up some of the photon's energy—the deflected photon is left with a reduced energy. [A] reduction of the energy of the photon implies an increase of wavelength. Qualitatively, we expect that photons that suffer the most violent collisions will be deflected through the largest angles and lose the most energy; and therefore such photons should emerge with the longest wavelength. And this is just what Compton found in his experiments."

> *Hans C. Ohanion and John T. Markert,* Physics for Engineers and Scientists,
> *Third Edition (New York: W. W. Norton, 2007), 1269–70*

8. "We currently know of 115 different elements, ranging form the simplest—hydrogen, containing one proton—to the most complex, called ununoctium and discovered in 1999, with 118 protons and 181 neutrons in its nucleus. . . .

"How and where did all these elements form? Were they always present in the universe, or were they created after the universe formed? Since the 1950s, astronomers have come to realize that the hydrogen and most of the helium in the universe are primordial—that is, these elements date from the very earliest times. . . . All other elements in our universe result from stellar nucleosynthesis—that is, they were formed by nuclear fusion in the hearts of stars.

"To test this idea, we must consider not just the list of different kinds of elements and isotopes but also their observed abundances. . . . Any theory proposed for the creation of the elements must reproduce these observed abundances. The most obvious feature is that the heavy elements are much less abundant than the most light elements. . . .

"The modern picture of element formation involves many different types of nuclear reactions occurring at many different stages of stellar evolution, from main-sequence stars all the way to supernovae. Light elements—from hydrogen to iron—are built first by fusion, then by alpha capture, with proton and neutron capture filling in the gaps. We are reassured of the basic soundness of our theories by [the following] evidence.

"[T]he rate at which various nuclei are captured and the rate at which they decay are known from laboratory experiments. When these rates are incorporated into detailed computer models of the nuclear processes occurring in stars and supernovae, the resulting elemental abundances agree extremely well, point by point, with the observational data [about the abundance of elements in the universe]. The match is remarkably good for elements up through iron and is still fairly close for heavier nuclei."

Eric Chaisson and Steve McMillan, Astronomy Today,
Fourth Edition (Upper Saddle River, NJ: Prentice Hall, 2002), 552–60

9.   "The [historic] temperatures are compared with results from climate models that participated in an exercise coordinated by the Intergovernmental Panel on Climate Change, or IPCC, for its 2007 Fourth Assessment Report. Nineteen models participated, from around the world, and they are all driven by the same scenarios only. Each model was run twice, once with natural climate forcings only, and once by natural plus human climate forcings [such as greenhouse gas emissions and soot from power plants]. . . .

"The model simulations do a fairly good job of capturing the temperature rise in the early part of the twentieth century, but only the runs that include the human impact on climate are able to reproduce and explain the warming in the last few decades. This [result] is considered to be the 'smoking gun,' proof that humans have already affected the climate of the Earth. . . ."

"What would it take for the global warming forecast to be substantially wrong? Is it possible, or does it seem likely, that humans could put as much CO_2 [carbon dioxide] in the air as we like without changing the Earth's climate, and the whole global warming issue could just go away?

"There are two obstacles to this possibility. First, there would have to be some other mechanism to explain the recent warming since the 1970s: some large perturbation to the energy budget of the Earth that no one has measured or conceived of yet. It takes a lot of energy to warm up the whole surface of the Earth including deep into the ocean, and it cannot happen just by random chaos. Certainly there will always be things about the natural world that are not perfectly understood, maybe even things about which we have no clue yet. But so far, in spite of intensive and highly motivated searching, no one has come up with an alternative source of energy to account for all that warming. This can be seen in the failure of the climate models without the human climate forcings to warm up enough.

"Second, there would have to be a reason to throw out the greenhouse effect theory, some explanation of why increasing CO_2 would not block outgoing IR [infrared] energy by absorbing in its bending vibrational mode, perhaps, or how some negative, compensating feedback might neutralize the warming tendency from the CO_2, somehow allowing the Earth to shed the excess energy without warming up.

"Overcoming either of these obstacles seems like a long shot, given how much intense, motivated searching has been done. Overcoming both obstacles together seems extremely unlikely to me."

David Archer, Global Warming: Understanding the Forecast,
2nd ed. (New York: Wiley, 2012), 143–44

10.   "[Since] there has been during the long course of ages much migration from one part of the world to another, owing to . . . climatal and geographical changes and to the many occasional and unknown means of dispersal, then we can understand, on the theory of descent with modification [i.e., evolution], most of the great leading facts in [the] distribution [of species]. . . . We see the full meaning of the wonderful fact, which must have struck every traveller, namely, that on the same continent, under the most diverse conditions, under heat and cold, on mountain and lowland, on deserts and marshes, most of the inhabitants within each great class are plainly related; for they will generally be descendants of the same progenitors and early colonists. . . .

"On this view of migration, with subsequent modification, we can see why oceanic islands should be inhabited by only few species, but of these, why many are peculiar or endemic forms. We clearly see why those animals which cannot cross wide spaces of ocean, as frogs and terrestrial mammals, should not inhabit oceanic islands; and why, on the other hand, new and peculiar species of bats, which can traverse the ocean, are often found on islands far distant from any continent. Such facts as the presence of peculiar species of bats, and the absence of all other mammals, on oceanic islands, are utterly inexplicable on the theory of independent acts of creation.

". . . [And again], it is a rule of high generality that the inhabitants of each area are related to the inhabitants of the nearest source whence immigrants might have been derived. We see this in nearly all the plants and animals of the Galapagos Archipelago, of Juan Fernandez, and of the other American islands being related in the most striking manner to the plants and animals of the neighbouring American mainland; and those of the Cape de Verde archipelago and other African islands to the African mainland. . . . [T]hese facts receive no explanation on the theory of creation."

Charles Darwin, On the Origin of Species, *Sixth Edition*
(London: John Murray, 1872), 418–19

Recognizing deductive argument forms

Objective: To give you practice recognizing deductive argument forms in difficult contexts.

Instructions: Read Chapter VI and complete Exercise Sets 6.1, 6.2, and 6.5 before beginning this activity. Then, complete each of the following steps in order.

1. *Form a small group, choose a name for your group, and write your group's name on ten sticky notes.* Be sure to leave some extra space on each sticky note for later steps.

2. *Working in a small group, identify the argument forms of the arguments in the box below.* Each argument uses at least one of the deductive argument forms described in Chapter VI. Some use deductive arguments in several steps, as explained in Rule 28. Write the argument form(s) used in each argument on a different sticky note.

3. *Stick your sticky notes on the board to show which argument follows which rule.* Your instructor will write the number of each argument on the board. Affix a sticky note to the board to show which argument form each argument uses.

4. *As a class, discuss the arguments about which different groups disagreed.* If there are arguments about which groups disagree, have each group explain their reasoning. Try to figure out which argument form(s) the argument really uses.

Final product: The final product of this assignment should be a board full of sticky notes, showing which argument forms each of the following arguments follow.

Variation: The arguments in the box below all have to do with philosophical topics and come from contemporary or historical philosophers. Therefore, not only can they help you practice analyzing deductive arguments (and some of them are *hard*—they make for good practice!), they also give you a small taste of what philosophical argument can look like. This is especially useful if your course is being offered through a philosophy department or if you plan to take philosophy courses in the future. Instructors who are not in a philosophy department might want to provide an alternative set of arguments for deductive analysis.

Variation: Instead of using the arguments below, have each group find or create an argument that follows exactly one of the rules from Chapter VI. Use those arguments as the basis for this activity.

Variation: After studying Appendix III and completing Exercise Sets 12.1 and 12.2, work in groups to create argument maps of the arguments below. To facilitate working on argument maps in groups, write numbers on index cards, which you can arrange and rearrange to try out different ways of mapping each argument.

Some Philosophical Arguments for Use in "Recognizing Deductive Argument Forms"

1. Although we rarely acknowledge it, the history of philosophy is really a great clash of personal temperaments. Professional philosophers are, when it comes to temperament, either "tender minded" or "tough minded." If a philosopher is tender minded, then he or she is going to be most tempted by philosophies that are rationalistic, religious, idealistic, and optimistic. On the other hand, a philosopher will be drawn to more empiricist, irreligious, skeptical, and pessimistic views if he or she is tough minded. Thus, professional philosophers will tend to be either rationalistic, religious, idealistic, and optimistic or empiricist, irreligious, skeptical, and pessimistic.

   Adapted from: William James, Pragmatism *(Indianapolis: Hackett Publishing Company, 1981), 8–10*

2. It is possible to find fault with any philosophical position, and yet it is impossible to say that my own philosophical position has any faults. It would, of course, be possible to find fault with my own philosophical position if I had one. But on the other hand, it is possible to find fault with my philosophical position *only* if I have one, which I do not.

   Adapted from: Nagarjuna, Nagarjuna's Vigrahavyavartani: The Dispeller of Disputes, *translated by Jan Westerhoff (New York: Oxford University Press, 2010), 29*

3. The first step to overcoming the fear of death is to recognize that neither our body nor our soul exists after death. If no part of us exists after death, neither as a soul nor as a body, then we can suffer no pain or harm in death. If we can suffer no pain or harm in death, then death is nothing to fear. Thus, death is nothing to fear.

    Adapted from: Epicurus, "Letter to Menoeceus," in The Epicurus Reader, *translated by Brad Inwood and Lloyd P. Gerson (Indianapolis: Hackett Publishing Company, 1994), 29*

4. You have said that justice involves doing good to our friends who are good and just and doing evil to those who are evil and our enemies. If you are right, then the just person will do evil to those who are unjust. Yet, doing evil to someone harms them, and harming something makes it worse. If, then, the just person does evil to those who are evil and unjust enemies, then those enemies will be made even worse. That is, they will be made even more evil and more unjust. Surely the just person does not, by acting justly, make others more *unjust!* So I am afraid that you are wrong about your definition of justice.

    Adapted from: Plato, Republic, *translated by C. D. C. Reeve (Indianapolis: Hackett Publishing Company, 2004), 11*

5. Let me tell you about the theories of our friend, Ivan Fyodorovitch. He has asserted that if someone does not believe in the immortality of the soul, as I do not, then that person is obliged to believe that nothing is immoral—not even cannibalism. Indeed, he thinks that for such a person, pure selfishness is the only reasonable path. So, it seems, I am obliged to believe that nothing is immoral.

    Adapted from: Fyodor Dostoevsky, The Brothers Karamazov, *translated by Constance Garnett (New York: Modern Library, 1996), 72*

6. If I understand you correctly, you are suggesting that the soul and the body must proceed, each according to their own laws, in such a way that they appear to interact with one another, but in fact do not. Now, this seems to me to be perfectly possible. Yet I regard it as nothing more than a hypothesis, for God, if He is all powerful, is not limited by what we can imagine. As we know that He is all powerful, we must acknowledge that he is not limited by our feeble imaginations, and we could regard this view of yours as more than a hypothesis only if God could not do more than what we can imagine.

    Adapted from: Damaris Cudworth, letter to G. W. Leibniz, March 29, 1704, in Women Philosophers of the Early Modern Period, *edited by Margaret Atherton (Indianapolis: Hackett Publishing Company, 1994), 83*

7.   Either the meaning of life is to be found in the pursuit of happiness or the pursuit of morality or it is to be found in something else—something that may not maximize our own happiness or the total amount of justice or goodness in the world. Some reflection on the kinds of activities that many of us deem most central to leading a meaningful life reveals that they are not the activities that lead to the greatest individual happiness or to the most moral life imaginable. A meaningful life, then, is to be found in something beyond the pursuit of happiness or morality, important as those things may be.

Adapted from: Susan Wolf, Meaning in Life and Why It Matters *(Princeton: Princeton University Press, 2010), 49*

8.   In order to establish knowledge on a firmer footing, I have temporarily persuaded myself that all of the familiar things of the world do not really exist. I have even temporarily persuaded myself that God does not exist. But can I believe that *I* do not exist? I cannot, for if I did not exist, then it would be impossible for me to have persuaded myself of anything or for me to believe that I do not exist. I must exist, after all, in order to persuade myself of something or to believe something. As long as I am considering whether I exist, then, it is evident that I cannot believe that I do not exist.

Adapted from: René Descartes, Meditations on First Philosophy, *Third Edition, translated by Donald A. Cress (Indianapolis: Hackett Publishing Company, 1993), 18*

9.   It is possible that I am nothing but a disembodied mind. If I could exist as a disembodied mind, then having a mind and having a body are two different things. Thus, having a mind and having a body are two different things. And yet, I find that I do have a body. If having a mind and having a body are two different things, and I have a body, then I must consist of two different parts—a body and a mind.

Adapted from: René Descartes, Meditations on First Philosophy, *Third Edition, translated by Donald A. Cress (Indianapolis: Hackett Publishing Company, 1993), 56*

10. Some things, like our opinions, desires, and actions, are in our control. Other things, like our health, our possessions, and our reputation, are beyond our control. With respect to things that lie beyond your control, you can either acknowledge that they are beyond your control or you can pine after them, pretending that they are within your control. You will be constantly disturbed and distressed if you pine after them as if they were in your control, but if you recognize that

they are beyond your control, no one can ever force you to do anything or prevent you from doing anything, and no one will be able to harm you. The choice, then, is up to you: You can have a life of constant distress or a life free from compulsion and harm. This lies within your control.

Adapted from: Epictetus, The Handbook (The Encheiridion), *translated by N. P. White (Indianapolis: Hackett Publishing Company, 1983), 11*

Compiling your research into an extended outline

Objective: To help you learn to compile shorter arguments on a specific topic into a single, extended outline for use in an argumentative essay or presentation.

Instructions: Read Chapter VII and complete Exercise Sets 7.2, 7.4, 7.6, 7.8, and 7.10 before beginning this activity. When you are ready, complete each of the following steps in order.

1. *Write down the question that you have been exploring in Exercise Sets 7.2, 7.4, 7.6, 7.8, and 7.10.* In Exercise Set 7.2, you identified several questions. In the exercise sets that followed, you explored one of those questions in detail. Write that question at the top of a piece of paper or the beginning of a document in a word processor.

2. *On the basis of the arguments and objections that you developed in Exercise Sets 7.4, 7.6, and 7.8, decide which answer to your question is best supported by arguments.* In Exercise Sets 7.4, 7.6, and 7.8, you considered arguments and objections related to one of the questions that you identified in Exercise Set 7.2. On the basis of all of those arguments, decide which answer to your question is best supported by arguments. Be sure to consider alternative answers to the question, which you identified in Exercise Set 7.10. Write this answer down. This answer will be the main conclusion of your extended argument.

3. *Identify the strongest argument(s) for your answer.* In Exercise Set 7.6, you developed at least two arguments for the answer that you have now chosen as your main conclusion. Write down your

strongest argument(s) for that answer, in premise-and-conclusion form.

4. *Identify the most important objections to your arguments.* In Exercise Set 7.8, you worked out at least one objection to the argument(s) that you chose in Step 3. Write down your objections to your chosen argument(s).

5. *Identify the strongest argument(s) against competing answers.* Write down the strongest argument(s) from Exercise Set 7.6 *against* each of the other plausible answers to your question, including the alternative answers that you identified in Exercise Set 7.10.

Final product: The final product of this activity should be a single document containing a statement of the question being considered, a statement of the answer that you think is best supported by arguments, premise-and-conclusion outlines of one or more strong arguments for that answer, clear statements of at least one objection to each of those arguments, and premise-and-conclusion outlines of strong arguments against alternative answers to the question being considered.

Improving a sample paper

Objective: To give you practice applying the rules from Chapter VIII to a sample paper.

Instructions: Read Chapter VIII before beginning this activity. Then, complete each of the following steps in order.

1. *Read the sample paper at the end of this assignment sheet.* You may want to annotate the paper to make later parts of this activity easier for you: that is, mark the main conclusion of the paper, each of the major arguments, any objections that the paper considers, and the author's responses to those objections.

2. *Write one or two paragraphs in response to each of the following questions about the paper.* Be as specific as possible in your responses, citing specific sentences or passages and offering concrete suggestions about how to improve the paper.

   a. Does the author's introduction get right to the point (Rule 34)? What changes could the author make in order to improve the introduction?

b. Does the paper make a definite claim (Rule 35)? Would you recommend any changes to clarify the main claim of the paper?

c. How well does this paper communicate its main argument(s)? Do the arguments in the paper follow all of the relevant rules from Chapters I through VI? What changes would you recommend to clarify the argument(s) and/or make them follow the relevant rules?

d. Does the paper detail and respond to objections (Rule 37)? What changes would you recommend to improve the author's handling of objections?

e. Does the paper state an appropriately modest conclusion (Rule 39)? What changes would you recommend to improve the paper's conclusion?

Final product: The final product of this assignment should be a written document of five to ten paragraphs. The document should provide concrete advice to the author of the sample paper.

Media Piracy Is Wrong

Since the beginning of time, people have debated whether it is morally wrong to download music, movies, and other media without paying for it. There are many arguments on both sides of the issue, and there will probably never be total agreement about it. Downloading media first became a major problem around the year 2000, when a software program called Napster made it possible for people to share MP3 files. Napster was eventually shut down by the courts, after a lawsuit by the recording companies. People's appetite for music couldn't be contained, though, and new file-sharing platforms developed, including gnutella and BitTorrent. Since then, people have begun downloading movies, TV shows, and other media too. In response, media companies started suing individual people who downloaded media files without paying for them, often imposing ridiculously high fines for minor offenses, such as downloading a few files. Many people thought that these lawsuits were overly harsh, and so the media companies discontinued them so as not to look bad. Although it did make the companies look bad, the companies were justified in bringing the lawsuits, because it is both illegal and morally wrong for people to download copyrighted media files without paying for them.

Downloading media without paying for it is wrong because it is a form of stealing. It is easy to see that downloading media files is stealing by noticing that downloading a movie without paying for it is like stealing a DVD from Walmart. It's true that the artists aren't going to suffer significantly from the loss of revenue from a single movie, just as losing a single DVD isn't going to affect the largest corporation in the world. Nonetheless, the DVD belongs to Walmart, and the song, movie, or whatever belongs to the artist(s) who created it. Just as stealing the DVD deprives Walmart of the right to control what happens to its property, so downloading media files deprives the artists of the right to control what happens to their property. Whenever one person takes another's property without the owner's permission, that is stealing. For instance, if a musician records a song and a record company gets hold of the recording and distributes it without the musician's permission, the record company has stolen the musician's intellectual property—even if the record company doesn't charge for the song. When people download a media file without paying for it, they are behaving much like that record company. They are undermining artists' control over their intellectual property. When a musician writes a song or a filmmaker makes a movie, that song or movie is the intellectual property of its creator. Since it is the creator's property, he or she gets to decide who can use the song or movie. Therefore, taking a song, movie, or whatever without the creator's permission is stealing, and stealing is morally wrong.

Not everyone finds this analogy convincing. Some people object that downloading media files isn't like stealing a DVD because downloading a file doesn't involve taking anything physical. When someone steals a DVD, on this view he or she is taking something away from Walmart. When one person downloads a media file from someone else's computer, the other person still has the media file. This objection doesn't work, though, because the difference between stealing a DVD and downloading a file isn't morally relevant.

Others might object to this argument by pointing out that even if downloading media files is a form of stealing, it is not morally wrong, because it does not harm anyone. In fact, some people argue that downloading media files benefits the artists because it encourages the people who download the files to go to concerts, buy t-shirts for their favorite bands, and so on. This is implausible, however. If giving away music for free boosted overall profits, then record companies and musicians would be happy about it. Instead, they are trying to stop it. Furthermore, this logic does not apply to the downloading of movies, television shows, or other forms of media. There are no concert tours for movies, and people rarely buy t-shirts or other memorabilia for their favorite movies and television shows in the way that they buy memorabilia for their favorite bands.

Besides, the reason that stealing is wrong is not only because it causes harm but also because it violates the owners' rights. Even if downloading media did benefit the artists, it would still be wrong because it is a violation of their rights.

One final objection is that many people download media files as a way of deciding whether they want to buy a song or a movie. This might make downloading media files okay if people deleted the media files after they downloaded them, but many people do not. Downloading a media file to "try it out" is like stealing a piece of clothing from a store in order to try it on at home. The more appropriate thing to do is to use one of the approved methods for "trying out" a song or movie, such as listening to samples online or renting the movie. This is like trying on a piece of clothing in the store, which everyone agrees is okay.

The main argument against downloading media files without paying for them is that doing so amounts to stealing, which is wrong. Downloading media is stealing because it undermines the artists' intellectual property rights, which give the artists the right to decide who can access their creations. The objections considered above attempt to show either that downloading media is not stealing or that in the case of media files, stealing is not wrong. Since none of these objections succeed, it is reasonable to conclude that downloading media files is wrong. People who download media files are therefore criminals, like burglars, muggers, and pirates. They ought to be forced to serve jail time, just like burglars and muggers.

Compiling a draft of an argumentative essay

Objective: To help you learn to compile shorter arguments on a specific topic into a single, extended argument for use in an argumentative essay or presentation.

Instructions: Read Chapter VIII; complete Exercise Sets 8.1, 8.2, 8.3, and 8.5; and do the "Compiling your research into an extended outline" activity (p. 470) before beginning this activity. When you are ready, complete each of the following steps in order.

1. *Write a brief introduction to your essay.* Your introduction should introduce the issue in a clear and engaging way (Rule 34). It should provide the reader with just enough background information to help them understand what the issue is and why it matters. Most importantly, it should clearly indicate the question that you will be answering and the answer that you will be arguing for (Rule 35). Use the question and the answer that you chose while completing the "Compiling your research into an extended outline" activity.

2. *Add the prose version of your strongest arguments for your main conclusion.* When you compiled your research into an extended outline, you identified one or more arguments as the strongest arguments for your answer. In exercise 8.3, you converted those arguments into prose paragraphs. Insert those paragraphs after your introduction, adding appropriate transitions between them.

3. *Add the objections and responses to each of your main arguments.* When you compiled your research into an extended outline, you identified one or more objections to each of the arguments for your main answer. In Exercise Set 8.5, you converted those objections into complete paragraphs and added responses to them. Add those objections to your essay, along with your response to them. Depending on the length of your arguments and objections, it might work best to include objections immediately after each argument. In other cases, you might prefer to give all of your arguments and then discuss all of your objections.

4. *Add arguments against any other plausible answers to the question answered in your essay.* If there are other very plausible answers to the question that you are answering in your essay, you might want to tell your readers why those answers are not as good as yours. When you compiled your research into an extended outline, you identified the strongest arguments against each of those answers. In exercise 8.3, you converted those arguments into prose paragraphs. Choose one or two plausible alternatives to your chosen answer, and add the arguments against them to your essay, using appropriate transitions.

5. *Write a brief conclusion to your essay.* Your conclusion should reiterate the main points of your essay. In particular, remind your reader of your main conclusion and the main arguments that you use to support that conclusion. And remember: don't claim more than you have shown (Rule 39)!

Final product: The final product of this activity will be a complete draft of an argumentative essay. This will be a big accomplishment—congratulations! Remember, though, that you're not done with the writing process. You still need to get feedback on your draft and use that feedback to make your essay even better (Rule 38).

Peer-review workshop

Objective: To give you practice applying the rules from Chapter VIII to provide constructive feedback on someone else's argumentative essay and use someone else's feedback to plan improvements to your own essay.

Instructions: Read Chapter VIII before beginning this activity. Then, complete each of the following steps in order.

1. *Choose an argumentative essay of your own to use for this activity.* This might be an essay that you wrote for the "Compiling a draft of an argumentative essay" activity (p. 474), an essay that you wrote for another class, or an essay you wrote for some other purpose.

2. *Exchange argumentative essays with a group of classmates.* Form a group of three or four people. Give one copy of your essay to each person in the group and get an essay from each person in the group.

3. *Write a detailed evaluation of your classmates' essays, using the peer-review worksheet at the end of this activity as a guide.* Your goal is to provide constructive feedback that will help your classmates know what they have done well and how they can improve their essays. Your evaluation should include concrete advice that is framed directly but constructively and politely. Your evaluation can take the form of a numbered list of responses to the prompts on the peer-review worksheet. You may also find it helpful to write some comments directly on your classmates' essays.

4. *Return your evaluations to your classmates and collect your peers' evaluations of your own essay.*

5. *Make a plan for revising your essay.* Read your classmates' evaluations of your essay. Decide which of their criticisms are worth addressing and which suggestions are worth taking. Make a list of specific changes that you intend to make to your draft to meet those criticisms and implement those suggestions.

Final product: The final product of this assignment consists of several documents. You should have two or three peer evaluations of your essay and a list of specific changes that you intend to make to your paper in light of those evaluations. Each evaluation should consist of a numbered list of responses to the prompts on the peer-review worksheet and, optionally, a copy of your essay with comments written directly on it. (Each member of your group should also have your evaluation of their essay.)

Peer-Review Worksheet

Instructions: Answer the following questions to provide feedback on a draft of a classmate's paper. Be as specific as possible in all of your answers.

1. Does the draft have an engaging opening? If so, what makes it engaging? If not, suggest a way to make it more engaging.

2. Is the draft's introduction an appropriate length? Does it include any sentences that are off topic, redundant, or overly long? Are there any topics that ought to be covered in the introduction, but aren't?

3. Does the draft contain a clear, definite statement of the paper's main thesis or proposal? In your own words, what do you think the paper's main thesis or proposal is?

4. On the draft itself, put an asterisk next to each of the paper's main arguments. Does the draft present these arguments clearly? If not, identify specific aspects of the draft's presentation that you find confusing or important assumptions that are left out.

5. Does the draft develop the main argument(s) in enough detail, or are there premises that need further explanation and/or support? If so, which premises are they?

6. What types of arguments are used in this paper (arguments by example, deductive arguments, analogies, etc.)? Do they follow the relevant rules in this book?

7. On the draft itself, put two asterisks next to each objection that the author considers. Does the draft explain each objection in detail? Do any of them need further development? If so, which ones?

8. On the draft itself, put three asterisks next to the author's response to each objection. Does the draft meet each objection that it raises? If not, which objections need to be addressed further, and how do you suggest the author address those objections?

9. Are there any other objections that you think the author should consider?

10. Are there alternative theses or proposals that you think the author should consider? If so, what are they, and why do you think they are important?

11. Does the draft contain an appropriate conclusion, which restates the paper's main points and avoids making overly bold claims?

12. If you could change just one thing about this draft, what would it be and why? Be as specific as possible.

13. What is the best thing about this draft? Be as specific as possible.

14. What other comments or suggestions do you have about how the author might improve this draft?

Writing opening lines

Objective: To give you practice writing openings for written essays and oral presentations.

Instructions: Read Rules 34 and 40 and complete Exercise Sets 8.1 and 9.1 before beginning this activity. Then, complete each of the following steps in order.

1. *Read the pieces provided by your instructor.* Your instructor will provide you with three editorials or op-eds from recent newspapers or magazines. Read each piece carefully.

2. *Write three openings for each of those pieces.* For each of the three pieces that your instructor gave you, imagine that you were going to write an essay or give an oral presentation arguing for the editorial or op-ed's main point. Write a hard lead for a written essay, a soft lead for a written essay, and an opening for an oral presentation of that piece.

3. *Share your openings with a group.* Form a group of five people. Have each member of the group share all three of his or her openings for each of the three pieces that your instructor gave you.

4. *Choose one opening for each piece.* As a group, choose the best opening for each piece, leaving you with a list of three openings for the entire group.

5. *Share your group's chosen openings with the class.* Share your group's openings with the rest of the class, including a few words about why you chose each one.

Final Product: The final product of this activity should be a written list of nine openings for each member of your group, consisting of one hard lead, one soft lead, and one presentation opening for each of the three pieces, as well as a list of the three openings that the group chose to share with the class.

Creating a visual aid

Objective: To give you practice applying Rule 44 from Chapter IX to create good visual aids for oral presentations.

Instructions: Read Chapter IX before beginning this activity. Then, complete each of the following steps in order.

1. *Choose an argumentative essay to use for this activity.* This might be an essay of your own, such as one that you wrote for the "Compiling a draft of an argumentative essay" activity (p. 474) or one that you wrote for another class. If your instructor allows it, you might also use an op-ed from a newspaper or an argumentative essay from a book or textbook.

2. *Create a visual aid for an oral presentation of the argument from your chosen essay.* Create a visual aid to accompany an oral presentation of the argument from the essay you picked in Step 1. This can take any form you want—a PowerPoint presentation, a handout, etc.

   Think very carefully about the structure and content of this visual aid. You might also look for advice online about making good use of the kind of visual aid you're planning to use. The visual aid should complement and enhance your presentation without making your oral presentation redundant.

3. *Write one or two pages explaining why you chose to design your visual aid as you did.* First, explain why you chose the form that you did. For instance, if you chose to draw your visual aid on a board as you talk, explain why you chose to do that rather than use PowerPoint. If you did (or didn't) use a handout (instead of or in addition to, say, PowerPoint), why (or why not)? Second, explain why you included the content that you did, rather than other content or no content at all. Be as specific as possible, even if that means discussing each slide separately.

Final product: The final product of this assignment consists of a copy of the essay you chose in Step 1, a hard copy of the visual aid you created in Step 2, and the one- to two-page explanatory document that you wrote for Step 3. If your visual aid is a PowerPoint presentation, provide a printout of your slides. If your visual aid is something that you would create during the presentation, such a series of drawings on a board, create a paper copy in advance to turn in to your instructor.

Oral presentations

Objective: To give you practice applying the rules from Chapter IX on oral arguments.

Instructions: Read Chapter IX before beginning this activity. Then, complete each of the following steps in order.

1. *Choose an argumentative essay to use for this activity.* This might be an essay of your own, such as one that you wrote for the "Compiling a draft of an argumentative essay" activity (p. 474) or one that you wrote for another class. If your instructor allows it, you might also use an op-ed from a newspaper or an argumentative essay from a book or textbook. Be sure to choose an essay whose basic argument you could present in about ten minutes.

2. *Prepare an oral presentation of the argument from that essay.* Follow the rules from Chapter IX to prepare a ten-minute oral presentation of the argument from the essay you chose in Step 1. You may need to simplify the argument a bit. Think carefully about which parts you can cut from the presentation while retaining the overall structure of the argument.

    You may want to complete the "Creating a visual aid" activity (p. 479) when preparing your visual aid.

3. *Deliver your oral presentation to your class.* Rehearse your presentation in advance so that you can *deliver* the presentation rather than reading from a page or a screen. Rehearsing your presentation also helps ensure that you can finish your presentation in the allotted time.

    Be sure to find out whether you are expected to take questions after your presentation. If so, think about the kinds of questions you're likely to get, and prepare some answers for them. In particular, be prepared to answer questions about the parts of the essay that you chose to cut in order to fit your presentation into the allotted time.

    Arrange to record your presentation. A video is best, since you can see and hear what you're doing, but even an audio recording made on a computer can be helpful. You can learn a lot about public speaking by watching or listening to your own presentation.

4. *Make a list of things that you did well and things that you could improve.* Watch or listen to the recording of your presentation. Then, create a list of things that you did well in the presentation and things that you could improve. For each item that you could improve, write a few sentences explaining what you could do differently to give a better presentation. Be as specific as possible.

Final product: The final product of this assignment should be an oral presentation of an argument, along with a set of notes for your presentation—or even a full, written-out version of the presentation, if that helps you feel prepared. Your final product should also include a recording of your presentation and a list of things that you did well, aspects of your presentation that you could improve, and specific things you could do to improve those aspects.

In-class debates

Objective: To give you practice applying all of the rules from this book in the context of an in-class debate.

Instructions: Reread Chapters I, VII, VIII, and IX before beginning this activity. Then, complete each of the following steps in order.

1. *Pair up with a debate partner.* Find out from your instructor whether you may choose your own debate partner or if your instructor will assign one to you.

2. *Identify a specific debate question.* Your instructor may assign a specific question for each pair or provide guidelines for choosing a question of your own. If you are choosing your own question, pick a question that interests both you and your debate partner.

3. *Assign each debater to argue for a different answer to the debate question.* In Step 2, you picked a specific question for your debate. Identify possible answers to that question (there may be more than two, of course), and choose one for each debater to defend. For the purposes of this activity, be sure that you and your partner are arguing for different answers. It's fine if you are arguing for an answer that you don't actually believe.

4. *Prepare a five-minute oral argument for your assigned answer.* Outside of class, prepare a five-minute oral argument for your assigned answer. This will probably take a bit of research. (See Chapter VII for guidance on researching your argument.) Be sure that your argument follows the rules in this book—especially the rules in Chapter I—and that your oral presentation follows the rules in Chapter IX.

5. *Join with another pair of debate partners to form a debate group of four people.* The other pair of partners need not be debating the same question that you are.

6. *Debate your partner in front of the rest of your debate group.* Pick one pair of debate partners to go first. Follow these steps to hold a structured debate on the topic:

   a. *Have each partner present his or her oral argument to the debate group.* Give each partner five uninterrupted minutes to present his or her argument to the group.

   b. *Have each partner offer a two-minute rebuttal to his or her partner's argument.* Give each partner two uninterrupted minutes to raise objections and ask questions about the other's argument.

   c. *Have each partner conclude with a two-minute response.* These responses can address objections, answer questions, and wrap up the case for each partner's view.

7. *Discuss the arguments and rebuttals as a group.* Spend five minutes discussing the arguments, questions, and objections as a group. See if you can decide on which answer is best.

8. *Repeat Steps 6 and 7 with the other pair of debate partners in your group.*

9. *(Optional) Have several pairs of partners from the class repeat their debate in front of the whole class.* Your instructor may pick several pairs of debate partners to repeat Step 6 in front of the class, with the whole class participating in the question-and-answer session. Use the class discussion to try to decide which answer is best.

Final product: The final product of this assignment should be a series of debates and discussions between you and your classmates. Your instructor may also ask you to turn in a written version of your initial oral argument.

Extended in-class group debates

Objective: To give you practice applying all of the rules from this book in the context of an extended series of in-class debates.

Instructions: Reread Chapters I, VII, VIII, and IX before beginning this activity. Then, complete each of the following steps in order.

1. *Identify a specific problem for the class to address.* Your entire class should identify a single problem that they would like to consider for this activity. This could be a problem in your school or community, or a more general problem of contemporary interest.

2. *Form debate groups of five people.* Find out from your instructor whether you may choose your own group or whether you will be assigned to a specific group.

3. *Prepare a five-minute oral argument for a proposed response to the assigned problem.* In Step 1, you identified a specific problem that your class would address. Think carefully about various possible responses to the problem, keeping the rules from Chapter VII in mind. Then, choose a specific proposal for responding to that problem, keeping Rule 35 in mind. Construct an argument for that proposal, following the rules from Chapter VIII. Then, develop a five-minute oral presentation of that argument, following the rules in Chapter IX.

4. *Hold a debate within your debate group to identify your group's strongest proposal.* Follow these steps to hold a structured debate in which your group identifies the strongest of the proposals that your group develops:

   a. *Have each member of the group present his or her oral argument.* Give each group member five uninterrupted minutes to present his or her argument to the debate group.

   b. *Discuss possible objections and revisions to each proposal.* Discuss each proposal as a group, raising objections, considering responses to those objections, and considering possible revisions to each proposal. Do your best to identify the strongest possible proposal that you can.

   c. *Choose a single proposal to use in the next round of debate.* Choose a single proposal to put forward as your group's proposal in the next round of debate. This could be one of the original proposals or a revised version that emerged during discussion. If your group can't reach a unanimous decision, you may need to vote on the best proposal.

5. *Prepare a ten-minute oral argument to present to the whole class.* Work with your debate group to prepare a ten-minute oral argument for the proposal that you chose in Step 4(c).

6. *Hold a debate as a class to identify the strongest proposal.* Follow these steps to hold a structured debate in which the whole class identifies the strongest of the groups' proposals:

   a. *Have each group present their oral argument.* Give each group ten uninterrupted minutes to present their argument to the entire class.

   b. *Hold a question-and-answer session about each group's proposals.* Immediately after each group's proposals, give the class five minutes to ask questions about the proposal.

   c. *Choose one proposal as the strongest.* If the class can't reach a unanimous decision about which proposal is the strongest, choose a single proposal by a class vote.

7. *(Optional) Propose revisions to the chosen proposal.* Hold a class discussion to consider revisions to the proposal that you chose in Step 6(c). These revisions may involve incorporating elements of the other proposals.

8. *Submit your proposal to an appropriate stakeholder.* Choose someone to produce a written version of the proposal that your class chose in Step 6(c). With your instructor's help, identify an appropriate person and send that person your class's proposal. For instance, if your proposals address a problem in your city, you might send the proposal to the mayor's office.

Final product: After two rounds of debate, the final product of this activity should be a written proposal for a response to address a specific problem. Your instructor may ask you to turn in additional materials, such as written versions of your oral arguments.

Relating rules and fallacies

Objective: To help you understand the connections between the rules in Chapters I through VI and the fallacies in Appendix I.

Instructions: Read Chapters I through VI and Appendix I before beginning this activity. When you are ready, complete each of the following steps in order.

1. *Make a table listing the fallacies in Appendix I along the left-hand side and the rules from Chapters I through VI along the top.* You can draw the table by hand or use a spreadsheet.

2. *Next to each fallacy, put an X in the column(s) corresponding to the rule(s) that each fallacy violates.* Most of the fallacies in Appendix I violate specific rules from Chapters I through VI of this book. In the row for each fallacy, put an X in the column for each of the specific rule(s) that the fallacy violates. A few of the fallacies do not directly violate any rule from this book. For those fallacies, you do not need to write anything down.

3. *Identify rules that are not associated with any of the fallacies in Appendix I.* Some of the columns in your table will not have any X's in them. These columns correspond to rules that are not associated with any of the fallacies listed on your table.

4. *Suggest names for arguments that violate each of the rules from Step 3.* For each rule that is not associated with a fallacy listed on your table, name a new fallacy that involves violating that rule. Add a new row to the bottom of your table for each of these new fallacies.

5. *Write a brief description of the fallacies you named in Step 4.* On a separate piece of paper, write a one- or two-sentence description of the fallacies from Step 4. If possible, give an example of an argument that commits that fallacy.

6. *Create a master table for the class by comparing your table with your classmates' tables.* Working in small groups or as an entire class, compare your tables with your classmates' tables. If there are any differences between your tables, try to resolve the differences through discussion. Once you have resolved your disagreements about which rules each fallacy violates, create a master table that shows the consensus about which fallacies violate which rules.

Final product: The final product of this assignment should be a table of fallacies and rules, showing all of the fallacies in Appendix I as well as new fallacies involving other rules from this book. This should be accompanied by a separate document containing brief descriptions and examples of any fallacies in the table that are not described in Appendix I. If you come up with some especially good names for fallacies not listed in this book, send them to us care of the publisher!

Identifying, reinterpreting, and revising fallacies

Objective: To help you learn to recognize, reinterpret, and avoid fallacies.

Instructions: Read Appendix I and complete Exercise Sets 10.1–10.4 before beginning this activity. When you are ready, complete each of the following steps in order.

1. *Bring six copies of a fallacious argument to class.* This could be a fallacious argument that you found on your own or one that you wrote yourself (e.g., while completing Exercise Set 10.3). Bring six copies of the argument on six separate pieces of paper. Do not write the name of the fallacy on the paper.

2. *Form a group of four or five people.* Your instructor may assign you to a group, or you may choose your own group.

3. *Choose two fallacious arguments from your group.* Each member of your group has brought one fallacious argument. Share the arguments with one another and then, as a group, choose two arguments that you will share with the other groups. These could be the most subtle, the most persuasive, or the most entertaining fallacies that your group has found or written.

4. *Distribute your two chosen arguments to other groups in the class.* Your group should have six copies of each of the arguments that you chose in Step 3. Give one copy to your instructor. Distribute the other five copies among five other groups in the class. During this step, your group should receive up to five arguments from various other groups in the class.

5. *Identify the fallacy committed by each of the arguments you received from the other groups.* In Step 4, you received several fallacious arguments from other groups in the class. As a group, decide which fallacy each argument commits.

6. *Suggest a way to reinterpret or improve each of the arguments you received in order to avoid committing a fallacy.* It is usually possible to reinterpret an argument in such a way that it avoids committing a fallacy, or at least to suggest additional premises that could be added to avoid the fallacy. Offer such a reinterpretation or revision of each argument from Step 4, just as you did in Exercise Sets 10.2 and 10.4.

7. *Compare your results with the rest of the class.* As a class, go through each of the arguments that were distributed in Step 4. Have each group that received that particular argument state which fallacy they think the argument commits and how they would reinterpret or revise it to avoid the fallacy. If there is disagreement, see if the class can resolve the disagreement through discussion.

Final product: The final product of this assignment should be a set of fallacious arguments, given to your group by other groups, each labeled with the name of the fallacy that the argument commits and accompanied by a suggestion for reinterpreting or revising the argument to avoid the fallacy.

Critical-thinking public service announcements

Objective: To help you learn to understand specific fallacies and strategies for avoiding them.

Instructions: Read Appendix I before beginning this activity. When you are ready, complete each of the following steps in order.

1. *Identify a type of fallacy to focus on for this activity.* Your instructor may assign you to focus on a specific type of fallacy (e.g., the straw man fallacy) or you may be allowed to choose your own kind of fallacy.

2. *Create a public service announcement about your chosen fallacy.* Follow the steps below to create a public service announcement (PSA) educating the public about the "dangers" of the fallacy you chose or were assigned and offering advice on how to avoid it. Think creatively about the format and content of your PSA. Whether it's a video, an audio recording, a brochure, a Web page, or something else, your PSA should explain the fallacy and offer advice about avoiding it.

3. (Optional) *Share your public service announcement with your class.* Share your final product with your classmates by distributing or presenting it in class or posting it online.

Final product: The final product of this assignment is a public service announcement about a specific fallacy. This may take the form of a pamphlet, a PowerPoint presentation, an audio recording, a video, or any other format that your instructor allows.

Defining key terms in an essay

Objective: To give you practice defining key terms in an argumentative essay.

Instructions: Read Appendix II and complete Exercise Sets 11.1 and 11.2 before beginning this activity. When you are ready, complete each of the following steps in order.

1. *Choose an argumentative essay of your own to use for this activity.* This might be an essay that you wrote for the "Compiling a draft of an argumentative essay" activity (p. 474), an essay that you wrote for another class, or an essay you wrote for some other purpose.

2. *Identify the thesis statement of your essay.* Find the thesis statement (i.e., the main conclusion) of the argumentative essay that you chose in Step 1. If the essay does not contain a clear statement of its conclusion, write your own statement of its conclusion.

3. *Provide a definition for the key terms in the essay's thesis statement.* Make a list of all of the most important terms in the essay's thesis statement. Then, provide a definition for each word on that list. Be sure the definitions follow the rules from Appendix II.

4. (Optional) *Exchange essays and definitions with a classmate and check to see that all of your classmate's definitions follow the rules from Appendix II.* Quickly skim your classmate's essay so that you have some idea of the context for these definitions. Then, look at each definition and decide how well it follows each of the rules from Appendix II. Write a brief paragraph summarizing how well the definitions follow those rules. If any of the definitions violate the rules, suggest better definitions.

Final product: The final product of this assignment should be a list of definitions for key terms in your essay's thesis statement. Optionally, it may also include a brief paragraph critiquing a classmate's definitions and suggesting improvement to those definitions.

Defining difficult terms

Objective: To give you practice defining difficult terms.

Instructions: Read Appendix II and complete Exercise Sets 11.1 and 11.2 before beginning this activity. When you are ready, complete each of the following steps in order.

1. *Form a group of four or five people.* Your instructor may assign you to a group, or you may be allowed to choose your own group.

2. *Identify two words that are difficult to define.* As a group, identify two words that are difficult to define. They should be difficult because they are abstract, vague, or loaded, not because they are rare or obscure words.

3. *Write your two words on the board.* Choose one person from your group to write your two words on the board or post them somewhere that everyone in the class can see them.

4. *Come up with definitions for all of the words on the board.* In Step 3, each group put two words on the board. As a group, come up with the best definitions you can for each word, keeping in mind the rules from Appendix II.

5. *Compare definitions from each group.* As a class, go through each of the words that were written on the board in Step 3. Have each

group share their definition of the word. After everyone has shared their definition for a given word, vote on the best definition. Optionally, see if you can combine definitions to make an even better definition.

Final Product: The final product of this assignment should be a list of words that are difficult to define, and proposed definitions for those words.

Argument mapping workshop

Objective: To give you practice mapping arguments and thinking about argument maps.

Instructions: Read Appendix III and complete Exercise Sets 12.1 and 12.2 before beginning this activity. Then, complete each of the following steps in order.

1. *Form a group of two to five people.* Find out from your instructor whether you may choose your own group or whether you will be assigned to a specific group.

2. *Write out a paragraph-length argument in plain English.* As a group, construct an argument on any topic that interests you. Write out your argument in plain English—that is, in the style in which the arguments from the exercise sets in Appendix III are written. Your argument should be about the length of a medium-sized paragraph. It should be simple enough that someone else could read it and draw an argument map of it in five or ten minutes.

3. *Draw an argument map of your argument on a separate piece of paper.* As a group, draw an argument map of the argument from Step 2. Draw your map on a different piece of paper than the one containing your written argument.

4. *Put your argument map in an envelope and pass the envelope and your argument to another group.* Place the argument map from Step 3, but not the written argument itself, in an envelope. Write your group members' names on the envelope, but do not seal it. Pass your written argument and the envelope to another group in the class. Be sure that your group receives an argument and envelope from another group.

5. *Draw an argument map of the argument you received in Step 4.* As a group, draw an argument map for the argument that you received in Step 4. Don't look at the argument map that's already in the envelope.

6. *Add your argument map to the envelope, and pass the argument and envelope to another group.* Add your argument map from Step 5 to the envelope that you received in Step 4. Then, pass the argument and envelope on to another group. Be sure that your group receives a new argument and envelope from another group.

7. *Repeat Step 6 as many times as you can in the time allotted.* Find out from your instructor how much time you have. Repeat Step 6 as many times as you can in that time.

8. *Return the envelopes and arguments to their creators.* Return each envelope and written argument to the group that originally wrote the argument.

9. *Compare the various argument maps of your argument.* Compare the other groups' maps of your argument. If the argument maps are not all identical, figure out how many different maps there are. Decide which argument maps are accurate representations of your argument and which are not. Choose one argument map as the best representation of your argument.

10. *(Optional) Draw the argument map of your argument on the board.* Choose one person to draw your group's map of your argument on the board. Choose another person to explain why your group mapped the argument as it did and how other groups mapped it (if they mapped it differently).

Final product: The final product of this activity is a written version of your argument and an envelope containing several different maps of the argument.

Variation: Instead of creating an argument together during Step 2, have each member of your group write his or her own argument before class. As a group, choose your favorite argument and then proceed to Step 3.

Developing your own arguments using argument maps

Objective: To give you practice mapping arguments and using argument maps to develop your own arguments.

Instructions: Read Appendix III and complete Exercise Sets 12.1 and 12.2 before beginning this activity. Then, complete each of the following steps in order.

1. *Choose an argumentative essay of your own to use for this activity.* This might be an essay that you wrote for the "Compiling a draft of an argumentative essay" activity (p. 474), an essay that you wrote for another class, or an essay you wrote for some other purpose.

2. *Draw an argument map for each of the major arguments in your essay.* If your essay contains only one, large argument, draw a single argument map. If your essay contains multiple arguments, draw a separate argument map for each argument.

3. *Highlight all of the premises on the argument maps that are not supported by other premises.* On each argument map, circle or highlight the numbers representing premises that are not supported by other premises—that is, premises that are not also subconclusions.

4. *Identify the unsupported premises that need more support.* Of the premises that you highlighted in Step 3, identify those that need more support (e.g., because they are controversial or because most readers might not know whether they are true).

5. *Develop and map arguments for each of the premises that need more support.* Develop an argument for each of the premises that you identified in Step 4. Add those arguments to your argument maps.

6. *Repeat Steps 3–5 until there are no more premises in need of more support.*

Final product: The final product of this activity is a (set of) argument map(s), along with new arguments devised to support selected premises in the original arguments.

Index

This thematic index offers a route to this book's main themes that is different from, but complementary to, the table of contents. Chiefly it concentrates on Part 1 of the *Workbook*, covering the original *Rulebook* text and all relevant tips and sample discussions in Part 1 of the *Workbook*. Pages from Parts 2 and 3 are indexed when they make substantive new additions to these themes.